D0876133

A PROGRAMMING METHODOLOGY IN COMPILER CONSTRUCTION
Part 2: Implementation

A PROGRAMMING METHODOLOGY IN COMPILER CONSTRUCTION

Part 2: Implementation

J. LEWI
K. DE VLAMINCK
J. HUENS
E. STEEGMANS

Computer Science Department,
Faculty of Applied Sciences,
Katholieke Universiteit Leuven,
Heverlee,
BELGIUM

1982

NORTH-HOLLAND PUBLISHING COMPANY — AMSTERDAM • NEW YORK • OXFORD

ISBN: 0 444 86339 7

Publishers:
NORTH-HOLLAND PUBLISHING COMPANY
AMSTERDAM • NEW YORK • OXFORD

Sole distributors for the U.S.A. and Canada:
ELSEVIERS SCIENCE PUBLISHING COMPANY, INC.
52 VANDERBILT AVENUE, NEW YORK, N.Y. 10017

PRINTED IN THE NETHERLANDS

ACKNOWLEDGEMENTS

The project LILA has been undertaken at the Computer Science Department of the Katholieke Universiteit Leuven. The project had two aspects : the study of a methodology to write compilers that meet the software engineering requirements and the implementation of a software tool LILA (a Language Implementation LAboratory) supporting the methodology.

We would like to express our appreciation to the Development Department of Siemens Oostkamp, especially to R. Majelijne and his team with whom we had an excellent collaboration during a number of years. We are indebted to M. Huybrechts who wrote an early version of LILA. We also thank L. Swinnen for her careful typing of the book.

Finally, we thank all the members of our department for the good atmosphere which made it possible to develop LILA to what it is today.

Johan Lewi
Karel De Vlaminck
Jean Huens
Eric Steegmans

Johan LEWI received an engineering degree in Electronics from the Katholieke Universiteit Leuven (Belgium). He has been associated with the Natuurkundig Laboratorium of Philips in Eindhoven (The Netherlands). Later he worked at the Research Laboratory of MBLE in Brussels where he was a member of the Algol 68 implementation group.

Since 1973 he has been professor at the Computer Science Department of the K.U.Leuven where he started the project LILA (a Language Implementation LAboratory).

He lectures on programming languages and compiler construction at the K.U.Leuven and the Vrije Universiteit Brussels.

Karel DE VLAMINCK received an engineering degree in Computer Science from the Katholieke Universiteit Leuven in 1975. To date he has been researcher at the Computer Science Department of the K.U.Leuven where he obtained his Ph.D. in 1980.

Until 1981, he has mostly been working on the design and implementation of LILA.

His current interests include software engineering, language processors, formal semantics and language design.

Jean HUENS became Technical Engineer in 1972 and in 1975 he obtained his engineering degree in Computer Science at the Katholieke Universiteit Leuven. He has been researcher at the Department of Computer Science of the K.U.Leuven and worked on the portability of compilers in the LILA project.

His current fields of interest include language processors, operating systems and software engineering tools for microprocessors.

Eric STEEGMANS received an engineering degree in Computer Science from the Katholieke Universiteit Leuven in 1978. Since then, he has been engaged in research at the Computer Science Department of the K.U.Leuven, where he became involved in the design and implementation of LILA.

His current fields of interest include language processors, programming languages and semantic specifications.

FOREWORD

One of the major problems in software development is the production of programs that meet the software engineering requirements of simplicity, reliability, adaptability, portability and efficiency. The production of such programs becomes manageable by introducing the adequate methodology and the appropriate tools supporting it. Such a methodology will reduce the software production costs not only in the design phase but also in the maintenance phase. Moreover, it will serve as a sound communication means within a software team, resulting in programs that are uniformly documented, commonly readable and maintainable.

This book describes a programming methodology in compiler construction. This methodology is supported by a software tool, called LILA, standing for Language Implementation LAboratory.

LILA and its underlying methodology promote the modular design and implementation of compilers. The main characteristic of LILA, which is responsible for this modularity, is related to the technique of syntax-directed compiler description. Such a description mainly consists of a number of so-called translation syntax modules. Semantic actions, attribute handling, object (constants, variables, types, procedures and functions) declarations and error recovery information can be specified local to each translation syntax module. LILA also supports the development of multipass compilers, each pass being described in a syntax-directed way.

One of the major design goals was to build a compiler writing system, which can be used in all its generative power, but which also allows a high degree of user interaction. This means that in the development of a compiler with LILA, a number of LILA decisions can be overridden, in order to meet very special requirements. In

such cases, step-wise overriding of default definitions has turned
out to be an adequate design philosophy.

A general problem in the development of compiler writing systems
is the production of compilers with error recovery. LILA offers an
elegant solution where the error recovery is mechanically produced
from the error recovery information in the LILA input.

LILA is a tool that helps to develop programs. Since this tool
is itself a program, one needs a methodology and a tool to develop
that program. The methodology described in this book is used to
design LILA. Therefore, LILA meets the same software engineering
requirements as the compilers produced by it. An original approach
in the design of LILA consists in describing LILA as a 17-pass compiler, each pass being described in a syntax-directed way. This
high-level description turned out to be a very elegant tool to document and to maintain the system.

The book is divided into six modules :
(1) A <u>tutorial</u> gives an overview of the different aspects of the
     methodology and of the generative power of the compiler writing
     system LILA.
(2) A number of <u>basic concepts</u>, that a user of the methodology of
     LILA needs to know, are discussed. These concepts are
     extracted from Part 1. Since both Part 1 and Part 2 serve dif-
     ferent purposes, they are made self-contained.
(3) A number of <u>case studies</u> with increasing complexity are worked
     out by means of LILA. For each case study, a number of design
     variants are developed and discussed.
(4) The treatment of <u>error recovery</u> with LILA is a feature that
     deserves special attention. Here, the error recovery strategy
     within the generated compilers is explained.
(5) The <u>design of LILA</u> is based on the LILA methodology itself.
     LILA has been documented as a 17-pass compiler, where each pass
     is described in a syntax-directed way.
(6) The <u>reference guide</u> gives an exhausitive list of the compiler
     generation features of LILA and specifies how these features
     must be written to be obtain a correct LILA input.

TABLE OF CONTENTS

INTRODUCTION

CRITERIA FOR SOFTWARE DEVELOPMENT

It is generally agreed upon that program quality is the most important factor to reduce software production costs. One of the most difficult tasks in software development is writing programs of high quality, i.e., programs that satisfy a number of software engineering criteria. Our software engineering criteria will be : simplicity, reliability, adaptability, portability and efficiency.

Simplicity is the program property that makes it possible to understand what programs do. It can be achieved by splitting up a complicated task into simpler ones (modules). This technique is called modular design. Obviously, each module must correspond to a specific task. In a modular design, we deal with two types of questions :
(1)   how does each module work individually ?
(2)   how do the modules work together ?
In a program that is modularly designed, each module should be individually verified, compiled, executed, checked and documented.

Reliability is highly related to simplicity, in the sense that both program qualities depend on the degree of modularity of the program. To date, there exist a number of well-known verification techniques, covering different aspects of reliability. Among these techniques are proofreading, compile-time checks, run-time checks, systematic testing and program correctness proofs.
Program correctness proofs and the use of compile-time checks are techniques to show the absence of programming errors. These techniques handle properties of programs statically. If such a property is verified or proved to be true, then this holds independently of any program run.

The techniques of systematic testing and the use of run-time checks
handle properties of programs dynamically. If such a property is
verified to be true at a particular program run, then it may be
false during the next run.

   Adaptability guarantees that programs can be modified and
extended at a reasonable cost. It is a programming aspect every
software designer has to cope with sooner or later.
In most software projects the maintenance phase is much longer than
the design and development phases. If no precautionary measures
have been taken during the design phase, the maintenance cost may
rise beyond proportion. Indeed, a modification of a program part
often introduces a number of errors which are difficult to localize,
because previously tested program parts may behave differently.
Adaptability is also promoted by the degree of modularity of the
program. The aspect of individuality of modules guarantees that
modification of a module implementation will not affect the other
modules. Only the modified module must again be verified, compiled,
checked and possibly proved to be correct.

   Portability is the property by which programs can be easily moved
from one computer environment to another.

   Efficiency is related to the amount of time and space needed for
a program to be executed.

   Obviously, there is always a trade-off to be made in meeting the
criteria of high quality programs. In this respect, simplicity,
reliability and adaptability have the highest priority.

TOOLS IN SOFTWARE DEVELOPMENT

   In large software projects, the construction of programs of high
quality is a difficult and tedious task. This task will become
manageable by introducing a programming methodology that promotes
simplicity, reliability and adaptability in the first place, and
portability and efficiency in the second place. Such a methodology
can be tuned towards a given application area, such as the development of compilers. An application-oriented methodology is in fact

the accumulation of an amount of experience and know-how about the application, gathered by many people and made accessible for any potential user working in that area.

A specific problem in a software team is related to the fact that the members of the team may have different ideas and requirements on program quality because of differences in training and background. This communication problem can be cured by a sound methodology. Such a methodology, commonly used among all the members of a software team, promotes the production of software that is readable and adaptable by any member of the team. This is an important aspect of software maintenance.

If a methodology has been established in a given application area, the next logical step is to design a software tool to support that methodology. The software tool must be such that the user is encouraged and/or forced to follow the underlying methodology. A simple illustration is the use of types in a programming language with strong typing. For example, in writing a Pascal variable declaration we specify a relation between the variable and the domain of values over which the variable is defined. For any applied occurrence of the variable, we are able to verify this rela-tion. The use of types in Pascal can be considered a methodology that promotes reliability. A tool supporting the use of strong typ-ing would be a Pascal compiler systematically checking the con-sistent use of types in Pascal programs.

LILA AS A TOOL IN COMPILER CONSTRUCTION

The methodology, described in this book, is supported by a software tool, called LILA, standing for a Language Implementation LAboratory. With LILA, we claim that one is able to produce com-pilers meeting the software requirements of simplicity, reliability, adaptability, portability and efficiency.

Let us first introduce a few definitions. A translation t is a set of pairs (x,E), where x is a string of symbols over some alpha-bet, called input vocabulary, and E is the contents of an environ-ment. This environment may contain e.g. real variables, array

variables and print files. We state that E is the translation of x.
The set of all strings x for which there exists an E, such that
(x,E) belongs to t, is called the <u>input</u> <u>language</u>.

Translations can be described by means of generative devices,
called <u>translation</u> <u>syntaxes</u>, and by means of recognizing devices,
called <u>transducers</u> ('transducer' is a general term including compilers and interpreters).
The translation syntax is the ideal tool to describe and document
translations, whereas the transducer is the automaton that maps
input strings x into E, if x belongs to the input language. If x
does not belong to the input language, error messages are produced.
Our methodology in compiler writing consists in building the translation syntax F and to produce the transducer B from it in a mechanical way. The translation defined by F, denoted t(F), must be identical to the translation defined by B, denoted t(B). The mapping of
translation syntaxes into transducers can be defined by means of a
finite set of generation rules, called the <u>generation</u> scheme. This
is illustrated in Fig. O.1.

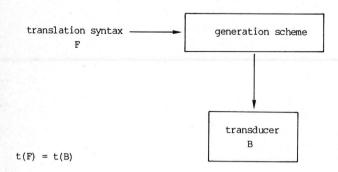

Fig. O.1.

In the literature, there exist translation syntaxes and transducers of different types, each type having different properties. The choice of the type of translation syntax and transducer is very important. In LILA, the translation syntaxes are of the type 'generalized Attributed Extended Context-Free (AECF)', whereas the transducers are of the type 'generalized Attributed Push-Down (APD)'. These formalisms are explained in Part 2. A more theoretical approach can be found in Part 1. The heart of LILA is a generation scheme that maps a generalized AECF translation syntax into its equivalent generalized APD transducer. This is illustrated in Fig. 0.2.

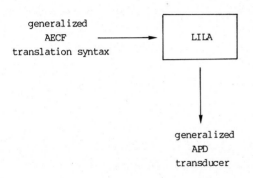

Fig. 0.2.

TWO-LEVEL STRUCTURE OF MODULARITY

The methodology of LILA supports a two-level structure of modularity. The first level is related to the syntax-oriented method of writing compilers. The translation syntax F is said to be a syntax-oriented description of the transducer B. A translation syntax consists of a number of syntax rules defining the input language. With each syntax rule a number of semantic actions and attributes are associated describing the translation. Such a syntax

rule together with the semantic actions and attributes involved,
constitutes a <u>syntax</u> <u>module</u>. Each syntax module treats the translation of a specific feature of the input language e.g., there will be
a module to treat assignments, expressions, terms and factors.
Also, each module can be written and verified independently from the
others and the interface between all modules is straightforward. To
each module in the translation syntax corresponds a transducer
module, called <u>transducer</u> <u>routine</u>. This is schematically illustrated in Fig. 0.3.

translation syntax

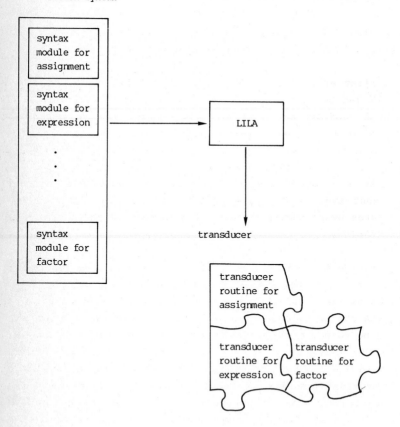

Fig. 0.3.

The <u>second level</u> is related to the possibility to describe transducers in several passes, resulting in multi-pass transducers. Each
pass of the transducer is described in a syntax-oriented way by
means of a translation syntax. The translation syntax of a transducer pass describes a specific function within the translation. It
can be designed, verified and tested independently from the others.
The interface between the different passes is simple and is part of
the input of LILA. This interface is such that the output of one
pass will be the input of an other pass. This is illustrated in
Fig. 0.4.

STEP-WISE OVERRIDING OF DEFAULT DEFINITIONS

Many design criteria and aspects of LILA have to do with human
engineering. A great effort is made to make LILA <u>flexible</u>.

Let us first explain what we mean by flexibility with respect to
LILA. LILA can be used at different levels of sophistication. The
lowest level consists in using the defaults for all the generation
features. This means that the user agrees with all the decisions
taken by LILA in the mechanical production process of transducers.
However, in some cases one wishes to override default decisions made
by LILA. As an example, the user may redefine the module for reading the input symbols in the generated transducer. The more work
the user takes over from LILA, the more know-how is needed about the
behavior of LILA.

One of the design principles of LILA is to build a compiler writing system which can be used in all its generative power, but which
also allows a high degree of user interaction (a number of decisions
made by LILA can be overridden). The highest level of user interaction would be to write the complete transducer by hand. Between the
lowest and highest level of user interaction, a whole range of possibilities exists. An interesting aspect of the design philosophy
in writing compilers with LILA is as follows. First, LILA is used in

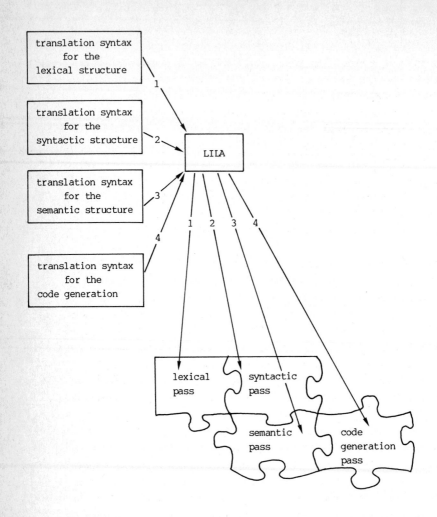

Fig. 0.4.

all its generative power. The generated transducer can be systematically verified and tested. Then, if necessary, LILA features may be
redefined one by one. Each time a LILA feature is redefined, the
new version of the generated transducer is tested only for that

redefined feature.

Step-wise overriding of default definitions makes it possible to produce several releases of a compiler. This is an important tool in the debugging phase and maintenance phase of compilers. An example of step-wise overriding of default definitions is the implementation of the lexical analyser in a compiler, produced by LILA. In a first step, the lexical analyser can be developed as a separate pass, the other pass being the syntax-semantic analysis. In a second step, the lexical analyser can be implemented as a compiler subroutine by overriding the read module of the syntax-semantic analyser.

DESIGN PHILOSOPHY OF LILA

LILA is a tool that helps to develop programs. Since this tool is itself a program, one needs a methodology and a tool to develop that program. The methodology described in this book is used in the design of LILA. Therefore, LILA meets exactly the same software engineering requirements as the transducers produced by it. Indeed, the tool is also simple, reliable, adaptable, portable and efficient.

An original approach in the design of LILA is the use of a high-level description of LILA as a 17-pass compiler, each pass being described in a syntax-oriented way. This high-level documentation turned out to be a very efficient tool to adapt and maintain the system LILA. As an example, the modification of LILA to produce compilers in PL/1 instead of Pascal has become an easy job.

The LILA methodology promotes the writing of compilers that are not only simple, reliable and adaptable, but also portable at a low cost, and efficient at compile-time as well as at run-time. As for compile-time efficiency, a great part of the LILA project was devoted to a systematic study of optimization, allowing the production of compilers which are optimized in time and space. The run-time efficiency of the generated compilers is dealt with by the semantic actions. Since the semantic actions are entirely written by the LILA user, there is no loss of run-time efficiency with respect to hand-

coded compilers.   Portability of compilers produced by LILA has two
aspects.

(1) LILA offers the user an excellent infrastructure to localize
     the machine-dependent run-time features within the compiler
     design.

(2) The compiler produced by LILA is generated in standard Pascal,
     which turned out to be a very portable language.

     The design of the compiler writing system LILA is characterized
by a trade-off between the degree of automation and the degree of
generality and flexibility.   If the degree of automation is too
high, the system becomes inflexible for many applications.   This
trade-off is strongly related to the aspect of human engineering of
software tools.   The authors believe in the usefulness and the need
of a compiler writing system that offers the appropriate infrastructure supporting a sound methodology in the construction of compilers, based on mathematical concepts.

ERROR RECOVERY

     A big problem in the development of compiler writing systems is
the production of compilers with error recovery.   Insertion of error
recovery by hand in the generated compiler is impractical and in
most cases impossible; it destroys the modular structure of the generated compiler.   Each time a new version of the compiler is generated, the entire insertion process has to be redone.   LILA offers
an elegant solution for this error recovery problem.   The error
recovery in compilers generated by LILA is mechanically produced
from the error recovery information in the LILA input.   The use of
this feature requires the knowledge of the error recovery strategy
imposed by LILA.

TEACHING

     LILA is also a didactic tool to support a course on compiler con-
struction, where the students experiment in both language and compiler design.   With the help of LILA, student projects with a degree
of complexity sufficiently high to illustrate compiler design in a
realistic way, can be worked out.

PART 1 VERSUS PART 2

LILA is an engineering product that is based on the theory of
syntaxes and translation syntaxes on the one hand, and the theory of
acceptors and transducers on the other hand. This is the subject of
Part 1, where a number of syntaxes, translation syntaxes, acceptors
and transducers with growing complexity are discussed. Also a
number of generation schemes from syntaxes to acceptors and from
translation syntaxes to transducers are described in all detail. In
Part 1, the emphasis is on the bridge between theory and practice in
the area of compiler construction, resulting in a methodology to
write compilers. In Part 2, the emphasis is mainly on the use of
the methodology and on the use of the system LILA, supporting this
methodology.

1. TUTORIAL

The main purpose of this tutorial is to give the reader a brief survey of a methodology in compiler construction as it is supported by the system LILA. Such a survey can best be given through an example : the design and implementation of a processor for the language called UNIT CONVERSION. This language was first described by J. Cohen [1973].

The methodology proposed in this book has many aspects. One of the most important aspects is modularity which is a way to control complexity in software development and to obtain programs that are reliable, readable, easy to maintain and to modify.

The language processor for UNIT CONVERSION explained here serves as a case study, illustrating the use of the compiler writing system LILA. One must keep in mind that the way UNIT CONVERSION is implemented is not the only possible way to implement language processors with LILA. Also, only a restricted set of the LILA features has been used in this case study. For example, error recovery (syntactically as well as semantically) is a very important feature in LILA. The subject of error recovery is treated in section 6. More case studies can be found in section 5. A complete survey of the possibilities of LILA is given in the Reference Guide (see Appendix).

Conceptually, the language processor for UNIT CONVERSION consists of four different phases : a low level syntax analysis, a low level semantic analysis, a high level syntax analysis and a high level semantic analysis.
Syntax and semantic analysis on the low level are usually performed in one single pass called the lexical analysis. High level syntax analysis is sometimes called parsing or syntax analysis,

whereas high level semantic analysis is often called <u>semantic analysis</u>. Both syntax and semantic analysis on the high level are usually performed in one single pass called the <u>syntax-semantic analysis</u>. The language processor for UNIT CONVERSION is illustrated in Fig. 1.1.

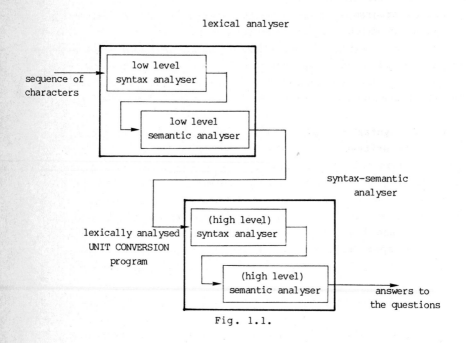

Fig. 1.1.

In the next four subsections, the design and implementation of the four phases of the language processor for UNIT CONVERSION are discussed. The order in which the phases are treated is slightly different from the order given above. Section 1.1 treats the (high level) syntax analyser; section 1.2 discusses the (high level) semantic analyser. The low level syntax analyser is covered in section 1.3 and the low level semantic analyser is explained in section 1.4. By following this order, we are able to introduce the language

UNIT CONVERSION at the same time we explain the language processor.

1.1. Syntax analysis

The role of the syntax analyser is to check if a UNIT CONVERSION program is syntactically correct, i.e., if it is legally built up from statements, assignments, questions, expressions, terms, factors, secondaries, primaries, identifiers, numbers, keywords and delimiters. The syntax analyser gives the answer 'yes', if the UNIT CONVERSION program at the input is syntactically correct, and 'no' otherwise, in which case error messages are produced.

The syntax analysis of UNIT CONVERSION is described by means of a syntax formalism called Extended Context-Free syntax, abbreviated ECF syntax. This formalism is explained at the same time it is used. ECF syntaxes are treated in more detail in section 2.

The ECF syntax for UNIT CONVERSION as it is described in this section, is written as a correct LILA input, from which LILA produces a syntax analyser in the form of a Pascal program. Each LILA input section starts with a LILA command and each LILA command starts with a number of '#' symbols, depending on the command level. Each portion of the LILA input beginning with the symbol '$' up to the end of the line is treated as a comment. The details of the LILA input specifications are given in the Reference Guide (see Appendix).

1.1.1. Input vocabulary

The input symbols of the syntax analyser are represented by integers. All the input symbols (in the form of integers) must be listed in the input vocabulary. In addition, each input symbol must be given a symbolic name. This name must be used to reference the input symbol in the syntax.
As an example,

```
┌─────┐
│  2  │
└─────┘
```

represents the input symbol "identifier".

There are two special elements in the input vocabulary for UNIT CONVERSION: "identifier" and "number". In the input of the syntax analyser all identifiers and numbers are replaced by the integers 2 and 3, respectively. This replacement is done by the lexical analyser, see section 1.3. A program transformed in this way, will be called a <u>lexically analysed program</u>. Notice that the input symbols of the syntax analyser are the terminal symbols of the ECF syntax.

###inputvocabulary rep(integer);

  "identifier" = 2

  "number" = 3

  "how" = 4   "many" = 5   "in" = 6
  "kg" = 7   "m"   = 8   "s" = 9

  "(" = 10   ")" = 11   "*" = 12   "+" = 13   "," = 14
  "-" = 15   "/" = 16   "=" = 17   "?" = 18   "^" = 19

1.1.2. Program

The first language construct in UNIT CONVERSION is the program. Its syntax analysis is described by the following ECF syntax rule :

  ##rule;
    <program> =
      <statement> ("," <statement>)*

In this formalism, (e)* must be read as 'processing e zero or more times'. The operator '*' is called the <u>reflexive and transitive closure set operator</u>.

The syntax analysis of a UNIT CONVERSION program is as follows. First, the syntax analysis of a statement is activated. This is followed by the processing of a comma symbol followed by the processing of a statement, zero or more times. The syntax analysis of a statement is discussed in section 1.1.3.

In the sequel, the following conventions will hold :

1) processing an input symbol means checking if the input head of the syntax analyser contains that input symbol. If the answer is yes then the next input symbol is read, otherwise an error message is produced.

2) processing a nonterminal symbol <A> means activating the syntax analysis for <A>. This syntax analysis can be found in the section where the ECF syntax rule <A> = e is defined. This is one of the aspects of modular design of compilers. In UNIT CONVERSION the nonterminal symbols are <program>, <statement>, <assignment>, <question>, <expression>, <term>, <factor>, <secondary> and <primary>.

1.1.3. Statement

The syntax analysis of a statement is described by the following ECF syntax rule :

```
##rule;
  <statement> =
    <assignment> | <question>
```

where '|' is called the union set operator.

Statements are either assignments or questions. The syntax analysis of a statement consists of detecting whether an assignment or a question is dealt with. In the first case, the syntax analysis of an assignment is activated, whereas in the second case, the syntax analysis of a question is performed. The syntax analysis of an assignment is defined in section 1.1.4; the syntax analysis of a question is defined in section 1.1.5.

1.1.4. Assignment

The syntax analysis of an assignment is described by the following ECF syntax rule :

```
##rule;
  <assignment> =
    "identifier" "=" <expression>
```

In UNIT CONVERSION, an identifier represents a unit which is program-defined. There are three language-defined units : the me- ter, the kilogram and the second, represented by the keywords 'm', 'kg' and 's', respectively (see section 1.1.10). Program-defined units come into existence by means of assignments.

The syntax analysis of an assignment consists of the processing of an identifier, followed by the processing of an equal symbol, followed by the processing of an expression. The syntax analysis of an expression is defined in section 1.1.6.

Examples of assignments are :

```
cm    = 0.01 * m,
inch = 2.54 * cm,
feet = 0.3048 * m,
yard = 0.9144 * m,
sqinch = inch * inch,
cuinch = inch ^ 3
```

1.1.5. Question

The syntax analysis of a question is described by the following ECF syntax rule :

```
##rule;
  <question> =
    "how" "many"  <expression>  "in"  <expression> "?"
```

The syntax analysis of a question consists of the processing of the keyword 'how', followed by the processing of the keyword 'many', followed by the processing of an expression, followed by the processing of the keyword 'in', followed by the processing of an ex- pression, followed by the processing of a question mark.

Examples of questions are :

```
how many inch in feet?,
how many inch in yard?,
how many feet in yard?,
how many sqinch in sqfeet?,
how many sqinch in m2?,
how many cuinch in m2 * m?,
how many m/s in (sqfeet/yard) / s?
```

1.1.6. Expression

The syntax analysis of an expression is described by the following ECF syntax rule :

```
##rule;
  <expression> =
    <term>
      ( "+" <term>  |  "-" <term> )*
```

The syntax analysis of an expression is as follows. First, the
syntax analysis of a term is activated. This is followed by the
processing of an adding operator followed by a term or the processing of a subtraction operator followed by a term, zero or more
times. The processing of a term is defined in section 1.1.7.

1.1.7. Term

The syntax analysis of a term is defined in terms of the processing of a factor, the multiplication operator '*' and the division
operator '/'. This is described by the following ECF syntax rule :

```
##rule;
  <term> =
    <factor>
      ( "*" <factor>  |  "/" <factor> )*
```

The processing of a factor is defined in section 1.1.8.

1.1.8. Factor

The processing of a factor is recursively defined in terms of the processing of a secondary, a factor and the exponentiation operator '^'. This is described by the following ECF syntax rule :

```
##rule;
  <factor> =
    <secondary>
       ( "^" <factor>   |   & )
```

The processing of a secondary is defined in section 1.1.9.

1.1.9. Secondary

The processing of a secondary is defined in terms of the processing of a primary and the negation operator '-'. This is described by the following ECF syntax rule :

```
##rule;
  <secondary> =
       "-" <primary>
    | <primary>
```

The processing of a primary is defined in section 1.1.10.

1.1.10. Primary

The processing of a primary is either the processing of an identifier, or the processing of a number, or the processing of one of the keywords 'kg', 'm' and 's', or the processing of an expression enclosed between parentheses. This is described by the following ECF syntax rule :

```
##rule;
  <primary> =
       "identifier"
    | "number"
    | "kg"
    | "m"
    | "s"
    | "(" <expression> ")"
```

The processing of an expression has been defined in section 1.1.6. Notice that the processing of expressions is recursively defined.

1.1.11. The syntax analyser for UNIT CONVERSION

The input of the syntax analyser is a sequence of elements of the input vocabulary, see section 1.1.1. The output of the syntax analyser will be 'yes', if the input is syntactically correct and 'no' otherwise, in which case error messages will be produced. The syntax analysis for UNIT CONVERSION is schematically illustrated in Fig. 1.2.

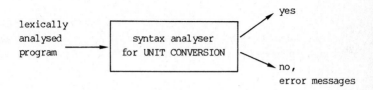

Fig. 1.2.

As it will be explained in section 2.5, the transformation of the ECF syntax of UNIT CONVERSION into a syntax analyser in the form of a Pascal program is performed by LILA. This is schematically illustrated in Fig. 1.3.

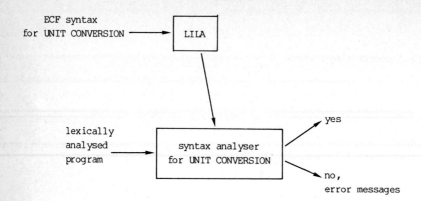

Fig. 1.3.

The <u>complete</u> <u>ECF</u> <u>syntax</u> <u>for</u> <u>UNIT</u> <u>CONVERSION</u> in the form of a LILA input is given below.

###inputvocabulary rep(integer);

  "identifier" = 2

  "number" = 3

  "how" = 4   "many" = 5   "in" = 6
  "kg" = 7   "m"   = 8   "s" = 9

  "(" = 10   ")" = 11   "*" = 12   "+" = 13   "," = 14
  "-" = 15   "/" = 16   "=" = 17   "?" = 18   "^" = 19

###syntax;

$ <u>Program</u>
  ##rule;
    <program> -
      <statement> ("," <statement>)*

```
$ Statement
  ##rule;
    <statement> =
      <assignment> | <question>



$ Assignment
  ##rule;
    <assignment> =
      "identifier" "=" <expression>



$ Question
  ##rule;
    <question> =
      "how" "many"  <expression>  "in"  <expression> "?"



$ Expression
  ##rule;
    <expression> =
      <term>
        ( "+" <term>  |  "-" <term> )*



$ Term
  ##rule;
    <term> =
      <factor>
        ( "*" <factor>  |  "/" <factor> )*

$ Factor
  ##rule;
    <factor> =
      <secondary>
        ( "^" <factor>   |  & )


$ Secondary
  ##rule;
    <secondary> =
        "-" <primary>
      | <primary>
```

```
$ Primary
  ##rule;
   <primary> =
       "identifier"
     | "number"
     | "kg"
     | "m"
     | "s"
     | "(" <expression> ")"



###globalinfo;

  ##parameter;
    output,infile
```

The globalinfo part of the LILA input is further explained in section 1.2. A detailed description can be found in the Reference Guide (see Appendix).

1.2. Semantic analysis

In section 1.1, we have discussed the syntax analyser for UNIT CONVERSION by means of an ECF syntax. This syntax analyser determines if a lexically analysed UNIT CONVERSION program is legally composed of statements, assignments, questions, expressions, terms, factors, primaries, secondaries, identifiers, numbers, keywords and delimiters.

In this section we are concerned not only with the syntactic aspect of UNIT CONVERSION, but also with the translation aspect. Each lexically analysed UNIT CONVERSION program must be translated into a sequence of answers to the questions specified in the UNIT CONVERSION program. Therefore, we will extend the syntax analyser with a number of actions, producing the answers for each syntactically correct UNIT CONVERSION program. These actions are called semantic actions and the processor is called a syntax-semantic analyser.

Conceptually, a syntax-semantic analyser consists of two phases : a syntactic phase, called syntax analyser and a semantic phase, called semantic analyser. This is schematically illustrated in Fig. 1.4.

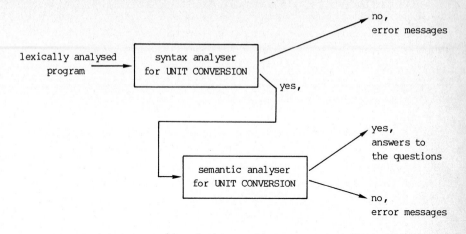

Fig. 1.4.

In this particular design of the UNIT CONVERSION compiler the syntax analysis and the semantic analysis, as it will be produced by LILA, are performed in one pass. This is illustrated in Fig. 1.5.

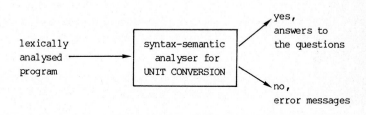

Fig. 1.5.

One elegant way to develop syntax-semantic analysers is the syntax-directed method. Then, we take the ECF syntax of the language and extend it with semantic actions, defining the translation. In order to control the information for the production of the translation, semantic actions deal with the so-called attribute

mechanism. Such an ECF syntax is then called a <u>generalized</u> <u>attri-</u>
<u>buted</u> <u>ECF</u> <u>translation</u> <u>syntax</u>, denoted generalized AECF translation
syntax. Generalized AECF translation syntaxes are treated in sec-
tion 4. From a generalized AECF translation syntax, LILA will produce a syntax-semantic analyser in the form of a Pascal program.
This is also explained in section 4.

The generalized AECF translation syntax for UNIT CONVERSION consists of
1) an input vocabulary,
2) generalized AECF translation syntax rules (simply called syntax
   rules),
3) definitions of semantic actions,
4) global information (globalinfo), containing the definitions of
   constants, types, variables, functions and procedures, which are
   global to all semantic action definitions,
5) attribute type definitions,
6) local information, containing the definitions of constants,
   types, variables, functions and procedures, which are local to a
   specific syntax rule.
In the generalized AECF translation syntax all declarations are
written in Pascal and the semantic actions must be Pascal statements.

1.2.1. Input vocabulary

The input of the syntax-semantic analyser for UNIT CONVERSION is
a lexically analysed program. This program is a sequence of input
symbols, where some of them are attributed. The input vocabulary
is :

```
###inputvocabulary  rep(integer);

  "identifier" = 2 : rep_name

  "number" = 3 : real

  "how" = 4     "many" = 5     "in" = 6
  "kg"  = 7     "m"   = 8      "s"  = 9

  "(" = 10    ")" = 11    "*" = 12    "+" = 13    "," = 14
```

"-" = 15   "/" = 16   "=" = 17   "?" = 18   "^" = 19

The attributed input symbols in UNIT CONVERSION are "identifier" and "number". Each "identifier" is attributed with a string of characters, which is the name of the identifier. Each "number" is attributed with a real value representing the value of the number. The type of the attribute of "identifier" is 'rep_name' and the type of the attribute of "number" is 'real'. The type 'rep_name' is defined in globalinfo (see section 1.2.13) as :

```
rep_name = packed array [1..idlength] of char;
```

An example of an "identifier" input symbol is :

```
2   'cm2'
```

where 2 is the integer representation and where 'cm2' is its attribute value. This attribute can be referenced in the semantic actions by :

```
@"identifier"
```

which denotes a variable of type 'rep_name'.
The representation of "identifier" can be obtained by :

```
%"identifier"
```

which denotes a constant of type 'integer'.

An example of a "number" input symbol is :

```
3   0.01
```

where 3 is the integer representation and where 0.01 is its attribute value. This attribute can be referenced in the semantic actions by :

```
@"number"
```

which denotes a variable of type 'real'.

Another example,

```
┌─────┐
│  4  │
└─────┘
```

is an input symbol "how", where 4 is the integer representation, referenced by %"how". Clearly, @"how" does not exist.

An example of a sequence of input symbols for the syntax-semantic analyser for UNIT CONVERSION is :

representation	attribute	input symbol
2	'cm2'	"identifier"
17		"="
10		"("
3	0.01	"number"
12		"*"
8		"m"
11		")"
19		"^"
3	2.00	"number"

The syntax-semantic analysis of UNIT CONVERSION is schematically illustrated in Fig. 1.6.

sequence of input symbols
representation   attribute

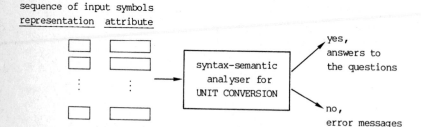

input for the semantic analyser

input for the syntax analyser

Fig. 1.6.

1.2.2. Attributes

In section 1.2.1, we associated attributes with input symbols. An attribute may also be associated with a nonterminal symbol. In UNIT CONVERSION, an attribute is associated with each expression, term, factor, secondary and primary. This attribute is of type 'rep_unit' and describes the dimension of mass, the dimension of length, the dimension of time and the conversion factor. The type 'rep_unit' is defined in globalinfo (see section 1.2.13) :

```
$ rep dimension
  rep_dimension = record
    mass   : integer;
    length : integer;
    time   : integer
  end;

$ rep unit
  rep_unit = record
    dimension  : rep_dimension;
    conversion : real
  end;
```

The calculation of the attribute of the nonterminal symbols <expression>, <term>, <factor>, <secondary> and <primary> is described in the sections covering their defining syntax rules, see sections 1.2.8 to 1.2.12.

A semantic action has access to the attribute of the input and nonterminal symbols that appear in the rule where the semantic action is defined. The access to the attribute of an input symbol is described in section 1.2.1. The attribute of a nonterminal symbol, e.g. <expression>, can be accessed by :

@<expression>

which denotes a variable of type 'rep_unit'.

1.2.3. Data structures in UNIT CONVERSION

The semantic actions in the syntax-semantic analysis deal with four program-defined types of data structures. These four types of data structures together with the operations defined on them, are summarized below. The actual representation of the types and the implementation of the operations are defined in globalinfo.

1) <u>rep unit</u>

```
procedure init_unit (var un:rep_unit; cv:real; m,l,t: integer);
procedure add_unit (var un1:rep_unit; un2:rep_unit);
procedure subtr_unit (var un1:rep_unit; un2:rep_unit);
procedure negate_unit (var un:rep_unit);
procedure mult_unit (var un1:rep_unit; un2:rep_unit);
procedure divide_unit (var un1:rep_unit; un2:rep_unit);
procedure exponentiate_unit ( var un1:rep_unit; un2:rep_unit);
function convert_unit( un1,un2:rep_unit): real;
procedure print_unit (un:rep_unit);
```

2) <u>rep dimension</u>

```
procedure init_dimension (var dim:rep_dimension; m,l,t:integer);
function equal_dimension (dim1,dim2:rep_dimension): boolean;
procedure add_dimension (var dim1:rep_dimension; dim2:rep_dimension);
procedure subtr_dimension (var dim1:rep_dimension; dim2:rep_dimension);
procedure mult_dimension( var dim:rep_dimension; ct:integer);
procedure print_dimension (dim:rep_dimension);
```

3) <u>rep symbtab</u>

```
var symbtab : rep_symbtab;
   { Creation of a location of type 'rep_symbtab' }
procedure add_symbtab (nm:rep_name; un:rep_unit);
function in_symbtab (nm:rep_name): boolean;
procedure take_symbtab (var un:rep_unit; nm:rep_name);
procedure print_symbtab;
```

4) <u>message</u>

```
procedure error (m:message);
```

1.2.4. <u>Program</u>

The syntax-semantic analysis of a lexically analysed UNIT CONVER-SION program is described by the following syntax rule :

```
##rule;
  <program> =
    init
      <statement>  ( "," <statement> )*
      final
```

```
##action;
  #init;
    symbtabp := 0;

    writeln(output,'ANSWERS TO THE QUESTIONS');
    writeln(output,'************************');
    writeln(output)

  #final;
    print_symbtab
```

The syntax-semantic analysis of a program is as follows. First, the semantic action 'init' is activated, then the first statement is processed, followed by zero or more times the processing of a comma symbol followed by a statement. Finally, the semantic action 'final' is activated. The processing of a statement is described in section 1.2.5. The semantic actions 'init' and 'final' are discussed below.

The semantic action 'init' initializes a table, called 'symbtab'. Each symbtab element consists of two fields : a name field to hold the identifiers and a unit field to hold the attributes 'mass', 'length', 'time' and 'conv'. The data structure 'symbtab' is defined and described by means of the following constant, type and variable declarations. They are part of globalinfo (see section 1.2.13).

```
##const;
  $ rep symbtab
    idlength =  8;
    maxsymbt = 10;


##type;
  $ rep dimension
    rep_dimension = record
      mass   : integer;
      length : integer;
      time   : integer
    end;

  $ rep unit
    rep_unit = record
      dimension  : rep_dimension;
      conversion : real
```

```
     end;

  $ rep symbtab
    rep_name = packed array [1..idlength] of char;
    rep_symbtab = array [0..maxsymbt] of record
       name : rep_name;
       unit : rep_unit
    end


##var;
  $ rep symbtab
    symbtab : rep_symbtab;
    symbtabp: 0..maxsymbt
```

The variable 'symbtabp' contains the index of the first free entry
in 'symbtab'.

The semantic action 'final' prints the contents of 'symbtab' for
debugging purposes.

1.2.5. Statement

The syntax-semantic analysis of a statement is described by the
following syntax rule :

```
##rule;
  <statement> =
    <assignment> | <question>
```

1.2.6. Assignment

The syntax-semantic analysis of an assignment is described by the
following syntax rule :

```
##rule;
  <assignment> =
    "identifier" "=" <expression> assign

##action;
  #assign;
    if  in_symbtab(@"identifier")
      then error(re_assignment)
      else add_symbtab( @"identifier", @<expression>)
```

The syntax-semantic analysis of an assignment is as follows. First, the processing of an identifier is performed, followed by the processing of an equal symbol. Then, the syntax-semantic analysis of an expression (see section 1.2.8) is activated followed by the activation of the semantic action 'assign'.

The key thought here is that we assume that as a result of the syntax-semantic analysis of an expression, the attribute value of that expression has been calculated and is associated with the non-terminal <expression>. In the definition of the syntax-semantic analysis of expression (see section 1.2.8), we will see that we can always make this assumption.

The semantic action 'assign' has access to the attribute of the terminal symbol "identifier" and of the nonterminal symbol <expression>. The semantic action 'assign' will take the attribute value of expression and store it at the appropriate entry in 'symbtab' for later use. This entry in 'symbtab' is calculated by means of the attribute value of "identifier". If the identifier is defined for the first time, a new entry in 'symbtab' is created, otherwise an error message is produced. The calculation of the entry in 'symbtab' is performed by the routine 'add_symbt', which is defined in globalinfo, see section 1.2.13.

1.2.7. Question

The syntax-semantic analysis of a question is described by the following syntax rule :

```
##rule;
  <question> =
    "how" "many"  <expression>  "in"  <expression> "?"  print_result

##action;
  #print_result;
    writeln(output, convert_unit(@<expression>1,@<expression>2):9)
```

The syntax-semantic analysis of a question is as follows. First, the processing of the keyword 'how' is activated, followed by the processing of the keyword 'many'. Then, the syntax-semantic analysis of an expression is activated, followed by processing the keyword 'in'. Thereafter, the syntax-semantic analysis of an expression is activated for a second time, followed by the processing

of a question mark, followed by the activation of the semantic action 'print_result'.

Again, the key thought here is that each time an expression has
been syntax-semantically analysed, its attribute value is available.

The semantic action 'print_result' checks for consistency of the
dimensions   of   the   units   described   by   @<expression>1   and
@<expression>2 and calculates the answer.

Here, @<expression>i denotes the attribute of the ith occurrence
of the nonterminal symbol <expression>, where i stands for any posi-
tive integer. Different occurrences of the same nonterminal symbol
in a syntax rule are numbered from left to right, starting from one.

1.2.8. Expression

The syntax-semantic analysis of an expression is described by the
following syntax rule :

```
##rule;
  <expression> =
    <term>   trans_et
       ( "+" <term> add  |  "-" <term> subtract )*

##attribute;
  rep_unit

##action;
  #trans_et;
    @<expression>   := @<term>1;

  #add;
    add_unit( @<expression>, @<term>2)

  #subtract;
    subtr_unit( @<expression>, @<term>3)
```

First, the syntax-semantic analysis of a term is activated, followed by the activation of the semantic action 'trans_et'; this action has access to the attribute associated with <term>1 and <ex-
pression>. Then, each time the operator '+' is processed, the
syntax-semantic analysis of a term is activated, followed by the activation of the semantic action 'add'. The semantic action 'add'
has access to the attribute of <expression>, <term>1 and <term>2.

Each time, the operator '-' is processed, the syntax-semantic analysis of a term is activated, followed by the activation of the semantic action 'subtract'. The semantic action 'subtract' has access to the attribute of <expression>, <term>1 and <term>3. The attribute of an expression is of type 'rep_unit' :

```
##attribute;
  rep_unit
```

The type 'rep_unit' is defined in globalinfo, see section 1.2.13.

In the calculation of the attribute value in the syntax rule for an expression, there is a loop invariant assertion : each time the semantic action 'add' ('subtract') is activated, the attribute value of the left operand of the adding (subtraction) operator will always be @<expression>, whereas the attribute value of the right operand will always be @<term>2 (respectively @<term>3). Therefore, the semantic action 'trans_et' will simply transfer @<term>1 to @<expression>.

1.2.9. Term

The syntax-semantic analysis of a term is described by the following syntax rule :

```
##rule;
  <term> =
    <factor>  trans_tf
      ( "*" <factor> multiply  |  "/" <factor> divide )*

  ##attribute;
    rep_unit

  ##action;
    #trans_tf;
      @<term>  := @<factor>1;




    #multiply;
      mult_unit( @<term>, @<factor>2)

    #divide;
      divide_unit( @<term>, @<factor>3)
```

This case is similar to the syntax-semantic analysis of an expression, see section 1.2.8.

1.2.10. Factor

The syntax-semantic analysis of a factor is described by the following syntax rule :

```
##rule;
  <factor> =
    <secondary>  trans_fs
      ( "^" <factor> exponentiate   | & )

  ##attribute;
    rep_unit

  ##action;
    #trans_fs;
      @<factor>1 := @<secondary>

    #exponentiate;
      exponentiate_unit( @<factor>1, @<factor>2)
```

The syntax rule for factor is recursively defined in terms of factor, in order to implement the association of exponent operators and their operands from right to left. This implementation would be more complex using an iterative definition of the syntax rule for factor. The syntax-semantic analysis of a factor is straightforward.

1.2.11. Secondary

The syntax-semantic analysis of a secondary is described by the following syntax rule :

```
##rule;
  <secondary> =
      "-" <primary>  negate
    | <primary>      trans_sp

  ##attribute;
    rep_unit
```

```
    ##action;
      #negate;
        negate_unit(@<primary>1);
        @<secondary> := @<primary>1


      #trans_sp;
        @<secondary> := @<primary>2
```

This case is straightforward.

1.2.12. Primary

The syntax-semantic analysis of a primary is described by the
following syntax rule :

```
  ##rule;
    <primary> =
        "identifier"  identifier
      | "number"      number
      | "kg"          mass_unit
      | "m"           length_unit
      | "s"           time_unit
      | "(" <expression> ")" trans_pe


    ##attribute;
      rep_unit



    ##action;
      #identifier;
        if  in_symbtab(@"identifier")
          then take_symbtab( @<primary>, @"identifier")
          else error(undef_unit)

      #number;
        init_unit( @<primary>,  @"number"{conv}, O{kg}, O{m}, O{s})

      #mass_unit;
        init_unit( @<primary>,  1.O{conv}, 1{kg}, O{m}, O{s})

      #length_unit;
        init_unit( @<primary>,  1.O{conv}, O{kg}, 1{m}, O{s})

      #time_unit;
        init_unit( @<primary>,  1.O{conv}, O{kg}, O{m}, 1{s})

      #trans_pe;
```

@<primary> := @<expression>

The syntax-semantic analysis of a primary either processes an identifier, in which case the semantic action 'identifier' is activated, or processes a number, in which case the semantic action 'number' is activated, or processes one of the keywords 'kg', 'm' or 's', in which case one of the semantic actions 'mass_unit', 'length_unit' or 'time_unit' is activated, or processes an expression between parentheses, in which case 'trans_pe' is activated.

The semantic action 'identifier' checks if the identifier has already been defined in symbtab. If the answer is yes, the attribute value is simply transmitted from the symbtab entry to the nonterminal <primary>. If the answer is no, an error message is produced.

The semantic action 'number' simply calculates @<primary> by means of @"number".

The semantic actions 'mass_unit', 'length_unit' and 'time_unit' initialize @<primary> to the unit of mass, the unit of length and the unit of time, respectively.

The semantic action 'trans_pe' transmits @<expression> to @<primary>.

1.2.13. Global information

The semantic actions make common use of constants, types, variables and routines (procedures and functions) defined in the global information (globalinfo).

```
###globalinfo;

  ##parameter;
   output,infile


  ##const;
    $ rep symbtab
      idlength =  8;
      maxsymbt = 10


  ##type;
    $ message
      message = (inv_terms, zero_divide, inv_exponent, undef_unit,
        inv_conversion, re_assignment, overfl_symbt);
```

```
$ rep_dimension
  rep_dimension = record
    mass   : integer;
    length : integer;
    time   : integer
  end;

$ rep_unit
  rep_unit = record
    dimension  : rep_dimension;
    conversion : real
  end;


$ rep_symbtab
  rep_name = packed array [1..idlength] of char;
  rep_symbtab = array [0..maxsymbt] of record
    name : rep_name;
    unit : rep_unit
  end


##var;
  $ rep_symbtab
    symbtab : rep_symbtab;
    symbtabp: 0..maxsymbt


##routine;
  $ message
    procedure error (m:message);
    begin
      nberrors := nberrors + 1;
      writeln(output,linenumber:4,'    ','*** ERROR ***');
      write(output,'      ');
      case  m  of
        inv_terms:
          writeln(output,'No corresponding dimensions for the ',
            'units in an addition or a subtraction.');
        zero_divide:
          writeln(output,'Attempt to divide by 0.');
        inv_exponent:
          writeln(output,'Exponent must be a number.');
        undef_unit:
          writeln(output,'Attempt to use an undefined unit.');
        inv_conversion:
          writeln(output,'No corresponding dimensions for ',
            'the units in a conversion.');
```

```
      re_assignment:
        writeln(output,'A language defined unit cannot be redefined.');
      overfl_symbt:
        writeln(output,'The number of units exceeds the allowed maximum.')
    end
  end; {error}


$ rep_dimension
  procedure init_dimension (var dim:rep_dimension; m,l,t:integer);
  begin
    dim.mass   := m;
    dim.length := l;
    dim.time   := t
  end; {init_dimension}


  procedure print_dimension (dim:rep_dimension);
  begin
    if (dim.mass <> 0) then begin
      write('kg');
      if (dim.mass <> 1)
        then write('^',dim.mass:1);
      if (dim.length <> 0) or (dim.time <> 0) then write('.')
    end;
    if (dim.length <> 0) then begin
      write('m');
      if (dim.length <> 1)
        then write('^',dim.length:1);
      if (dim.time <> 0) then write('.')
    end;
    if (dim.time <> 0) then begin
      write('s');
      if (dim.time <> 1)
        then write('^',dim.time:1)
    end
  end; {print_dimension}


  function equal_dimension (dim1,dim2:rep_dimension): boolean;
  begin
    equal_dimension :=
          (dim1.mass   = dim2.mass)
      and (dim1.length = dim2.length)
      and (dim1.time   = dim2.time)
  end; {equal_dimension}


  procedure add_dimension (var dim1:rep_dimension; dim2:rep_dimension);
  begin
    dim1.mass   := dim1.mass   + dim2.mass;
    dim1.length := dim1.length + dim2.length;
```

```
    dim1.time    := dim1.time    + dim2.time
end; {add_dimension}


procedure subtr_dimension (var dim1:rep_dimension; dim2:rep_dimension);
begin
    dim1.mass    := dim1.mass    - dim2.mass  ;
    dim1.length := dim1.length - dim2.length;
    dim1.time    := dim1.time    - dim2.time
end; {subtr_dimension}


procedure mult_dimension( var dim:rep_dimension; ct:integer);
begin
    dim.mass    := dim.mass    * ct;
    dim.length := dim.length * ct;
    dim.time    := dim.time    * ct
end; {mult_dimension}
```

$ rep_unit
```
procedure init_unit (var un:rep_unit; cv:real; m,l,t: integer);
begin
    init_dimension( un.dimension, m, l, t);
    un.conversion := cv
end; {init_unit}


procedure add_unit (var un1:rep_unit; un2:rep_unit);
begin
    if  equal_dimension( un1.dimension, un2.dimension)
        then un1.conversion := un1.conversion + un2.conversion
        else error(inv_terms)
end; {add_unit}


procedure subtr_unit (var un1:rep_unit; un2:rep_unit);
begin
    if  equal_dimension( un1.dimension, un2.dimension)
        then un1.conversion := un1.conversion - un2.conversion
        else error(inv_terms)
end; {subtr_unit}


procedure negate_unit (var un:rep_unit);
begin    un.conversion := - un.conversion
end; {negate_unit}


procedure mult_unit (var un1:rep_unit; un2:rep_unit);
begin
    add_dimension( un1.dimension, un2.dimension);
    un1.conversion := un1.conversion * un2.conversion
end; {mult_unit}
```

```
procedure divide_unit (var un1:rep_unit; un2:rep_unit);
begin
  subtr_dimension( un1.dimension, un2.dimension);
  if (un2.conversion = 0.0)  then error(zero_divide)
  else un1.conversion := un1.conversion / un2.conversion
end; {divide_unit}


procedure exponentiate_unit ( var un1:rep_unit; un2:rep_unit);
var nul_dimension: rep_dimension;
function power(x:real; y:integer): real;
var z : real;
begin
  if (y < 0) then begin
    if (x = 0.0) then error(zero_divide)
    else x := 1.0 / x;
    y := -y
  end;
  z := 1;
  while (y > 0) do begin
    while not odd(y) do begin
      y := y div 2;
      x := sqr(x)
    end;
    y := y - 1;
    z := x * z
  end;
  power := z
end; {power}
begin
  init_dimension( nul_dimension,  0{kg}, 0{m}, 0{s});
  if  equal_dimension( un2.dimension, nul_dimension) then begin
    mult_dimension( un1.dimension, round(un2.conversion));
    un1.conversion := power( un1.conversion, round(un2.conversion))
  end
  else error(inv_exponent)
end; {exponentiate_unit}

function convert_unit( un1,un2:rep_unit): real;
begin
  if  equal_dimension( un1.dimension, un2.dimension)
    then divide_unit( un2, un1)
    else error(inv_conversion);
  convert_unit := un2.conversion
end; {convert_unit}

procedure print_unit (un:rep_unit);
begin
```

```
    write(un.conversion:9,' ');
    print_dimension (un.dimension)
  end; {print_unit}


$ rep symbtab
  procedure add_symbtab (nm:rep_name; un:rep_unit);
  begin
    if (symbtabp = maxsymbt) then error(overfl_symbt)
    else begin
      with  symbtab[symbtabp]  do begin
        name := nm;
        unit := un
      end;
      symbtabp := symbtabp + 1
    end
  end; {add_symbtab}


  function in_symbtab (nm:rep_name): boolean;
  var i : -1..maxsymbt;
  begin
    symbtab[symbtabp].name := nm;
    i := -1;
    repeat i := i + 1  until  (symbtab[i].name = nm);
    in_symbtab := (i < symbtabp)
  end; {in_symbtab}


  procedure take_symbtab (var un:rep_unit; nm:rep_name);
  var i : -1..maxsymbt;
  begin
    i := -1;
    repeat i := i + 1  until  (symbtab[i].name = nm);
    un := symbtab[i].unit
  end; {take_symbtab}


  procedure print_symbtab;
  var i:0..maxsymbt;
  begin
    writeln(output);
    writeln(output,'SYMBOL TABLE');
    writeln(output,'************');
    writeln(output);
    for i:=0 to symbtabp-1 do
      with  symbtab[i]  do begin
        write(output, name, ' = ');
        print_unit (unit);
        writeln(output)
      end
  end {print_symbtab}
```

1.2.14. The syntax-semantic analyser for UNIT CONVERSION

From the generalized AECF translation syntax for UNIT CONVERSION, LILA produces the syntax-semantic analyser in the form of a Pascal program. This is illustrated in Fig. 1.7. The basic principles of this generation are explained in section 4.

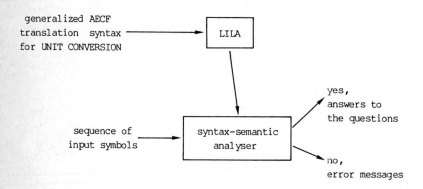

Fig. 1.7.

The skeleton of the generalized AECF translation syntax of UNIT CONVERSION, as it forms the input of LILA, has the following structure :

###inputvocabulary rep(integer);

```
description of the input symbols of
the syntax-semantic analyser.
<input symbol name> = code : type
```

```
###syntax;
  ##rule;
```
┌───┐
│ syntax rule of the form '<A> = e'   │
└───┘

```
  ##attribute;
```
┌───┐
│ type of the attribute of A   │
└───┘

```
  ##const;
```
┌───┐
│ local constant definitions   │
└───┘

```
  ##type;
```
┌───┐
│ local type definitions   │
└───┘

a number of times

```
  ##var;
```
┌───┐
│ local variable definitions   │
└───┘

```
  ##routine;
```
┌───┐
│ local procedure and function definitions │
└───┘

```
  ##action;
```
┌───┐
│ definitions of semantic actions   │
│ applied in e of the syntax rule.   │
└───┘

```
###globalinfo;
  ##parameter;
```
┌───┐
│ program parameters (files)   │
└───┘

```
  ##const;
```
┌───┐
│ global constant definitions   │
└───┘

```
  ##type;
```
┌───┐
│ global type definitions   │
└───┘

```
  ##var;
```
┌───┐
│ global variable definitions   │
└───┘

```
  ##routine;
```
┌───┐
│ global procedure and function definitions │
└───┘

Now follows the complete LILA input for the syntax-semantic analyser of UNIT CONVERSION.

```
###inputvocabulary  rep(integer);

  "identifier" = 2 : rep_name

  "number" = 3 : real

  "how" = 4     "many" = 5     "in" = 6
  "kg"  = 7     "m"    = 8     "s"  = 9

  "(" = 10   ")" = 11    "*" = 12    "+" = 13    "," = 14
  "-" = 15   "/" = 16    "=" = 17    "?" = 18    "^" = 19



###syntax;

$ Program
  ##rule;
    <program> =
      init
        <statement>  ( "," <statement> )*
      final

    ##action;
      #init;
        symbtabp := 0;

        writeln(output,'ANSWERS TO THE QUESTIONS');
        writeln(output,'************************');
        writeln(output)

      #final;
        print_symbtab



$ Statement
  ##rule;
    <statement> =
      <assignment> | <question>


$ Assignment
```

```
##rule;
  <assignment> =
    "identifier" "=" <expression> assign

  ##action;
    #assign;
      if  in_symbtab(@"identifier")
        then error(re_assignment)
        else add_symbtab( @"identifier", @<expression>)


$ Question
  ##rule;
    <question> =
      "how" "many"  <expression>  "in"  <expression> "?"  print_result

    ##action;
      #print_result;
        writeln(output, convert_unit(@<expression>1,@<expression>2):9)


$ Expression
  ##rule;
    <expression> =
      <term>   trans_et
        ( "+" <term> add  |  "-" <term> subtract )*

    ##attribute;
      rep_unit

    ##action;
      #trans_et;
        @<expression>  := @<term>1;

      #add;
        add_unit( @<expression>, @<term>2)

      #subtract;
        subtr_unit( @<expression>, @<term>3)


$ Term
  ##rule;
    <term> =
      <factor>   trans_tf
        ( "*" <factor> multiply |  "/" <factor> divide )*

    ##attribute;
      rep_unit
```

```
##action;
  #trans_tf;
    @<term>  := @<factor>1;

  #multiply;
    mult_unit( @<term>, @<factor>2)

  #divide;
    divide_unit( @<term>, @<factor>3)
```

$ <u>Factor</u>
```
  ##rule;
    <factor> =
      <secondary>  trans_fs
        ( "^" <factor> exponentiate    |  & )

  ##attribute;
    rep_unit

  ##action;
    #trans_fs;
      @<factor>1 := @<secondary>

    #exponentiate;
      exponentiate_unit( @<factor>1, @<factor>2)
```

$ <u>Secondary</u>
```
  ##rule;
    <secondary> =
        "-" <primary>  negate
      | <primary>        trans_sp

  ##attribute;
    rep_unit

  ##action;
    #negate;
      negate_unit(@<primary>1);
      @<secondary> := @<primary>1

    #trans_sp;
      @<secondary> := @<primary>2
```

$ <u>Primary</u>
```
  ##rule;
    <primary> =
```

```
       "identifier"  identifier
    |  "number"      number
    |  "kg"          mass_unit
    |  "m"           length_unit
    |  "s"           time_unit
    |  "(" <expression> ")" trans_pe

  ##attribute;
    rep_unit

  ##action;
    #identifier;
      if  in_symbtab(@"identifier")
        then take_symbtab( @<primary>, @"identifier")
        else error(undef_unit)

    #number;
      init_unit( @<primary>,  @"number"{conv}, 0{kg}, 0{m}, 0{s})

    #mass_unit;
      init_unit( @<primary>,  1.0{conv}, 1{kg}, 0{m}, 0{s})

    #length_unit;
      init_unit( @<primary>,  1.0{conv}, 0{kg}, 1{m}, 0{s})
    #time_unit;
      init_unit( @<primary>,  1.0{conv}, 0{kg}, 0{m}, 1{s})

    #trans_pe;
      @<primary> := @<expression>


###globalinfo;

  ##parameter;
    output,infile


  ##const;
    $ rep symbtab
      idlength =  8;
      maxsymbt = 10


  ##type;
    $ message
      message = (inv_terms, zero_divide, inv_exponent, undef_unit,
        inv_conversion, re_assignment, overfl_symbt);

    $ rep dimension
```

```
    rep_dimension = record
      mass    : integer;
      length : integer;
      time    : integer
    end;


$ rep_unit
  rep_unit = record
    dimension  : rep_dimension;
    conversion : real
  end;


$ rep_symbtab
  rep_name = packed array [1..idlength] of char;
  rep_symbtab = array [0..maxsymbt] of record
    name : rep_name;
    unit : rep_unit
  end


##var;
  $ rep_symbtab
    symbtab : rep_symbtab;
    symbtabp: 0..maxsymbt



##routine;
  $ message
    procedure error (m:message);
    begin
      nberrors := nberrors + 1;
      writeln(output,linenumber:4,'    ','*** ERROR ***');
      write(output,'        ');
      case  m  of
        inv_terms:
          writeln(output,'No corresponding dimensions for the ',
            'units in an addition or a subtraction.');
        zero_divide:
          writeln(output,'Attempt to divide by 0.');
        inv_exponent:
          writeln(output,'Exponent must be a number.');
        undef_unit:
          writeln(output,'Attempt to use an undefined unit.');
        inv_conversion:
          writeln(output,'No corresponding dimensions for ',
            'the units in a conversion.');
        re_assignment:
          writeln(output,'A language defined unit cannot be redefined.');
```

```
      overfl_symbt:
         writeln(output,'The number of units exceeds the allowed maximum.')
      end
   end; {error}


$ rep_dimension
   procedure init_dimension (var dim:rep_dimension; m,l,t:integer);
   begin
     dim.mass   := m;
     dim.length := l;
     dim.time   := t
   end; {init_dimension}




   procedure print_dimension (dim:rep_dimension);
   begin
     if (dim.mass <> 0) then begin
       write('kg');
       if (dim.mass <> 1)
         then write('^',dim.mass:1);
       if (dim.length <> 0) or (dim.time <> 0) then write('.')
     end;
     if (dim.length <> 0) then begin
       write('m');
       if (dim.length <> 1)
         then write('^',dim.length:1);
       if (dim.time <> 0) then write('.')
     end;
     if (dim.time <> 0) then begin
       write('s');
       if (dim.time <> 1)
         then write('^',dim.time:1)
     end
   end; {print_dimension}

   function equal_dimension (dim1,dim2:rep_dimension): boolean;
   begin
     equal_dimension :=
           (dim1.mass   = dim2.mass)
       and (dim1.length = dim2.length)
       and (dim1.time   = dim2.time)
   end; {equal_dimension}

   procedure add_dimension (var dim1:rep_dimension; dim2:rep_dimension);
   begin
     dim1.mass   := dim1.mass   + dim2.mass;
     dim1.length := dim1.length + dim2.length;
```

```
    dim1.time    := dim1.time   + dim2.time
  end; {add_dimension}

  procedure subtr_dimension (var dim1:rep_dimension; dim2:rep_dimension);
  begin
    dim1.mass    := dim1.mass   - dim2.mass  ;
    dim1.length := dim1.length - dim2.length;
    dim1.time    := dim1.time   - dim2.time
  end; {subtr_dimension}


  procedure mult_dimension( var dim:rep_dimension; ct:integer);
  begin
    dim.mass    := dim.mass   * ct;
    dim.length := dim.length * ct;
    dim.time    := dim.time   * ct
  end; {mult_dimension}


$ rep unit
  procedure init_unit (var un:rep_unit; cv:real; m,l,t: integer);
  begin
    init_dimension( un.dimension, m, l, t);
    un.conversion := cv
  end; {init_unit}

  procedure add_unit (var un1:rep_unit; un2:rep_unit);
  begin
    if  equal_dimension( un1.dimension, un2.dimension)
      then un1.conversion := un1.conversion + un2.conversion
      else error(inv_terms)
  end; {add_unit}

  procedure subtr_unit (var un1:rep_unit; un2:rep_unit);
  begin
    if  equal_dimension( un1.dimension, un2.dimension)
      then un1.conversion := un1.conversion - un2.conversion
      else error(inv_terms)
  end; {subtr_unit}

  procedure negate_unit (var un:rep_unit);
  begin  un.conversion := - un.conversion
  end; {negate_unit}

  procedure mult_unit (var un1:rep_unit; un2:rep_unit);
  begin
    add_dimension( un1.dimension, un2.dimension);
    un1.conversion := un1.conversion * un2.conversion
  end; {mult_unit}
```

```
procedure divide_unit (var un1:rep_unit; un2:rep_unit);
begin
   subtr_dimension( un1.dimension, un2.dimension);
   if (un2.conversion = 0.0)  then error(zero_divide)
   else un1.conversion := un1.conversion / un2.conversion
end; {divide_unit}

procedure exponentiate_unit ( var un1:rep_unit; un2:rep_unit);
var nul_dimension: rep_dimension;
function power(x:real; y:integer): real;
var z : real;
begin
   if (y < 0) then begin
      if (x = 0.0) then error(zero_divide)
      else x := 1.0 / x;
      y := -y
   end;
   z := 1;
   while (y > 0) do begin
      while not odd(y) do begin
         y := y div 2;
         x := sqr(x)
      end;
      y := y - 1;
      z := x * z
   end;
   power := z
end; {power}
begin
   init_dimension( nul_dimension,  0{kg}, 0{m}, 0{s});
   if  equal_dimension( un2.dimension, nul_dimension) then begin
      mult_dimension( un1.dimension, round(un2.conversion));
      un1.conversion := power( un1.conversion, round(un2.conversion))
   end
   else error(inv_exponent)
end; {exponentiate_unit}

function convert_unit( un1,un2:rep_unit): real;
begin
   if  equal_dimension( un1.dimension, un2.dimension)
      then divide_unit( un2, un1)
      else error(inv_conversion);
   convert_unit := un2.conversion
end; {convert_unit}

procedure print_unit (un:rep_unit);
begin
   write(un.conversion:9,' ');
   print_dimension (un.dimension)
```

```
  end; {print_unit}


$ rep_symbtab
  procedure add_symbtab (nm:rep_name; un:rep_unit);
  begin
    if (symbtabp = maxsymbt) then error(overfl_symbt)
    else begin
      with  symbtab[symbtabp]  do begin
        name := nm;
        unit := un
      end;
      symbtabp := symbtabp + 1
    end
  end; {add_symbtab}

  function in_symbtab (nm:rep_name): boolean;
  var i : -1..maxsymbt;
  begin
    symbtab[symbtabp].name := nm;
    i := -1;
    repeat  i := i + 1  until  (symbtab[i].name = nm);
    in_symbtab := (i < symbtabp)
  end; {in_symbtab}

  procedure take_symbtab (var un:rep_unit; nm:rep_name);
  var i : -1..maxsymbt;
  begin
    i := -1;
    repeat  i := i + 1  until  (symbtab[i].name = nm);
    un := symbtab[i].unit
  end; {take_symbtab}

  procedure print_symbtab;
  var i:0..maxsymbt;
  begin
    writeln(output);
    writeln(output,'SYMBOL TABLE');
    writeln(output,'************');
    writeln(output);
    for i:=0 to symbtabp-1 do
      with  symbtab[i]  do begin
        write(output, name, ' = ');
        print_unit (unit);
        writeln(output)
      end
  end {print_symbtab}
```

The following ilustrates the execution of the UNIT CONVERSION interpreter. The input is :

```
cm = 0.01 * m, inch = 2.54 * cm, feet = 0.3048 * m,
how many inch in feet?,

yard = 0.9144 * m,
how many inch in yard?,
how many feet in yard?,

sqinch = inch * inch, sqfeet = feet * feet,
how many sqinch in sqfeet?,

cuinch = inch ^ 3, m2 = m * m, m3 = m ^ 3,
how many sqinch in m2?,
how many cuinch in m2 * m?,

how many m/s in (sqfeet/yard) / s?
```

The following results are produced :

```
ANSWERS TO THE QUESTIONS
************************

  1.20e+01
  3.60e+01
  3.00e+00
  1.44e+02
  1.55e+03
  6.10e+04
  1.02e-01

SYMBOL TABLE
************

cm       =  1.00e-02 m
inch     =  2.54e-02 m
feet     =  3.05e-01 m
yard     =  9.14e-01 m
sqinch   =  6.45e-04 m^2
sqfeet   =  9.29e-02 m^2
cuinch   =  1.64e-05 m^3
m2       =  1.00e+00 m^2
m3       =  1.00e+00 m^3
```

1.3. Lexical analysis, syntactic phase

The task of the lexical analyser is to produce the appropriate sequence of input symbols for the syntax-semantic analyser. The input of the lexical analyser is a sequence of characters.

As for the syntax-semantic analyser, the lexical analyser consists of two conceptually separated phases : the syntactic phase and the semantic phase. The syntactic phase of the lexical analyser gives the answer 'yes', if the input string of characters is lexically correct, and 'no' otherwise, in which case error messages are produced. The semantic phase of the lexical analyser is responsible for the production of output symbols, possibly attributed, which will be the input for the syntax-semantic analyser. This is schematically illustrated in Fig. 1.8.

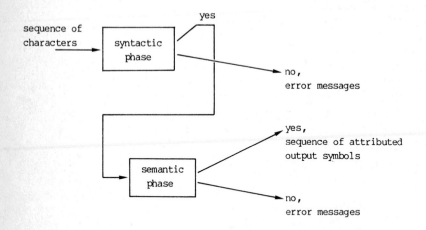

Fig. 1.8.

Actually, the syntactic phase and semantic phase of the lexical analyser are performed in one pass. This is illustrated in Fig. 1.9.

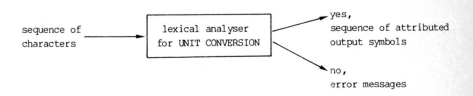

```
sequence of              lexical analyser          yes,
characters               for UNIT CONVERSION        sequence of attributed
                                                    output symbols

                                                    no,
                                                    error messages
```

Fig. 1.9.

As for the syntax analyser (see section 1.1), the syntactic phase of the lexical analyser is described by means of an ECF syntax.

1.3.1. Input vocabulary

The input symbols of the syntactic phase of the lexical analyser, together with their representation are listed in the inputvocabulary. We are free to choose the names of the input symbols, whereas their representation must correspond to the character representation of the computer on which the lexical analyser will run. E.g., for the blanc character, the symbolic name is "bl" and the representation is 32, which is the ASCII code for a space. More details about the inputvocabulary can be found in the Reference Guide (see Appendix).

inputvocabulary rep(char), file(input);

"bl"= 32	"(" = 40	")" = 41	"*" = 42	"+" = 43	"," = 44
"-" = 45	"." = 46	"/" = 47	"0" = 48	"1" = 49	"2" = 50
"3" = 51	"4" = 52	"5" = 53	"6" = 54	"7" = 55	"8" = 56
"9" = 57	"=" = 61	"?" = 63	"^" = 94	"a" = 97	"b" = 98
"c" = 99	"d" =100	"e" =101	"f" =102	"g" =103	"h" =104
"i" =105	"j" =106	"k" =107	"l" =108	"m" =109	"n" =110
"o" =111	"p" =112	"q" =113	"r" =114	"s" =115	"t" =116
"u" =117	"v" =118	"w" =119	"x" =120	"y" =121	"z" =122

1.3.2. Program

At the lexical level, a UNIT CONVERSION program consists of identifiers, keywords, numbers and delimiters. This is described by the
following ECF syntax rule :

```
##rule;
  <program> =
    ( ( <identifier keyword>
    | <number>
    | &
    )
    <delimiter>
    )*
```

Here, the metasyntactic symbol '&' denotes the empty alternative.

1.3.3. Identifier keyword

Identifiers and keywords are strings of letters and digits, the
first element of the string being a letter. This is described by
the following ECF syntax rule :

```
##rule;
  <identifier keyword> =
    <letter>
      ( <letter>  |  <digit>  )*
```

1.3.4. Number

Numbers in UNIT CONVERSION consist of an integer part and possibly a fractional part. . This is described by the following ECF syntax rule :

```
##rule;
  <number> =
    <digit>+
      ( "."  <digit>+
      | &
      )
```

Here, (e)+ must be read as 'one or more times the processing of e'. The metasyntactic operator '+' is called the <u>positive closure set operator</u>.

1.3.5. <u>Delimiter</u>

The delimiters in UNIT CONVERSION are listed in the following ECF syntax rule :

```
##rule;
  <delimiter> =
      ","  |  "="  |  "?"  |  "-"  |  "+"  |  "*"
    |  "/"  |  "^"  |  "("  |  ")"  |  "bl"
```

1.3.6. <u>Letter</u>

The ECF syntax rule defining a letter is :

```
##rule;
  <letter> =
      "a"  |  "b"  |  "c"  |  "d"  |  "e"  |  "f"  |  "g"  |  "h"  |  "i"
    |  "j"  |  "k"  |  "l"  |  "m"  |  "n"  |  "o"  |  "p"  |  "q"  |  "r"
    |  "s"  |  "t"  |  "u"  |  "v"  |  "w"  |  "x"  |  "y"  |  "z"
```

1.3.7. <u>Digit</u>

The ECF syntax rule defining a digit is :

```
##rule;
  <digit> =
      "0"  |  "1"  |  "2"  |  "3"  |  "4"
    |  "5"  |  "6"  |  "7"  |  "8"  |  "9"
```

1.3.8. <u>The ECF syntax describing the syntactic phase of the lexical analyser</u>

The complete ECF syntax, as it is used as input for LILA to produce the syntactic phase of the lexical analyser, is given below :

```
###inputvocabulary  rep(char), file(input);
```

```
"bl"= 32    "(" = 40    ")" = 41    "*" = 42    "+" = 43    "," = 44
"-" = 45    "." = 46    "/" = 47    "0" = 48    "1" = 49    "2" = 50
"3" = 51    "4" = 52    "5" = 53    "6" = 54    "7" = 55    "8" = 56
"9" = 57    "=" = 61    "?" = 63    "^" = 94    "a" = 97    "b" = 98
"c" = 99    "d" =100    "e" =101    "f" =102    "g" =103    "h" =104
"i" =105    "j" =106    "k" =107    "l" =108    "m" =109    "n" =110
"o" =111    "p" =112    "q" =113    "r" =114    "s" =115    "t" =116
"u" =117    "v" =118    "w" =119    "x" =120    "y" =121    "z" =122
```

```
###syntax;
```

```
$ Program
  ##rule;
    <program> =
      ( ( <identifier keyword>
      | <number>
      | &
      )
      <delimiter>
    )*
```

```
$ Identifier or Keyword
  ##rule;
    <identifier keyword> =
      <letter>
      ( <letter> | <digit> )*
```

```
$ Constant
  ##rule;
    <number> =
      <digit>+
      ( "." <digit>+
      | &
      )
```

```
$ Delimiter
  ##rule;
    <delimiter> =
        ","  | "="  | "?"  | "-"  | "+"  | "*"
      | "/"  | "^"  | "("  | ")"  | "bl"
```

```
$ Letter
 ##rule;
   <letter> =
       "a"  |  "b"  |  "c"  |  "d"  |  "e"  |  "f"  |  "g"  |  "h"  |  "i"
     |  "j"  |  "k"  |  "l"  |  "m"  |  "n"  |  "o"  |  "p"  |  "q"  |  "r"
     |  "s"  |  "t"  |  "u"  |  "v"  |  "w"  |  "x"  |  "y"  |  "z"


$ Digit
 ##rule;
   <digit> =
       "0"  |  "1"  |  "2"  |  "3"  |  "4"
     |  "5"  |  "6"  |  "7"  |  "8"  |  "9"



###globalinfo;


  ##parameter;
    input, output
```

The generation of the syntactic phase of the lexical analyser by means of LILA is illustrated in Fig. 1.10.

In contrast with the ECF syntax given in section 1.1, the ECF syntax describing the syntactic phase of the lexical analyser only deals with iterative structures; it does not use recursivity. Such an ECF syntax is also called a regular syntax. The processor produced by LILA is then called a finite-state acceptor. The subject of regular syntaxes and finite-state acceptors in relation to compiler generation is thoroughly discussed in Part 1.

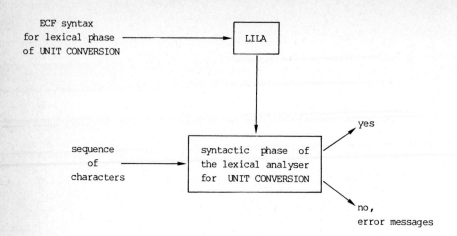

Fig. 1.10.

1.4.   Lexical analysis, syntax-semantic phase (nonoptimized version)

The syntactic phase of the lexical analyser, as it is described
in section 1.3, checks if the input sequence of characters is a le-
gal UNIT CONVERSION program at the lexical level. What we actually
want is a processor producing a sequence of attributed output symbols satisfying the input format of the syntax-semantic analyser,
see section 1.2. As for the description of the syntax-semantic analyser, the description of the lexical analyser is syntax-directed.
We take the ECF syntax of section 1.3 and add semantic actions to
it. These semantic actions are responsible for the production of
the attributed output symbols. Also, local and global information
is added, together with semantic action definitions and attribute
type definitions. Such a syntax has been called a generalized AECF
translation syntax (see section 1.2).

1.4.1. Input vocabulary

The input vocabulary lists the input symbols, together with their representations. Clearly, the input symbols of a lexical analyser have no attributes.

###inputvocabulary rep(char), file(input);

"bl"= 32	"(" = 40	")" = 41	"*" = 42	"+" = 43	"," = 44
"-" = 45	"." = 46	"/" = 47	"0" = 48	"1" = 49	"2" = 50
"3" = 51	"4" = 52	"5" = 53	"6" = 54	"7" = 55	"8" = 56
"9" = 57	"=" = 61	"?" = 63	"^" = 94	"a" = 97	"b" = 98
"c" = 99	"d" =100	"e" =101	"f" =102	"g" =103	"h" =104
"i" =105	"j" =106	"k" =107	"l" =108	"m" =109	"n" =110
"o" =111	"p" =112	"q" =113	"r" =114	"s" =115	"t" =116
"u" =117	"v" =118	"w" =119	"x" =120	"y" =121	"z" =122

1.4.2. Output vocabulary

The output vocabulary describes the attributed output symbols to be produced by the lexical analyser of UNIT CONVERSION. As for the input vocabulary, the output vocabulary lists the output symbols, with their integer representations and the types of their corresponding attributes, if any.

###outputvocabulary rep(integer);

[identifier] = 2 : rep_name

[number] = 3 : real

[how] = 4	[many] = 5	[in] = 6
[kg] = 7	[m] = 8	[s] = 9

[(] = 10	[)] = 11	[*] = 12	[+] = 13	[,] = 14
[-] = 15	[/] = 16	[=] = 17	[?] = 18	[^] = 19

As an example, the output symbol [identifier] has an attribute of type 'rep_name'. The type 'rep_name' is defined in globalinfo, see section 1.4.9. Output symbols will always be enclosed between '[' and ']'. This makes it possible to distinguish the input symbol "+" from the output symbol [+].

The attribute of an output symbol can be accessed in the semantic actions. As an example, the attribute of the output symbol [identifier] is accessed by :

  @[identifier]

which denotes a variable of type 'rep_name'. This variable is local to the rule where it is used.
The representation of the output symbol [identifier] can be obtained by :

  %[identifier]

which denotes a constant of type 'integer'.
Clearly, the output vocabulary of the lexical analyser must be identical to the input vocabulary of the syntax-semantic analyser.

1.4.3. Program

The lexical analysis of a UNIT CONVERSION program is described by the following syntax rule :

```
##rule;
 <program> =
   ( ( <identifier keyword>
     | <number>
     | &
     )
     <delimiter>
   )*
```

The lexical analysis of a UNIT CONVERSION program is straightforward.

1.4.4.   Identifier keyword

The lexical analysis of an identifier or a keyword is described by the following syntax rule :

```
##rule;
 <identifier keyword> =
   <letter> init_name
     ( <letter> add_letter | <digit> add_digit )*
   out_idkey
```

```
##var;
  nb_chars : 1..maxint

##action;
  #init_name;
    @[identifier] := '          ';
    @[identifier] [1] := @<letter>1;
    nb_chars := 1

  #add_letter;
    nb_chars := nb_chars + 1;
    if (nb_chars <= idlength)
      then @[identifier] [nb_chars] := @<letter>2

  #add_digit;
    nb_chars := nb_chars + 1;
    if (nb_chars <= idlength)
      then @[identifier] [nb_chars] := @<digit>

  #out_idkey;
    if (nb_chars > idlength) then error(iden_truncated);
    if      ( @[identifier]='how    ' ) then out(%[how])
    else if ( @[identifier]='many   ' ) then out(%[many])
    else if ( @[identifier]='in     ' ) then out(%[in])
    else if ( @[identifier]='kg     ' ) then out(%[kg])
    else if ( @[identifier]='m      ' ) then out(%[m])
    else if ( @[identifier]='s      ' ) then out(%[s])
    else out(%[identifier])
```

This syntax rule determines that an identifier or a keyword is a string of letters and digits, the first element of the string being a letter. If the string is a keyword, one of the symbols [how], [many], [in], [kg], [m] or [s] is produced. If it is an identifier, an output symbol [identifier], attributed with the string, is produced.

The lexical analysis of an identifier or a keyword activates the processing of <letter>, calculating the attribute value, which is a letter (see section 1.4.7) and then activates the semantic action 'init_name'. The semantic action 'init_name' has access to an attribute variable @[identifier]. The semantic action 'init_name' initializes @[identifier] with the value of @<letter>1.

Then, for each letter or digit being processed, @[identifier] is filled up with the value of @<letter>2 or @<digit> by the semantic actions 'add_letter' and 'add_digit', respectively.

Finally, the semantic action 'out_idkey' is activated producing one of the output symbols [identifier], [how], [many], [in], [kg], [m] and [s].

In LILA, the production of an output symbol, e.g. [identifier], is performed by the standard procedure 'out'. The procedure call :

```
out(%[identifier])
```

produces an output symbol [identifier], i.e., the representation is %[identifier] and the attribute value is @[identifier]. This attribute value must have been calculated prior to the activation of out. Notice that @[identifier] is local to the syntax rule and is commonly accessible by any semantic action involved in that syntax rule.

1.4.5. Number

The lexical analysis of a number is described by the following syntax rule :

```
##rule;
  <number> =
    init_value
      (  <digit> whole_value  )+
        ( "." (  <digit> fract_value    )+
        | &
        )
    out_number

##var;
  scale : real

##action;
  #init_value;
    @[number] := 0.0;
    scale    := 0.1

  #whole_value;
    @[number] := @[number]*10 + ( ord(@<digit>1) - ord('0') )

  #fract_value;
    @[number] := @[number] + (ord(@<digit>2) - ord('0'))*scale;
    scale    := scale/10

  #out_number;
    out(%[number])
```

This syntax rule determines that a number consists of an integer part and possibly a fractional part. An output symbol [number], attributed with its value, will be produced.

The lexical analysis of a number activates the semantic action 'init_value', which initializes the attribute variable @[number] and the scale factor.

For each digit of the integer part, the attribute @[number] is calculated in terms of its previous value and the value of @<digit>1.

For each digit of the fractional part, the attribute @[number] is calculated in terms of its previous value, the attribute @<digit>2 and the scale factor.

Finally, the semantic action 'out_number' is activated producing an output symbol [number].

1.4.6. Delimiter

The lexical analysis of a delimiter is described by the following syntax rule :

```
##rule;
  <delimiter> =
     "," out_cm  |  "=" out_eq  |  "?" out_qm  |  "-" out_mi
   | "+" out_pl  |  "*" out_mu  |  "/" out_di  |  "^" out_ex
   | "(" out_op  |  ")" out_cp  |  "bl"

  ##action;
    #out_cm;  out(%[,])        #out_eq;  out(%[=])
    #out_qm;  out(%[?])        #out_mi;  out(%[-])
    #out_pl;  out(%[+])        #out_mu;  out(%[*])
    #out_di;  out(%[/])        #out_ex;  out(%[^])
    #out_op;  out(%[(])        #out_cp;  out(%[)])
```

The lexical analysis of a delimiter simply produces an output symbol for each delimiter. In the optimized version (see section 1.5), the syntax rule for <delimiter> is written in a more compact way, giving rise to a more efficient lexical analysis of delimiters.

1.4.7. Letter

The lexical analysis of a letter is described by the following syntax rule :

```
##rule;
  <letter> =
        "a" gen_a  |   "b" gen_b  |   "c" gen_c  |   "d" gen_d
      | "e" gen_e  |   "f" gen_f  |   "g" gen_g  |   "h" gen_h
      | "i" gen_i  |   "j" gen_j  |   "k" gen_k  |   "l" gen_l
      | "m" gen_m  |   "n" gen_n  |   "o" gen_o  |   "p" gen_p
      | "q" gen_q  |   "r" gen_r  |   "s" gen_s  |   "t" gen_t
      | "u" gen_u  |   "v" gen_v  |   "w" gen_w  |   "x" gen_x
      | "y" gen_y  |   "z" gen_z

##attribute;
  char

##action;
  #gen_a;  @<letter> := 'a'          #gen_b;  @<letter> := 'b'
  #gen_c;  @<letter> := 'c'          #gen_d;  @<letter> := 'd'
  #gen_e;  @<letter> := 'e'          #gen_f;  @<letter> := 'f'
  #gen_g;  @<letter> := 'g'          #gen_h;  @<letter> := 'h'
  #gen_i;  @<letter> := 'i'          #gen_j;  @<letter> := 'j'
  #gen_k;  @<letter> := 'k'          #gen_l;  @<letter> := 'l'
  #gen_m;  @<letter> := 'm'          #gen_n;  @<letter> := 'n'
  #gen_o;  @<letter> := 'o'          #gen_p;  @<letter> := 'p'
  #gen_q;  @<letter> := 'q'          #gen_r;  @<letter> := 'r'
  #gen_s;  @<letter> := 's'          #gen_t;  @<letter> := 't'
  #gen_u;  @<letter> := 'u'          #gen_v;  @<letter> := 'v'
  #gen_w;  @<letter> := 'w'          #gen_x;  @<letter> := 'x'
  #gen_y;  @<letter> := 'y'          #gen_z;  @<letter> := 'z'
```

The lexical analysis of letter calculates the attribute value of the nonterminal <letter>. In the optimized version (see section 1.5), the syntax rule for <letter> is written in a more compact form, giving rise to a more efficient lexical analysis of letters.

1.4.8. Digit

The lexical analysis of a digit is described by the following syntax rule :

```
##rule;
  <digit> =
```

```
        "0"  gen_0   |   "1"  gen_1   |   "2"  gen_2   |   "3"  gen_3
    |   "4"  gen_4   |   "5"  gen_5   |   "6"  gen_6   |   "7"  gen_7
    |   "8"  gen_8   |   "9"  gen_9

##attribute;
  char


##action;
  #gen_0;   @<digit> := '0'        #gen_1;   @<digit> := '1'
  #gen_2;   @<digit> := '2'        #gen_3;   @<digit> := '3'
  #gen_4;   @<digit> := '4'        #gen_5;   @<digit> := '5'
  #gen_6;   @<digit> := '6'        #gen_7;   @<digit> := '7'
  #gen_8;   @<digit> := '8'        #gen_9;   @<digit> := '9'
```

The lexical analysis of a digit calculates the attribute value of
the nonterminal <digit>. In the optimized version (see section
1.5), the syntax rule for <digit> is written in a more compact way,
giving rise to a more efficient lexical analysis of digits.

1.4.9. Global information

Global information (globalinfo) contains the definitions of constants, types, variables and routines (functions and procedures)
which are global to all semantic actions.

```
###globalinfo;


  ##parameter;
    input, output, outfile



  ##const;
    idlength = 8


  ##type;
    rep_name = packed array [1..idlength] of char;

    message = (iden_truncated)


  ##routine;
    procedure error (m:message);
    begin
```

```
    nberrors := nberrors + 1;
    writeln(output,linenumber:4,'    ','*** ERROR ***');
    write(output,'        ');
    case m of
      iden_truncated :
        writeln('Identifier truncated to ',idlength:2,' char''s')
    end
  end {error}
```

1.4.10.
The lexical analyser for UNIT CONVERSION (nonoptimized version)

The complete LILA input describing the lexical analysis of UNIT
CONVERSION is given below.

###inputvocabulary rep(char), file(input);

```
"bl"= 32    "(" = 40    ")" = 41    "*" = 42    "+" = 43    "," = 44
"-" = 45    "." = 46    "/" = 47    "0" = 48    "1" = 49    "2" = 50
"3" = 51    "4" = 52    "5" = 53    "6" = 54    "7" = 55    "8" = 56
"9" = 57    "=" = 61    "?" = 63    "^" = 94    "a" = 97    "b" = 98
"c" = 99    "d" =100    "e" =101    "f" =102    "g" =103    "h" =104
"i" =105    "j" =106    "k" =107    "l" =108    "m" =109    "n" =110
"o" =111    "p" =112    "q" =113    "r" =114    "s" =115    "t" =116
"u" =117    "v" =118    "w" =119    "x" =120    "y" =121    "z" =122
```

###outputvocabulary rep(integer);

```
    [identifier] = 2 : rep_name

    [number] = 3 : real

    [how]   = 4      [many] = 5      [in] = 6
    [kg]    = 7      [m]    = 8      [s]  = 9

    [(] = 10     [)] = 11    [*] = 12    [+] = 13    [,] = 14
    [-] = 15     [/] = 16    [=] = 17    [?] = 18    [^] = 19
```

###syntax;

$ <u>Program</u>
  ##rule;

```
<program> =
  ( ( <identifier keyword>
    | <number>
    | &
    )
    <delimiter>
  )*
```

$ Identifier or Keyword
  ##rule;
```
   <identifier keyword> =
     <letter> init_name
       ( <letter> add_letter | <digit> add_digit )*
     out_idkey
```

  ##var;
```
   nb_chars : 1..maxint
```

  ##action;
```
   #init_name;
     @[identifier] := '         ';
     @[identifier] [1] := @<letter>1;
     nb_chars := 1


   #add_letter;
     nb_chars := nb_chars + 1;
     if (nb_chars <= idlength)
       then @[identifier] [nb_chars] := @<letter>2

   #add_digit;
     nb_chars := nb_chars + 1;
     if (nb_chars <= idlength)
       then @[identifier] [nb_chars] := @<digit>

   #out_idkey;
     if (nb_chars > idlength) then error(iden_truncated);
     if      ( @[identifier]='how   ' ) then out(%[how])
     else if ( @[identifier]='many  ' ) then out(%[many])
     else if ( @[identifier]='in    ' ) then out(%[in])
     else if ( @[identifier]='kg    ' ) then out(%[kg])
     else if ( @[identifier]='m     ' ) then out(%[m])
     else if ( @[identifier]='s     ' ) then out(%[s])
     else out(%[identifier])
```

$ Constant
  ##rule;

```
<number> =
  init_value
    (  <digit> whole_value  )+
      ( "."  (  <digit> fract_value   )+
      | &
      )
  out_number

##var;
  scale : real

##action;
  #init_value;
    @[number] := 0.0;
    scale     := 0.1

  #whole_value;
    @[number] := @[number]*10 + ( ord(@<digit>1) - ord('0') )



  #fract_value;
    @[number] := @[number] + (ord(@<digit>2) - ord('0'))*scale;
    scale     := scale/10

  #out_number;
    out(%[number])
```

$ <u>Delimiter</u>
```
##rule;
  <delimiter> =
      ","  out_cm  |   "=" out_eq  |   "?" out_qm  |   "-" out_mi
    | "+" out_pl  |   "*" out_mu  |   "/" out_di  |   "^" out_ex
    | "(" out_op  |   ")" out_cp  |   "bl"

  ##action;
    #out_cm;  out(%[,])          #out_eq;  out(%[=])
    #out_qm;  out(%[?])          #out_mi;  out(%[-])
    #out_pl;  out(%[+])          #out_mu;  out(%[*])
    #out_di;  out(%[/])          #out_ex;  out(%[^])
    #out_op;  out(%[(])          #out_cp;  out(%[)])
```

$ <u>Letter</u>
```
##rule;
  <letter> =
      "a" gen_a  |   "b" gen_b  |   "c" gen_c  |   "d" gen_d
```

```
     | "e" gen_e   |   "f" gen_f   |   "g" gen_g   |   "h" gen_h
     | "i" gen_i   |   "j" gen_j   |   "k" gen_k   |   "l" gen_l
     | "m" gen_m   |   "n" gen_n   |   "o" gen_o   |   "p" gen_p
     | "q" gen_q   |   "r" gen_r   |   "s" gen_s   |   "t" gen_t
     | "u" gen_u   |   "v" gen_v   |   "w" gen_w   |   "x" gen_x
     | "y" gen_y   |   "z" gen_z


  ##attribute;
    char


  ##action;
    #gen_a;   @<letter> := 'a'        #gen_b;   @<letter> := 'b'
    #gen_c;   @<letter> := 'c'        #gen_d;   @<letter> := 'd'
    #gen_e;   @<letter> := 'e'        #gen_f;   @<letter> := 'f'
    #gen_g;   @<letter> := 'g'        #gen_h;   @<letter> := 'h'
    #gen_i;   @<letter> := 'i'        #gen_j;   @<letter> := 'j'
    #gen_k;   @<letter> := 'k'        #gen_l;   @<letter> := 'l'
    #gen_m;   @<letter> := 'm'        #gen_n;   @<letter> := 'n'
    #gen_o;   @<letter> := 'o'        #gen_p;   @<letter> := 'p'
    #gen_q;   @<letter> := 'q'        #gen_r;   @<letter> := 'r'
    #gen_s;   @<letter> := 's'        #gen_t;   @<letter> := 't'
    #gen_u;   @<letter> := 'u'        #gen_v;   @<letter> := 'v'
    #gen_w;   @<letter> := 'w'        #gen_x;   @<letter> := 'x'
    #gen_y;   @<letter> := 'y'        #gen_z;   @<letter> := 'z'


$ Digit
  ##rule;
    <digit> =
        "0" gen_0   |   "1" gen_1   |   "2" gen_2   |   "3" gen_3
      | "4" gen_4   |   "5" gen_5   |   "6" gen_6   |   "7" gen_7
      | "8" gen_8   |   "9" gen_9


  ##attribute;
    char


  ##action;
    #gen_0;   @<digit> := '0'        #gen_1;   @<digit> := '1'
    #gen_2;   @<digit> := '2'        #gen_3;   @<digit> := '3'
    #gen_4;   @<digit> := '4'        #gen_5;   @<digit> := '5'
    #gen_6;   @<digit> := '6'        #gen_7;   @<digit> := '7'
    #gen_8;   @<digit> := '8'        #gen_9;   @<digit> := '9'



###globalinfo;
```

```
##parameter;
  input, output, outfile


##const;
  idlength = 8


##type;
  rep_name = packed array [1..idlength] of char;

  message = (iden_truncated)


##routine;
  procedure error (m:message);
  begin
    nberrors := nberrors + 1;
    writeln(output,linenumber:4,'   ','*** ERROR ***');
    write(output,'       ');
    case  m  of
      iden_truncated :
        writeln('Identifier truncated to ',idlength:2,' char''s')
    end
  end {error}
```

1.5. Lexical analysis, syntax-semantic phase (optimized version)

The lexical analysis described in section 1.4, can be written in
a more compact way by making use of the LILA standard variable
'inp'.

This variable represents the input head of the lexical analyser
as it is produced by LILA. The variable 'inp' contains the input
symbol currently under the input head. It is a record variable with
two fields : one for the representation of the input symbol (inp.c)
and one for the attribute value (inp.a). The variable 'inp' is global to all semantic action definitions.

1.5.1. Identifier keyword

The lexical analysis of an identifier or a keyword in the optimized version is described by the following syntax rule :

```
##rule;
  <identifier keyword> =
    init_name  <letter>
      (  add_name ( <letter> | <digit> )  )*
    out_idkey

  ##var;
    nb_chars : 1..maxint

  ##action;
    #init_name;
      @[identifier] := '          ';
      @[identifier] [1] := inp.c;
      nb_chars := 1

    #add_name;
      nb_chars := nb_chars + 1;
      if (nb_chars <= idlength)
        then @[identifier] [nb_chars] := inp.c



    #out_idkey;
      if (nb_chars > idlength) then error(iden_truncated);
      if      ( @[identifier]='how     ' ) then out(%[how])
      else if ( @[identifier]='many    ' ) then out(%[many])
      else if ( @[identifier]='in      ' ) then out(%[in])
      else if ( @[identifier]='kg      ' ) then out(%[kg])
      else if ( @[identifier]='m       ' ) then out(%[m])
      else if ( @[identifier]='s       ' ) then out(%[s])
      else out(%[identifier])
```

When the semantic action 'init_name' is activated, the input symbol under the input head of the lexical analyser is a letter. In
the semantic action 'init_name', we may write

```
@[identifier][1] := inp.c
```

When the semantic action 'add_name' is activated, the input symbol under the input head is either a letter or a digit. In the semantic action 'add_name', we may write

```
@[identifier][nb_chars] := inp.c
```

In this way, the nonterminal symbols <letter> and <digit> need not be attributed. This makes their syntax rules extremely simple :

```
##rule;
  <letter> =
    "a"  |  "b"  |  "c"  |  "d"  |  "e"  |  "f"  |  "g"  |  "h"  |  "i"
  | "j"  |  "k"  |  "l"  |  "m"  |  "n"  |  "o"  |  "p"  |  "q"  |  "r"
  | "s"  |  "t"  |  "u"  |  "v"  |  "w"  |  "x"  |  "y"  |  "z"
```

```
##rule;
  <digit> =
    "0"  |  "1"  |  "2"  |  "3"  |  "4"
  | "5"  |  "6"  |  "7"  |  "8"  |  "9"
```

Notice that the semantic action init_name precedes the nonterminal symbol <letter>. Indeed, the processing of a letter is something like :

```
if the input head contains a letter
  then read next symbol
  else error
fi
```

1.5.2. Number

The lexical analysis of a number in the optimized version is described by the following syntax rule :

```
##rule;
  <number> =
    init_value
      (  whole_value <digit>  )+
      ( "."  (  fract_value <digit>  )+
      | &
      )
    out_number

  ##var;
    scale : real
```

```
##action;
  #init_value;
    @[number] := 0.0;
    scale     := 0.1

  #whole_value;
    @[number] := @[number]*10 + ( ord(inp.c) - ord('0') )

  #fract_value;
    @[number] := @[number] + (ord(inp.c) - ord('0'))*scale;
    scale     := scale/10

  #out_number;
    out(%[number])
```

The optimization is similar to the one performed in the analysis of an identifier or a keyword.

1.5.3. Delimiter

The lexical analysis of a delimiter in the optimized version is described by the following syntax rule :

```
##rule;
  <delimiter> =
      out_delimiter
        ( ","  |  "="  |  "?"  |  "-"  |  "+"  |  "*"
        |  "/"  |  "^"  |  "("  |  ")"  )
      |  "bl"

##action;
  #out_delimiter;
    out( ord(inp.c) )
```

When the semantic action 'out_delimiter' is activated, 'inp' contains a delimiter. Since we are free to choose the representation of the output delimiter symbols, we have taken the integer that corresponds with the character representation of the corresponding input delimiter symbol.

As an example, the representation of the output symbol [(] is the integer 40 and the representation of the input symbol "(" is the character with internal code 40. In this way, the production of output symbols for delimiters is greatly simplified.

1.5.4. The lexical analyser for UNIT CONVERSION (optimized version)

The complete generalized AECF translation syntax, optimized version, describing the lexical analysis of UNIT CONVERSION is given below.

###inputvocabulary rep(char), file(input);

"bl"= 32	"(" = 40	")" = 41	"*" = 42	"+" = 43	"," = 44
"-" = 45	"." = 46	"/" = 47	"0" = 48	"1" = 49	"2" = 50
"3" = 51	"4" = 52	"5" = 53	"6" = 54	"7" = 55	"8" = 56
"9" = 57	"=" = 61	"?" = 63	"^" = 94	"a" = 97	"b" = 98
"c" = 99	"d" =100	"e" =101	"f" =102	"g" =103	"h" =104
"i" =105	"j" =106	"k" =107	"l" =108	"m" =109	"n" =110
"o" =111	"p" =112	"q" =113	"r" =114	"s" =115	"t" =116
"u" =117	"v" =118	"w" =119	"x" =120	"y" =121	"z" =122

###outputvocabulary rep(integer);

[identifier] = 2 : rep_name

[number] = 3 : real

[how] = 4	[many] = 5	[in] = 6
[kg] = 7	[m] = 8	[s] = 9

[(] = 40	[)] = 41	[*] = 42	[+] = 43	[,] = 44
[-] = 45	[/] = 47	[=] = 61	[?] = 63	[^] = 94

###syntax;

$ <u>Program</u>
  ##rule;
    <program> =
      ((<identifier keyword>
        | <number>
        | &
)
        <delimiter>
)*

$ <u>Identifier or Keyword</u>
  ##rule;
    <identifier keyword> =

```
    init_name  <letter>
      (  add_name ( <letter> | <digit> )  )*
    out_idkey

##var;
   nb_chars : 1..maxint

##action;
   #init_name;
     @[identifier] := '        ';
     @[identifier] [1] := inp.c;
     nb_chars := 1

   #add_name;
     nb_chars := nb_chars + 1;
     if (nb_chars <= idlength)
       then @[identifier] [nb_chars] := inp.c

   #out_idkey;
     if (nb_chars > idlength) then error(iden_truncated);
     if      ( @[identifier]='how     ' ) then out(%[how])
     else if ( @[identifier]='many    ' ) then out(%[many])
     else if ( @[identifier]='in      ' ) then out(%[in])
     else if ( @[identifier]='kg      ' ) then out(%[kg])
     else if ( @[identifier]='m       ' ) then out(%[m])
     else if ( @[identifier]='s       ' ) then out(%[s])
     else out(%[identifier])
```

$ Constant
```
##rule;
   <number> =
     init_value
       (  whole_value <digit>  )+
         ( "."  (  fract_value <digit>  )+
         | &
         )
     out_number

##var;
   scale : real

##action;
   #init_value;
     @[number] := 0.0;
     scale     := 0.1

   #whole_value;
```

```
        @[number] := @[number]*10 + ( ord(inp.c) - ord('0') )

    #fract_value;
        @[number] := @[number] + (ord(inp.c) - ord('0'))*scale;
        scale     := scale/10

    #out_number;
        out(%[number])
```

$ Delimiter
```
  ##rule;
    <delimiter> =
        out_delimiter
          ( ","  |  "="  |  "?"  |  "-"  |  "+"  |  "*"
          | "/"  |  "^"  |  "("  |  ")"  )
      | "bl"

  ##action;
    #out_delimiter;
        out( ord(inp.c) )
```

$ Letter
```
  ##rule;
    <letter> =
        "a"  |  "b"  |  "c"  |  "d"  |  "e"  |  "f"  |  "g"  |  "h"  |  "i"
      | "j"  |  "k"  |  "l"  |  "m"  |  "n"  |  "o"  |  "p"  |  "q"  |  "r"
      | "s"  |  "t"  |  "u"  |  "v"  |  "w"  |  "x"  |  "y"  |  "z"
```

$ Digit
```
  ##rule;
    <digit> =
        "0"  |  "1"  |  "2"  |  "3"  |  "4"
      | "5"  |  "6"  |  "7"  |  "8"  |  "9"



###globalinfo;



  ##parameter;
    input, output, outfile



  ##const;
    idlength = 8
```

```
##type;
  rep_name = packed array [1..idlength] of char;

  message = (iden_truncated)


##routine;
  procedure error (m:message);
  begin
    nberrors := nberrors + 1;
    writeln(output,linenumber:4,'   ','*** ERROR ***');
    write(output,'      ');
    case  m  of
      iden_truncated :
        writeln('Identifier truncated to ',idlength:2,' char''s')
    end
  end {error}
```

2. ELL(1) PARSER

2.1. Introduction

The language definition tools can be divided in two categories : the generative devices called syntaxes and the recognizing devices called parsers, also called acceptors or syntax analysers. In sections 2.2 and 2.3, we will discuss the generative properties of two particular types of syntax, namely the regular syntax (RE syntax) and the extended context-free syntax (ECF syntax). In section 2.4, we will treat the recognizing behavior of a particular type of parser, namely the ELL(1) parser.

Roughly speaking, an ECF syntax G generates strings w over some alphabet VT from an axiom, called the start symbol, over several sentential forms by means of successive generation steps. At each generation step, a syntax rule in G is applied. The language defined by G is the set of all strings over VT that can be generated in this way. This language is denoted L(G) and the strings w are called sentences of L(G).

Roughly speaking, an ELL(1) parser A maps the set of strings over the alphabet VT into the set {yes,no} by means of successive parsing steps. At each parsing step, a parsing rule is applied. The language accepted by A consists of the input strings which are mapped into yes. This language is denoted L(A) and the strings w accepted by A are called sentences of L(A).

Moreover, an ECF syntax G generates for each sentence of L(G) a syntactic structure in the form of e.g., a derivation tree. The ELL(1) parser A recognizes for each input string, that belongs to L(A), its syntactic structure.

Given an ECF syntax G defining a language L(G) over some alphabet
VT.   The question now is how can we <u>produce</u> <u>mechanically</u> an ELL(1)
parser A from G such that L = L(G) = L(A) and such that for each
sentence of L, the syntactic structure generated by G is identical
to the one recognized by A.   This is schematically illustrated in
Fig. 2.1.

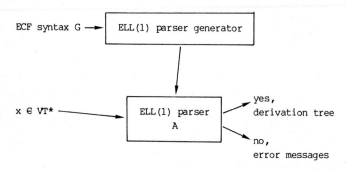

Fig. 2.1.

In section 2.5, we will discuss the mechanical production of
ELL(1) parsers from ECF syntaxes.   This production is only possible
for ECF syntaxes satisfying a number of conditions, called <u>ELL(1)</u>
<u>conditions</u>.

2.2. Regular syntax

The first formalism to define languages we will discuss is the
<u>regular syntax</u>, denoted <u>RE syntax</u>.   The RE syntax is a generative
device of the simplest form.   It is the basic model used in defining
the lexical structure of programming languages.   Such a lexical
structure defines the grouping of individual characters into elemen-
tary constructs, called tokens.   Examples of tokens are identifiers,
numbers, keywords and operators.

As it will become clear later, the definition power of the RE
syntax is too restricted for a great number of applications.   It is

a well-known fact that the RE syntax cannot deal with languages having nested structures, such as Algol begin-end blocks, conditional
statements and for-statements. We need a more powerful formalism
such as the extended context-free syntax (section 2.3).

A RE syntax G defines a language, denoted L(G). It uses a set VT
of <u>terminal</u> <u>symbols</u>. VT is the vocabulary over which the language
is defined. The class of languages defined by a RE syntax is known
as the class of the RE languages. A language is regular if and only
if it is $\emptyset$, $\{\&\}$ or $\{a_i\}$, where $\&$ is the empty string and a_i is a
terminal symbol, or if it can be obtained from these by a finite
number of applications of the set operations union, concatenation
and closure.

Definition

   A regular (RE) syntax is a 2-tuple G = (VT,e), where

1) VT is a finite set of <u>terminal</u> <u>symbols</u>
   VT = $\{a_1,a_2,\ldots,a_n\}$

2) e is a regular (RE) expression.
   e is a rule determining which string of terminal symbols belongs
   to L(G) and which does not. RE expressions and the languages
   they define are recursively defined by the scheme below. In this
   scheme RE expressions are composed of smaller modules. To each
   RE expression corresponds a language and to each composition rule
   for RE expressions corresponds a composition rule for languages.
   The language defined by a RE expression e is denoted L(e). The
   empty language is defined by the absence of a RE expression.

<u>Axiomatic</u> <u>rules</u>

1) $\&$ is a RE expression.
   $\&$ is the notation for the <u>empty</u> <u>string</u>.
   L($\&$) denotes $\{\&\}$, the set containing only the empty string.

2) $a_i \in$ VT is a RE expression.
   a_i is a <u>terminal</u> <u>symbol</u>.
   L(a_i) denotes the set $\{a_i\}$.

Composition rules

We assume that $e, e_1, e_2, \ldots, e_n$ are RE expressions,

3) $(e_1|e_2| \ldots |e_n)$ is a RE expression, $n>1$

$$L((e_1|e_2| \ldots |e_n)) = U_{1 \leq i \leq n} L(e_i)$$

The symbol | is called the <u>union set</u> operator.
$(e_1|e_2|\ldots|e_n)$ is read 'e_1 or e_2 ... or e_n'.

4) $e_1 e_2 \ldots e_n$ is a RE expression, $n>1$

$$L(e_1 e_2 \ldots e_n) = L(e_1).L(e_2). \ldots .L(e_n)$$

The symbol . is called the <u>product set</u> operator or <u>concatenation</u>
operator. As it is common practice, the product set operator
will not be written explicitly in RE expressions.
$e_1 e_2 \ldots e_n$ is read 'e_1 concatenated with e_2 ... concatenated
with e_n'.

5) $(e)*$ is a RE expression

$$L((e)*) = L(e)*$$
$$L(e)* = L(e)^0 \cup L(e)^1 \cup L(e)^2 \cup \ldots \cup L(e)^i \cup \ldots$$
$$L(e)* = U_{0 \leq i < \infty} L(e)^i$$

The symbol * is called the <u>closure set</u> operator.
Note that $L(e)^0 = \{\&\}$
$(e)*$ is read 'zero or more times e'.

6) $(e)^+$ is a RE expression

$$L((e)^+) = L(e)^+$$
$$L(e)^+ = U_{1 \leq i < \infty} L(e)^i$$

The symbol $+$ is called the <u>positive closure set</u> operator.
$(e)^+$ is read 'one or more times e'.

The set operators |, ., * and $+$, the notation & for the empty string and the parentheses are called the <u>metasyntactical</u> <u>symbols</u> of the RE syntax.

Notational conventions

1) <u>Redundant</u> <u>parentheses</u>

As a shorthand notation, we shall remove redundant parentheses from RE expressions. To avoid ambiguity, we assume that the monadic set operators ($*$,$^+$) have a higher priority than concatenation, and that concatenation has a higher priority than union. As an example, the RE expression "a"|"b" "c" stands for ("a"|("b" "c")) and not for (("a"|"b") "c").

2) <u>Terminal</u> <u>symbols</u>

The terminal symbols are represented by character strings enclosed between double quotes ("). Without these quotes, RE expressions can be ambiguous for two reasons :
- the product set operator is implicit, and
- the terminal symbols &, |, $*$, $^+$, (and) would have the same representation as the corresponding metasyntactical symbols of the RE syntax.

In the sequel, we will delete the double quote symbols wherever the context clearly determines the meaning of the RE expression.

Simple examples of RE expressions

e = "a""b"
L(e) = {ab}

e = ("a"|"b")$*$ which is a shorthand notation for e = (("a"|"b"))$*$
L(e) = {a,b}$*$

e = ("a"|"b")("c"|"d")$*$ which is a shorthand notation for e = ("a"|"b")(("c"|"d"))$*$
L(e) = {a,b}.{c,d}$*$
L(e) is the set of all strings over {c,d} preceded by one of the

symbols a or b.

e = ("a"|"b"|"c"| ... |"z")
L(e) = {a,b,c, ...,z}

e = "a"$^+$("b"|&)"c"$^+$ which is a shorthand notation for e = ("a")$^+$("b"|&)("c")$^+$
L(e) = {$a^n bc^m$|n,m$\geq$1} U {$a^n c^m$|n,m$\geq$1}

e = "a"(("+"|"-"|"*"|"/")"a")*
L(e) is the set of the simple arithmetic expressions composed of the binary operators +, -, * and / and of the single letter operand a. The operators +, -, * and / all have the same priority. Notice the difference in level between the arithmetic operator "*" and the set operator *.

EXAMPLE : The RE syntax for the floating point representation of real numbers

G_f = (VT,<REAL_NUMB>)
VT = {0,1,2,3,4,5,6,7,8,9,.,E,+,-}
<REAL_NUMB> is the name for the RE expression defining the set of floating point representations of real numbers.

```
<REAL_NUMB> = (<DIG>+ "." <DIG>* "E"
               |"E"
               |"." <DIG>+ "E"
              )(("+"
               |"-"
               )<DIG>
              |<DIG>
              )<DIG>*
```
<DIG> stands for ("0"|"1"|"2"|"3"|"4"|"5"|"6"|"7"|"8"|"9")

Strings of the language L(G_f) are, e.g., 5.7E+3, 5.E-7, 7.3E3, E-3. Note that .E+5 is not allowed by the syntax G_f. The expressions <DIG>* and <DIG>$^+$ are shorthand notations for (<DIG>)* and (<DIG>)$^+$, respectively.

The RE expression <REAL_NUMB> is constructed by the definition
scheme as follows :

step	RE expression	applied rule	on step(s)
(1)	"0"	(2)	
(2)	"1"	(2)	
.			
.			
.			
(10)	"9"	(2)	
(11)	<DIG> = ("0"|"1"|"2"|"3"|"4"| "5"|"6"|"7"|"8"|"9")	(3)	(1),(2),...,(10)
(12)	<DIG>$^+$	(6)	(11)
(13)	"."	(2)	
(14)	<DIG>*	(5)	(11)
(15)	"E"	(2)	
(16)	<A> = <DIG>$^+$ "." <DIG>* "E"	(4)	(12),(13),(14),(15)
(17)	<B> = "." <DIG>$^+$ "E"	(4)	(13),(12),(15)
(18)	(<A>|"E"|<B>)	(3)	(16),(15),(17)
(19)	"+"	(2)	
(20)	"-"	(2)	
(21)	("+"|"-")	(3)	(19),(20)
(22)	("+"|"-")<DIG>	(4)	(21),(11)
(23)	(("+"|"-")<DIG>|<DIG>)	(3)	(22),(11)
(24)	<REAL_NUMB>= (<DIG>$^+$ "." <DIG>* "E" |"E" |"." <DIG>+ "E")(("+" |"-")<DIG> |<DIG>)<DIG>*	(4)	(18),(23),(14)

Relations in RE syntaxes

RE subexpression

    The relation <u>RE subexpression</u> is a relation on RE expressions. We assume that $e, e_1, e_2, \ldots, e_n$ are RE expressions. The relation RE subexpression is defined by the following rules :

1) e_k is a RE subexpression of $(e_1 | e_2 | \ldots | e_n)$ with $n > 1$, for any k, $1 \le k \le n$.

2) e_k is a RE subexpression of $e_1 e_2 \ldots e_n$ with $n > 1$, for any k, $1 \le k \le n$.

3) e is a RE subexpression of $(e)*$.

4) e is a RE subexpression of $(e)^+$.

5) The relation RE subexpression is reflexive :
each RE expression e is a RE subexpression of itself.

6) & is a RE subexpression of any RE expression.

7) The relation RE subexpression is transitive :
if e_1 is a RE subexpression of e_2 and e_2 is a RE subexpression of e_3, then e_1 is a RE subexpression of e_3.

The relation RE subexpression will be used in the definition of the relation directly derives => , which is given below.

The relation RE subexpression is illustrated by the following examples :

e = "a""b"
&, "a""b", "a" and "b" are RE subexpressions of e.

e = (("a"|"b"))*

&, $(("a"|"b"))*$, $("a"|"b")$, "a" and "b" are RE subexpressions of e.

e = $("a"|"b")(("c"|"d"))*$
&, $("a"|"b")(("c"|"d"))*$, $("a"|"b")$, $(("c"|"d"))*$, $("c"|"d")$, "a", "b", "c" and "d" are RE subexpressions of e.

Produces

The relation ->, pronounced <u>produces</u>, is a relation on RE expressions. We assume that $e, e_1, \ldots, e_n$ are RE expressions. The relation -> is defined by the following rules :

1) $(e_1|e_2| \ldots |e_n)$ -> e_k, for any k, $1 \leq k \leq n$ with $n > 1$.

2) $(e)*$ -> $\underbrace{ee \ldots e}_{k \text{ times}}$ with $k \geq 0$.

3) $(e)^+$ -> $\underbrace{ee \ldots e}_{k \text{ times}}$ with $k \geq 1$.

Directly derives

The relation =>, pronounced <u>directly derives</u>, is a relation on RE expressions. Given two RE expressions e_1 and e_2, $e_1 => e_2$ if e_1 can be written as xyz and e_2 as xvz, with y -> v and x, y and z are RE subexpressions of e_1 (x and z may be empty).

The relation =>1, pronounced <u>leftmost directly derives</u>, is a relation on RE expressions. Given two RE expressions e_1 and e_2, $e_1 =>1 e_2$ if $e_1 => e_2$ ($e_1 = xyz$ and $e_2 = xvz$) and y is the leftmost RE subexpression in e_1 for which there is a v such that y -> v.

We call =>k the <u>k-fold product</u>, =>+ the <u>transitive closure</u>, =>* the <u>reflexive and transitive closure</u> of the relation =>. In the same way, we have $=>1^k$, $=>1^+$, $=>1*$.

The relations defined above are illustrated by the following examples :

```
("a""b"|"c") => "a""b"
"a"("b"|"c"|&)"d" => "a""b""d"
"a"("b"|"c"|&)"d" => "a""c""d"
"a"("b"|"c"|&)"d" => "a""d"
"a"(("b""a"|"c"))*"d" => "a""d"
"a"(("b""a"|"c"))*"d" =>
        "a"("b""a"|"c")("b""a"|"c")("b""a"|"c")("b""a"|"c")"d"
("a")*("b"|"c"|"d")("f")+ => ("a")*"b"("f")+
("a")*("b"|"c"|"d")("f")+ => ("a")*("b"|"c"|"d")"f"
("a")*("b"|"c"|"d")("f")+ => "a""a""a"("b"|"c"|"d")("f")+
```

Notice that e = "a"(("b""a"|"c"))* "d" $\neq$> "a"("b""a")* "d" since x
                    ‾   ‾‾‾‾‾‾‾‾‾‾‾ ‾‾‾   ‾ ‾‾‾‾‾‾‾ ‾‾‾
                    x   y   z   x   v   z
and z are no RE subexpressions of e.

Also e = ("a"|("b")*|"c") $\neq$> ("a"|"b""b""b"|"c") since x and z are
         ‾‾‾ ‾‾‾‾‾‾ ‾‾‾   ‾‾‾ ‾‾‾‾‾‾‾‾‾‾‾ ‾‾‾
          x   y   z   x   v   z
no RE subexpressions of e.


```
"a"("b"|"c"|&)"d" =>1 "a""d"
("a")*("b"|"c"|"d")("f")+ =>1 ("b"|"c"|"d")("f")+
("a")*("b"|"c"|"d")("f")+ =>1 "a""a""a""a""a"("b"|"c"|"d")("f")+
("b"|"c")("b"|"c")("b"|"c") =>1 "b"("b"|"c")("b"|"c")
"a"("b"|"c"|&)"d" =>* "a""d"
("a")*("b"|"c"|"d")("f")+ =>* "b""f"
("a")*("b"|"c"|"d")("f")+ =>* "a""b""f"
("a")*("b"|"c"|"d")("f")+ =>* "a""a""a""a""b""f""f""f""f""f""f""f""f"
(("b"|"c"))*("a")+ =>1 ("b"|"c")("b"|"c")("a")+ =>1
                    "b"("b"|"c")("a")+ =>1
                    "b""c"("a")+ =>1
                    "b""c""a""a""a""a"
```

Sentential form

A <u>sentential</u> <u>form</u> in G=(VT,e) is a RE expression x such that e =>* x.

Derivation

A <u>derivation</u> of a sentential form w in G=(VT,e) is a sequence of sentential forms e = $x_0, x_1, \ldots, x_i, \ldots, x_n$ = w with for all i, $0 \leq i < n$, x_i => x_{i+1}. A derivation of a sentential form w in G is not uniquely defined. Therefore, we define a <u>leftmost</u> <u>derivation</u> of a sentential form w in G as a derivation with for all i, $0 \leq i < n$, x_i =>l x_{i+1}. Informally, in a leftmost derivation, x_{i+1} is derived from x_i by rewriting the leftmost RE subexpression y in x_i by v, such that y -> v.

Note that in a leftmost derivation there exist two types of ordering : a left to right order and a hierarchical order which is due to the fact that in the definition of directly derives x, y and z must be RE subexpressions of e_1.

Sentence

A <u>sentence</u> in G=(VT,e) is a sentential form w such that w ∈ VT*.

Language

The <u>language</u> generated by G, denoted L(G), is the set of all sentences in G : L(G) = {w|e =>* w, w ∈ VT*}. The class of languages which can be defined by a RE syntax is the class of the RE languages.

The definitions of <u>leftmost</u> <u>derivation</u>, <u>sentential</u> <u>form</u> and <u>sentence</u> are illustrated in the following RE syntax G=(VT,e):
VT = {a,+,-}

```
e = "a"(("+"|"-")"a")*
```

The leftmost derivation of a+a-a+a in G is as follows :
```
"a"(("+"|"-")"a")* =>l
"a"("+"|"-")"a"("+"|"-")"a"("+"|"-")"a" =>l
"a" "+" "a"("+"|"-")"a"("+"|"-")"a" =>l
"a" "+" "a" "-" "a"("+"|"-")"a" =>l
"a" "+" "a" "-" "a" "+" "a"
```
The string a+a-a+a is a sentential form in G. We write :
```
    e =>* a+a-a+a
```
The string a+a-a+a is also a sentence in G. We write :
```
    a+a-a+a ∈ L(G)
```


Derivation tree

   As for any type of syntax, a RE syntax G=(VT,e) serves two purposes : (1) it determines which string over VT belongs to L(G) and
which does not, and (2) it associates with each sentence of L(G) a
<u>syntactic</u> <u>structure</u>.

   As mentioned earlier, the RE syntax is a language definition
model which is simple in its concepts but restrictive in its definition power. The RE syntax defines languages whose sentences have a
linear syntactic structure. Given a RE syntax G=(VT,e), a <u>deriva-</u>
<u>tion</u> <u>tree</u> of a sentence $w = a_{i_1} a_{i_2} \ldots a_{i_n}$ in G is a labeled
ordered tree consisting of a root and n direct descendants labeled
$a_{i_1}, a_{i_2}, \ldots, a_{i_n}$ in this order, where $a_{i_k} \in (VT \cup \{\&\})$ for any k,
$1 \le k \le n$. As a convention, the root of the derivation tree will be
labeled with the name, if any, given to the RE expression e.

The definition of <u>derivation</u> <u>tree</u> is illustrated by the following
example :
```
Gf = (VT,<REAL_NUMB>)
VT ={0,1,2,3,4,5,6,7,8,9,.,E,+,-}
```

```
<REAL_NUMB> = (<DIG>+ "." <DIG>* "E"
              |"E"
              |"." <DIG>+ "E"
              )(("+"
                |"-"
                )<DIG>
               |<DIG>
              )<DIG>*
<DIG> stands for ("0"|"1"|"2"|"3"|"4"|"5"|"6"|"7"|"8"|"9")
```

The derivation tree of 123.45E+67 in G_f is shown in Fig. 2.2

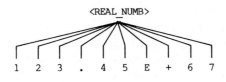

Fig. 2.2.

2.3. Extended context-free syntax

In section 2.2, we have discussed the RE syntax. The RE syntax is an ideal device to describe <u>iterative</u> <u>structures</u> such as the lexical structure of programming languages. However, for describing <u>nested</u> <u>structures</u> the model is inadequate. Nesting in programming languages is a very common feature. Examples of language constructs having a nested structure are conditional statements, begin-end blocks and while-do statements.

To describe languages with nested structures, a syntax model is needed that can handle <u>recursive</u> <u>definitions</u>. The <u>extended</u> <u>context-free</u> <u>syntax</u>, denoted <u>ECF</u> <u>syntax</u>, is a good candidate for a generative device to handle both iterative and recursive definitions.

An ECF syntax makes use of two finite disjoint sets of symbols :

the set of terminal symbols, denoted VT, and the set of nonterminal symbols, denoted VN. VT is the alphabet over which the language is defined. VN is used in the generation mechanism of the syntax as it will become clear later. The heart of the ECF syntax is a finite set of rules describing how the sentences of the language are to be generated.

Definition

An ECF syntax is a 4-tuple, $G = (VT, VN, A_0, P)$, where

1) VT is a finite set of terminal symbols.
   $VT = \{a_1, a_2, \ldots a_n\}$

2) VN is a finite set of nonterminal symbols.
   $VN = \{A_0, A_1, A_2, \ldots, A_m\}$
   $VT \; ^\wedge \; VN = \emptyset$

3) A_0 is the start symbol of G.
   $A_0 \in VN$

4) P is a finite set of ECF syntax rules.
   Each rule is of the form $A_j = e_j$, where A_j belongs to VN and e_j is an ECF expression defined below.
   There is one ECF syntax rule for each nonterminal symbol in VN.

ECF expressions are defined by means of three axiomatic rules and four composition rules.

Axiomatic rules

1) & is an ECF expression.
   & is the notation for the empty string.

2) a_i is an ECF expression.
   a_i is a terminal symbol.

3) A_j is an ECF expression.
   A_j is a nonterminal symbol.

Composition <u>rules</u>

We assume that $e, e_1, e_2, \ldots, e_n$ are ECF expressions,

4) $(e_1 | e_2 | \ldots | e_n)$ is an ECF expression, $n > 1$.

5) $e_1 e_2 \ldots e_n$ is an ECF expression, $n > 1$.

6) $(e)*$ is an ECF expression.

7) $(e)^+$ is an ECF expression.

Notice that the definition of ECF expression differs from the definition of RE expression in that a rule for nonterminal symbols is added.

The notational conventions about redundant parentheses and terminal symbols, introduced for RE expressions (see section 2.2) are also valid for ECF expressions. Nonterminal symbols are represented by character strings enclosed between the symbols '<' and '>'.

EXAMPLE : The ECF syntax for Pico-Algol.

G_{pico} = ($VT_{pico}, VN_{pico}, PICO, P_{pico}$)
VT_{pico} = {identifier,number,+,-,*,/,=,(,),;,.,:=,begin,end,integer,
         boolean,print,if,then,else,fi,true,false,do,od,for,from,to}
VN_{pico} = {PICO,DECLARATION,STATEMENT,E,T,F}
P_{pico} = {<PICO> = "begin"
              (<DECLARATION> ";")*
              <STATEMENT> (";" <STATEMENT>)*
          "end" ".",

      <DECLARATION> = "integer" "identifier" (& | "=" <E>)
               | "boolean" "identifier" (& | "=" <E>),

      <STATEMENT> =

```
                "do" <STATEMENT> ( ";" <STATEMENT> )* "od"
              | "identifier" ":=" <E>
              | "print" <E>
              | "if" <E>
                 "then" <STATEMENT>
                 "else" <STATEMENT>
                 "fi"
              | "for" "identifier" "from" <E> "to" <E>
                 "do" <STATEMENT> ( ";" <STATEMENT> )* "od",

      <E> = <T> ( "+" <T>
                | "-" <T> )*,

      <T> = <F> ( "*" <F>
                | "/" <F> )*,

      <F> = "identifier"
          | "number"
          | "true"
          | "false"
          | "(" <E> ")"
      }
```

Relations in ECF syntaxes

ECF subexpression

   The relation <u>ECF</u> <u>subexpression</u> is a relation on ECF expressions.
The definition of this relation is identical to the definition of RE
subexpression, where RE is systematically replaced by ECF.

Produces

The relation ->, pronounced produces, is a relation between VN
and (VT U VN)*. Suppose A=e is a rule in P of G. We have A -> v if
A ∈ VN and v is a sentence in the RE syntax G' = (VT U VN,e).

Each ECF syntax rule A=e can be considered a scheme of rules,
standing for a number (possibly infinite) of rules of the form A=w,
where w is a string of terminal and nonterminal symbols. The string
w is then an element defined by the RE syntax G' = (VT U VN,e).
G' is called an associated RE syntax of G.

Directly derives

The relation =>, pronounced directly derives, is a relation on
(VT U VN)*. Given two strings e_1 and e_2, e_1 => e_2 if e_1 can be
written as xAz and e_2 as xvz with A -> v (x and z may be empty).

Leftmost directly derives

The relation =>1, pronounced leftmost directly derives, is a
relation on (VT U VN)*. Given two strings e_1 and e_2, e_1 =>1 e_2 if
e_1 => e_2 (e_1 = xAz and e_2 = xvz), A is the leftmost nonterminal in
e_1 and A -> v.

The k-fold product, the transitive closure and the reflexive and
transitive closure of the relations => and =>1 are defined in the
usual way.

Sentential form

A sentential form in G = (VT,VN,A_0,P) is an element x belonging
to (VT U VN)* such that A_0 =>* x.

Derivation

A <u>derivation</u> of a sentential form w in G = (VT, VN, A_0, P) is a sequence of sentential forms $A_0 = x_0, x_1, \ldots, x_n = w$ with for all i, $0 \leq i < n$, $x_i \Rightarrow x_{i+1}$. A derivation of a sentential form w in G is not uniquely defined. Therefore, we define a <u>leftmost derivation</u> of a sentential form w in G, as a derivation with for all i, $0 \leq i < n$, $x_i \Rightarrow^1 x_{i+1}$. Informally, in a leftmost derivation, x_{i+1} is derived from x_i by rewriting the leftmost nonterminal A in x_i by v, such that A -> v.

Sentence

A <u>sentence</u> in G = (VT, VN, A_0, P) is a sentential form w such that w ∈ VT*.

Language

The language generated by G, denoted L(G), is the set of all sentences in G : L(G) = {w|A_0 =>* w, w ∈ VT*}. The class of languages which can be defined by an ECF syntax is the class of the ECF languages.

Example of a derivation

Consider the ECF syntax G = (VT, VN, E, P)

VT = {a,b,c,+,-,*,/,(,)}
VN = {E,T,F}
P = {<E> = <T>(("+"|"-") <T>)*,
     <T> = <F>(("*"|"/") <F>)*,
     <F> = "a"|"b"|"c"|"("<E>")"
     }

The leftmost derivation of the sentence a+b-a*c in G is :

```
E =>1
T + T - T =>1
F + T - T =>1
a + T - T =>1
a + F - T =>1
a + b - T =>1
a + b - F * F =>1
a + b - a * F =>1
a + b - a * c
```

We have the relations :

```
E =>1* a+b-a*c
E =>1+ a+b-a*c
a+b-a*c ∈ L(G)
```

G defines the set of the simple arithmetic expressions with four binary operators +, -, * and /, three primitive operands a, b and c, and the parentheses. G assigns to the operators * and / a priority which is higher than that of the operators + and -.

Derivation tree

A <u>derivation tree</u> in an ECF syntax $G(A_0) = (VT,VN,A_0,P)$ is a labeled ordered tree D such that

1) The root of D is labeled A_0.

2) If $D_1,D_2, \ldots ,D_k$ are subtrees of D, starting from the direct descendants of the root, and the root of D_j is labeled X_j ($1 \leq j \leq k$), then the labeled tree consisting of the root of D and the roots of $D_1,D_2, \ldots ,D_k$ is a derivation tree in the associated RE syntax $G = (VT \cup VN,e_0)$.
If $X_j \in VN$, then D_j must be a derivation tree in $G(X_j) = (VT,VN,X_j,P)$ and if $X_j \in VT \cup \{\&\}$, then D_j is a terminal node labeled X_j.

Given an ECF syntax G. The derivation tree and the leftmost derivation of a sentence in G are equivalent notations describing the syntactic structure of the sentence. From the derivation tree, one can derive the leftmost derivation and vice versa.

Interior frontier

An <u>interior</u> <u>frontier</u> of a derivation tree is a string obtained by concatenating the labels of the nodes (in the order from left to right), such that (1) no two nodes are on the same path and (2) no other node can be added without violating (1).

Terminal frontier

The <u>terminal</u> <u>frontier</u> of a derivation tree is a string obtained by concatenating the labels of the leaves (in the order from left to right) of the derivation tree.

Ambiguous ECF syntax

An ECF syntax G is said to be <u>ambiguous</u> if L(G) contains a sentence for which there is more than one distinct derivation tree (leftmost derivation) in G.

Reduced ECF syntax

An ECF syntax G is said to be <u>reduced</u> if the following two conditions are fulfilled :
1) each nonterminal symbol derives at least one element of VT*.
2) each nonterminal symbol appears at least once in a sentential form in G.
Formally, we have
1) $\forall A_j \in VN$, $A_j \Rightarrow^* w$ for some $w \in VT*$
2) $\forall A_j \in VN$, $\exists x$, such that $A_0 \Rightarrow^* x$ and x contains A_j.
Unless specified otherwise, we will always assume an ECF syntax to be reduced.

Example of a derivation tree


```
G = (VT,VN,E,P)
VT = {a,b,c,+,-,*,/,(,)}
VN = {E,T,F}
P = {<E> = <T>(("+"|"-")<T>)*,
     <T> = <F>(("*"|"/")<F>)*,
     <F> = "a"|"b"|"c"|"("<E>")"
    }
```

The derivation tree of a+b-a*c in G is illustrated in Fig. 2.3.

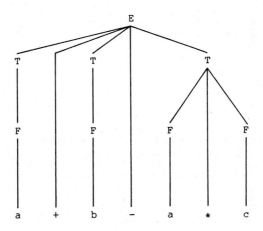

Fig. 2.3.

Examples of interior frontiers are : E, F+T-a*F, a+F-a*c. The string a+b-a*c is the terminal frontier of the derivation tree.

Iterative versus recursive definition

   The following example illustrates how languages can be defined in
many different ways. G_{rec} and G_{it} define the set of simple arithmetic expressions (without parentheses).

G_{rec} = $(VT_{rec}, VN_{rec}, E_{rec}, P_{rec})$ G_{it} = $(VT_{it}, VN_{it}, E_{it}, P_{it})$

VT_{rec} = $\{a, b, c, +, -, *, /\}$ VT_{it} = VT_{rec}

VN_{rec} = $\{E_{rec}, T_{rec}, F_{rec}\}$ VN_{it} = $\{E_{it}, T_{it}, F_{it}\}$

P_{rec} = {<E_{rec}> =   <E_{rec}>"+"<T_{rec}> P_{it} = {<E_{it}> = <T_{it}>(("+"

                |<E_{rec}>"-"<T_{rec}> |"-"

                |<T_{rec}>,   )<T_{it}>

)*,

       <T_{rec}> =   <T_{rec}>"*"<F_{rec}>   <T_{it}> = <F_{it}>(("*"

                |<T_{rec}>"/"<F_{rec}> |"/"

                |<F_{rec}>,   )<F_{it}>

)*,

       <F_{rec}> =   "a"   <F_{it}> =   "a"

                |"b" |"b"

                |"c" |"c"

    }   }

The derivation tree of the sentence a+b-a*b/c in G_{rec} is shown in
Fig. 2.4 and the derivation tree of the same sentence in G_{it} is
shown in Fig. 2.5.

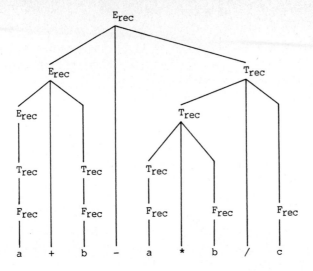

Fig. 2.4.

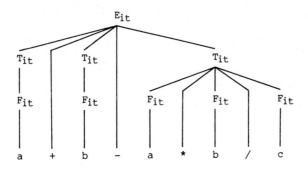

Fig. 2.5.

It is important to see that the sets $L(G_{rec})$ and $L(G_{it})$ are
identical but that the derivation trees in G_{rec} and G_{it} for the same
sentence a+b-a*b/c are different.

The ECF syntax of the ECF syntax rules

$$G_{ecf} = (VT_{ecf}, VN_{ecf}, Z, P_{ecf})$$
$$VT_{ecf} = \{terminal, nonterminal, |, *, +, (,), \&, =\}$$
$$VN_{ecf} = \{Z, E\}$$
$$P_{ecf} = \{<Z> = \text{"nonterminal" "=" } <E>,$$

```
        <E> = "&"                        1
            | "terminal"                 2
            | "nonterminal"              3     rule numbers in the
            | "(" <E> ("|" <E>)+ ")"     4     definition scheme
            | <E>+                       5     of ECF expression
            | "(" <E> ")" "*"            6
            | "(" <E> ")" "+"            7
        }
```

ECF expressions are often defined in a slightly different way.
Then the definition of ECF expressions is analogous to the definition of arithmetic expressions.

$$G'_{ecf} = (VT'_{ecf}, VN'_{ecf}, Z, P'_{ecf})$$
$$VT'_{ecf} = \{terminal, nonterminal, |, *, +, (,), \&, =\}$$
$$VN'_{ecf} = \{Z, E, T, F, G\}$$
$$P'_{ecf} = \{<Z> = \text{"nonterminal" "=" } <E>,$$

```
        <E> = <T>("|" <T>)*,
        <T> = <F>+,
        <F> = <G> "*"
            |<G> "+"
            |<G>,
        <G> = "&"
            |"terminal"
            |"nonterminal"
            |"(" <E> ")"
        }
```

2.4. ELL(1) parser

In section 2.3, we have discussed a particular type of generative device to define languages, namely the ECF syntax. Let L be a language defined by an ECF syntax G = (VT,VN,A_0,P). We have L = L(G). Remember that G generates for each sentence of L(G) a syntactic structure, represented in the form of e.g., a derivation tree.

In the present section, we will discuss a particular type of recognizing device, namely the ELL(1) parser. Given a vocabulary VT, an ELL(1) parser A maps the set of strings over VT into the set {yes,no}. The language accepted by A consists of all those input strings which are mapped into yes. This language is denoted L(A).

In order to build an ELL(1) parser for a given language L with vocabulary VT, we will first define L by means of an ECF syntax G. Then, we will construct an ELL(1) parser A for the language L = L(G) such that L = L(G) = L(A) and such that for each input string, accepted by A, its syntactic structure (defined in G) is recognized. As we will see later, the ELL(1) parser A can be directly produced from the ECF syntax G.

An ELL(1) parser has the following properties :
1) it is derived from an ECF syntax,
2) it scans the input string from Left to right,
3) it produces a Left parser, which means that the syntactic structure is recognized from top to bottom. Take the derivation tree as a representation of the syntactic structure, then the syntactic structure is recognized from the root towards the leaves of the tree,
4) it recognizes the input string with a lookahead string of length 1.

All these properties are thoroughly discussed in Part 1.

An ELL(1) parser A is composed of four elements :
1) the input tape which is a sequence of tape squares, each tape square containing exactly one input symbol of a finite set VT. Each string of input symbols will always be terminated by an end

<u>marker</u>, represented by the symbol "#".

2) the <u>input head</u> which can read one symbol at a given instance of
   time. At each read action, the input head moves one square to
   the right.

3) the <u>pushdown list</u> which is an auxiliary memory of the type last-
   in first-out.

4) the <u>finite control</u> containing a finite set of accepting rules,
   dictating the behavior of A.

As it has been explained in Part 1, the accepting rules of the finite control of the ELL(1) parser can be represented in many ways,
such as :

1) a mapping,

2) a program, where the pushdown list is explicit,

3) a program, where the pushdown list is implicit.

Here, we will only give a practical view on ELL(1) parsers. For
this reason, we will discuss the ELL(1) parser with the accepting
rules in the form of a program with implicit pushdown list.

In all three cases, it is important to observe the mechanical aspect
in the development of the ELL(1) parser A from the ECF syntax rules
of G. The mechanical production of ELL(1) parsers of type (3) from
ECF syntaxes is discussed in section 2.5. More about ELL(1) parsers
of type (1) and (2), together with their mechanical production can
be found in Part 1.

ELL(1) parser with implicit pushdown list

The structure of an ELL(1) parser in the form of a program with
implicit pushdown list is best explained by a simple example : the
parsing of simple arithmetic expressions.

The simple arithmetic expressions for which we will develop an
ELL(1) parser, are defined by the ECF syntax $G_a = (VT_a, VN_a, E, P_a)$.

```
VTa = {a,b,c,+,-,*,/,(,)}
VNa = {E,F,T}
E is the start symbol of Ga
Pa = {<E> = <T>("+" <T>
                |"-" <T>
                )*,
       <T> = <F>("*" <F>
                |"/" <F>
                )*,
     <F> = "a"
          |"b"
          |"c"
          |"(" <E> ")"
     }
```

G_a is a generative device. It generates any simple arithmetic expression and associates with it a syntactic structure. The language generated by G_a is denoted $L(G_a)$. As an example, a*(b+c) is a sentence in $L(G_a)$. Its syntactic structure in the form of a derivation tree is pictured in Fig. 2.6.

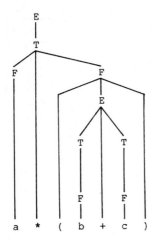

Fig. 2.6.

The syntactic structure in the form of a leftmost derivation is the
following sequence :

E,T,F*F,a*F,a*(E),a*(T+T),a*(F+T),a*(b+T),a*(b+F),a*(b+c)

Our purpose is to construct an ELL(1) parser A_a for the simple
arithmetic expressions as they are defined by G_a. The input of A_a
is the set of all strings over VT_a. The set VT_a* is mapped by A_a
into the set {yes,no}, where $L(A_a)$ is the set of those strings which
are mapped into yes.
The ELL(1) parser A_a is such that
1) $L(A_a) = L(G_a) = L_a$
2) For each element of L_a, the syntactic structure recognized by A_a
   is identical with the syntactic structure generated by G_a.
3) For each element of $VT*-L_a$, an error message is produced.
   If the above conditions are fulfilled, the definitions G_a and A_a
are said to be equivalent. This is illustrated in Fig. 2.7.

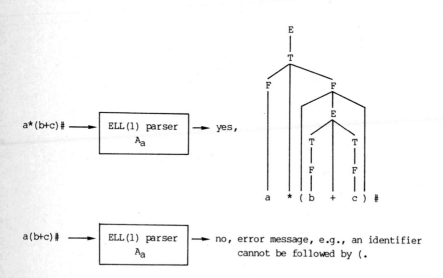

a*(b+c)# ⟶ | ELL(1) parser A_a | ⟶ yes,

a(b+c)# ⟶ | ELL(1) parser A_a | ⟶ no, error message, e.g., an identifier
                                         cannot be followed by (.

Fig. 2.7.

The ELL(1) parser A_a for the simple arithmetic expressions is
represented by a program, where the pushdown list is implemented by
means of the implicit stack of the recursive procedure mechanism
available in the language in which the ELL(1) parser is written.
The ELL(1) parser A_a can be directly obtained from the ECF syntax
G_a. The complete generation scheme of ELL(1) parsers from ECF syntaxes is discussed in section 2.5.

The ELL(1) parser A_a mainly consists of three so-called <u>parsing rou-</u>
<u>tines</u> E, T and F, corresponding to the ECF syntax rules for expres-
sion, term and factor, respectively.

In a first pass, the ELL(1) parser is written in a systematic
(pseudo automatic) way. In a second pass, a number of trivial
optimizations are performed. These optimizations consist in deleting the text which is contained within

ELL(1) parser program


```
proc ELL(1) parser = void :
begin
    char in := co this character variable represents the
                  input head of the ELL(1) parser.
                  This variable is initialized with
                  the leftmost symbol of the input
                  string co;
    proc read = void : co the next symbol in the input
                           string is stored in the variable
                           'in' co;
    proc error = void : co the appropriate error message
                            is produced. The parser halts co;
    proc accept = void : co the input string has been accepted.
                             Some appropriate action is performed.
                             The parser halts co;
        proc E = void : co                              co;
```

```
      proc T = void : co            defined below            co;
      proc F = void : co                                     co;
      E;
      if in = "#"
         then accept
         else error
      fi
end
```

expression

The ELL(1) parsing routine E for the ECF syntax rule

```
      <E> = <T>("+"<T>
                |"-"<T>
                )*
```

is the following :

```
      proc E = void :
         begin
           T;
           while in ϵ {+,-}
             do case in
                    when "+"
                       if in = "+"
                          then read
                          else error
                       fi;
                       T
                    otherwise
                       if in = "-"
                          then read
                          else error
                       fi;
                       T
                esac
             od
```

    <u>end</u>

<u>term</u>

The ELL(1) parsing routine T for the ECF syntax rule

        <T> = <F>("*"<F>
                  |"/"<F>
)*

is analogous with the parsing routine for expression.

<u>factor</u>

The ELL(1) parsing routine F for the ECF syntax rule

        <F> = "a"
             |"b"
             |"c"
             |"("<E>")"

is the following :

    <u>proc</u> F = <u>void</u> :
      <u>case</u> in
          <u>when</u> "a"
              ┌─────────────┐
              │<u>if</u> in = "a"│
              │ <u>then</u>┌─────┤
              │   │read │
              │ <u>else</u>│error│
              ├──┐ └─────┘
              │<u>fi</u>│
          <u>when</u> "b"
              ┌─────────────┐
              │<u>if</u> in = "b"│
              │ <u>then</u>┌─────┤
              │   │read │
              │ <u>else</u>│error│
              ├──┐ └─────┘
              │<u>fi</u>│
          <u>when</u> "c"
              ┌─────────────┐
              │<u>if</u> in = "c"│
              └──┐   ┌────

```
         then read
         else error
      fi
   otherwise
      if in = "("
         then read
         else error
      fi;
      E;
      if in = ")"
         then read
         else error
      fi
   esac
```

The different moves of the ELL(1) parser, when parsing the input string a*(b+c), are displayed in Fig. 2.8. Notice that, conceptually, the ELL(1) parser produces a syntactic structure (e.g., a derivation tree) for each input string that is accepted. In practice, this derivation tree need not to be completely constructed. The input head is represented by ^.

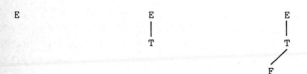

```
E               E               E
                |               |
                T               T
                               /
                              F


a * ( b + c ) #   a * ( b + c ) #   a * ( b + c ) #
^                     ^                   ^
```

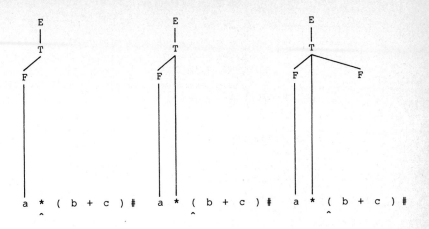

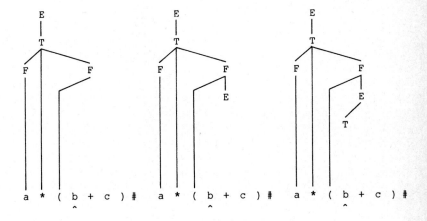

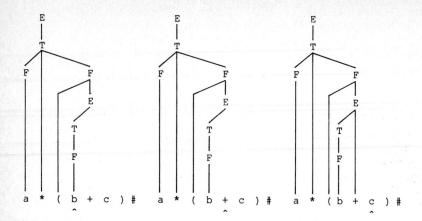

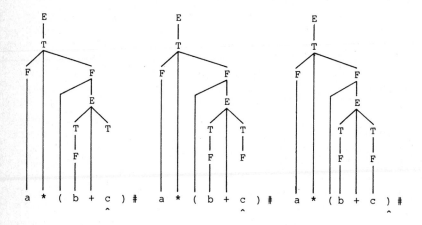

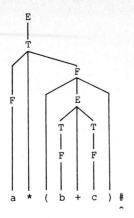

Fig. 2.8.

2.5. Generation of ELL(1) parsers

Given an ECF syntax G defining a language L(G) over some alphabet
VT. We will investigate how we can produce an ELL(1) parser A from
an ECF syntax G in a mechanical way with A and G being equivalent.
By equivalence of A and G, we mean that L = L(G) = L(A) and that for
each sentence of L the syntactic structure defined by G is identical
to the one recognized by A.

The mechanical generation of ELL(1) parsers from ECF syntaxes is
described by means of a so-called generation scheme. This is
schematically illustrated in Fig. 2.9.

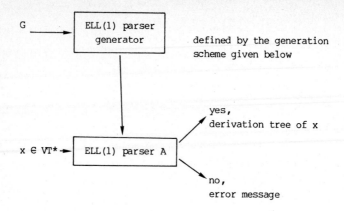

Fig. 2.9

Generation scheme

Given an ECF syntax $G = (VT, VN, A_0, P)$, where

$$VT = \{a_1, a_2, \ldots, a_n\}$$
$$VN = \{A_0, A_1, \ldots, A_m\}$$

A_0 is the start symbol of G

$$P = \{A_0 = e_0,$$
$$\quad A_1 = e_1,$$
$$\quad \ldots$$
$$\quad A_m = e_m$$
$$\quad \}$$

where e_i $(1 \leq i \leq m)$ is an ECF expression.

The ELL(1) parser A is produced from G by the generation scheme below.

```
proc ELL(1) parser = void :
begin
  char in := co this character variable represents the
                input head of the ELL(1) parser.
                This variable is initialized with
                the leftmost symbol of the input
                string co;
```

```
proc read = void :
   co the next symbol in the input string is put in the
      variable 'in' (the input head is moved one symbol
      to the right). co;
proc error = void :
   co this routine produces appropriate error messages.
      Hereafter, the parser halts co;
proc accept = void :
   co the input string has been accepted. Some appropri-
      ate actions are performed. Hereafter, the parser
      halts co;


A(A0=e0);
A(A1=e1);
   .
   .
   .
A(Aj=ej);
   .
   .
   .
A(Am=em);
A0;
if in = "#"
   then accept
   else error
fi
end
```

For each ECF syntax rule $A_j = e_j$ in G, we produce an ELL(1) **pars-ing routine**, denoted $A(A_j=e_j)$, for the nonterminal A_j as follows :

```
Aj = ej ∈ P    ->    proc Aj = void :
                         begin
                             A(ej)
                         end
```

The body of the ELL(1) parsing routine A_j is denoted $A(e_j)$. This body is modularly produced by means of the following three axiomatic rules and four composition rules

Production of the body of an ELL(1) parsing routine.

Axiomatic rules

ECF expression -> parser module

1)   & -> skip

2) $a_i \in$ VT -> if in = a_i
                 then read
                 else error
            fi

2') $A_j \in$ VN -> A_j
      This is the call of the ELL(1) parsing routine generated for A_j.

Composition rules

   Suppose A(e) represents the parser module for the ECF expression
e, with e possibly indexed.

ECF expression -> parser module

3) $(e_1|e_2| \ldots |e_n)$ -> case in
                           when DIRSYMB(e_1)
                              A(e_1)
                           when DIRSYMB(e_2)
                              A(e_2)
                           ...
                           when DIRSYMB(e_{n-1})
                              A(e_{n-1})
                           otherwise
                              A(e_n)
                     esac

   DIRSYMB(e_i) with $1 \leq i < n$ stands for the set of all terminal symbols which may occur initially under the input head for the
   ELL(1) parser module A(e_i). These symbols are called direction
   symbols, since they determine the ELL(1) parsing module to be

applied. The sets DIRSYMB(e_i) for all i ($1 \leq i < n$) are calculated from the ECF syntax G in a mechanical way. The calculation of these sets is performed prior to the generation of the ELL(1) parser. The definition of DIRSYMB is given below, whereas the practical algorithms to calculate DIRSYMB are described in section 7.

4) $e_1 e_2 \ldots e_n$ -> A(e_1);A(e_2); ... ;A(e_n)

5) (e)* -> <u>while</u> in $\in$ DIRSYMB(e)
       <u>do</u> A(e) <u>od</u>

6) (e)$^+$ -> <u>repeat</u> A(e) <u>until</u> in $\notin$ DIRSYMB(e)

The generation scheme on which LILA is based is an elaborated version of the generation scheme given above. LILA generates ELL(1) parsers (transducers) which are optimized up to a high extent. Among these optimizations are the trivial ones, in the example below represented by

Optimizations in LILA are thoroughly discussed in section 7.

EXAMPLE : The ELL(1) parser for PICO-ALGOL


```
proc ELL(1) parser = void :
begin
    char in := co ... co;
    proc read = void : co ... co;
    proc error = void : co ... co;
    proc accept = void : co ... co;
    proc PICO = void : co                         co;
    proc DECLARATION = void : co                  co;
    proc STATEMENT = void : co   defined below    co;
    proc E = void : co                            co;
    proc T = void : co                            co;
    proc F = void : co                            co;
```

```
      PICO;
      if in = "#"
        then accept
        else error
      fi
    end
    proc PICO = void :
      begin
        if in = "begin"
          then read
          else error
        fi;
        while in ∈ {integer,boolean}
          do DECLARATION;
             if in = ";"
               then read
               else error
             fi
          od;
        STATEMENT;
        while in = ";"
          do if in = ";"
               then read
               else error
             fi ;
             STATEMENT
          od;
        if in = "end"
          then read
          else error
        fi;
        if in = "."
          then read
          else error
        fi
      end


    proc DECLARATION = void :
      case in
        when "integer"
          if in = "integer"
            then read
            else error
          fi ;
          if in = "identifier"
            then read
            else error
```

```
  fi;
  case in
    when ";"
      skip
    otherwise
      if in = "="
        then read
        else error
      fi;
      E
  esac
otherwise
  if in = "boolean"
    then read
    else error
  fi;
  if in = "identifier"
    then read
    else error
  fi;
  case in
    when ";"
      skip
    otherwise
      if in = "="
        then read
        else error
      fi;
      E
  esac
esac


proc E = void :
  begin
    T;
    while in ∈ {+,-}
      do case in
          when "+"
              if in = "+"
                then read
                else error
              fi;
              T
          otherwise
              if in = "-"
                then read
                else error
```

```
          | fi | ;
            T
        esac
    od
  end


proc F = void :
  case in
    when "identifier"
      | if in = "identifier" |
          then | read |
          else | error |
      | fi |
    when "number"
      | if in = "number" |
          then | read |
          else | error |
      | fi |
    when "true"
      | if in = "true" |
          then | read |
          else | error |
      | fi |
    when "false"
      | if in = "false" |
          then | read |
          else | error |
      | fi |
    otherwise
      if in = "("
          then read
          else error
      fi;
      E;
      if in = ")"
          then read
          else error
      fi
  esac
```

The ELL(1) parsing routines for STATEMENT and T are left to the reader.

The definition of DIRSYMB and the ELL(1) conditions

Definition of DIRSYMB

DIRSYMB(e), where e is an occurrence of an ECF expression in the right hand side of an ECF syntax rule, is the set of all possible lookahead symbols (symbols under the input head), when the ELL(1) parser module A(e) is in its initial state.

DIRSYMB(e) = if EMPTY(e)
                then FIRST(e) U FOLLOW(e)
                else FIRST(e)
       fi

Definition of FIRST

Given an ECF expression e, FIRST(e) specifies the set of symbols in VT that may start any string in L(e). The function FIRST is recursively defined by the following scheme of rules.

Axiomatic rules

1) FIRST(&) = $\emptyset$

2) FIRST(a_i) = {a_i}, where $a_i \in$ VT

2') FIRST(A_j) = FIRST(e_j) where $A_j \in$ VN and $A_j = e \in$ P. Note that FIRST(A_j) is the set of terminal symbols that may start any terminal string derivable from e_j. FIRST(e_j) is derived from the transitive closure on the relation FIRST_DIRECT. For the transitive closure algorithm see Warshall [1962]. FIRST_DIRECT is the set of terminal and nonterminal symbols that can directly start e_j. The definition schemes of FIRST_DIRECT(e) and FIRST(e) are identical, except for rule (2'), which becomes : FIRST_DIRECT(A_j) = {A_j}. A practical algorithm to calculate this transitive closure can be found in section 7.

Composition rules

3) $\text{FIRST}((e_1|e_2| \ \ldots \ |e_n)) = \bigcup_{1 \le i \le n}\text{FIRST}(e_i)$

4) $\text{FIRST}(e_1 e_2 \ \ldots \ e_n) = \underline{\text{if}}$ not $\text{EMPTY}(e_1)$
                                   $\underline{\text{then}}$ $\text{FIRST}(e_1)$
                                   $\underline{\text{else}}$ $\text{FIRST}(e_1) \cup \text{FIRST}(e_2 \ \ldots \ e_n)$
                            $\underline{\text{fi}}$

5) $\text{FIRST}((e)*) = \text{FIRST}(e)$

6) $\text{FIRST}((e)^+) = \text{FIRST}(e)$

Example of FIRST

$G = (VT, VN, E, P)$

$VT = \{a,b,c,+,*,(,)\}$
$VN = \{E,T,F\}$
$P = \{<E> = <T>("+"<T>)*,$
      $<T> = <F>("*"<F>)*,$
      $<F> = "a"|"b"|"c"|"("<E>")"$
      $\}$

$\text{FIRST}(E) = \text{FIRST}(T(+T)*)$
$\text{FIRST\_DIRECT}(T(+T)*) = \{T\}$
$\text{FIRST\_DIRECT}(F(*F)*) = \{F\}$
$\text{FIRST\_DIRECT}(a|b|c|(E)) = \{a,b,c,(\}$

By applying the transitive closure on FIRST_DIRECT, we become
$\text{FIRST}(T(+T)*) = \{a,b,c,(\}$

Definition of EMPTY

  EMPTY(e) specifies the Boolean value $\underline{\text{true}}$ if the ECF expression e
defines a language L(e) containing &. It returns $\underline{\text{false}}$ otherwise.

The function EMPTY is defined by the following scheme of rules.

Axiomatic rules

1) EMPTY($\&$) = $\underline{\text{true}}$

2) EMPTY(a_i) = $\underline{\text{false}}$, where $a_i \in$ VT

2') EMPTY(A_j) = EMPTY(e_j), where $A_j \in$ VN and $A_j = e_j \in$ P. Notice that this is a recursive definition.

Composition rules

3) EMPTY(($e_1 | e_2 | \ \ldots \ | e_n$)) = $\text{OR}_{1 \leq i \leq n}$ EMPTY(e_i)

4) EMPTY($e_1 e_2 \ \ldots \ e_n$) = $\text{AND}_{1 \leq i \leq n}$ EMPTY(e_i)

5) EMPTY((e)*) = $\underline{\text{true}}$

6) EMPTY((e)$^+$) = EMPTY(e)

A practical algorithm to calculate EMPTY can be found in section 7.

Example of EMPTY

$G = (VT, VN, E, P)$
$VT = \{a, b, c, +, *, (,)\}$
$VN = \{E, T, F\}$
$P = \{<E> = <T>("+"<T>)^*,$
       $<T> = <F>("*"<F>)^*,$
       $<F> = "a" | "b" | "c" | "("<E>")"$
       $\}$

EMPTY(E) = EMPTY(T) AND $\underline{\text{true}}$
EMPTY(T) = EMPTY(F) AND $\underline{\text{true}}$
EMPTY(F) = $\underline{\text{false}}$ OR $\underline{\text{false}}$ OR $\underline{\text{false}}$ OR $\underline{\text{false}}$ AND EMPTY(E) AND $\underline{\text{false}}$

EMPTY(E) = <u>false</u>
EMPTY(T) = <u>false</u>
EMPTY(F) = <u>false</u>

Definition of FOLLOW

FOLLOW(e), where e is an occurrence of an ECF expression in the right hand side of an ECF syntax rule, is the set of all lookahead symbols, when the ELL(1) parser module A(e) is in its final state.

The scheme of rules defining FOLLOW is different in nature from the schemes defining EMPTY and FIRST. FOLLOW(e) is defined by the right context of an occurrence of e.

1) $(e_1|e_2| \ldots |e_n)$

   For all i, $1 \leq i \leq n$, FOLLOW(e_i) = FOLLOW($(e_1|e_2| \ldots |e_n)$)

2) $e_1e_2 \ldots e_n$

   For all i, $1 \leq i < n$, FOLLOW(e_i) = <u>if</u> EMPTY(e_{i+1})

   $\qquad\qquad\qquad\qquad\qquad\qquad$ <u>then</u> FIRST(e_{i+1}) U FOLLOW(e_{i+1})

   $\qquad\qquad\qquad\qquad\qquad\qquad$ <u>else</u> FIRST(e_{i+1})

   $\qquad\qquad\qquad\qquad\qquad$ <u>fi</u>

   FOLLOW(e_n) = FOLLOW($e_1e_2 \ldots e_n$)

3) $(e)^x$, where x stands for one of the monadic set operators * and +.

   FOLLOW(e) = FIRST(e) U FOLLOW($(e)^x$)

4) Assume that e_j is the right part of an ECF syntax rule $A_j=e_j \in P$. FOLLOW(e_j) is the union of FOLLOW(A_j) for any occurrence of A_j in the right-hand side of an ECF syntax rule in P. In addition, FOLLOW(A_0) contains also #.

Analogous to FIRST and FIRST_DIRECT, FOLLOW(A_j) is obtained from the relation FOLLOW_DIRECT by the transitive closure operation. A practical algorithm to calculate FOLLOW can be found in section 7.

Example of FOLLOW

G = (VT,VN,E,P)

VT = {a,b,c,+,*,(,)}
VN = {E,T,F}
P = {<E> = <T>("+"<T>)*,
     <T> = <F>("*"<F>)*,
     <F> = "a"|"b"|"c"|"("<E>")"
           $\underbrace{\quad\quad}_{e_1}$ $\underbrace{\quad\quad}_{e_2\ e_3}$
     }
FOLLOW(e_1) = {*,+,),#}
FOLLOW(e_2) = {a,b,c,(}
FOLLOW(e_3) = {)}}

The ELL(1) conditions

Consider the generation scheme, which generates an ELL(1) parser A from an ECF syntax G. The ELL(1) parser A is equivalent with the ECF syntax G only if G satisfies a number of conditions, called ELL(1) conditions.

Take composition rule (3)

$(e_1|e_2|$ ... $|e_n)$ -> <u>case</u> in
            <u>when</u> DIRSYMB(e_1)
                A(e_1)
            <u>when</u> DIRSYMB(e_2)
                A(e_2)
            ...
            <u>when</u> DIRSYMB(e_{n-1})
                A(e_{n-1})
            <u>otherwise</u>
                A(e_n)
        <u>esac</u>

The sets DIRSYMB(e_1), DIRSYMB(e_2), ... ,DIRSYMB(e_n) must be disjoint, otherwise the language defined by $(e_1|e_2|$ ... $|e_n)$ is not

identical to the language defined by $A((e_1|e_2| \ldots |e_n))$. Clearly,
if e.g., DIRSYMB(e_1) and DIRSYMB(e_2) contain a common symbol, then
with this symbol under the input head, the module $A(e_2)$ will never
apply.

Take composition rule (6) :

    (e)* -> <u>while</u> in $\in$ DIRSYMB(e)
               <u>do</u> A(e) <u>od</u>

   The sets DIRSYMB(e) and FOLLOW((e)*) must be disjoint, otherwise
the language defined by (e)* is not identical to the language
defined by A((e)*). Clearly, if DIRSYMB(e) and FOLLOW((e)*) contain
a common symbol, the while clause will not be left.

Take composition rule (7) :

    (e)$^+$ -> <u>repeat</u> A(e) <u>until</u> in $\notin$ DIRSYMB(e)

This is analogous to the ELL(1) condition for composition rule (6).

3. ELL(1) TRANSDUCER

3.1. Introduction

In section 2, we have discussed two language definition tools :
the ECF syntax (section 2.3), which is a generative device and the
ELL(1) parser (section 2.4), which is a recognizing device. In section 2.5, we learned how to produce mechanically an ELL(1) parser A
from an ECF syntax G, with both A and G being equivalent.

In the present section, we are concerned with the definition
tools of translations. A translation t is a set of pairs (x,E),
where x is a string over some input vocabulary V_{in} and E is the contents of a given environment. This environment may contain e.g., a
sequence of output symbols, a sequence of intermediate instructions
or a real variable. In this way, the definition of translation is
kept very general. The set of all strings x for which there is a
translation element (x,E) in t, is called the input language L_{in}.
As for languages, translations can be defined by generative devices
and by recognizing devices.

The generative device is derived from the ECF syntax as follows.
Given a translation t with input language L_{in}. First, we construct
an ECF syntax G such that $L(G) = L_{in}$. Then, we add semantic actions
on the syntax rules, which calculate the contents E of the environment for each sentence x being generated. By definition, (x,E) is
an element of the translation t. This new definition tool is called
the generalized ECF translation syntax. It will be discussed in
section 3.2.

The recognizing device is derived from the ELL(1) parser as follows. Given a translation t with input language L_{in}. First, we
construct an ELL(1) parser A such that $L(A) = L_{in}$. Then, we add
semantic actions on the parsing rules, which calculate the contents

119

E of the environment for each input string x being accepted. By
definition, (x,E) is an element of the translation t. This new
definition tool is called the ELL(1) transducer. It will be discussed in section 3.3.

Notice that the ECF syntax and the ELL(1) parser are special
cases of the generalized ECF translation syntax and the ELL(1)
transducer, with an empty set of semantic actions and an empty
environment.

Section 3.4 will cover the mechanical generation of ELL(1) transducers from generalized ECF translation syntaxes.

3.2.   Generalized Extended Context-free translation syntax

The generalized ECF translation syntax is the underlying formalism for the syntax-directed description of a translation, as it will
be the input for LILA.

A generalized ECF translation syntax F is a generative device
that defines a set (possibly infinite) of pairs (x,E), where x is a
string over the input vocabulary and E is the contents of the
environment. This set of pairs is called the translation defined by
F and is denoted t(F). E is said to be the translation of x.

A generalized ECF translation syntax makes use of three sets of
symbols : the set of input symbols, denoted V_{in}, the set of nonterminal symbols, denoted VN, and the set of semantic action symbols,
denoted V_{action}. V_{in} is the alphabet over which the language to be
translated, is defined. VN is used in the generation mechanism of
the generalized ECF translation syntax and V_{action} contains the
names of the semantic actions performing the translation. The heart
of the generalized ECF translation syntax is a finite set of rules
describing how elements of the translation, i.e. pairs (x,E), are to
be generated. Furthermore, a generalized ECF translation syntax
contains a finite set D of semantic action definitions and a finite
set G of definitions of objects (such as constants, variables, functions, procedures, types) which are global to all the semantic
actions.

Definition

A generalized ECF translation syntax is a 7-tuple, $F = (V_{in}, V_{action}, VN, A_0, P, G, D)$, where

1) V_{in} is a finite set of input symbols, V_{in} is called the input vocabulary.
   $V_{in} = \{a_1, a_2, \ldots, a_n\}$

2) V_{action} is a finite set of semantic action symbols. V_{action} is called the semantic action vocabulary.
   $V_{action} = \{r_1, r_2, \ldots, r_k\}$

3) VN is a finite set of nonterminal symbols.
   $VN = \{A_0, A_1, A_2, \ldots, A_m\}$

4) A_0 is the start symbol of F.
   $A_0 \in VN$.

5) P is a finite set of generalized ECF translation rules.
   Each rule is of the form $A_j = s_j$, where A_j belongs to VN and s_j is a generalized ECF translation expression. There is one generalized ECF translation rule for each nonterminal symbol in VN.

The definition of generalized ECF translation expression is identical to the definition of ECF expression (see section 2.3), except for the axiomatic rule (0).

Axiomatic rules

0) r is a generalized ECF translation expression.
   $r \in V_{action}$, r is called an applied occurrence of a semantic action.

1) & is a generalized ECF translation expression.
   & is the notation for the empty string.

2) a_i is a generalized ECF translation expression.
   $a_i \in V_{in}$

3) A_j is a generalized ECF translation expression.

   $A_j \in VN$

Composition rules

We assume that $s, s_1, s_2, \ldots, s_n$ are generalized ECF translation expressions,

4) $(s_1 | s_2 | \ldots | s_n)$ is a generalized ECF translation expression, $n > 1$.

5) $s_1 s_2 \ldots s_n$ is a generalized ECF translation expression, $n > 1$.

6) $(s)^*$ is a generalized ECF translation expression.

7) $(s)^+$ is a generalized ECF translation expression.

6) G is a finite set of declarations which are global to all semantic action definitions.

7) D is a finite set of semantic action definitions. It associates with each semantic action symbol r in V_{action} a description of the action; r is called the defining occurrence of a semantic action.

Metalanguage

The metalanguage of a generalized ECF translation syntax $F = (V_{in}, V_{action}, VN, A_0, P, G, D)$ is the language in which the actions in D and the declarations in G are written. As it will be explained later, the metalanguage is the language in which the ELL(1) transducers are written.

Environment

Given a generalized ECF translation syntax $F = (V_{in}, V_{action}, VN, A_0, P, G, D)$ defining the translation t(F). The environment of F consists of the variables declared in G (program-defined

variables) as well as the variables declared in the metalanguage
(language-defined variables). The contents of the environment is
denoted E. At the start of each generation, the environment is in
the initial state E_0. In our model, E_0 is metalanguage defined.

Produces

The relation ->, pronounced <u>produces</u>, is a relation on pairs of
strings over (V_{in} U VN U V_{action}) and the contents of the environment. For each rule A=s in P and for each semantic action symbol r
in V_{action}, we have :

1) $(A,E)->(v,E)$, where v is a sentence in the RE syntax G' = (V_{in} U
   VN U V_{action}, s).

2) $(r,E)->(\&,E')$, where the contents E of the environment is altered
   into E' by the execution of the semantic action r.

Directly derives

The relation =>, pronounced <u>directly derives</u>, is a relation on
pairs of strings over (V_{in} U VN U V_{action}) and the contents of the
environment. Given two pairs (s_1,E_1) and (s_2,E_2), (s_1,E_1) =>
(s_2,E_2) if s_1 can be written as xyz and s_2 as xvz with $(y,E_1)->$
(v,E_2).

Leftmost directly derives

The relation =>1, pronounced <u>leftmost directly derives</u>, is a
relation on pairs of strings over (V_{in} U VN U V_{action}) and the contents of the environment. Given two pairs (s_1,E_1) and (s_2,E_2). We
have (s_1,E_1) =>1 (s_2,E_2) if (s_1,E_1) => (s_2,E_2), s_1=xyz, s_2=xvz, y is
the leftmost nonterminal or semantic action symbol in s_1 and (y,E_1)
-> (v,E_2).

The <u>k-fold product</u> =>^{k}, the <u>transitive closure</u> =>$^+$ and the
<u>reflexive and transitive closure</u> =>* of the relation => are defined
in the usual way. The same is true for =>1^k, =>1$^+$ and =>1*.

Translation form

   A <u>translation</u> <u>form</u> in $F = (V_{in}, V_{action}, VN, A_0, P, G, D)$ is a pair (x, E) such that $(A_0, E_0) =>1^* (x, E)$.

Leftmost derivation

   A <u>leftmost</u> <u>derivation</u> of a translation form (x, E) in $F = (V_{in}, V_{action}, VN, A_0, P, G, D)$ is a sequence of pairs $(A_0, E_0) = x_0, x_1,$ ... , x_i, ... , $x_n = (x, E)$ with for all i, $0 \le i < n$, $x_i =>1 x_{i+1}$.

Terminal translation form

   A <u>terminal</u> <u>translation</u> <u>form</u> in $F = (V_{in}, V_{action}, VN, A_0, P, G, D)$ is a translation form (w, E) such that $w \in V_{in}^*$.

Translation

   The <u>translation</u> defined in F is the set of all terminal translation forms in F; $t(F) = \{(w, E) \mid (A_0, E_0) =>1^* (w, E), w \in V_{in}^*\}$. Notice that the set $\{(w, E) \mid (A_0, E_0) =>^* (w, E), w \in V_{in}^*\}$ is not necessarily identical to t(F) as defined above. The reason is that the contents of the environment generally depends on the order in which semantic actions are evaluated. Since we are used to read from left to right, we have chosen for the definition based on the relation $=>1$.

Derivation tree

   Given a generalized ECF translation syntax $F = (V_{in}, V_{action}, VN, A_0, P, G, D)$ and let D be a derivation tree (see section 2.3) of w in the ECF syntax $G = (V_{in} \cup V_{action}, VN, A_0, P)$. Let v be a string of input symbols derived from w by replacing all semantic action symbols by &. We call D a <u>derivation</u> <u>tree</u> of v in F.

Interior and terminal frontier

These definitions are identical to the ones given in section 2.3.

Semantic action evaluation

Given a derivation tree D in a generalized ECF translation syntax F. The derivation tree D is traversed recursive descent from left to right. Each time an r node is encountered, where r is a semantic action symbol, the semantic action for r is activated, possibly modifying the contents of the environment. The semantic action evaluation is described by the recursive procedure evaluate_subtree :

```
proc evaluate_subtree = (tree NODE) void :
  for each direct descendant Xᵢ of NODE from left to right
    do if Xᵢ ∈ VN
        then evaluate_subtree (iᵗʰ descendant of NODE)
        else if Xᵢ ∈ V_action
              then activate the semantic action Xᵢ
              else co Xᵢ is an input symbol or
                    the empty string symbol & co
            fi
    fi
  od
```

Translation

A translation in F, denoted t(F), can also be defined as the set of all pairs (w,E) where w is a string of input symbols and E is the contents of the environment after the semantic action evaluation of the derivation tree of w in F.

Ambiguous generalized ECF translation syntax

A generalized ECF translation syntax F is said to be ambiguous if its input syntax G is ambiguous. The definition of ambiguous ECF syntax is given in section 2.3.

Reduced generalized ECF translation syntax

A generalized ECF translation syntax F is <u>reduced</u> if its input syntax G is reduced. The definition of reduced ECF syntax is given in section 2.3.

Input syntax

The <u>input</u> <u>syntax</u> of a generalized ECF translation syntax $F = (V_{in}, V_{action}, VN, A_O, P, G, D)$ is the ECF syntax $G = (V_{in}, VN, A_O, P')$ where P' is obtained from P by replacing all semantic action symbols by the empty string symbol &. L(G) defines all the possible strings w over V_{in} for which there is a terminal translation form (w,E) in F.

Example

The generalized ECF translation syntax F_a for the translation of simple arithmetic expressions into postfix notation is given below.

$F_a = (V_{in}, V_{action}, VN_a, E, P_a, G_a, D_a)$

$V_{in} = \{a, b, c, +, -, *, /, (,)\}$
$V_{action} = \{PLUS, MINUS, TIMES, DIVIDE,$
$\qquad\qquad ASYMBOL, BSYMBOL, CSYMBOL\}$
$VN_a = \{E, T, F\}$
E is the start symbol of F_a
$P_a = \{$<E> = <T> ("+" <T> PLUS
$\qquad\qquad\qquad$ |"-" <T> MINUS
$\qquad\qquad\qquad$)*,
$\qquad\quad$<T> = <F> ("*" <F> TIMES
$\qquad\qquad\qquad$ |"/" <F> DIVIDE
$\qquad\qquad\qquad$)*,
$\qquad\quad$<F> = "a" ASYMBOL
$\qquad\qquad\quad$ |"b" BSYMBOL
$\qquad\qquad\quad$ |"c" CSYMBOL
$\qquad\qquad\quad$ |"(" <E> ")" $\}$

$G_a = \{ \}$
$D_a = \{\underline{action}$ PLUS = $\underline{void}$: write ("+");
      $\underline{action}$ MINUS = $\underline{void}$: write ("-");
      $\underline{action}$ TIMES = $\underline{void}$: write ("*");
      $\underline{action}$ DIVIDE = $\underline{void}$: write ("/");
      $\underline{action}$ ASYMBOL = $\underline{void}$: write ("a");
      $\underline{action}$ BSYMBOL = $\underline{void}$: write ("b");
      $\underline{action}$ CSYMBOL = $\underline{void}$: write ("c") $\}$

The derivation tree of the input string 'a*(b+c)' in F_a is pictured in fig. 3.1. After semantic evaluation of the derivation tree in fig. 3.1, the environment (which is an output file) contains the string abc+*. The pair (a*(b+c), abc+*) is an element of the translation $t(F_a)$.

The leftmost derivation of the terminal translation form (a*(b+c), abc+*) is given below.

```
(<E>,&) =>1
(<T>,&) =>1
(<F>"*"<F> TIMES,&) =>1
("a" ASYMBOL "*" <F> TIMES,&) =>1
("a" "*" <F> TIMES,a) =>1
("a" "*" "(" <E> ")" TIMES,a) =>1
("a" "*" "(" <T> "+" <T> PLUS ")" TIMES,a) =>1
("a" "*" "(" <F> "+" <T> PLUS ")" TIMES,a) =>1
("a" "*" "(" "b" BSYMBOL "+" <T> PLUS ")" TIMES,a) =>1
("a" "*" "(" "b" "+" <T> PLUS ")" TIMES,ab) =>1
("a" "*" "(" "b" "+" <F> PLUS ")" TIMES,ab) =>1
("a" "*" "(" "b" "+" "c" CSYMBOL PLUS ")" TIMES,ab) =>1
("a" "*" "(" "b" "+" "c" PLUS ")" TIMES,abc) =>1
("a" "*" "(" "b" "+" "c" ")" TIMES,abc+) =>1
("a" "*" "(" "b" "+" "c" ")",abc+*)
```

In each pair (x,y), x is a string over $(V_{in} \cup VN \cup V_{action})$ and y is the contents of a print file (environment).

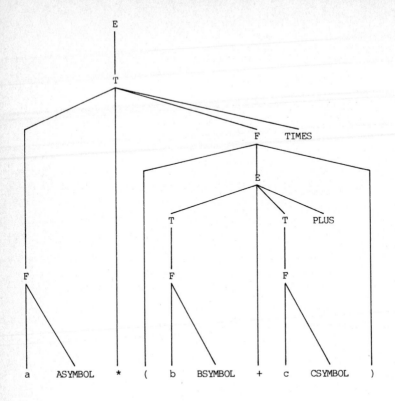

Fig. 3.1.

The input syntax of F_a is G_a:

$G_a = (V_{in}, VN_a, E, P_a)$
$V_{in} = \{a,b,c,+,-,*,/,(,)\}$
$VN_a = \{E,T,F\}$
$P_a = \{\langle E\rangle = \langle T\rangle \ ("+" \ \langle T\rangle$
$\qquad\qquad\qquad\quad |"-" \ \langle T\rangle$
$\qquad\qquad\qquad)*,$
$\qquad\quad \langle T\rangle = \langle F\rangle \ ("*" \ \langle F\rangle$
$\qquad\qquad\qquad\quad |"/" \ \langle F\rangle$
$\qquad\qquad\qquad)*,$

```
<F> = "a"
    |"b"
    |"c"
    |"(" <E> ")"
}
```

$L(G_a)$ is the set of all strings over V_{in}, for which there is a translation in $t(F_a)$. $L(G_a)$ is the input language of F_a.

EXAMPLE : The translation of arithmetic expressions into three-address instructions.

The translation of arithmetic expressions into three-address instructions is described by the generalized ECF translation syntax $F = (V_{in}, V_{action}, VN, PROG, P, G, D)$, given below.

Notice that the semantic actions do not calculate the values of the arithmetic expressions but calculate the attributes of these values in order to produce three-address instructions.
A three-address instruction consists of the following six fields :
1) the operation field,
2) the type field for the left operand,
3) the type field for the right operand,
4) the access field for the left operand,
5) the access field for the right operand and
6) the access field for the result.

In our example, three-address instructions have four possible operations : plus, minus, times and divide. There are two kinds of attributes to be calculated : <u>type</u> and <u>access</u>. These attributes will be the actual parameters of the three-address instructions to be generated. In our example, the types are restricted to <u>int</u> and <u>real</u>.

An access attribute consists of two fields : a class field and a specification field. The class field specifies in which run-time space the value will reside and the specification field gives the relative address in that space. To keep the storage allocation simple, we have two run-time spaces : the <u>working</u> <u>space</u> (worksp) and the <u>table</u> <u>of</u> <u>constants</u> (constab). In the working space the addresses are calculated statically in such a way that at run-time the values are stored stackwise.

The type and access information must be seen as a static (at translation-<u>time</u>) description of run-time values, i.e., values that come into existence during the execution of the generated three-address instructions. For example, (real, (constab, 3)) describes a real value that is stored in the table of constants at relative address 3, and (int, (worksp, 5)) describes an integer value that is stored in the working space at relative address 5.

In the generalized ECF translation syntax given below, intct and realct are input symbols. We suppose that they represent indices of entries in the table of constants.

As an example, consider the string of terminal symbols

"intct" "+" "realct" "*" "intct" "-" "realct"
  0   1   3   4

The table of constants is :

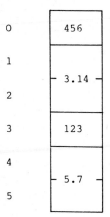

0	456
1	— 3.14 —
2	
3	123
4	— 5.7 —
5	

With each occurrence of "intct" and "realct" an index of an entry in the table of constants is associated in one or another way. In section 4.2, we will see that input symbols can be attributed. The same translation of arithmetic expressions into three-address instructions will be worked out with a generalized attributed ECF translation syntax in section 4.2.

The translation of the above string of input symbols is then :

```
times (real,
       int,
       (constab,1),
       (constab,3),
       (worksp,0))
 plus (int,
       real,
       (constab,0),
       (worksp,0),
       (worksp,0))
minus (real,
       real,
       (worksp,0),
       (constab,4),
       (worksp,0))
```

Notice that the attributes type and access are calculated by the semantic actions and that this calculation has a recursive aspect. Therefore, the semantic actions use a stack, called <u>semanticstack</u>. Upon this stack, a number of primitive actions are defined : popstack, pushstack and initstack.

The control of the calculation of the attributes type and access is based on some sort of invariant relation. Each time one of the semantic actions ADD, SUBTRACT, MULTIPLY and DIVIDE, is activated, the attributes of the right and left operand are the top and the top but one element of semanticstack. In order to make this relation always true, the semantic actions ADD, SUBTRACT, MULTIPLY and DIVIDE, will replace both stack elements by a new element, representing the attribute of the result of the operations plus, minus, times and divide, respectively. Also, the semantic actions TREAT_INTCT and TREAT_REALCT will produce an element on the top of semanticstack.

$F = (V_{in}, V_{action}, VN, PROG, P, G, D)$
$V_{in} = \{+, -, *, /, (,), intct, realct\}$
$V_{action} = \{ADD, SUBTRACT, MULTIPLY, DIVIDE, TREAT\_INTCT, TREAT\_REALCT, INIT\}$
$VN = \{PROG, E, T, F\}$
$P = \{<PROG> = INIT <E>,$

```
      <E> = <T> ("+" <T> ADD
                |"-" <T> SUBTRACT
                )*,
      <T> = <F> ("*" <F> MULTIPLY
```

```
              |"/" <F> DIVIDE
              )*,
     <F> = "intct" TREAT_INTCT
           |"realct" TREAT_REALCT
           |"(" <E> ")"
     }


G = {mode attribute = struct (type type,
                              access access);
     mode type = (int,real);
     mode access = struct (class class,
                           int spec);
     mode class = (worksp, constab);

     int stackmax = co some integer constant co;
     [1:stackmax] attribute semanticstack;
     int topstack;
     proc popstack = (ref attribute x) void :
       if topstack = 0
         then stackunderflow
         else x := semanticstack[topstack];
              topstack -:= 1
       fi;
     proc pushstack = (attribute x) void :
       begin
         topstack +:= 1;
         if topstack > stackmax
           then stackoverflow
         fi;
         semanticstack[topstack] := x
       end;
     proc stackoverflow = void :
       co an error message is printed and the transducer halts co;
     proc stackunderflow = void :
       co an error message is printed and the transducer halts co;

     attribute attribute_left, attribute_right;
     type type_left, type_right, type_result;
     access access_left, access_right, access_result;
```

```
proc balance_type = (type leftoperand, type rightoperand) type :
  co the result of this routine is described by the type table below :
```

	int	real
int	int	real
real	real	real

left operand | right operand

```
  co;
```

```
proc size = (type type) int :
  co this routine determines the number of basic memory cells a value of
     a given type occupies. This routine illustrates how machine—dependent
     features in an implementation can be localized. In our example,
     size(int) = 1 and size(real) = 2.
  co;
int workp
}
```

```
D = {action INIT = void :
       begin
         topstack := 0;
         workp := 0;
       end;


     action ADD = void :
       begin
         popstack (attribute_right);
         popstack (attribute_left);
         type_left := type of attribute_left;
         type_right := type of attribute_right;
         access_left := access of attribute_left;
         access_right := access of attribute_right;
         type_result := balance_type (type_left, type_right);
         if class of access_left = worksp
           then access_result := access_left;
                workp := spec of access_left + size (type_result)
           else if class of access_right = worksp
                  then access_result := access_right;
                       workp := spec of access_right + size (type_result)
                  else access_result := (worksp,workp);
                       workp +:= size (type_result)
                fi
```

```
      fi;
    write ("plus (", type_left, ", ",
                     type_right, ", ",
                     access_left, ", ",
                     access_right, ", ",
                     access_result, ") ");
    pushstack((type_result, access_result))
  end;


action SUBTRACT = void :
  begin
    popstack (attribute_right);
    popstack (attribute_left);
    type_left := type of attribute_left;
    type_right := type of attribute_right;
    access_left := access of attribute_left;
    access_right := access of attribute_right;
    type_result := balance_type (type_left, type_right);
    if class of access_left = worksp
      then access_result := access_left;
           workp := spec of access_left + size (type_result)
      else if class of access_right = worksp
           then access_result := access_right;
                workp := spec of access_right + size (type_result)
           else access_result := (worksp,workp);
                workp + := size (type_result)
           fi
    fi;
    write ("minus (", type_left, ", ",
                      type_right, ", ",
                      access_left, ", ",
                      access_right, ", ",
                      access_result, ", ",
    pushstack((type_result,access_result))
  end;


action MULTIPLY = void :
  begin
    popstack (attribute_right);
    popstack (attribute_left);
    type_left := type of attribute_left;
    type_right := type of attribute_right;
    access_left := access of attribute_left;
    access_right := access of attribute_right;
    type_result := balance_type (type_left, type_right);
    if class of access_left = worksp
      then access_result := access_left;
```

```
          workp := spec of access_left + size (type_result)
     else if class of access_right = worksp
           then access_result := access_right;
                workp := spec of access_right + size (type_result)
           else access_result := (worksp,workp);
                workp +:= size (type_result)
        fi
  fi;
  write ("times (", type_left, ", ",
                    type_right, ", ",
                    access_left, ", ",
                    access_right, ", ",
                    access_result, ") ");
  pushstack((type_result, access_result))
end;


action DIVIDE = void :
  begin
    popstack (attribute_right);
    popstack (attribute_left);
    type_left := type of attribute_left;
    type_right := type of attribute_right;
    access_left := access of attribute_left;
    access_right := access of attribute_right;
    type_result := real;
    if class of access_left = worksp
      then access_result := access_left;
           workp := spec of access_left + size (type_result)
      else if class of access_right = worksp
             then access_result := access_right;
                  workp := spec of access_right + size (type_result)
             else access_result := (worksp,workp);
                  workp +:= size (type_result)
          fi
    fi;
    write ("divide (", type_left, ", ",
                       type_right, ", ",
                       access_left, ", ",
                       access_right, ", ",
                       access_result, ") ");
    pushstack((type_result, access_result))
  end;


action TREAT_INTCT = void :
  pushstack ((int, (constab,
                  co index of the entry of the constant table where the
```

```
                    integer constant is stored co)));

   action TREAT_REALCT = void :
      pushstack ((real, (constab,
                        co index of the entry of the constant table where the
                           real constant is stored co)))
   }
```

Design of a generalized ECF translation syntax

A generalized ECF translation syntax will be designed in two steps. In a first step, the input language L of the translation is defined by means of an ECF syntax G. In a second step, we add the appropriate semantic actions and global information, resulting in a generalized ECF translation syntax F. This is illustrated by means of an example : the translation of simple arithmetic expressions into reversed polish notation.

step 1

The input language L_a of the translation is the set of simple arithmetic expressions. L_a is defined by the following ECF syntax :

$G_a = (VT_a, VN, E, P_a)$

$VT_a = \{a,b,c,+,-,*,/,(,)\}$
$VN_a = \{E,T,F\}$
E is the start symbol of G_a
$P_a = \{$<E> = <T> ("+" <T>
                |"-" <T>
)*,
       <T> = <F> ("*" <F>
                |"/" <F>
)*,
       <F> = "a"
           |"b"
           |"c"
           |"(" <E> ")" }

<u>step</u> <u>2</u>

We add semantic actions and global information to G_a to obtain the generalized ECF translation syntax F_a.

$F_a = (V_{in}, V_{action}, VN_a, E, P_a, G_a, D_a)$

$V_{in} = \{a, b, c, +, -, *, /, (,)\}$
$V_{action} = \{PLUS, MINUS, TIMES, DIVIDE,$
$\qquad\qquad ASYMBOL, BSYMBOL, CSYMBOL\}$
$VN_a = \{E, T, F\}$
E is the start symbol of F_a
$P_a = \{$<E> = <T> ("+" <T> PLUS
$\qquad\qquad\qquad$ |"-" <T> MINUS
$\qquad\qquad\qquad$)*,
$\qquad$ <T> = <F> ("*" <F> TIMES
$\qquad\qquad\qquad$ |"/" <F> DIVIDE
$\qquad\qquad\qquad$)*,
$\qquad$ <F> = "a" ASYMBOL
$\qquad\qquad$ |"b" BSYMBOL
$\qquad\qquad$ |"c" CSYMBOL
$\qquad\qquad$ |"(" <E> ")" $\}$
$G_a = \{ \}$
$D_a = \{$<u>action</u> PLUS = <u>void</u> : write ("+");
$\qquad$ <u>action</u> MINUS = <u>void</u> : write ("-");
$\qquad$ <u>action</u> TIMES = <u>void</u> : write ("*");
$\qquad$ <u>action</u> DIVIDE = <u>void</u> : write ("/");
$\qquad$ <u>action</u> ASYMBOL = <u>void</u> : write ("a");
$\qquad$ <u>action</u> BSYMBOL = <u>void</u> : write ("b");
$\qquad$ <u>action</u> CSYMBOL = <u>void</u> : write ("c") $\}$

3.3. <u>ELL(1) transducer</u>

In section 3.2, we have discussed a particular type of generative device to define translations, namely the generalized ECF translation syntax.

In the present section, we will discuss a particular type of recognizing device, namely the <u>ELL(1)</u> <u>transducer</u>. Given an input vocabulary V_{in} and an environment, an ELL(1) transducer B maps the set of strings over V_{in} into $(V_E \cup \{no\})$, where V_E represents the set of all possible contents of the environment. The set of input strings which are mapped into V_E, is called the <u>input language</u> of

the translation.
The set of pairs (x,E), where the input string x is mapped into a contents E of the environment, is called the translation defined by B. It is denoted t(B).

An Ell(1) transducer B is composed of five elements :

1) the input tape which is a sequence of tape squares, each tape square containing exactly one input symbol of an input vocabulary V_{in}. Input strings will always be terminated by the end marker, represented by the symbol '#'.

2) the input head which reads one symbol at a given instance of time. At each read action, the input head moves one square to the right.

3) the pushdown list which is an auxiliary memory of the type last-in first-out. It is used by the underlying ELL(1) parser of B.

4) the finite control containing a finite set of transducing rules, dictating the behavior of B.

5) the environment, the contents of which can be altered by the transducing rules.

As for the accepting rules of an ELL(1) parser, the transducing rules of the finite control of an ELL(1) transducer can be represented in different forms, such as
1) a mapping,
2) a program, where the pushdown list is explicit,
3) a program, where the pushdown list is implicit. An implicit pushdown list means that the pushdown list is implemented by means of the stack of the recursive procedure mechanism available in the metalanguage.
In this book, we will only discuss ELL(1) transducers of type (3). ELL(1) transducers of types (1) and (2) are discussed in Part 1.

ELL(1) transducer with implicit pushdown list

The ELL(1) transducer in the form of a program with implicit pushdown list can best be explained by means of an example : the translation of simple arithmetic expressions into reversed polish notation. More complex examples can be found in section 5.
The translation of simple arithmetic expressions into reversed polish notation is defined by the following generalized ECF translation syntax F_a.

$F_a = (V_{in}, V_{action}, VN_a, E, P_a, G_a, D_a)$

$V_{in} = \{a,b,c,+,-,*,/,(,)\}$
$V_{action} = \{PLUS, MINUS, TIMES, DIVIDE,$
          $ASYMBOL, BSYMBOL, CSYMBOL\}$
$VN_a = \{E, T, F\}$
E is the start symbol of F_a
$P_a = \{<E> = <T>$ ("+" $<T>$ PLUS
              |"-" $<T>$ MINUS
)*,

      $<T> = <F>$ ("*" $<F>$ TIMES
              |"/" $<F>$ DIVIDE
)*,

      $<F> =$ "a" ASYMBOL
          |"b" BSYMBOL
          |"c" CSYMBOL
          |"(" $<E>$ ")" }
$G_a = \{ \}$
$D_a = \{$action PLUS = void : write ("+");
      action MINUS = void : write ("-");
      action TIMES = void : write ("*");
      action DIVIDE = void : write ("/");
      action ASYMBOL = void : write ("a");
      action BSYMBOL = void : write ("b");
      action CSYMBOL = void : write ("c") }

The main idea is to develop a methodology to write the ELL(1) transducer B_a, using the generalized ECF translation syntax F_a as a guide. In section 3.4, we will see that the ELL(1) transducer B_a with implicit pushdown list can be obtained from the generalized ECF translation syntax F_a in a mechanical way.

Notice that the generalized ECF translation syntax is a very compact and readable description of the ELL(1) transducer. The description is also very flexible and can easily be modified and extended. Furthermore, the syntax-directed description F_a is very close to the definition of reversed polish notation of simple arithmetic expressions.

The ELL(1) transducer B_a mainly consists of three so-called ELL(1) <u>transducing</u> <u>routines</u> E, T and F. There is a transducing routine for each generalized ECF translation syntax rule in F_a.

```
proc ELL(1) transducer = void :
begin
    char in := co ... co;
    proc read = void : co ... co;
    proc error = void : co ... co;
    proc accept = void : co ... co;
    proc E = void : co ┌──────────────────────┐ co;
    proc T = void : co  │    defined below     │ co;
    proc F = void : co └──────────────────────┘ co;
    action PLUS = void : write ("+");
    action MINUS = void : write ("-");
    action TIMES = void : write ("*");
    action DIVIDE = void : write ("/");
    action ASYMBOL = void : write ("a");
    action BSYMBOL = void : write ("b");
    action CSYMBOL = void : write ("c") }
    E;
    if in = "#"
       then accept
       else error
    fi
end
```

<u>expression</u>

The ELL(1) transducing routine E for the generalized ECF translation syntax rule :

```
<E> = <T> ("+" <T> PLUS
          |"-" <T> MINUS
          )*
```

is the following :

```
proc E = void :
  begin
    T;
    while in ∈ {+,-}
      do case in
            when "+"
                if in = "+"
                  then read
                  else error
                fi;
                T;
                PLUS
            otherwise
                if in = "-"
                  then read
                  else error
                fi;
                T;
                MINUS
         esac
      od
  end
```

term

The ELL(1) transducing routine T for the generalized ECF translation syntax rule :

```
<T> = <F> ("*" <F> TIMES
          |"/" <F> DIVIDE
          )*
```

is the following :

```
proc T = void :
  begin
    F;
    while in ∈ {*,/}
      do case in
           when "*"
                ┌─────────────────┐
                │ if in = "*"     │
                │   then │ read │ │
                │   else │ error│ │
                │ fi;             │
                └─────────────────┘
                F;
                TIMES
           otherwise
                ┌─────────────────┐
                │ if in = "/"     │
                │   then │ read │ │
                │   else │ error│ │
                │ fi;             │
                └─────────────────┘
                F;
                DIVIDE
         esac
      od
  end
```

factor

The ELL(1) transducing routine F for the generalized ECF translation syntax rule :

```
<F> = "a" ASYMBOL
     |"b" BSYMBOL
     |"c" CSYMBOL
     |"(" <E> ")"
```

is the following :

```
proc F = void :
  case in
    when "a"
      if in = "a"
        then read
        else error
      fi;
      ASYMBOL
    when "b"
      if in = "b"
        then read
        else error
      fi;
      BSYMBOL
    when "c"
      if in = "c"
        then read
        else error
      fi;
      CSYMBOL
    otherwise
      if in = "("
        then read
        else error
      fi;
      E;
      if in = ")"
        then read
        else error
      fi
  esac
```

The different moves of the ELL(1) transducer when translating the input string a∗(b+c) are displayed in fig. 3.2.

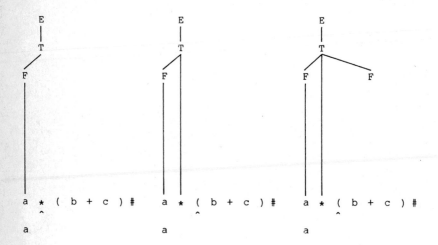

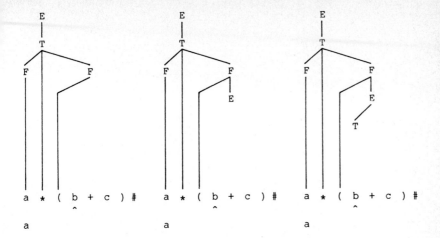

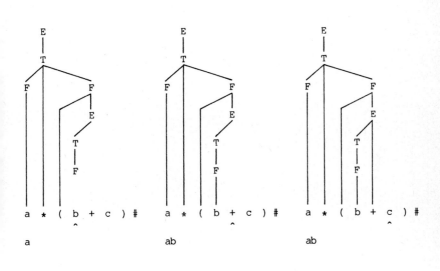

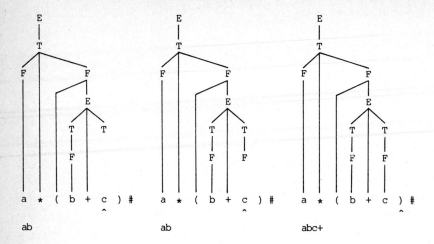

ab   ab   abc+

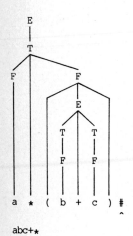

abc+*

Fig. 3.2.

Two-pass ELL(1) transducer

The ELL(1) transducer described so far is a one-pass transducer. Practically, this means that the entire derivation tree has not to be built and stored in memory. Syntactic and semantic analysis is performed in one pass.

Conceptually, each ELL(1) transducer can be separated into a syntactic pass (syntactic analyser) and a semantic pass (semantic analyser). Given a generalized ECF translation syntax F. The syntactic analyser is an <u>ELL(1) parser</u> A which can be produced mechanically from the input syntax G of F. The syntactic analyser produces a derivation tree in F for each input string that belongs to L(G).

The semantic analyser traverses the derivation tree recursive descent from left to right, activating the semantic actions. The semantic pass is called <u>semantic action evaluation</u>.

Notice the duality between the generation of a translation element (w,E) in a generalized ECF translation syntax and the production of (w,E) by its corresponding two-pass ELL(1) transducer. The only difference is that in the generalized ECF translation syntax, the derivation tree for w is <u>generated</u>, whereas in the ELL(1) transducer the derivation tree is <u>recognized</u>.

The behavior of a two-pas ELL(1) transducer B is illustrated in fig. 3.3.

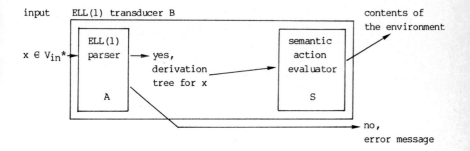

Fig. 3.3.

With LILA one is able to built one-pass as well as multi-pass compilers. This is illustrated by the case studies in section 5.

3.4.   Generation of ELL(1) transducers

Here, we will investigate how we can produce an ELL(1) transducer
B from a generalized ECF translation syntax F in a mechanical way,
with B and F being equivalent, i.e., t(B) = t(F). The ELL(1) transducer will be in the form of a program with the pushdown list being
implicit. The generation of ELL(1) transducers is pictured in fig.
3.4.

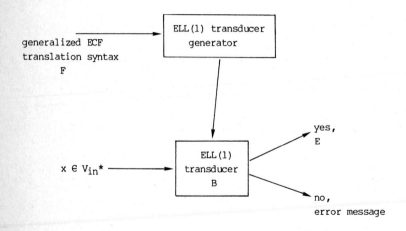

Fig. 3.4

Given a generalized ECF translation syntax $F = (V_{in}, V_{action}, VN,$
$A_0, P, G, D)$.

$V_{in} = \{a_1, a_2, \ldots, a_n\}$

$V_{action} = \{r_1, r_2, \ldots, r_k\}$

$VN = \{A_0, A_1, \ldots, A_m\}$

A_0 is the start symbol of F

$P = \{A_0 = s_0,$

$\qquad A_1 = s_1,$

$\qquad \ldots$

$\qquad A_m = s_m\}$

G is the set of global definitions

D is the set of semantic action definitions

Generation scheme

The ELL(1) transducer B as it is produced from F by the genera-tion scheme, is given below.

<u>proc</u> ELL(1) transducer B = <u>void</u> :
<u>begin</u>
  <u>char</u> in := <u>co</u> leftmost symbol of the input string <u>co</u>;
  <u>proc</u> read = <u>void</u> :
    <u>co</u> the next symbol in the input string is put in the variable
      'in' (the input head is moved one symbol to the right).
    <u>co</u>;
  <u>proc</u> error = <u>void</u> :
    <u>co</u> this routine produces an appropriate error message.
      Thereafter, the ELL(1) transducer halts.
    <u>co</u>;
  <u>proc</u> accept = <u>void</u> :
    <u>co</u> the input string has been transduced. Some appropriate
      actions are performed. Thereafter, the ELL(1) transducer
      halts.
    <u>co</u>;

```
┌──────────┐
│          │
│   G      │
│          │
└──────────┘;

┌──────────┐
│          │
│   D      │
│          │
└──────────┘;
```

$B(A_0 = s_0);$
$B(A_1 = s_1);$

    .

```
      .
      .
  B(Aj = sj);
      .
      .
      .
  B(Am = sm);
  A0;
  if in = "#"
    then accept
    else error
  fi
end
```

For each generalized ECF translation syntax rule $A_j = s_j$ in P of
F, we produce a routine called ELL(1) <u>transducing</u> <u>routine</u>, denoted
$B(A_j = s_j)$, as follows :

$A_j = s_j \in P$ -> <u>proc</u> A_j = <u>void</u> :
                         begin
                              $B(s_j)$
                         end

The body of the ELL(1) transducing routine A_j is denoted $B(s_j)$.
This body is produced in a modular way by means of the following
four axiomatic rules and four composition rules.

<u>Axiomatic rules</u>

<u>generalized ECF translation expression</u> -> <u>transducer module</u>

0) r -> r <u>co</u> this is the call of the semantic action r <u>co</u>

1) & -> <u>skip</u> <u>co</u> this is the empty statement <u>co</u>

2) $a_i \in V_{in}$ -> <u>if</u> in = a_i
                       then read
                       else error
                    fi

2') $A_j \in VN \rightarrow A_j$

This is the call of the ELL(1) transducing routine generated for A_j.

Composition rules

Suppose B(s) represents the transducer module for the generalized ECF translation expression s, with s possibly indexed.

3) $(s_1|s_2| \ldots |s_n) \rightarrow \underline{case}$ in

$\qquad$ $\underline{when}$ DIRSYMB(s_1)

$\qquad$ $\quad$ B(s_1)

$\qquad$ $\underline{when}$ DIRSYMB(s_2)

$\qquad$ $\quad$ B(s_2)

$\qquad$ ...

$\qquad$ $\underline{when}$ DIRSYMB(s_{n-1})

$\qquad$ $\quad$ B(s_{n-1})

$\qquad$ $\underline{otherwise}$

$\qquad$ $\quad$ B(s_n)

$\qquad$ esac

DIRSYMB (s_i) with $1 \leq i < n$ stands for the set of all input symbols which may occur initially under the input head for the transducer module B(s_i). These symbols are called <u>direction symbols</u>. The sets DIRSYMB(s_i) for all i ($1 \leq i < n$) are calculated from the generalized ECF translation syntax F in a mechanical way, prior to the generation of the ELL(1) transducer. The definition of DIRSYMB is given below.

4) $s_1 s_2 \ldots s_n \rightarrow$ B(s_1);B(s_2); $\ldots$;B(s_n)

5) $(s)* \rightarrow \underline{while}$ in $\in$ DIRSYMB(s)

$\qquad$ $\underline{do}$ B(s) $\underline{od}$

6) $(s)^+ \rightarrow \underline{repeat}$ B(s) $\underline{until}$ in $\notin$ DIRSYMB(s)

The definition of DIRSYMB and the ELL(1) conditions

The definitions of DIRSYMB, FIRST, EMPTY and FOLLOW for generalized ECF translation expressions are nearly identical to the
corresponding definitions for ECF expressions (see section 2.5).

Definition of DIRSYMB

DIRSYMB(s) = if EMPTY(s)
                  then FIRST(s) U FOLLOW(s)
                  else FIRST(s)
             fi

Definition of FIRST

(0) FIRST (r) = Ø
For the rules (1) to (6) see definition of FIRST(e) in section 2.5.

Definition of EMPTY

(0) EMPTY (r) = true
For the rules (1) to (6) see definition of EMPTY(e) in section 2.5.

Definition of FOLLOW

This is identical to the definition of FOLLOW(e) in section 2.5.

The ELL(1) conditions

Consider the generation scheme, which generates an ELL(1) transducer
B from a generalized ECF translation syntax F. B and F are
equivalent if F satisfies a number of conditions called ELL(1) conditions.
The ELL(1) conditions for ELL(1) transducers are identical to those
for ELL(1) parsers, see section 2.5.

Underlying parser

Given a generalized ECF translation syntax F, from which an ELL(1) transducer B is derived, t(F) = t(B). From F, we produce the input syntax G, from which an ELL(1) parser A is derived, L(G) = L(A). The ELL(1) parser A is called the underlying parser of B. This is illustrated by fig. 3.5.

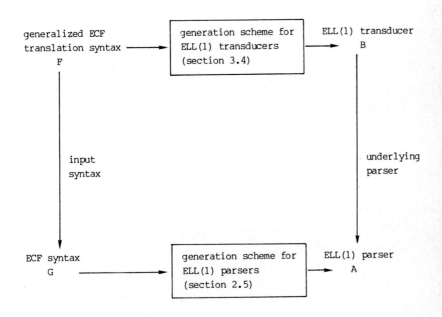

Fig. 3.5.

4. ATTRIBUTES

4.1. Introduction

In section 3 we have treated the generalized ECF translation syntax, which differs mainly from the ECF syntax (section 2) by the presence of the semantic actions. Except for trivial examples, the semantic actions deal with a bulk of information in order to produce the translation of the input strings. One part of this information is of a global nature, while another part is closely related to the nested structure of the input language. This kind of information is called the semantic-stack information, since it must be treated by means of a pushdown list in one way or another.

Many experiences in compiler design have shown that the management of the semantic-stack information may grow out of control very rapidly and may form a serious bottleneck for further correction, modification and extension of the compiler. Therefore, an adequate methodology together with a flexible formalism is needed to describe and implement semantic-stack information in a modular way. An adequate tool for this purpose is the technique of attributes.

The attributed syntax is a formalism that forces the implementor to treat semantic-stack information local to each syntax module. In this respect, attribute handling is a technique that promotes modular programming.

Here, we will discuss one particular type of attributed syntax : the generalized attributed ECF (AECF) translation syntax. Also, a generation scheme is given to produce mechanically attributed ELL(1) transducers from generalized AECF translation syntaxes. The theoretical background of the generalized AECF translation syntax and the attributed ELL(1) transducer can be found in Part 1.

155

4.2. Generalized Attributed Extended Context-free translation syntax

In section 2.3, we introduced the ECF syntax, which is a generative device to define languages. By adding semantic actions on the ECF syntax, we obtained the generalized ECF translation syntax, which is a generative device to define translations. This has been discussed in section 3.2. On the generalized ECF translation syntax, we will now superimpose the attribute mechanism, resulting in a generative device, called generalized AECF translation syntax.

Attributed context-free syntaxes were first described in Knuth [1968], which covered many interesting theoretical properties. Our starting point was Knuth's attribute mechanism, which we tuned into a practical tool. The result is the generalized AECF translation syntax. The step-wise transformation from the attributes of Knuth into the LILA attribute mechanism is thoroughly discussed in Part 1.

As for generalized ECF translation syntaxes, the generalized AECF translation syntax consists of a finite set of input symbols V_{in}, a finite set of semantic action symbols V_{action}, a finite set of nonterminal symbols VN, global information G and a finite set of semantic action definitions D. Now, input symbols and nonterminal symbols may be attributed.

In contrast with the attributes of Knuth, the LILA attributes are calculated by the semantic actions in attribute variables, which are associated with those nodes of a derivation tree, which are labelled with a nonterminal and a terminal symbol. This is explained below. Such an attribute variable is then identified within the semantic actions by means of the name of the terminal or nonterminal symbol. The types of these variables are described by a finite set of attribute declarations V_{att}.

As we will discuss later, attributes are calculated in an attributed derivation tree by a process called semantic action evaluation. The flow of information during this attribute handling may have two directions. Roughly speaking, attributes may be calculated from the root downwards, these attributes are called inherited, and attributes may be calculated from the leaves upwards, they are called <u>synthesized</u>.

Definition

A <u>generalized</u> <u>attributed</u> <u>extended</u> <u>context-free</u> <u>translation</u> <u>syntax</u>, denoted <u>generalized</u> <u>AECF</u> <u>translation</u> <u>syntax</u> is an 8-tuple, $F = (V_{in}, V_{action}, VN, V_{att}, A_0, P, G, D)$, where

1) V_{in} is a finite set of <u>input</u> <u>symbols</u>, V_{in} is called the <u>input</u> <u>vocabulary</u>.

2) V_{action} is a finite set of <u>semantic</u> <u>action</u> symbols, V_{action} is called the <u>semantic</u> <u>action</u> <u>vocabulary</u>.

3) VN is a finite set of <u>nonterminal</u> <u>symbols</u>.

4) V_{att} is a finite set of <u>attribute</u> <u>declarations</u>. Input symbols and nonterminal symbols may be attributed. This is specified by means of <u>attribute</u> <u>declarations</u> which have the following form :

    X <u>inher</u> $t_1 I_1, t_2 I_2, \ldots, t_n I_n,$
       <u>synth</u> $t_1' S_1, t_2' S_2, \ldots, t_k' S_k;$

where X is a symbol in $(V_{in} \cup VN)$, $t_1, t_2, \ldots, t_1', t_2', \ldots$ are type specifications, $I_1, I_2, \ldots, I_n$ are inherited attributes of X and $S_1, S_2, \ldots, S_k$ are synthesized attributes of X. The keyword <u>inher</u> stands for <u>inherited</u> and <u>synth</u> for <u>synthesized</u>. The set of inherited attributes of X is denoted $I(X) = \{I_1, I_2, \ldots, I_n\}$. The set of synthesized attributes of X is denoted $S(X) = \{S_1, S_2, \ldots, S_k\}$. The set of attributes of X is denoted $A(X) = I(X) \cup S(X)$. For any X, an attribute is either inherited or synthesized, $I(X) \cap S(X) = \emptyset$ for all $X \in (V_{in} \cup VN)$. If a given X does not occur in V_{att}, it means that X has no attributes associated with it. In our syntax model, input symbols and the start symbol A_0 never have inherited attributes. Thus, $I(X) = \emptyset$ for all X in V_{in} and $I(A_0) = \emptyset$. As it will be explained later, inherited attributes are calculated in the derivation tree from the root downwards (top-down), whereas synthesized attributes are calculated from the leaves upwards (bottom-up).

5) A_0 is the <u>start</u> <u>symbol</u> of F, $A_0 \in VN$.

6) P is a finite set of <u>generalized</u> AECF <u>translation</u> <u>syntax</u> <u>rules</u>. Each syntax rule is of the form $A_j = s_j$, where A_j belongs to VN and s_j is a <u>generalized</u> <u>ECF</u> <u>translation</u> <u>expression</u> as it is defined in section 3.2.

7) G is a finite set of <u>declarations</u> which are <u>global</u> to all semantic action definitions.

8) D is a finite set of <u>semantic</u> <u>action</u> <u>definitions</u>. It associates with each semantic action symbol r in V_{action} a description of the action. The semantic action symbols in D are said to be <u>defining</u> <u>occurrences</u> of the semantic actions. A semantic action definition may refer to attributes of occurrences of terminal and nonterminal symbols in a generalized AECF translation syntax rule $A_j = s_j$. Such a reference has the form of an attribute variable v <u>of</u> X_k, where v is an attribute associated with X according to the attribute declarations V_{att} and where X_k denotes the kth occurrence of the symbol X in the generalized AECF translation syntax rule $A_j = s_j$. If there is only one occurrence of X in the syntax rule, v <u>of</u> X_1 may be written as v <u>of</u> X.

Scope

Each occurrence of a terminal and nonterminal symbol X in a generalized AECF translation syntax rule has a well-defined zone, outside which the semantic actions have no access to the attributes associated with X. This zone is called the <u>scope</u> of X. This is analogous to the concept of scope for the defining occurrences of identifiers in block-structured programming languages. The definition of scope is based on the notion of <u>block</u>. Given a generalized AECF translation syntax rule A = s,

1) A = s itself constitutes a block.

2) for each generalized ECF translation subexpression of the form $(s_1|s_2| \ldots |s_n)$ in s, each expression $s_1, s_2, \ldots, s_n$ forms a block.

3) for each generalized ECF translation subexpression of the form (s)* or (s)$^+$, s forms a block.

The scope of an occurrence of a nonterminal or terminal symbol X in a generalized AECF translation syntax rule, is the smallest block enclosing X with inclusion of all inner blocks. The scope rule can now be formulated as follows. Given a syntax rule A = s, each semantic action whose call is in the scope of an occurrence of a terminal or nonterminal symbol X, may access the attributes associated with X. The definition of scope is illustrated for the rule :

$$X = r_1 X_1 \; (X_2 r_2 | X_3 r_3 \; (X_4 r_4)^*) \; X_5 r_5$$

X is a nonterminal symbol. X_1, X_2, X_3, X_4 and X_5 are occurrences of terminal or nonterminal symbols. r_1, r_2, r_3, r_4 and r_5 are semantic action symbols. The semantic action r_1 has access to the attributes of X, X_1 and X_5. The semantic action r_4 has access to the attributes of X, X_1, X_3, X_4 and X_5. The block structure for the syntax rule for X and the access rights for the semantic actions r_1 and r_4 are illustrated in Fig. 4.1.

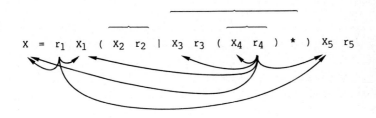

Fig. 4.1.

Derivation tree

A <u>derivation</u> <u>tree</u> in a generalized AECF translation syntax
$F = (V_{in}, V_{action}, VN, V_{att}, A_0, P, G, D)$ is a derivation tree in the ECF
syntax $G = (V_{in} \cup V_{action}, VN, A_0, P)$. The notion of derivation tree
in an ECF syntax has been defined in section 2.3.

Attributed derivation tree

An attributed derivation tree in a generalized AECF translation
syntax F is a derivation tree in F, where with each node, labelled
with an input symbol or a nonterminal symbol, the attribute variables (as they are defined in V_{att}) for that input or nonterminal
symbol are associated.

Metalanguage

The metalanguage of a generalized AECF translation syntax
$F = (V_{in}, V_{action}, VN, V_{att}, A_0, P, G, D)$ is the language in which the
actions in D, the declarations in G and the attribute declarations
in V_{att} are written. The metalanguage is identical with the
language in which the attributed ELL(1) transducers (see section
4.3) will be written.

Environment

Given a generalized AECF translation syntax $F = (V_{in},
V_{action}, VN, V_{att}, A_0, P, G, D)$. We call <u>environment</u> the set of all vari-
ables declared in G (program-defined variables) as well as the variables declared in the metalanguage (language-defined variables).
The contents of the environment at a given moment of semantic action
evaluation in F is denoted E. At the start of the semantic action
evaluation (described below), the environment is in the initial
state E_0. Each time a semantic action is activated, the contents E
of the environment may change. In our model, E_0 is metalanguage
defined.

Semantic action evaluation

The process by which the contents E of the environment and the attribute variables for a given attributed derivation tree D are calculated is called <u>semantic action evaluation</u>.

Given an attributed derivation tree D in a generalized AECF translation syntax. D is traversed recursive descent from left to right. When a node labelled r is encountered, where r is a semantic action symbol, the semantic action r is activated, calculating the attribute variables and possibly modifying the contents E of the environment. The semantic action evaluation is described by the recursive procedure evaluate_subtree.

<u>proc</u> evaluate_subtree = (<u>tree</u> NODE) <u>void</u> :
  <u>for</u> each direct descendant X_i of NODE from left to right
    <u>do</u> <u>if</u> $X_i \in VN$
          <u>then</u> evaluate_subtree (i^{th} descendant of NODE)
        <u>else</u> <u>if</u> $X_i \in V_{action}$
             <u>then</u> activate the semantic action X_i
            <u>else</u> <u>co</u> X_i is an input symbol or & <u>co</u>;
                 Initialize the synthesized attributes of X_i, if $X_i \in V_{in}$
          <u>fi</u>
     <u>fi</u>
  <u>od</u>

The flow of information can be illustrated by describing how an attribute variable of a node in the attributed derivation tree can be calculated in terms of other attribute variables. Therefore, we will consider two situations : the node as a father and the node as a son.

<u>Synthesized attributes</u> S_j of a nonterminal node, labeled X, are calculated when this node is in the position of a father. This calculation, specified by a semantic action r, is defined in terms of the attributes of the direct descendants Y of X, the inherited attributes I of X, together with the other synthesized attributes of X. This information flow is illustrated in the Fig. 4.2.

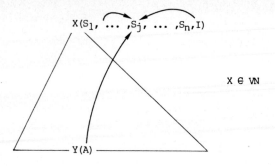

$$X(S_1, \ldots ,S_j, \ldots ,S_n,I)$$

$$X \in VN$$

$$Y(A)$$

Fig. 4.2.

Notice that the root, labelled with the start symbol A_0, has no inherited attributes. The information flow is illustrated in Fig. 4.3.

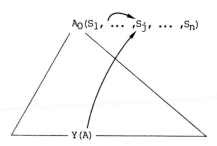

$$A_0(S_1, \ldots ,S_j, \ldots ,S_n)$$

$$Y(A)$$

Fig. 4.3.

The <u>inherited</u> <u>attributes</u> I_j of a node, labeled Y, are calculated when this node is in the position of a son. This calculation, specified by a semantic action r, is defined in terms of the synthesized attributes S of Y, the other inherited attributes of Y and the attributes A of its father X and its brothers Z and W. This information flow is illustrated in Fig. 4.4.

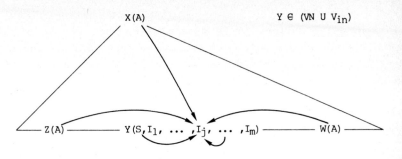

Fig. 4.4.

Remember that Y has no inherited attributes when it is an input symbol. Then, there is no information flow into this node. This is illustrated in Fig. 4.5.

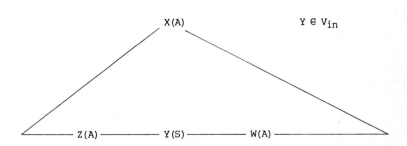

Fig. 4.5.

From fig. 4.2 to 4.5 we clearly see that synthesized attributes are used to transfer information from bottom to top, whereas inherited attributes are used to transfer information from top to bottom or sideways. The transfer of information between attributes of the same symbol makes it also possible to reverse the information flow.

Translation

   The translation defined in F, denoted t(F), is the set of all
pairs (w,E) where w is a string of attributed input symbols and E is
the contents of the environment after a semantic action evaluation
on the attributed derivation tree of w in F.

Input syntax

   The input syntax of a generalized AECF translation syntax F =
$(V_{in}, V_{action}, VN, V_{att}, A_0, P, G, D)$ is the ECF syntax G = (V_{in}, VN, A_0, P'),
where P' is obtained from P by replacing all semantic action symbols
by &. The input syntax G of F defines the set of strings x over
V_{in}, for which there is a pair (x,E) in t(F). This set of strings
is called the input language.

Ambiguous generalized AECF translation syntax

   A generalized AECF translation syntax F is ambiguous if the input
syntax G of F is ambiguous.

Reduced generalized AECF translation syntax.

   A generalized AECF translation syntax F = $(V_{in}, V_{action}, VN, V_{att},$
$A_0, P, G, D)$ is reduced if the input syntax G of F is reduced.

EXAMPLE : The generalized AECF translation syntax for the translation of simple arithmetic expressions into three-address instructions.

   The translation of simple arithmetic expressions into three-
address instructions has already been worked out by means of a generalized ECF translation syntax (see section 3.2). There, the

attributes <u>type</u> and <u>access</u> were controlled by means of a (compile-time) pushdown list. Here, the same translation will be defined by means of a generalized AECF translation syntax, where the type and access information will be controlled by means of the attribute mechanism. The synthesized attributes type and access are associated with the nonterminal symbols E, T and F. Furthermore, the input symbols realct and intct will be attributed with indexes into a table of constants where the real and integer values have been stored. As an example, the attributed input string for the expression 456 + 3.14 * 123 - 5.7 is given in Fig. 4.6.

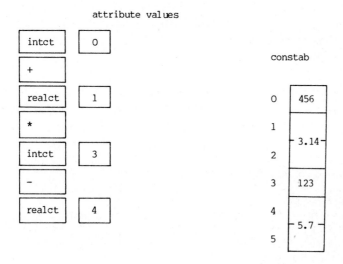

Fig. 4.6.

The translation of the attributed input string of fig. 4.6. is given in Fig. 4.7.

```
        times    (real,
                 int,
                 (constab, 1),
                 (constab, 3),
                 (worksp, 0))
        plus     (int,
                 real,
                 (constab, 0),
                 (worksp, 0),
                 (worksp, 0))
        minus    (real,
                 real,
                 (worksp, 0),
                 (constab, 4),
                 (worksp, 0))
```

Fig. 4.7.

The generalized AECF translation syntax F_a, defining the translation of the simple arithmetic expressions into three-address
instructions, is given below.

$F_a = (V_{in}, V_{action}, VN, V_{att}, PROG, P, G, D)$

$V_{in} = \{+, -, *, /, (,), intct, realct\}$
$V_{action} = \{ADD, SUBTRACT, MULTIPLY, DIVIDE, TREAT\_INTCT, TREAT\_REALCT,$
$\qquad\qquad TRANS\_T\_E, TRANS\_F\_T, TRANS\_E\_F, INIT\}$
$VN = \{PROG, E, T, F\}$
$V_{att} = \{E, T, F$ synth type type,
$\qquad\qquad\qquad$ access access;
$\qquad\quad$ intct, realct synth int constabp;
$\qquad$ }
$P = \{<PROG> = INIT <E>,$
$\qquad <E> = <T> TRANS\_T\_E$
$\qquad\qquad\qquad ("+" <T> ADD$
$\qquad\qquad\qquad |"-" <T> SUBTRACT$
$\qquad\qquad\qquad)*,$
$\qquad <T> = <F> TRANS\_F\_T$
$\qquad\qquad\qquad ("*" <F> MULTIPLY$
$\qquad\qquad\qquad |"/" <F> DIVIDE$
$\qquad\qquad\qquad)*,$
$\qquad <F> = "intct" TREAT\_INTCT$
$\qquad\qquad |"realct" TREAT\_REALCT$

```
            |"(" <E> ")" TRANS_E_F
      }


G = {mode access = struct (class class,
                              int spec);
      mode type = (int,real);
      mode class = (worksp,constab);
      type type_result;
      access access_result;
      proc balance_type = (type leftoperand, type rightoperand) type :
        co the result of this routine is described by the type table below :
```

	left operand	right operand	
		int	real
----------	-----	-----	------
int		int	real
real		real	real

```
      co;


      proc size = (type type) int :
        co this routine determines the number of basic memory cells a value of
           a given type occupies. This routine illustrates how machine-dependent
           features in an implementation can be localized. In our example,
           size(int) = 1 and size(real) = 2.
        co;
      int workp
      }


D = {action INIT = void :
        workp := 0;

      action ADD = void :
        begin
          type_result := balance_type (type of E, type of T_2);
          if class of access of E = worksp
            then access_result := access of E;
                 workp := spec of access of E + size (type_result)
            else if class of access of T_2 = worksp
                   then access_result := access of T_2;
                        workp := spec of access of T_2 + size (type_result)
                   else access_result := (worksp,workp);
                        workp +:= size (type_result)
                 fi
          fi;
```

```
        write ("plus (", type of E, ", ",
                        type of T_2, ", ",
                        access of E, ", ",
                        access of T_2, ", ",
                        access_result, ")" );
        type of E := type_result;
        access of E := access_result
      end;


  action SUBTRACT = void :
    begin
      type_result := balance_type (type of E, type of T_3);
      if class of access of E = worksp
        then access_result := access of E;
             workp := spec of access of E + size (type_result)
        else if class of access of T_3 = worksp
                then access_result := access of T_3;
                     workp := spec of access of T_3 + size (type_result)
                else access_result := (worksp,workp);
                     workp +:= size (type_result)
             fi
      fi;
      write ("minus (", type of E, ", ",
                        type of T_3, ", ",
                        access of E, ", ",
                        access of T_3, ", ",
                        access_result, ")" );
      type of E := type_result;
      access of E := access_result
    end;


  action MULTIPLY = void :
    begin
      type_result := balance_type (type of T, type of F_2);
      if class of access of T = worksp
        then access_result := access of T;
             workp := spec of access of T + size (type_result)
        else if class of access of F_2 = worksp
                then access_result := access of F_2;
                     workp := spec of access of F_2 + size (type_result)
                else access_result := (worksp,workp);
                     workp +:= size (type_result)
             fi
      fi;
      write ("times (", type of T, ", ",
                        type of F_2, ", ",
                        access of T, ", ",
                        access of F_2, ", ",
```

```
                        access_result, ")" );
    type of T := type_result;
    access of T := access_result
  end;


action DIVIDE = void :
  begin
    type_result := real;
    if class of access of T = worksp
      then access_result := access of T;
           workp := spec of access of T + size (type_result)
      else if class of access of F_3 = worksp
              then access_result := access of F_3;
                   workp := spec of access of F_3 + size (type_result)
              else access_result := (worksp,workp);
                   workp +:= size (type_result)
           fi
    fi;
    write ("divide (", type of T, ", ",
                       type of F_3, ", ",
                       access of T, ", ",
                       access of F_3, ", ",
                       access_result, ")" );
    type of T := type_result;
    access of T := access_result
  end;


action TREAT_INTCT = void :
  begin
    type of F := int;
    access of F := (constab, constabp of intct)
  end;


action TREAT_REALCT = void :
  begin
    type of F := real;
    access of F := (constab, constabp of realct)
  end;


action TRANS_T_E = void :
  begin
    type of E := type of T_1;
    access of E := access of T_1
  end;
```

```
action TRANS_F_T = void :
  begin
    type of T := type of F_1;
    access of T := access of F_1
  end;

action TRANS_E_F = void :
  begin
    type of F := type of E;
    access of F := access of E
  end
}
```

The input syntax of F_a is

G_a = (V_{in},VN,PROG,P)
V_{in} = {+,-,*,/,(,),intct,realct}
VN = {PROG,E,T,F}
P = {<PROG> = <E>,
```
    <E> = <T>
            ("+" <T>
            |"-" <T>
            )*,
    <T> = <F>
            ("*" <F>
            |"/" <F>
            )*,
    <F> = "intct"
          |"realct"
          |"(" <E> ")"
    }
```

As an illustration of the semantic action evaluation, take the following syntax rule from P of F_a :

```
    <E> = <T> TRANS_T_E
            ("+" <T> ADD
            |"-" <T> SUBTRACT
            )*
```

The derivation tree in F_a is illustrated in Fig. 4.8.

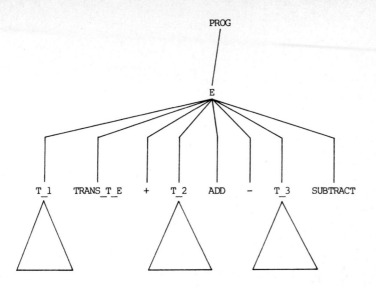

Fig. 4.8.

The attributes associated with the nonterminal symbols E and T
are type and access. Notice that the attribute variables associated
with the nodes in the attributed derivation tree have no initial
values. The semantic actions refer to the attribute variables by
writing e.g., type of T_1, access of T_1, type of T_2, access of
T_2, class of access of T_1. The attributed derivation tree is
schematically illustrated in Fig. 4.9.

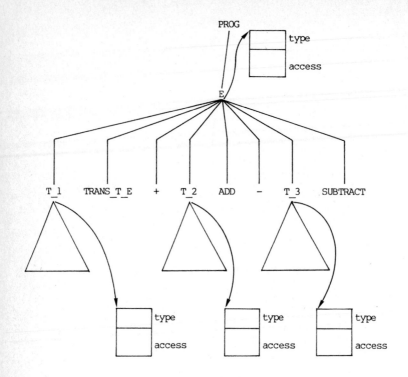

Fig. 4.9.

The semantic action evaluator will traverse the attributed derivation tree recursive descent from left to right, activating semantic actions. These semantic actions may calculate attribute variables and possibly modify the contents E of the environment.

After the semantic action evaluation of the subtree with root, e.g., T_1, we assume that the type and access values have been calculated properly and stored in the attribute variables associated with T_1. This assumption can be verified by inspection of the syntax rule defining T. The semantic action TRANS_T_E will simply transfer these values from T_1 to E. This is schematically illustrated in Fig. 4.10.

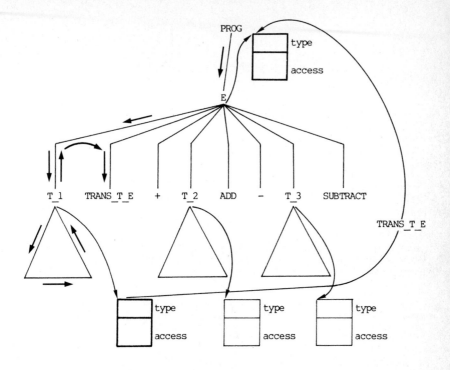

Fig. 4.10.

Each time the subtree with roots T_2 and T_3 is semantically evaluated, the type and access values are assumed to be available in the attribute variables associated with respectively T_2 and T_3. The invariant assertion is then that for each ADD and SUBTRACT action, the type and access values of the left operand will always be available in E, whereas the type and access values of the right operand will always be available in T_2 in the case of ADD and T_3 in the case of SUBTRACT. Finally, the type and access values of the result will always be available in E. Consequently, any time we need the type and access of an expression E, we can assume that after the semantic evaluation of E, the type and access values are available in E. This is schematically illustrated in Fig. 4.11.

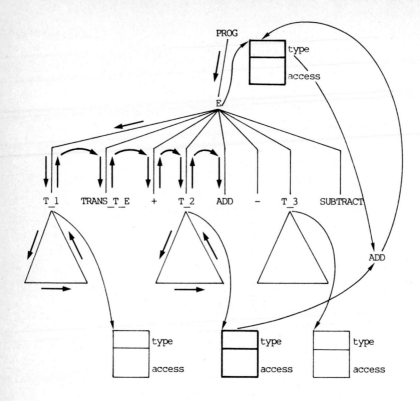

Fig. 4.11.

Design of a generalized AECF translation syntax

As for generalized ECF translation syntaxes, a generalized AECF
translation syntax is designed in two steps. This is illustrated by
means of the example : the translation of simple arithmetic expressions into three-address instructions.

step 1

The input language of the translation is the set of the simple arithmetic expressions. It is defined by means of the ECF syntax G_a.

step 2

To define the translation of simple arithmetic expressions into three-address instructions, the ECF syntax G_a is extended with semantic actions, attributes and global information. The result will be the generalized AECF translation syntax F_a.

4.3.   Attributed ELL(1) transducer

In section 4.2, we have discussed a particular type of generative device to define translations, namely the generalized AECF translation syntax. Let t be a translation defined by a generalized AECF translation syntax $F = (V_{in}, V_{action}, VN, V_{att}, A_0, P, G, D)$. We have $t = t(F)$.

In the present section, we will discuss a particular type of recognizing device, namely the attributed ELL(1) transducer. As for an ELL(1) transducer (see section 3.3) an attributed ELL(1) transducer maps the set of strings over V_{in} into the set $(V_E \cup \{no\})$, where V_E is the set of all possible contents of the environment. The set of input strings which are mapped into V_E, is called the input language of the translation. The set of pairs (x, E), where the input string x is mapped into a contents E of the environment, is called the translation defined by B. It is denoted $t(B)$.

An attributed ELL(1) transducer B is composed of six elements.

1) the input tape which is a sequence of tape squares, each tape square containing exactly one input symbol of an input vocabulary V_{in}.
Input strings will always be terminated by the end marker, represented by the symbol #.

2) the <u>input</u> <u>head</u> which reads one symbol at a given instance of time. At each read action, the input head moves one square to the right.

3) the <u>pushdown</u> <u>list</u> which is an auxiliary memory of the type last-in first-out. It is used by the underlying ELL(1) parser of B.

4) the <u>attributed</u> <u>pushdown</u> <u>list</u> which is an auxiliary memory of the type last-in first-out to deal with the attributes in B.

5) the <u>finite</u> <u>control</u> containing a finite set of transducing rules, dictating the behavior of B.

6) the <u>environment</u>, the contents of which can be altered by the transducing rules of B.

As for the ELL(1) parser and the ELL(1) transducer, the transducing rules of the attributed ELL(1) transducer can be represented in different forms, such as
1) a mapping,
2) a program, where the pushdown list and the attributed pushdown list are explicit,
3) a program, where the pushdown list and the attributed pushdown list are implicit.
In this book, we will only discuss attributed ELL(1) transducers of type (3). Attributed ELL(1) transducers of types (1) and (2) are discussed in Part 1.

Attributed ELL(1) transducer with implicit pushdown list and implicit attributed pushdown list

The attributed ELL(1) transducer in the form of a program with implicit pushdown list and implicit attributed pushdown list can be best explained by means of an example : the translation of simple arithmetic expressions into three-address instructions. More complex examples can be found in section 5. The translation is defined by the following generalized AECF translation syntax F_a.

$F_a = (V_{in}, V_{action}, VN, V_{att}, PROG, P, G, D)$

$V_{in} = \{+,-,*,/,(,),intct,realct\}$
$V_{action} = \{ADD,SUBTRACT,MULTIPLY,DIVIDE,TREAT\_INTCT,TREAT\_REALCT,$
$\qquad\qquad TRANS\_T\_E,TRANS\_F\_T,TRANS\_E\_F,INIT\}$
$VN = \{PROG,E,T,F\}$
$V_{att} = \{E,T,F$ synth type type,
$\qquad\qquad\qquad$ access access;
$\qquad\quad$ intct,realct synth int constabp;
$\qquad\quad \}$
$P = \{$<PROG> = INIT <E>,
$\qquad$<E> = <T> TRANS_T_E
$\qquad\qquad\qquad$ ("+" <T> ADD
$\qquad\qquad\qquad$ |"-" <T> SUBTRACT
$\qquad\qquad\qquad$)*,
$\qquad\quad$<T> = <F> TRANS_F_T
$\qquad\qquad\qquad$ ("*" <F> MULTIPLY
$\qquad\qquad\qquad$ |"/" <F> DIVIDE
$\qquad\qquad\qquad$)*,
$\qquad\quad$<F> = "intct" TREAT_INTCT
$\qquad\qquad\quad$ |"realct" TREAT_REALCT
$\qquad\qquad\quad$ |"(" <E> ")" TRANS_E_F
$\qquad \}$
$G = \{$defined in section 4.2$\}$
$D = \{$defined in section 4.2$\}$

The ELL(1) transducer B_a is represented by a program, where the pushdown list and attributed pushdown list have been implemented by means of the implicit stack of the recursive procedure mechanism available in the metalanguage. In section 4.4, we will see that the attributed ELL(1) transducer B_a can be obtained from the generalized AECF translation syntax F_a in a mechanical way.

The attributed ELL(1) transducer B_a mainly consists of three ELL(1) transducing routines E, T and F. There is an ELL(1) transducing routine for each generalized AECF translation syntax rule in F_a.

proc attributed ELL(1) transducer program B = void :
$\quad$ begin
$\qquad$ struct (char c, in-attribute a) in :=
$\qquad\quad$ co the variable 'in' contains the leftmost input symbol
$\qquad\qquad$ (possibly attributed) of the input string co;
$\qquad\quad$ proc read = void :
$\qquad\qquad$ co the next input symbol (possibly attributed) is read in

```
         the variable 'in' co;
proc error = void : co ... co;
proc accept = void : co ... co;
mode E-attribute = nonterminal;
mode T-attribute = nonterminal;
mode F-attribute = nonterminal;
mode nonterminal = struct (type type,
                           access access);
mode intct-attribute = terminal;
mode realct-attribute = terminal;
mode terminal = struct (int constabp);
mode in-attribute = union (intct-attribute,realct-attribute);
```

```
┌──────────┐
│          │
│   G      │
│          │ ;
└──────────┘
```

```
proc $PROG = void : co        ┌─────────────────┐  co;
proc $E = (ref E-attribute E) void : co  │              │  co;
proc $T = (ref T-attribute T) void : co  │ defined below│  co;
proc $F = (ref F-attribute F) void : co  │              │  co;
$PROG;                        └─────────────────┘
if c of in = "#"
   then read
   else error
fi
end
```

```
proc $PROG = void :
  begin
    E-attribute E;
```

```
┌──────────────┐
│ macro copy   │
│  of INIT     │ ;
└──────────────┘
```

```
    $E(E)
end
```

```
proc $E = (ref E-attribute E) void :
  begin
    T-attribute T_1;
    $T(T_1);
```

```
┌──────────────────┐
│ macro copy       │
│  of TRANS_T_E    │ ;
└──────────────────┘
```

```
    while c of in in {+,-}
```

```
   do case c of in
        when "+"
             T-attribute T_2;
             read;
             $T(T_2);
```

```
             ┌─────────────────────┐
             │    macro copy       │
             │    of ADD           │
             └─────────────────────┘
```

```
        otherwise
             T-attribute T_3;
             if c of in = "-"
                then read
                else error
             fi;
                $T(T_3);
```

```
                ┌─────────────────────┐
                │   macro copy        │
                │   of SUBTRACT       │
                └─────────────────────┘
```

```
        esac
     od
end
```

```
proc $T = (ref T-attribute T) void :
   begin
      F-attribute F_1;
      $F(F_1);
```

```
      ┌─────────────────────┐
      │  macro copy         │
      │  of TRANS_F_T       │  ;
      └─────────────────────┘
```

```
      while c of in in {*,/}
         do case c of in
              when "*"
                   F-attribute F_2;
                   read;
                   $F(F_2);
```

```
                   ┌─────────────────────┐
                   │   macro copy        │
                   │   of MULTIPLY       │
                   └─────────────────────┘
```

```
              otherwise
                   F-attribute F_3;
                   if c of in = "-"
                      then read
```

```
            else error
        fi;
          $F(F_3);
```

```
          ┌─────────────────┐
          │  macro copy     │
          │  of DIVIDE      │
          └─────────────────┘
```

```
        esac
      od
  end


proc $F = (ref F-attribute F) void :
  case c of in
    when "intct"
      intct-attribute intct;
      if c of in = "intct"
        then intct := a of in;
             read
        else error
      fi;
```

```
      ┌──────────────────────┐
      │  macro copy          │
      │  of TREAT_INTCT      │
      └──────────────────────┘
```

```
    when "realct"
      realct-attribute realct;
      if c of in = "realct"
        then realct := a of in;
             read
        else error
      fi;
```

```
      ┌──────────────────────┐
      │  macro copy          │
      │  of TREAT_REALCT     │
      └──────────────────────┘
```

```
    otherwise
      E-attribute E;
      if c of in = "("
        then read
        else error
      fi;
      $E(E);
      if c of in = ")"
        then read
        else error
      fi;
```

```
┌─────────────────────┐
│   macro copy        │
│   of TRANS_E_F      │
└─────────────────────┘
```

<u>esac</u>

Two-pass attributed ELL(1) transducer

The attributed ELL(1) transducer described so far is a one-pass transducer. As for ELL(1) transducers, each attributed ELL(1) transducer B can be conceptually separated into a syntactic pass (syntactic analyser) and a semantic pass (semantic analyser).

Given a generalized AECF translation syntax F. The syntactic analyser is an <u>ELL(1)</u> <u>parser</u> A which can be produced mechanically from the input syntax G of F. The syntactic analyser produces a derivation tree in F for each input string that belongs to L(G). Then, the derivation tree produced by A is attributed. The semantic analyser traverses the attributed derivation tree recursive descent from left to right, activating the semantic actions. During this tree traversal the attributes and the contents E of the environment are calculated. The semantic pass is called <u>semantic action evaluator</u>.

Notice the duality between the generation of a translation element (w,E) in a generalized AECF translation syntax and the production of (w,E) by its corresponding two-pass attributed ELL(1) transducer.
There are two differences. The attributed derivation tree for w is <u>generated</u> in the generalized AECF translation syntax and the attributes of the input symbols are initialized. The attributed derivation tree for w is <u>recognized</u> in the two-pass attributed ELL(1) transducer and the attribute values of the input symbols are taken from the transducer input.

Observe that the ELL(1) parser recognizes the derivation tree with the same strategy which is used by the semantic action evaluator to calculate the attributes. This is the reason why ELL(1) parsing and semantic action evaluation can be performed in one single pass.

The behavior of a two-pass attributed ELL(1) transducer B is illustrated in Fig. 4.12.

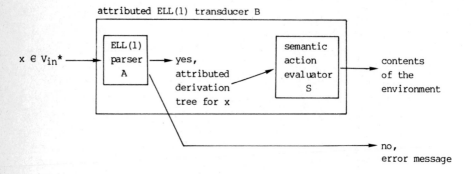

attributed ELL(1) transducer B

$x \in V_{in}^*$ → ELL(1) parser A → yes, attributed derivation tree for x → semantic action evaluator S → contents of the environment

→ no, error message

Fig. 4.12.

4.4. Generation of attributed ELL(1) transducers

The mechanical production of an attributed ELL(1) transducer in the form of a program from a generalized AECF translation syntax is described by means of the generation scheme below. The generation of attributed ELL(1) transducers is pictured in Fig. 4.13.

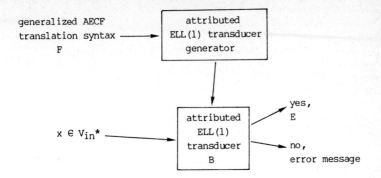

Fig. 4.13

Given a generalized AECF translation syntax $F = (V_{in}, V_{action}, VN, V_{att}, A_0, P, G, D)$, where

$V_{in} = \{a_1, a_2, \ldots, a_n\}$
$V_{action} = \{r_1, r_2, \ldots, r_k\}$
$VN = \{A_0, A_1, \ldots, A_m\}$
V_{att} is a finite set of attribute declarations
A_0 is the start symbol
$P = \{A_0 = s_0,$
    $A_1 = s_1,$
    $\ldots$
    $A_m = s_m$
    $\}$
G is the set of global definitions
D is the set of semantic action definitions.

Generation scheme

The attributed ELL(1) transducer B as it is produced from F by the generation scheme, is given below.

```
proc attributed ELL(1) transducer B = void :
begin
  struct (char c, in-attribute a) in :=
```

<u>co</u> the variable 'in' contains the leftmost input symbol
   (possibly attributed) of the input string <u>co</u>;
<u>proc</u> read = <u>void</u> :
   <u>co</u> the next input symbol (possibly attributed) is read in the
   variable 'in' <u>co</u>;
<u>proc</u> error = <u>void</u> : <u>co</u> ... <u>co</u>;
<u>proc</u> accept = <u>void</u> : <u>co</u> ... <u>co</u>;

<u>mode</u> A_0-attribute = <u>co</u>   <u>co</u>;
<u>mode</u> A_1-attribute = <u>co</u>   <u>co</u>;

   .
   .
   .
                                         derived
<u>mode</u> A_m-attribute = <u>co</u>   from   <u>co</u>;
                                         V_{att}

<u>mode</u> a_1-attribute = <u>co</u>   <u>co</u>;

<u>mode</u> a_2-attribute = <u>co</u>   <u>co</u>;

   .
   .
   .

<u>mode</u> a_n-attribute = <u>co</u>   <u>co</u>;

<u>mode</u> in-attribute = <u>union</u>(a_1-attribute,a_2-attribute, ... ,a_n-attribute);

   G   ;

<u>proc</u> \$$A_0$ = (<u>ref</u> A_0-attribute A_0) <u>void</u> : <u>co</u>   <u>co</u>;
<u>proc</u> \$$A_1$ =(<u>ref</u> A_1-attribute A_1) <u>void</u> : <u>co</u> defined   <u>co</u>;
                                           by the
   .   generation
   .   scheme
   .

<u>proc</u> \$$A_m$ = (<u>ref</u> A_m-attribute A_m) <u>void</u> : <u>co</u>   <u>co</u>;
A_0-attribute A_0;
\$$A_0$($A_0$);
<u>if</u> c <u>of</u> in = '#'
   <u>then</u> accept

<u>else</u> error
<u>fi</u>
<u>end</u>

For each generalized AECF translation syntax rule $A_j = s_j$ in P of F, we produce an <u>ELL(1) transducing routine</u> $\$A_j$.

$A_j = s_j$ in P -> <u>proc</u> $\$A_j$ =(<u>ref</u> A_j <u>attribute</u> A_j) <u>void</u> :
     <u>begin</u>
      X_1-<u>attribute</u> X_1;
      X_2-<u>attribute</u> X_2;
      .
      .
      .
      X_t-<u>attribute</u> X_t;
      $B(s_j)$
     <u>end</u>

$X_1, X_2, \ldots, X_t$ denote all input and nonterminal symbols that occur in block s_j with exclusion of its inner blocks and for which there is an attribute declaration in V_{att}.

The parameter binding mechanism between formal and actual parameters is <u>call</u> <u>by</u> <u>value</u> (<u>in</u> parameters) for inherited attributes of A_j and <u>call</u> <u>by</u> <u>result</u> (<u>out</u> parameters) for synthesized attributes.

The body $B(s_j)$ of the routine $\$A_j$ is produced in a modular way by means of the following four axiomatic rules and four composition rules.

Axiomatic <u>rules</u>

<u>generalized</u> <u>ECF</u> <u>translation</u> <u>expression</u> -> <u>program</u> <u>module</u>

0) $r \in V_{action}$ -> $D[r]$
  This is the copy of the body of the semantic action definition r specified in D.

1) & -> skip

2) $a_i \in V_{in}$ -> <u>if</u> c <u>of</u> in = a_i
                     <u>then</u> a_i := a <u>of</u> in;
                          read
                     <u>else</u> error
                 <u>fi</u>

2') $A_j \in VN$ -> $\$A_j(A_j)$
This is the call of the ELL(1) transducing routine $\$A_j$ with the attribute variable A_j as actual parameter.

Composition <u>rules</u>

Suppose B(s) represents the program module for the generalized ECF translation expression s, with s possibly indexed.

3) $(s_1|s_2| \ \ldots \ |s_n)$ -> <u>case</u> c <u>of</u> in
                     <u>when</u> DIRSYMB(s_1)
                         $\underline{X_{11}}$-attribute X_{11};
                         $\underline{X_{12}}$-attribute X_{12};
                           .
                           .
                           .
                         $\underline{X_{1t_1}}$-attribute X_{1t_1};
                         B(s_1)
                     <u>when</u> DIRSYMB(s_2)
                         $\underline{X_{21}}$-attribute X_{21};
                         $\underline{X_{22}}$-attribute X_{22};
                           .
                           .
                           .
                         $\underline{X_{2t_2}}$-attribute X_{2t_2};
                         B(s_2)
                         ...
                     <u>otherwise</u>
                         $\underline{X_{n1}}$-attribute X_{n1};
                         $\underline{X_{n2}}$-attribute X_{n2};
                           .
                           .
                           .

$$\underline{X}_{nt_n}\text{-attribute } X_{nt_n};$$
$$B(s_n)$$

      <u>esac</u>

$X_{j1}, X_{j2}, \ldots, X_{jt_j}$ denote all input and nonterminal symbols that occur in block s_j with exclusion of its inner blocks and for which there is an attribute declaration in V_{att}. For the definition of block and inner block see section 4.1.

4) $s_1 s_2 \ldots s_n \rightarrow B(s_1); B(s_2); \ldots ; B(s_n)$

5) $(s)* \rightarrow$ <u>while</u> c <u>of</u> in $\in$ DIRSYMB(s)
              <u>do</u> $\underline{X}_1$-attribute $X_1;$
                  $\underline{X}_2$-attribute $X_2;$
                  .
                  .
                  .
                  $\underline{X}_t$-attribute $X_t;$
                  $B(s)$
              <u>od</u>

$X_1, X_2, \ldots, X_t$ denote all input and nonterminal symbols that occur in block s with exclusion of its inner blocks and for which there is an attribute declaration in V_{att}.

6) $(s)^+ \rightarrow$ <u>repeat</u>
                $\underline{X}_1$-attribute $X_1;$
                $\underline{X}_2$-attribute $X_2;$
                .
                .
                .
                $\underline{X}_t$-attribute $X_t;$
                $B(s)$
          <u>until</u> in $\notin$ DIRSYMB(s)

$X_1, X_2, \ldots, X_t$ denote all input and nonterminal symbols that occur in block s with exclusion of its inner blocks and for which there is an attribute declaration in V_{att}.

The definition of DIRSYMB and the ELL(1) conditions

The definitions of DIRSYMB, FIRST, EMPTY, FOLLOW and the ELL(1) conditions for generalized ECF translation expressions are given in section 3.4.

Underlying parser

Given a generalized AECF translation syntax F, from which an attributed ELL(1) transducer B is derived, t(F) = t(B). From F, we can produce the input syntax G, from which an ELL(1) parser A is derived, L(G) = L(A). The ELL(1) parser A is called the underlying parser of B. This is illustrated in Fig. 4.14.

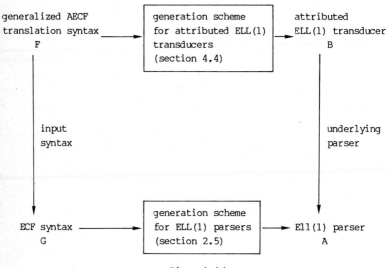

Fig. 4.14.

4.5. Differences between concepts and implementation

The generation scheme for attributed ELL(1) transducers, discussed in section 4.4, is an appropriate vehicle to understand the
basic concepts and the behavior of LILA, a Language Implementation
LAboratory. Actually, this generation scheme is the skeleton on
which a number of additional features must be attached in order to
obtain a practical and user-friendly software engineering tool.

Now follows a list of additional features implemented in LILA.
Each of them is briefly commented. This list is not exhaustive. A
complete description of the LILA input is given in the Reference
Guide in the appendix. The case studies in section 5 illustrate
systematically how these features must be used.

Pascal as the representation language of LILA

The language in which the transducers are generated by LILA is
Pascal. This means that all semantic actions, attribute declara-
tions, local declarations and global declarations must be written in
Pascal.

The choice of Pascal as representation language has some advan-
tages and drawbacks for the design of LILA. The major advantage of
Pascal as a representation language is the portability of the generated transducers as far as standard Pascal is used in the LILA
input. The major drawback of Pascal as a representation language
follows from the restrictions imposed by Pascal. As an example,
there is no call by result parameter binding mechanism. So, the
attribute mechanism in LILA is implemented by means of a call by
variable. This means that the control on the inherited and synthesized properties of attributes does not exist in LILA. Another
serious restriction is the complete lack of any support to use the
principles of abstract data types and information hiding.

Error recovery

The transducers produced by the generation scheme in section 4.4
will halt as soon as a syntactic error is encountered. Of course,

this situation is not a realistic one. LILA offers an elegant solution where the error recovery is mechanically produced from error
recovery information which is local to the translation syntax rules.

Local information

   Objects such as constants, variables, types, procedures and functions, can be declared local to a translation syntax rule.

Prologue and epilogue

   Each of these LILA input parts defines a number of statements to
be executed respectively before and after the activation of the generated transducer.

Global options

   As an example, one can specify in the LILA input by means of the
global options whether the generated transducer must have the form
of a Pascal program or a Pascal procedure.

Follow information

   The follow set defines the input symbols that can follow any sentence of the input language. This follow set is used for example
when the generated transducer (e.g. a lexical analyser) is to be
used as a subroutine of another transducer. Both transducers can be
generated by LILA; this is illustrated in section 5.

Input and output symbol representation

   In the input and output vocabulary parts of LILA, the representation (ASCII, EBCDIC or any other code) of the input and output symbols has to be specified.

Overriding facilities

Stepwise overriding of LILA definitions makes it possible to produce compilers gradually. In a first step, the compiler can be produced by using all the generation facilities of LILA. In a later
stage of development of the transducer, LILA definitions such as the
read, write and error modules, may become user-defined.

Multi-pass facilities

LILA offers the user the possibility to produce different passes
of a compiler. The interfaces between the passes are kept very simple.

5. CASE STUDIES

In this section, we will illustrate the methodology in compiler construction as it is supported by LILA. For this purpose, a number of case studies with growing complexity are discussed.

Important aspects of the LILA methodology are :

1) two-level structure of modularity

The first level of modularity stems from the syntax-oriented description of the compiler. The attribute mechanism plays an important role here.

The second level of modularity is based on the organization of the compiler in several passes, each of which is described in a syntax-oriented way. Each pass can be developed (designed, verified, tested and documented) with LILA as an individual module.

2) stepwise overriding of LILA default definitions

LILA is designed to allow a high degree of user interaction. Therefore, a number of LILA decisions can be overridden by the LILA user. As an example, the module for reading input symbols by the generated transducer is LILA-defined. The LILA user is able to override the default read module definition, when, e.g., he wants the transducer to read input symbols from a tree-structured or a table-structured data set.

The design philosophy consists in writing a compiler by using LILA in all its generative power. The generated compiler will be systematically verified and tested. Then, if necessary, LILA default features will be redefined one by one. Each time a LILA

feature is overridden, the new version of the generated transducer is tested only for that specific feature. The more work
the user takes over from LILA, the more know-how is needed about
the behavior of LILA.

Stepwise overriding of LILA features makes it possible to produce compilers in successive releases. This is an important
aspect in debugging and maintaining compilers.

3) concept of 'package' ('abstract data type')

In a syntax-directed description, it is wise to specify the
different packages used in the semantic actions. A package consists of a description of a data structure by means of the definitions of the allowable actions (procedures, functions, operators) defined on it. The package may contain local definitions
of constants, types, variables, procedures and functions, which
are not accessible outside the package.

Since the metalanguage of LILA (i.e. the language in which we
write the semantic action definitions, attributes, local and global information) is Pascal, the methodology of using packages is
not supported by LILA (ADA as a metalanguage of LILA would be
more appropriate). In the present version of LILA, this methodology aspect is restricted to an indication of the packages in
the form of comments as part of the documentation.

The case studies illustrate the use of LILA and its underlying
methodology to design and maintain compilers. For each case study,
a number of design variants are discussed, showing that there is
more than one way to design a compiler with LILA. The choice of the
appropriate design characteristics is merely a matter of experience.
In this way, each case study reflects a specific experience in
designing compilers with LILA.

The LILA methodology, as described above, promotes the writing of
compilers which are simple, reliable, adaptable, portable and efficient.

By portability, we mean that the machine-dependent run-time features of the compiler are localized so that the compiler can be adapted for another machine at a low cost. The portability of the compiler program itself is related to the portability of standard Pascal, since LILA generates Pascal programs. The case studies will illustrate the portability aspects of run-time features.

As for efficiency, we must distinguish between compile-time efficiency and run-time efficiency. In the design of LILA, a great effort is devoted to the optimization of program generation. LILA generates Pascal programs which are highly optimized in time and space. The run-time efficiency of the generated compilers is dealt with by the semantic actions. Since the semantic actions are entirely written by the LILA user, there is no loss of run-time efficiency with respect to hand-coded compilers.

All these aspects of the LILA methodology are illustrated by five case studies:

1) Postfix transformer

2) Binary number representation

3) Formatter

4) Arithmetic expressions

5) Pico Algol

Each case study is worked out with LILA. An exhaustive description of the LILA input is given in the Reference Guide (see Appendix).

5.1. Postfix Transformer

The postfix transformer is an example of a one-pass transducer, translating infix arithmetic expressions into reversed polish notation. Although the example is simple, it already illustrates a number of interesting characteristics of LILA.

The input of the postfix transformer is a single line containing the infix arithmetic expression terminated by a dot. No spaces are allowed within the input (the treatment of spaces is illustrated in the formatter, see section 5.3). Similarly, the output of the postfix transformer is a single line, containing the postfix arithmetic expression terminated by a dot. This is illustrated in Fig. 5.1.

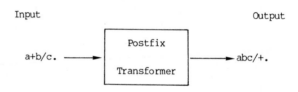

Input   Output

a+b/c. ────────►   Postfix Transformer   ────────► abc/+.

Fig. 5.1.

The postfix transformer is designed in two steps. In a first step, the syntax analyser of the postfix transformer is designed. The syntax analyser is discussed in section 5.1.1. Hereafter, semantic actions performing the translation of the infix arithmetic expression into reversed polish notation, are added. The semantic actions can be implemented in several ways. This is illustrated in sections 5.1.2, 5.1.3 and 5.1.4, each section describing a specific implementation of the semantic actions.

5.1.1. The Postfix Transformer : Syntax Analysis.

The syntax analyser of the postfix transformer will check whether the infix expression at the input is syntactically correct. A syntax-directed description of the syntax analyser in the form of a LILA input is given below.

```
$$$$$$$$$$$$$$$$$$$$$$$$$$$$$$$$$$$$$$$$$$$$$$$$$$$$$$$$$$$$$$$$$$$$$$$$$$$$$$$$$$$$$
$   LILA INPUT                                                                   $
$                                                                               $
$      The Postfix Transformer : Syntax Analysis                                 $
$$$$$$$$$$$$$$$$$$$$$$$$$$$$$$$$$$$$$$$$$$$$$$$$$$$$$$$$$$$$$$$$$$$$$$$$$$$$$$$$$$$$$
```

```
###inputvocabulary  rep(char), file(input);
```

"(" = 40	")" = 41	"eoln"=32	"." = 46	"*" = 42	"+" = 43
"-" = 45	"/" = 47	"0" = 48	"1" = 49	"2" = 50	"3" = 51
"4" = 52	"5" = 53	"6" = 54	"7" = 55	"8" = 56	"9" = 57
"a" = 97	"b" = 98	"c" = 99	"d" =100	"e" =101	"f" =102
"g" =103	"h" =104	"i" =105	"j" =106	"k" =107	"l" =108
"m" =109	"n" =110	"o" =111	"p" =112	"q" =113	"r" =114
"s" =115	"t" =116	"u" =117	"v" =118	"w" =119	"x" =120
"y" =121	"z" =122				

```
###syntax;
```

```
$ Definition of a program
  ##rule;
    <program> =
      <expression>   "." "eoln"

$ Definition of an expression
  ##rule;
    <expression> =
      <term>
        ( "+" <term>
        | "-" <term>
        )*

$ Definition of a term
  ##rule;
    <term> =
      <factor>
        ( "*" <factor>
        | "/" <factor>
        )*

$ Definition of a factor
  ##rule;
    <factor> =
        ( <digit> | <letter> )
      | "(" <expression> ")"
```

$ <u>Definition of a letter</u>
  ##rule;
    <letter> =
       "a" | "b" | "c" | "d" | "e" | "f" | "g" | "h" | "i" | "j"
     | "k" | "l" | "m" | "n" | "o" | "p" | "q" | "r" | "s" | "t"
     | "u" | "v" | "w" | "x" | "y" | "z"

$ <u>Definition of a digit</u>
  ##rule;
    <digit> =
       "0" | "1" | "2" | "3" | "4" | "5" | "6" | "7" | "8" | "9"

###globalinfo;

  ##parameter;
    input, output

The input vocabulary of the postfix transformer lists all the
symbols (characters) which can appear in a syntactically correct
infix expression. The input symbols are represented in ASCII.

Because the input vocabulary consists of non-attributed characters, the input file of the postfix transformer is a Pascal <u>text</u>
file. Such a file consists of a number of lines, each line terminated by an end-of-line character. Therefore, an input symbol
"eoln" representing the end-of-line character is added to the input
vocabulary.

5.1.2. The Postfix Transformer : Version 1

In this version, the postfix transformer is described by means of
an <u>output</u> <u>vocabulary</u>. The output vocabulary lists all the symbols
(characters) from which the postfix expression is constructed.
Notice that the output vocabulary is a subset of the input vocabulary because of two reasons:

1) The parentheses are not part of the output vocabulary, since
   reversed polish notation is parentheses-free.

2) The end-of-line character is omitted in the output vocabulary.
   It is generated automatically by means of a <u>writeln</u> statement.
   This statement is inserted in the generated program by LILA.
   It will be executed whenever the end-of-line input symbol is

read.

$$
$ LILA INPUT $
$ $
$ The Postfix Transformer : Version 1 $
$$

###inputvocabulary rep(char), file(input);

```
"(" = 40    ")" = 41    "eoln"=32   "." = 46    "*" = 42    "+" = 43
"-" = 45    "/" = 47    "0" = 48    "1" = 49    "2" = 50    "3" = 51
"4" = 52    "5" = 53    "6" = 54    "7" = 55    "8" = 56    "9" = 57
"a" = 97    "b" = 98    "c" = 99    "d" =100    "e" =101    "f" =102
"g" =103    "h" =104    "i" =105    "j" =106    "k" =107    "l" =108
"m" =109    "n" =110    "o" =111    "p" =112    "q" =113    "r" =114
"s" =115    "t" =116    "u" =117    "v" =118    "w" =119    "x" =120
"y" =121    "z" =122
```


###outputvocabulary rep(char), file(output);

```
                                    [.] = 46    [*] = 42    [+] = 43
[-] = 45    [/] = 47    [0] = 48    [1] = 49    [2] = 50    [3] = 51
[4] = 52    [5] = 53    [6] = 54    [7] = 55    [8] = 56    [9] = 57
[a] = 97    [b] = 98    [c] = 99    [d] =100    [e] =101    [f] =102
[g] =103    [h] =104    [i] =105    [j] =106    [k] =107    [l] =108
[m] =109    [n] =110    [o] =111    [p] =112    [q] =113    [r] =114
[s] =115    [t] =116    [u] =117    [v] =118    [w] =119    [x] =120
[y] =121    [z] =122
```


###syntax;

$ Definition of a program
  ##rule;
    <program> =
      <expression> out_dot "." "eoln"

    ##action;
      #out_dot;
        out(%[.])

$ Transformation of an expression
  ##rule;
    <expression> =

```
    <term>
      ( "+" <term>  out_plus
      | "-" <term>  out_minus
      )*

  ##action;
    #out_plus;
      out(%[+])

    #out_minus;
      out(%[-])
```

$ Transformation of a term
```
  ##rule;
    <term> =
      <factor>
        ( "*" <factor>  out_times
        | "/" <factor>  out_divide
        )*

  ##action;
    #out_times;
      out(%[*])

    #out_divide;
      out(%[/])
```

$ Transformation of a factor
```
  ##rule;
    <factor> =
        ( <digit> | <letter> )
      | "(" <expression> ")"
```

$ Definition of a letter
```
  ##rule;
    <letter> =
        "a" out_a  |  "b" out_b  |  "c" out_c  |  "d" out_d  |  "e" out_e
      | "f" out_f  |  "g" out_g  |  "h" out_h  |  "i" out_i  |  "j" out_j
      | "k" out_k  |  "l" out_l  |  "m" out_m  |  "n" out_n  |  "o" out_o
      | "p" out_p  |  "q" out_q  |  "r" out_r  |  "s" out_s  |  "t" out_t
      | "u" out_u  |  "v" out_v  |  "w" out_w  |  "x" out_x  |  "y" out_y
      | "z" out_z

  ##action;
    #out_a; out(%[a])        #out_b; out(%[b])       #out_c; out(%[c])
    #out_d; out(%[d])        #out_e; out(%[e])       #out_f; out(%[f])
    #out_g; out(%[g])        #out_h; out(%[h])       #out_i; out(%[i])
    #out_j; out(%[j])        #out_k; out(%[k])       #out_l; out(%[l])
```

```
    #out_m;  out(%[m])        #out_n;  out(%[n])      #out_o;  out(%[o])
    #out_p;  out(%[p])        #out_q;  out(%[q])      #out_r;  out(%[r])
    #out_s;  out(%[s])        #out_t;  out(%[t])      #out_u;  out(%[u])
    #out_v;  out(%[v])        #out_w;  out(%[w])      #out_x;  out(%[x])
    #out_y;  out(%[y])        #out_z;  out(%[z])
```

$ Definition of a digit
```
  ##rule;
    <digit> =
         "0" out_0  |  "1" out_1  |  "2" out_2  |  "3" out_3  |  "4" out_4
      |  "5" out_5  |  "6" out_6  |  "7" out_7  |  "8" out_8  |  "9" out_9

    ##action;
    #out_0;  out(%[0])        #out_1;  out(%[1])      #out_2;  out(%[2])
    #out_3;  out(%[3])        #out_4;  out(%[4])      #out_5;  out(%[5])
    #out_6;  out(%[6])        #out_7;  out(%[7])      #out_8;  out(%[8])
    #out_9;  out(%[9])
```

```
###global info;

  ##parameter;
    input, output
```

5.1.3.   The Postfix Transformer : Version 2

In this version, the postfix transformer is still described by
means of an output vocabulary, but output symbols are produced in a
more efficient way by directly controlling the input head variable
'inp'. This optimization is based on the fact that the representation of the input symbols and the corresponding output symbols are
identical. As an example, take the production of a letter in the
postfix transformer. Since the representations of the letters are
identical in both the input vocabulary and the output vocabulary, we
can simply write :

```
    out (inp.c)
```

whenever a letter has to be produced. Notice that the semantic
action to produce a letter must now <u>preceed</u> the analysis of a
letter, i.e. the semantic action must be activated when the input
head contains a letter. Indeed, LILA generates for a non-attributed
terminal symbol a_i the following program module (see the generation

schemes in sections 2,3 and 4):

  <u>if</u> (inp.c = a$_i$)
    <u>then</u> read <u>co</u> The next input symbol is under the input head <u>co</u>
    <u>else</u> error


```
$$$$$$$$$$$$$$$$$$$$$$$$$$$$$$$$$$$$$$$$$$$$$$$$$$$$$$$$$$$$$$$$$$$$$$$$$$$$$$$$$$$$$$$
$    LILA INPUT                                                                    $
$                                                                                  $
$       The Postfix Transformer : Version 2                                        $
$$$$$$$$$$$$$$$$$$$$$$$$$$$$$$$$$$$$$$$$$$$$$$$$$$$$$$$$$$$$$$$$$$$$$$$$$$$$$$$$$$$$$$$
```

###inputvocabulary rep(char), file(input);

```
"(" = 40    ")" = 41    "eoln"=32   "." = 46    "*" = 42    "+" = 43
"-" = 45    "/" = 47    "0" = 48    "1" = 49    "2" = 50    "3" = 51
"4" = 52    "5" = 53    "6" = 54    "7" = 55    "8" = 56    "9" = 57
"a" = 97    "b" = 98    "c" = 99    "d" =100    "e" =101    "f" =102
"g" =103    "h" =104    "i" =105    "j" =106    "k" =107    "l" =108
"m" =109    "n" =110    "o" =111    "p" =112    "q" =113    "r" =114
"s" =115    "t" =116    "u" =117    "v" =118    "w" =119    "x" =120
"y" =121    "z" =122
```

###outputvocabulary rep(char), file(output);

```
                                    [.] = 46    [*] = 42    [+] = 43
[-] = 45    [/] = 47    [0] = 48    [1] = 49    [2] = 50    [3] = 51
[4] = 52    [5] = 53    [6] = 54    [7] = 55    [8] = 56    [9] = 57
[a] = 97    [b] = 98    [c] = 99    [d] =100    [e] =101    [f] =102
[g] =103    [h] =104    [i] =105    [j] =106    [k] =107    [l] =108
[m] =109    [n] =110    [o] =111    [p] =112    [q] =113    [r] =114
[s] =115    [t] =116    [u] =117    [v] =118    [w] =119    [x] =120
[y] =121    [z] =122
```

###syntax;

$ <u>Definition of a program</u>
  ##rule;
    <program> =
      <expression> out_dot "." "eoln"

    ##action;
     #out_dot;
      out(%[.])

$ <u>Transformation of an expression</u>
```
  ##rule;
    <expression> =
      <term>
        ( "+" <term>   out_plus
        | "-" <term>   out_minus
        )*

    ##action;
      #out_plus;
        out(%[+])

      #out_minus;
        out(%[-])
```

$ <u>Transformation of a term</u>
```
  ##rule;
    <term> =
      <factor>
        ( "*" <factor>   out_times
        | "/" <factor>   out_divide
        )*

    ##action;
      #out_times;
        out(%[*])

      #out_divide;
        out(%[/])
```

$ <u>Transformation of a factor</u>
```
  ##rule;
    <factor> =
        out_symbol ( <digit> | <letter> )
      | "(" <expression> ")"

    ##action;
      #out_symbol;
        out(inp.c)
```

$ <u>Definition of a letter</u>
```
  ##rule;
    <letter> =
        "a" | "b" | "c" | "d" | "e" | "f" | "g" | "h" | "i" | "j"
      | "k" | "l" | "m" | "n" | "o" | "p" | "q" | "r" | "s" | "t"
      | "u" | "v" | "w" | "x" | "y" | "z"
```

$ <u>Definition of a digit</u>

```
##rule;
  <digit> =
    "0" | "1" | "2" | "3" | "4" | "5" | "6" | "7" | "8" | "9"


###globalinfo;

  ##parameter;
    input, output
```

5.1.4. The Postfix Transformer : Version 3

In contrast with the previous versions of the postfix
transformer, where an output vocabulary has been used to produce the
reversed polish notation, this version will directly use the Pascal
<u>write</u> procedure. The use of an output vocabulary augments readabil-
ity, whereas the use of the Pascal write procedure augments efficiency. It is up to the LILA user to decide which way he wants to
go.

```
$$$$$$$$$$$$$$$$$$$$$$$$$$$$$$$$$$$$$$$$$$$$$$$$$$$$$$$$$$$$$$$$$$$$$$$$$$$$$$$$$$$$
$   LILA INPUT                                                                  $
$                                                                              $
$      The Postfix Transformer : Version 3                                     $
$$$$$$$$$$$$$$$$$$$$$$$$$$$$$$$$$$$$$$$$$$$$$$$$$$$$$$$$$$$$$$$$$$$$$$$$$$$$$$$$$$$$


###inputvocabulary  rep(char), file(input);

  "(" = 40    ")" = 41    "eoln"=32   "." = 46    "*" = 42    "+" = 43
  "-" = 45    "/" = 47    "0" = 48    "1" = 49    "2" = 50    "3" = 51
  "4" = 52    "5" = 53    "6" = 54    "7" = 55    "8" = 56    "9" = 57
  "a" = 97    "b" = 98    "c" = 99    "d" =100    "e" =101    "f" =102
  "g" =103    "h" =104    "i" =105    "j" =106    "k" =107    "l" =108
  "m" =109    "n" =110    "o" =111    "p" =112    "q" =113    "r" =114
  "s" =115    "t" =116    "u" =117    "v" =118    "w" =119    "x" =120
  "y" =121    "z" =122


###syntax;

$ Definition of a program
  ##rule;
    <program> =
      <expression>    out_dot    "." "eoln"
```

```
      ##action;
        #out_dot;
          writeln('.')
```

$ Transformation of an expression
```
    ##rule;
      <expression> =
        <term>
          ( "+" <term>   out_plus
          | "-" <term>   out_minus
          )*

      ##action;
        #out_plus;
          write('+')

        #out_minus;
          write('-')
```

$ Transformation of a term
```
    ##rule;
      <term> =
        <factor>
          ( "*" <factor>   out_times
          | "/" <factor>   out_divide
          )*

      ##action;
        #out_times;
          write('*')

        #out_divide;
          write('/')
```

$ Transformation of a factor
```
    ##rule;
      <factor> =
          out_symbol ( <digit> | <letter> )
        | "(" <expression> ")"

      ##action;
        #out_symbol;
          write(output, inp.c)
```

$ Definition of a letter
```
    ##rule;
      <letter> =
          "a" | "b" | "c" | "d" | "e" | "f" | "g" | "h" | "i" | "j"
```

```
        | "k" | "l" | "m" | "n" | "o" | "p" | "q" | "r" | "s" | "t"
        | "u" | "v" | "w" | "x" | "y" | "z"
```

$ <u>Definition of a digit</u>
```
  ##rule;
    <digit> =
      "0" | "1" | "2" | "3" | "4" | "5" | "6" | "7" | "8" | "9"
```


```
###global info;
```

```
  ##parameter;
    input, output
```

5.2. Binary Number Representation

The interpreter for a binary number representation is a simple example of a one-pass transducer, illustrating the use of the attribute mechanism. The transducer transforms a binary number representation into a real value. This is illustrated in Fig. 5.2.

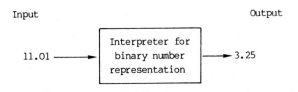

Fig. 5.2.

In sections 5.2.1 and 5.2.2, two different implementations of the interpreter for a binary number representation are given. They illustrate the trade-off between an iterative and a recursive definition of the syntax rules and its influence upon the semantic actions. In section 5.2.1, both the integer part and the fractional part of a binary number representation are defined iteratively, whereas in section 5.2.2, the fractional part of a binary number representation is defined recursively.

In both versions, a synthesized attribute is associated with the integer part and the fractional part of a binary number representation. This attribute represents the real value of that part.

5.2.1. Interpreter for a binary number representation : Version 1

In this version, both the integer part and the fractional part of a binary number representation are defined iteratively.

```
$$$$$$$$$$$$$$$$$$$$$$$$$$$$$$$$$$$$$$$$$$$$$$$$$$$$$$$$$$$$$$$$$$$$$$$$$$$$$$$$$$$$$$
$    LILA INPUT                                                                  $
$                                                                               $
$        Interpreter for a binary number representation : Version 1             $
$$$$$$$$$$$$$$$$$$$$$$$$$$$$$$$$$$$$$$$$$$$$$$$$$$$$$$$$$$$$$$$$$$$$$$$$$$$$$$$$$$$$$$
```

```
###inputvocabulary  rep(char), file(input);

  "0" = 48    "1" = 49    "." = 46    "eoln" = 32


###syntax;
```

$ Treatment of the binary number representation
```
  ##rule;
    <number> =
      <integer part> "." <fract part> "eoln"  calc_value

    ##action;
      #calc_value;
        writeln(output);
        writeln(output, 'real value :'
                     , @<integer part> + @<fract part>:15)
```

$ Calculation of the integer part value
```
  ##rule;
    <integer part> =
      <bit> first_bit  ( <bit> next_bit )*

    ##attribute;
      real

    ##action;
      #first_bit;
        @<integer part> := @<bit>1

      #next_bit;
        @<integer part> := @<integer part> * 2  +  @<bit>2
```

$ Calculation of the fractional part value
```
  ##rule;
    <fract part> =
      <bit> first_bit  ( <bit> next_bit )*

    ##attribute;
      real
```

```
    ##var;
      scale : real

    ##action;
      #first_bit;
        scale := 1/2;
        @<fract part> := @<bit>1 * scale

      #next_bit;
        scale := scale / 2;
        @<fract part> := @<fract part>  +  @<bit>2 * scale

$ Calculation of a bit value
  ##rule;
    <bit> =
        "0" bit_0
      | "1" bit_1

    ##attribute;
      real

    ##action;
      #bit_0;
        @<bit> := 0.0

      #bit_1;
        @<bit> := 1.0


###globalinfo;

    ##parameter;
      input, output
```

5.2.2. Interpreter for a binary number representation : Version 2

In the previous version, the syntax rule for the fractional part has been defined iteratively. An alternative and more natural definition is obtained by using a right recursive syntax rule, since it is easier to calculate the value of the fractional part from right to left.

```
$$$$$$$$$$$$$$$$$$$$$$$$$$$$$$$$$$$$$$$$$$$$$$$$$$$$$$$$$$$$$$$$$$$$$$$$$$$$$$$$$$$$
$    LILA INPUT                                                                 $
$                                                                              $
$        Interpreter for a binary number representation : Version 2            $
$$$$$$$$$$$$$$$$$$$$$$$$$$$$$$$$$$$$$$$$$$$$$$$$$$$$$$$$$$$$$$$$$$$$$$$$$$$$$$$$$$$$
```

```
###inputvocabulary  rep(char), file(input);

  "0" = 48    "1" = 49    "." = 46    "eoln" = 32
```

```
###syntax;
```

```
$ Treatment of the binary number representation.
  ##rule;
    <number> =
      <integer part> "." <fract part> "eoln"  calc_value

    ##action;
      #calc_value;
        writeln(output);
        writeln(output, 'real value :'
                    , @<integer part> + @<fract part>:15)
```

```
$ Calculation of the integer part value
  ##rule;
    <integer part> =
      <bit> first_bit  ( <bit> next_bit )*

    ##attribute;
      real

    ##action;
      #first_bit;
        @<integer part> := @<bit>1

      #next_bit;
        @<integer part> := @<integer part> * 2  +  @<bit>2
```

```
$ Calculation of the fractional part value
  ##rule;
    <fract part> =
      <bit>
        ( & calc_simple
        | <fract part> calc_compound
        )
```

```
        ##attribute;
          real

        ##action;
          #calc_simple;
            @<fract part>1 := @<bit> / 2

          #calc_compound;
            @<fract part>1 := @<bit> / 2  +  @<fract part>2 / 2
```

$ Calculation of a bit value
```
  ##rule;
    <bit> =
        "0" bit_0
      | "1" bit_1

      ##attribute;
        real

      ##action;
        #bit_0;
          @<bit> := 0.0

        #bit_1;
          @<bit> := 1.0


###globalinfo;

    ##parameter;
      input, output
```

5.3. Formatter

The formatter is a transducer that transforms a program containing conditional statements and assignment statements with free-
format into a formatted program. Conditional statements can be
nested with arbitrary depth. The free-format allows blanks at any
place, even within keywords. Blanks are not significant. For reasons of simplicity, variables and constants in this case study are
restricted to one character.

As an example, take the free-format program :

```
'if' a 'then' 'if' b 'then' c   :=1;   d:=0     'else'   c  := 2 'fi'
      'else' c:=3
'fi';
x     := 5
```

The formatted program is :

```
'if' a
  'then' 'if' b
            'then' c := 1;
                   d := 0
            'else' c := 2
         'fi'
  'else' c := 3
'fi';
x := 5
```

In sections 5.3.2, 5.3.3 and 5.3.4, three different implementations of the formatter are given. They illustrate the second level
structure of modularity in transducers generated with LILA. In section 5.3.1, the data structure 'output' used in the generation of
formatted lines, is described.

5.3.1. The data structure 'output'

The output file of the formatter is defined as a **textfile**, named
'output'. This file is organized as a sequence of **lines**. Each line
is of an infinite length. Only one line, called the current line,

can be accessed at a given instance of time.

Each line is divided into columns, numbered from left to right starting from 1. Each column may contain exactly one character. The 'cursor' is a variable containing the current column number of the current line, i.e. the column in which the next character has to be written.

The following four operations are defined on the data structure 'output' :

- <u>procedure</u> newline;
    A new line is added to the file 'output'. The cursor is positioned on the first column. This new line becomes the current line.

- <u>procedure</u> adv_cursor (c : column_number);
    The cursor is positioned on column number C. The columns between the old value and the new value of the cursor are filled up with blanks. If the old value of the cursor is greater than the new value, the cursor is positioned on the column number C on a new line of the output file. This new line becomes the current line.

- <u>procedure</u> write_char (c : char);
    The character C is written on the current line at the current cursor position. The cursor is moved one column to the right.

- <u>procedure</u> write_string (s : string);
    The string S is written on the current line starting from the current cursor position. Trailing blanks within the string S are not taken into account. The cursor is moved n columns to the right, where n is the length of the string minus the number of trailing blanks.

5.3.2. <u>Formatter : Version 1</u>

In this version, the formatter is described as a one-pass transducer, without any form of separate lexical analysis. As a consequence, the ECF syntax upon which the description of the transducer

is based, is defined in terms of single characters : the blank symbol, letters, digits, the quote symbol, the colon symbol, the semicolon symbol and the equal symbol. Notice that, in contrast with
the previous examples, the input symbol "eoln" is not part of the
input vocabulary. Because the input of the formatter is a text
file, an end-of-line in the input is treated as a space, as it is
defined in Pascal.

```
$$$$$$$$$$$$$$$$$$$$$$$$$$$$$$$$$$$$$$$$$$$$$$$$$$$$$$$$$$$$$$$$$$$$$$$$$$$$$$$$$$$$$$$$
$   LILA INPUT                                                                     $
$                                                                                  $
$      Formatter : Version 1      (Underlying ECF syntax)                          $
$$$$$$$$$$$$$$$$$$$$$$$$$$$$$$$$$$$$$$$$$$$$$$$$$$$$$$$$$$$$$$$$$$$$$$$$$$$$$$$$$$$$$$$$


###inputvocabulary  rep(char), file(input);

    "a" = 97    "b" = 98    "c" = 99    "d" =100    "e" =101    "f" =102
    "g" =103    "h" =104    "i" =105    "j" =106    "k" =107    "l" =108
    "m" =109    "n" =110    "o" =111    "p" =112    "q" =113    "r" =114
    "s" =115    "t" =116    "u" =117    "v" =118    "w" =119    "x" =120
    "y" =121    "z" =122

    "0" = 48    "1" = 49    "2" = 50    "3" = 51    "4" = 52    "5" = 53
    "6" = 54    "7" = 55    "8" = 56    "9" = 57

    "bl"= 32    "'" = 39    ":" = 58    ";" = 59    "=" = 61


###syntax;

  ##rule;
    <program> =
      <blanks>  <statement list>

  ##rule;
    <statement list> =
      <statement>  ( ";" <blanks> <statement> )*

  ##rule;
    <statement> =
        <if statement>
      | <assign statement>

  ##rule;
    <if statement> =
      <if> <variable>
```

```
          <then> <statement list>
          <else> <statement list>
        <fi>

##rule;
  <assign statement> =
    <variable>   ":" <blanks> "=" <blanks>
      ( <constant> | <variable> )

##rule;
  <variable> =
    <letter>

##rule;
  <constant> =
    <digit>

##rule;
  <if> =
    "'" <blanks>
      "i" <blanks> "f" <blanks>
    "'" <blanks>

##rule;
  <then> =
    "'" <blanks>
      "t" <blanks> "h"  <blanks> "e"  <blanks> "n" <blanks>
    "'" <blanks>

##rule;
  <else> =
    "'" <blanks>
      "e"  <blanks> "l"  <blanks> "s"  <blanks> "e" <blanks>
    "'" <blanks>

##rule;
  <fi> =
    "'" <blanks>
      "f"  <blanks> "i" <blanks>
    "'" <blanks>

##rule;
  <letter> =
      ( "a" | "b" | "c" | "d" | "e" | "f" | "g" | "h" | "i"
      | "j" | "k" | "l" | "m" | "n" | "o" | "p" | "q" | "r"
      | "s" | "t" | "u" | "v" | "w" | "x" | "y" | "z" )
    <blanks>
```

```
##rule;
  <digit> =
      ( "0" | "1" | "2" | "3" | "4" | "5" | "6" | "7" | "8" | "9" )
    <blanks>

##rule;
  <blanks> = "bl" *
```

After having defined the ECF syntax of a free-format program, semantic actions are added to produce the formatted program. The semantic actions of the formatter will use the inherited attribute 'column_number'. This attribute indicates from which column of the current line the corresponding formatted part must be written.

```
$$$$$$$$$$$$$$$$$$$$$$$$$$$$$$$$$$$$$$$$$$$$$$$$$$$$$$$$$$$$$$$$$$$$$$$$$$$$$$$$$$$$
$    LILA INPUT                                                                 $
$                                                                              $
$       Formatter : Version 1                                                   $
$$$$$$$$$$$$$$$$$$$$$$$$$$$$$$$$$$$$$$$$$$$$$$$$$$$$$$$$$$$$$$$$$$$$$$$$$$$$$$$$$$$$


###inputvocabulary  rep(char), file(input);

  "a" = 97    "b" = 98    "c" = 99    "d" =100    "e" =101    "f" =102
  "g" =103    "h" =104    "i" =105    "j" =106    "k" =107    "l" =108
  "m" =109    "n" =110    "o" =111    "p" =112    "q" =113    "r" =114
  "s" =115    "t" =116    "u" =117    "v" =118    "w" =119    "x" =120
  "y" =121    "z" =122


  "0" = 48    "1" = 49    "2" = 50    "3" = 51    "4" = 52    "5" = 53
  "6" = 54    "7" = 55    "8" = 56    "9" = 57


  "bl"= 32    "'" = 39    ":" = 58    ";" = 59    "=" = 61


###syntax;

$ Formatting of a program
  ##rule;
    <program> =
      init <blanks>
        <statement list>
      final

    ##action;
```

```
        #init;
          newline;
          @<statement list> := 1

        #final;
        .  newline

$ Formatting of a statement list
  ##rule;
    <statement list> =
      pass_sl  <statement>
        (  ";" write_sem  <blanks>  pass_s2 <statement> )*

    ##attribute;
      column_number

    ##action;
      #write_sem;
        write_char(';');
        newline

      #pass_sl;
        @<statement>1 := @<statement list>

      #pass_s2;
        @<statement>2 := @<statement list>

$ Formatting of a statement
  ##rule;
    <statement> =
        pass_is  <if statement>
      | pass_as  <assign statement>

    ##attribute;
      column_number

    ##action;
      #pass_as;
        @<assign statement> := @<statement>

      #pass_is;
        @<if statement> := @<statement>

$ Formatting of an if statement
  ##rule;
    <if statement> =
      <if> write_if  pos_variable <variable>
        <then> write_then  pos_sl <statement list>
```

```
      <else> write_else   pos_s2 <statement list>
    <fi> write_fi

##attribute;
  column_number

##const;
  var_indentation  = 5;
  then_indentation = 2;
  else_indentation = 2;
  statl_indentation= 9

##action;
  #write_if;
    adv_cursor(@<if statement>);
    write_string('''if''  ')

  #pos_variable;
    @<variable> := @<if statement> + var_indentation

  #write_then;
    newline;
    adv_cursor(@<if statement> + then_indentation);
    write_string('''then''')

  #pos_sl;
    @<statement list>1 := @<if statement> + statl_indentation

  #write_else;
    newline;
    adv_cursor(@<if statement> + else_indentation);
    write_string('''else''')

  #pos_s2;
    @<statement list>2 := @<if statement> + statl_indentation

  #write_fi;
    newline;
    adv_cursor(@<if statement>);
    write_string('''fi''  ')

$ Formatting of an assignment statement
##rule;
   <assign statement> =
     pass_av <variable>
       ":" <blanks> "=" <blanks>  write_assign
       ( pos_constant <constant>  | pos_variable <variable> )
```

```
##attribute;
  column_number


##const;
  const_indentation = 5;
  var_indentation   = 5;
  ass_indentation   = 2


##action;
  #pass_av;
    @<variable>1 := @<assign statement>

  #write_assign;
    adv_cursor(@<assign statement> + ass_indentation);
    write_string(':=     ')

  #pos_constant;
    @<constant> := @<assign statement> + const_indentation

  #pos_variable;
    @<variable>2 := @<assign statement> + var_indentation
```

$ Formatting of a variable
```
  ##rule;
    <variable> =
      write_variable  <letter>

  ##attribute;
    column_number

  ##action;
    #write_variable;
      adv_cursor(@<variable>);
      write_char(inp.c)
```

$ Formatting of a constant
```
  ##rule;
    <constant> =
      write_constant  <digit>

  ##attribute;
    column_number

  ##action;
    #write_constant;
      adv_cursor(@<constant>);
      write_char(inp.c)
```

```
$ Definition of the keyword if
  ##rule;
    <if> =
      "'" <blanks>
        "i" <blanks>  "f" <blanks>
      "'" <blanks>

$ Definition of the keyword then
  ##rule;
    <then> =
      "'" <blanks>
        "t" <blanks> "h"  <blanks> "e"  <blanks> "n" <blanks>
      "'" <blanks>

$ Definition of the keyword else
  ##rule;
    <else> =
      "'" <blanks>
        "e" <blanks> "l"  <blanks> "s"  <blanks> "e" <blanks>
      "'" <blanks>

$ Definition of the keyword fi
  ##rule;
    <fi> =
      "'" <blanks>
        "f" <blanks>  "i" <blanks>
      "'" <blanks>

$ Definition of a letter
  ##rule;
    <letter> =
        ( "a" | "b" | "c" | "d" | "e" | "f" | "g" | "h" | "i"
        | "j" | "k" | "l" | "m" | "n" | "o" | "p" | "q" | "r"
        | "s" | "t" | "u" | "v" | "w" | "x" | "y" | "z" )
      <blanks>

$ Definition of a digit
  ##rule;
    <digit> =
        ( "0" | "1" | "2" | "3" | "4" | "5" | "6" | "7" | "8" | "9" )
      <blanks>

$ Definition of a sequence of blanks
  ##rule;
    <blanks> = "bl" *


###globalinfo;
```

```
##parameter;
  input, output

##const;
  $ Output
    str_length = 6

##type;
  $ Output
    string = packed array [1..str_length] of char;

    column_number = 1..maxint

##var;
  $ Output
    cursor : column_number

##routine;
  $ Output
    procedure newline;
    begin
      writeln(output);
      cursor := 1
    end; {newline}

    procedure adv_cursor (c:column_number);
    var i:column_number;
    begin
      if (cursor > c) then newline;
      for i:=cursor to c-1 do
        write(output, ' ');
      cursor := c
    end; {adv_cursor}

    procedure write_char (c:char);
    begin
      write(output, c);
      cursor := cursor + 1
    end; {write_char}

    procedure write_string (s:string);
    var i,length : 1..str_length;
    begin
      length := str_length;
      while (s[length] = ' ') and (length > 1) do
        length := length - 1;
      for i:=1 to length do
        write_char(s[i])
```

```
     end {write_string}
```


5.3.3. Formatter : Version 2

The drawback of the previous version of the formatter is the lack of one of the two-level structures of modularity. Only the first level structure of modularity, which is related to syntax modules, is present. A second level structure of modularity can be introduced by preprocessing the blanks in the input string. The preprocessing of blanks is a simple case of what is called lexical analysis.

The ECF syntax upon which this version of the formatter is based, is still defined in terms of single characters. However, the blank symbols disappear as terminal symbols from the underlying ECF syntax.

```
$$$$$$$$$$$$$$$$$$$$$$$$$$$$$$$$$$$$$$$$$$$$$$$$$$$$$$$$$$$$$$$$$$$$$$$$$$$$$$$$$$$$
$   LILA INPUT                                                                  $
$                                                                              $
$       Formatter : Version 2      (Underlying ECF syntax)                     $
$$$$$$$$$$$$$$$$$$$$$$$$$$$$$$$$$$$$$$$$$$$$$$$$$$$$$$$$$$$$$$$$$$$$$$$$$$$$$$$$$$$$


###inputvocabulary  rep(char), file(input);

  "a" = 97   "b" = 98   "c" = 99   "d" =100   "e" =101   "f" =102
  "g" =103   "h" =104   "i" =105   "j" =106   "k" =107   "l" =108
  "m" =109   "n" =110   "o" =111   "p" =112   "q" =113   "r" =114
  "s" =115   "t" =116   "u" =117   "v" =118   "w" =119   "x" =120
  "y" =121   "z" =122

  "0" = 48   "1" = 49   "2" = 50   "3" = 51   "4" = 52   "5" = 53
  "6" = 54   "7" = 55   "8" = 56   "9" = 57

  "'" = 39   ":" = 58   ";" = 59   "=" = 61


###syntax;

  ##rule;
    <program> =
      <statement list>

  ##rule;
```

```
  <statement list> =
    <statement>  ( ";" <statement> )*

##rule;
  <statement> =
      <if statement>
    | <assign statement>

##rule;
  <if statement> =
    <if> <variable>
      <then> <statement list>
      <else> <statement list>
    <fi>

##rule;
  <assign statement> =
    <variable>  ":" "="  ( <constant> | <variable> )

##rule;
  <variable> =
    <letter>

##rule;
  <constant> =
    <digit>

##rule;
  <if> =
    "'" "i" "f" "'"

##rule;
  <then> =
    "'" "t" "h" "e" "n" "'"

##rule;
  <else> =
    "'" "e" "l" "s" "e" "'"

##rule;
  <fi> =
    "'" "f" "i" "'"

##rule;
  <letter> =
      "a" | "b" | "c" | "d" | "e" | "f" | "g" | "h" | "i"
    | "j" | "k" | "l" | "m" | "n" | "o" | "p" | "q" | "r"
    | "s" | "t" | "u" | "v" | "w" | "x" | "y" | "z"
```

```
##rule;
 <digit> =
    "0" | "1" | "2" | "3" | "4" | "5" | "6" | "7" | "8" | "9"
```

The preprocessing of the blanks will be performed in the read action of the formatter. Therefore, the LILA default read module has to be overridden. As it is explained in the Reference Guide, the LILA default read module provides for the definitions of

- the input file 'input'

- the input head 'inp'

- 'linenumb'

- an operation with name 'readin', to read the next input symbol.

In overriding the LILA default read module, the LILA user provides for the definitions of these components. In this case study, only the operation to read the next input symbol differs from the LILA default operation; it has to skip all the blanks in the input stream.

The input head 'inp' and the global variable 'linenumb' are defined in globalinfo. We refer to the Reference Guide in Appendix for more details about the structure of the input head 'inp'. The operation to read the next input symbol is defined in the read routine part of the LILA input. Notice that a virtual end-of-file symbol is generated in the read routine, whenever the end of the input file is reached. The LILA default representation of the virtual end-of-file symbol is 0.

Before the formatting actually starts, the variables 'inp' and 'linenumb' must be initialized in the prologue of globalinfo.

```
$$$$$$$$$$$$$$$$$$$$$$$$$$$$$$$$$$$$$$$$$$$$$$$$$$$$$$$$$$$$$$$$$$$$$$$$$$$$$$$$$$$$
$   LILA INPUT                                                                 $
$                                                                             $
$      Formatter : Version 2                                                  $
$$$$$$$$$$$$$$$$$$$$$$$$$$$$$$$$$$$$$$$$$$$$$$$$$$$$$$$$$$$$$$$$$$$$$$$$$$$$$$$$$$$$


###inputvocabulary  rep(char), file(input);
```

```
"a" = 97    "b" = 98    "c" = 99    "d" =100    "e" =101    "f" =102
"g" =103    "h" =104    "i" =105    "j" =106    "k" =107    "l" =108
"m" =109    "n" =110    "o" =111    "p" =112    "q" =113    "r" =114
"s" =115    "t" =116    "u" =117    "v" =118    "w" =119    "x" =120
"y" =121    "z" =122

"0" = 48    "1" = 49    "2" = 50    "3" = 51    "4" = 52    "5" = 53
"6" = 54    "7" = 55    "8" = 56    "9" = 57

"'" = 39    ":" = 58    ";" = 59    "=" = 61
```

```
###syntax;

$ Formatting of a program
  ##rule;
    <program> =
      init
        <statement list>
      final

    ##action;
      #init;
        newline;
        @<statement list> := 1

      #final;
        newline

$ Formatting of a statement list
  ##rule;
    <statement list> =
      pass_s1  <statement>
        ( ";" write_sem  pass_s2 <statement> )*

    ##attribute;
      column_number

    ##action;
      #write_sem;
        write_char(';');
        newline

      #pass_s1;
        @<statement>1 := @<statement list>

      #pass_s2;
        @<statement>2 := @<statement list>
```

```
$ Formatting of a statement
  ##rule;
    <statement> =
        pass_is  <if statement>
      | pass_as  <assign statement>

  ##attribute;
    column_number

  ##action;
    #pass_as;
      @<assign statement> := @<statement>

    #pass_is;
      @<if statement> := @<statement>

$ Formatting of an if statement
  ##rule;
    <if statement> =
      <if> write_if  pos_variable <variable>
        <then> write_then  pos_sl <statement list>
        <else> write_else  pos_s2 <statement list>
      <fi> write_fi

  ##attribute;
    column_number

  ##const;
    var_indentation  = 5;
    then_indentation = 2;
    else_indentation = 2;
    statl_indentation= 9

  ##action;
    #write_if;
      adv_cursor(@<if statement>);
      write_string('''if''  ')

    #pos_variable;
      @<variable> := @<if statement> + var_indentation

    #write_then;
      newline;
      adv_cursor(@<if statement> + then_indentation);
      write_string('''then''')

    #pos_sl;
      @<statement list>1 := @<if statement> + statl_indentation
```

```
     #write_else;
       newline;
       adv_cursor(@<if statement> + else_indentation);
       write_string('''else''')

     #pos_s2;
       @<statement list>2 := @<if statement> + statl_indentation

     #write_fi;
       newline;
       adv_cursor(@<if statement>);
       write_string('''fi''  ')
```

$ Formatting of an assignment statement
```
  ##rule;
    <assign statement> =
      pass_av <variable>
        ":" "="  write_assign
        ( pos_constant <constant>  | pos_variable <variable> )

  ##attribute;
    column_number

  ##const;
    const_indentation = 5;
    var_indentation   = 5;
    ass_indentation   = 2

  ##action;
    #pass_av;
      @<variable>1 := @<assign statement>

    #write_assign;
      adv_cursor(@<assign statement> + ass_indentation);
      write_string(':=     ')

    #pos_constant;
      @<constant> := @<assign statement> + const_indentation

    #pos_variable;
      @<variable>2 := @<assign statement> + var_indentation
```

$ Formatting of a variable
```
  ##rule;
    <variable> =
      write_variable  <letter>

  ##attribute;
```

```
      column_number

  ##action;
    #write_variable;
      adv_cursor(@<variable>);
      write_char(inp.c)
```

$ Formatting of a constant
```
  ##rule;
    <constant> =
      write_constant  <digit>

    ##attribute;
      column_number

    ##action;
      #write_constant;
        adv_cursor(@<constant>);
        write_char(inp.c)
```

$ Definition of the keyword if
```
  ##rule;
    <if> =
      "'" "i" "f" "'"
```

$ Definition of the keyword then
```
  ##rule;
    <then> =
      "'" "t" "h" "e" "n" "'"
```

$ Definition of the keyword else
```
  ##rule;
    <else> =
      "'" "e" "l" "s" "e" "'"
```

$ Definition of the keyword fi
```
  ##rule;
    <fi> =
      "'" "f" "i" "'"
```

$ Definition of a letter
```
  ##rule;
    <letter> =
        "a" | "b" | "c" | "d" | "e" | "f" | "g" | "h" | "i"
      | "j" | "k" | "l" | "m" | "n" | "o" | "p" | "q" | "r"
      | "s" | "t" | "u" | "v" | "w" | "x" | "y" | "z"
```

$ Definition of a digit

```
  ##rule;
    <digit> =
       "0" | "1" | "2" | "3" | "4" | "5" | "6" | "7" | "8" | "9"


###globalinfo;

  ##parameter;
    input, output

  ##const;
    $ Output
      str_length = 6

  ##type;
    $ Output
      string = packed array [1..str_length] of char;

      column_number = 1..maxint

  ##var;
    $ Output
      cursor : column_number;

    $ Lexical Analysis
      inp : record
               c:char
             end;
      linenumb : integer

  ##routine;
    $ Output
      procedure newline;
      begin
        writeln(output);
        cursor := 1
      end; {newline}

      procedure adv_cursor (c:column_number);
      var i:column_number;
      begin
        if (cursor > c) then newline;
        for i:=cursor to c-1 do
          write(output, ' ');
        cursor := c
      end; {adv_cursor}

      procedure write_char (c:char);
```

```
      begin
        write(output, c);
        cursor := cursor + 1
      end; {write_char}

      procedure write_string (s:string);
      var i,length : 1..str_length;
      begin
        length := str_length;
        while (s[length] = ' ') and (length > 1) do
          length := length - 1;
        for i:=1 to length do
          write_char(s[i])
      end {write_string}

  ##prologue;
    $ Lexical Analysis
      linenumb := 1;
      readin


###readroutine;

  repeat
    if eof(input) then inp.c := chr(0)
    else begin
      if eoln(input) then linenumb := linenumb + 1;
      read(input, inp.c)
    end
  until (inp.c <> ' ')
```

5.3.4. Formatter : Version 3

The lexical analysis in the formatter can go a step further. The
lexical analyser will then produce attributed input symbols for the
syntax-semantic analyser. These attributed input symbols are :
"constant" which is attributed with a constant, and "identifier"
which is attributed with an identifier name. The other input symbols are : ":=", ";", "if", "then", "else" and "fi". They have no
attributes.

```
$$$$$$$$$$$$$$$$$$$$$$$$$$$$$$$$$$$$$$$$$$$$$$$$$$$$$$$$$$$$$$$$$$$$$$$$$$$$$$$$$$$$
$    LILA INPUT                                                                 $
$                                                                              $
$      Formatter : Version 3      (Underlying ECF syntax)                      $
```

$$$

```
###inputvocabulary  rep(char);

  ":=" = 2    ";" = 3

  "constant" = 4

  "identifier" = 5

  "if" = 6    "then" = 7    "else" = 8    "fi" = 9


###syntax;

  ##rule;
    <program> =
      <statement list>

  ##rule;
    <statement list> =
      <statement>  ( ";" <statement> )*

  ##rule;
    <statement> =
        <if statement>
      | <assign statement>

  ##rule;
    <if statement> =
      "if" <variable>
        "then" <statement list>
        "else" <statement list>
      "fi"

  ##rule;
    <assign statement> =
      <variable>  ":="  ( <constant> | <variable> )

  ##rule;
    <variable> =
      "identifier"

  ##rule;
    <constant> =
      "constant"
```

The read module, which has to be redefined by the LILA user, consists in scanning the input string until a lexically analysed input
symbol, possibly attributed, is found, which is then passed on to
the input head of the syntax-semantic analyser of the formatter.
Recall that the input head of the syntax-semantic analyser is a
record with two fields:

a) a field $\underline{c}$ containing the representation of the input symbol.

b) a field $\underline{a}$ containing the attribute of the input symbol. This
   field is a variant over all the different types of the attributes of the input symbols.

```
$$$$$$$$$$$$$$$$$$$$$$$$$$$$$$$$$$$$$$$$$$$$$$$$$$$$$$$$$$$$$$$$$$$$$$$$$$$$$$$$$$$
$   LILA INPUT                                                                 $
$                                                                             $
$      Formatter : Version 3                                                   $
$$$$$$$$$$$$$$$$$$$$$$$$$$$$$$$$$$$$$$$$$$$$$$$$$$$$$$$$$$$$$$$$$$$$$$$$$$$$$$$$$$$
```

```
###inputvocabulary  rep(char);

  ":=" = 2    ";" = 3

  "constant" = 4 : char

  "identifier" = 5 : char

  "if" = 6    "then" = 7    "else" = 8    "fi" = 9


###syntax;

$ Formatting of a program
  ##rule;
    <program> =
      init
        <statement list>
      final

    ##action;
    #init;
```

```
        newline;
        @<statement list> := 1

      #final;
        newline

$ Formatting of a statement list
  ##rule;
    <statement list> =
      pass_sl  <statement>
        ( ";" write_sem  pass_s2 <statement> )*

    ##attribute;
      column_number

    ##action;
      #write_sem;
        write_char(';');
        newline

      #pass_sl;
        @<statement>1 := @<statement list>

      #pass_s2;
        @<statement>2 := @<statement list>

$ Formatting of a statement
  ##rule;
    <statement> =
        pass_is  <if statement>
      | pass_as  <assign statement>

    ##attribute;
      column_number

    ##action;
      #pass_as;
        @<assign statement> := @<statement>

      #pass_is;
        @<if statement> := @<statement>

$ Formatting of an if statement
  ##rule;
    <if statement> =
      "if" write_if  pos_variable <variable>
        "then" write_then  pos_sl <statement list>
        "else" write_else  pos_s2 <statement list>
```

```
      "fi" write_fi

   ##attribute;
      column_number

   ##const;
      var_indentation  = 5;
      then_indentation = 2;
      else_indentation = 2;
      statl_indentation= 9

   ##action;
      #write_if;
         adv_cursor(@<if statement>);
         write_string('''if''  ')

      #pos_variable;
         @<variable> := @<if statement> + var_indentation

      #write_then;
         newline;
         adv_cursor(@<if statement> + then_indentation);
         write_string('''then''')

      #pos_sl;
         @<statement list>l := @<if statement> + statl_indentation

      #write_else;
         newline;
         adv_cursor(@<if statement> + else_indentation);
         write_string('''else''')

      #pos_s2;
         @<statement list>2 := @<if statement> + statl_indentation

      #write_fi;
         newline;
         adv_cursor(@<if statement>);
         write_string('''fi''  ')

$ Formatting of an assignment statement
   ##rule;
      <assign statement> =
         pass_av <variable>
            ":=" write_assign
            ( pos_constant <constant>  | pos_variable <variable> )

      ##attribute;
```

```
        column_number

    ##const;
       const_indentation = 5;
       var_indentation   = 5;
       ass_indentation   = 2

    ##action;
       #pass_av;
         @<variable>1 := @<assign statement>

       #write_assign;
         adv_cursor(@<assign statement> + ass_indentation);
         write_string(':=    ')

       #pos_constant;
         @<constant> := @<assign statement> + const_indentation

       #pos_variable;
         @<variable>2 := @<assign statement> + var_indentation

$ Formatting of a variable
  ##rule;
     <variable> =
       "identifier"  write_variable

    ##attribute;
       column_number

    ##action;
       #write_variable;
         adv_cursor(@<variable>);
         write_char(@"identifier")

$ Formatting of a constant
  ##rule;
     <constant> =
       "constant"  write_constant

    ##attribute;
       column_number

    ##action;
       #write_constant;
         adv_cursor(@<constant>);
         write_char(@"constant")
```

```
###globalinfo;

   ##parameter;
     input, output

   ##const;
     $ Output
       str_length = 6

   ##type;
     $ Output
       string = packed array [1..str_length] of char;

       column_number = 1..maxint;

     $ Lexical Analysis
       nb_attr = 1..1;
       attr1_tp= char;
       inp_type = record
         c : char;
         a : record
           case  nb_attr  of
             1 : (char:attr1_tp)
         end
       end
         { The declaration of inp_type is an imitation of the default
           definition generated by LILA. The declaration  could  have
           been written in a more compact way. }

   ##var;
     $ Output
       cursor : column_number;

     $ Lexical Analysis
       inp : inp_type;
       linenumb : integer;

       ch : char;

       keyname : packed array [1..4] of char;
       nb_char : 0..maxint

   ##routine;
     $ Output
       procedure newline;
       begin
         writeln(output);
         cursor := 1
```

```
      end; {newline}

      procedure adv_cursor (c:column_number);
      var i:column_number;
      begin
        if (cursor > c) then newline;
        for i:=cursor to c-1 do
          write(output, ' ');
        cursor := c
      end; {adv_cursor}

      procedure write_char (c:char);
      begin
        write(output, c);
        cursor := cursor + 1
      end; {write_char}

      procedure write_string (s:string);
      var i,length : 1..str_length;
      begin
        length := str_length;
        while (s[length] = ' ') and (length > 1) do
          length := length - 1;
        for i:=1 to length do
          write_char(s[i])
      end; {write_string}

    $ Lexical Analysis
      procedure next_char;
      begin
        repeat
          if eof(input) then ch := chr(0)
          else begin
            if eoln(input) then linenumb := linenumb + 1;
            read(input, ch)
          end
        until (ch <> ' ')
      end  {next_char}

  ##prologue;
    $ Lexical Analysis
      linenumb := 1;
      readin

###readroutine;

  next_char;
  if ('a' <= ch) and (ch <= 'z') then begin
```

```
  inp.c      := %"identifier";
  inp.a.char:= ch
end
else if ('0' <= ch) and (ch <= '9') then begin
  inp.c      := %"constant";
  inp.a.char:= ch
end
else if (ch = ';') then    inp.c := %";"
else if (ch = ':') then begin
  next_char;
  if (ch <> '=') then begin
    writeln(output);
    writeln(output, linenumb:4, ' *** ERROR *** : ',
      'Invalid character after colon.');
    goto 9999  {Stop}
  end
  else inp.c := %":="
end
else if (ch = '''') then begin
  keyname := '    ';
  nb_char := 0;
  next_char;
  while ('a' <= ch) and (ch <= 'z')  do begin
    if (nb_char >= 4) then begin
      writeln(output);
      writeln(output, linenumb:4, ' *** ERROR *** : ',
        'Invalid keyword; name exceeds maximum length.');
      goto 9999  {Stop}
    end
    else begin
      nb_char := nb_char + 1;
      keyname [nb_char] := ch;
      next_char
    end
  end;
  if (ch <> '''') then begin
    writeln(output);
    writeln(output, linenumb:4, ' *** ERROR *** : ',
      'Invalid keyword; the end character is not a quote.');
    goto 9999
  end;
       if (keyname = 'if  ') then inp.c := %"if"
  else if (keyname = 'then') then inp.c := %"then"
  else if (keyname = 'else') then inp.c := %"else"
  else if (keyname = 'fi  ') then inp.c := %"fi"
  else begin
    writeln(output);
    writeln(output, linenumb:4, ' *** ERROR *** : ',
```

```
            'Invalid keyword; undefined name.');
        goto 9999   {Stop}
      end
  end
else if (ch = chr(0)) then inp.c := chr(0)
else begin
  writeln(output);
  writeln(output, linenumb:4, ' *** ERROR *** : ',
      'Invalid symbol.');
  goto 9999   {Stop}
end
```

5.4. Arithmetic Expressions

This case study discusses the implementation of an interpreter for simple arithmetic expressions by means of LILA. The statements to be interpreted are print statements and assign statements.

An example of an input for the interpreter is the following :

```
a = 111 + 11;
print value of a;
aa = 11 * (a - 1);
print value of aa;
print value of (aa + a) / 10;
```

The answers produced during interpretation are given below :

```
122
1331
145
```

This case study illustrates the stepwise development of a transducer by means of LILA. Furthermore, a great deal of attention is devoted to the aspect of error recovery at the semantic level.

5.4.1. Error recovery at the semantic level

An important aspect in the design of a transducer is the treatment of semantic errors. One of the most important characteristics of high quality error treatment is to avoid an accumulation of error messages. This means that a specific semantic error may not lead to a wild production of error messages.

In the interpreter for arithmetic expressions, high quality error treatment has been obtained by introducing an appropriate data structure to represent the value of an arithmetic expression. Basically, the value of an expression is either an integer or undefined. An example of an expression having an undefined value, is an expression in which an uninitialized variable is used. The representation of an integer is then described in Pascal as:

```
type rep_value = record
      case def:boolean of
         true : (value : integer);
         false: ( )
    end;
```

5.4.2. The stepwise development of the interpreter

Conceptually, the interpreter for arithmetic expressions consists of two successive passes : a lexical analyser and a syntax-semantic analyser. In a first step, the lexical analyser and the syntax-semantic analyser will be implemented and tested as two separate program modules. This is illustrated in Fig. 5.3.

Two-Pass Interpreter

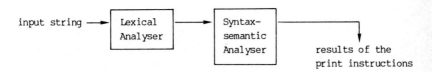

Fig. 5.3.

In a second step, the lexical analyser will be integrated in the syntax-semantic analyser such that the lexical analyser will override the read module of the syntax-semantic analyser. This is illustrated in Fig. 5.4.

One-Pass Interpreter

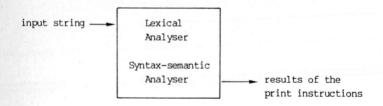

Fig. 5.4.

   Notice that the lexical analyser is now a subroutine producing
the next attributed input symbol for the syntax-semantic analyser.

5.4.3.   Two-Pass Interpreter

5.4.3.1.   The Lexical Analyser

   The task of the lexical analyser is to produce attributed output
symbols, which will become the attributed input symbols for the
syntax-semantic analyser.   These attributed output symbols are
[identifier] which is attributed with an identifier name, and [con-
stant] which is attributed with an integer value.   The other output
symbols are the keywords [print], [value] and [of], and the delimiters [(], [)], [*], [+], [-], [/], [;] and [=].   The output symbols
are produced on the LILA default output file, called 'outfile'.

   Notice that the ECF syntax rules defining the lexical structure
of identifiers, keywords and constants, do not satisfy the ELL(1)
conditions.   An ELL(1) ECF syntax is possible, but would be complex,
unreadable, and therefore unpractical.   However, the ELL(1) transducer generated by LILA will perform correctly, since all the
letters and digits (digits), not separated from one another, are
considered to be part of the same identifier or keyword (constant).
This follows from the generation schemes discussed in sections 2, 3
and 4.   The let option has been specified in the LILA input, in
order to force the generation of an ELL(1) transducer even if its
translation syntax does not satisfy the ELL(1) conditions.

The data structure 'rep_value'

In the lexical analyser, the following operations defined on the data structure 'rep_value', are used to attribute the output symbol [constant] :

- <u>procedure</u> initun_value (<u>var</u> v : rep_value);
      V is initialized with the undefined value.

- <u>procedure</u> init_value (<u>var</u> v : rep_value; i : integer);
      V is initialized with the integer I.


```
$$$$$$$$$$$$$$$$$$$$$$$$$$$$$$$$$$$$$$$$$$$$$$$$$$$$$$$$$$$$$$$$$$$$$$$$$$$$$$$$$$$
$    LILA INPUT                                                                $
$                                                                             $
$       Interpreter for Arithmetic expressions : Lexical Analyser             $
$$$$$$$$$$$$$$$$$$$$$$$$$$$$$$$$$$$$$$$$$$$$$$$$$$$$$$$$$$$$$$$$$$$$$$$$$$$$$$$$$$$
```


###options let;

###inputvocabulary   rep(char), file(input);

```
   " " = 32    "(" = 40    ")" = 41    "*" = 42    "+" = 43    "-" = 45
   "/" = 47    ";" = 59    "=" = 61


   "0" = 48    "1" = 49    "2" = 50    "3" = 51    "4" = 52    "5" = 53
   "6" = 54    "7" = 55    "8" = 56    "9" = 57


   "a" = 97    "b" = 98    "c" = 99    "d" =100    "e" =101    "f" =102
   "g" =103    "h" =104    "i" =105    "j" =106    "k" =107    "l" =108
   "m" =109    "n" =110    "o" =111    "p" =112    "q" =113    "r" =114
   "s" =115    "t" =116    "u" =117    "v" =118    "w" =119    "x" =120
   "y" =121    "z" =122
```


###outputvocabulary rep(char);

   [identifier] = 2 : rep_name

   [constant] = 3 : rep_value

   [print] = 4   [value] = 5   [of] = 6

```
[(] = 40    [)] = 41    [*] = 42    [+] = 43    [-] = 45
[/] = 47    [;] = 59    [=] = 61
```

###syntax;

$ Definition of a program at the lexical level
  ##rule;
    <program> =
      (<identifier keyword>
      | <constant>
      | <delimiter>
      | " "+
)*

$ Analysis of an identifier or a keyword
  ##rule;
    <identifier keyword> =
      init_name <letter>
        (add_name (<letter> | <digit>))*
      out_idenkey

    ##var;
    nb_char : 0..maxint

    ##action;
     #init_name;
       @[identifier] := '   ';
       @[identifier] [1] := inp.c;
       nb_char:= 1

     #add_name;
       nb_char := nb_char + 1;
       if (nb_char <= idlength)
         then @[identifier] [nb_char] := inp.c

     #out_idenkey;
       if (nb_char > idlength) then error(iden_trunc);
            if (@[identifier] = 'value   ') then out(%[value])
       else if (@[identifier] = 'print   ') then out(%[print])
       else if (@[identifier] = 'of   ') then out(%[of])
       else out(%[identifier])

$ Analysis of a constant
  ##rule;
    <constant> =
      init_value
        (value <digit>)+
```
```

```
        out_constant

    ##var;
      value : integer

    ##action;
      #init_value;
        value := 0

      #value;
        if (value <> -1) then
          if (value + 1) <= (maxint div 10)
            then value := value*10 + (ord(inp.c) - ord('0'))
            else begin
              error(maxconst_exc);
              value := -1
            end

      #out_constant;
        if (value = -1)
          then initun_value(@[constant])
          else init_value(@[constant], value);
        out(%[constant])

$ Analysis of a delimiter
  ##rule;
    <delimiter> =
      out_delimiter
        ( "*" | "/" | "+" | "-" | "(" | ")" | "=" | ";" )

    ##action;
      #out_delimiter;
        out(inp.c)

$ Definition of a letter
  ##rule;
    <letter> =
        "a" | "b" | "c" | "d" | "e" | "f" | "g" | "h" | "i"
      | "j" | "k" | "l" | "m" | "n" | "o" | "p" | "q" | "r"
      | "s" | "t" | "u" | "v" | "w" | "x" | "y" | "z"

$ Definition of a digit
  ##rule;
    <digit> =
      "0" | "1" | "2" | "3" | "4" | "5" | "6" | "7" | "8" | "9"


###globalinfo;
```

```
##parameter;
  input, output, outfile.

##const;
  $ Rep name
    idlength = 8

##type;
  $ Message
    message = (maxconst_exc, iden_trunc);

  $ Rep Value
    rep_value = record
      case  def:boolean  of
        true : ( value:integer);
        false: ( )
    end;

  $ Rep name
    rep_name = packed array [1..idlength] of char

##routine;
  $ Message
    procedure error (m:message);
    begin
      writeln(output);
      writeln(output, linenumb:3, ' --> ERROR');
      write  (output,'        ');
      case  m  of
        maxconst_exc:
          write(output, 'Constant exceeds maximum value');
          iden_trunc:
            write(output, 'Identifier truncated to ',idlength:1,' characters')
      end;
      writeln(output)
    end; {error}

  $ Rep value
    procedure initun_value (var v:rep_value);
    begin
      v.def := false
    end; {initun_value}

    procedure init_value ( var v:rep_value; i:integer);
    begin
      v.def := true;
      v.value := i
    end {init_value}
```

5.4.3.2. The Syntax-semantic Analyser

The syntax-semantic analyser is the heart of the interpreter. It will calculate the values of the arithmetic expressions and either save them in a table, called 'symbtab', or print the values on the standard file 'output'. The input symbols for the syntax-semantic analyser will be on the LILA default input file, called 'infile'. Before discussing the implementation of the syntax-semantic analyser in more detail, we will first describe the data structures and the actions defined on them.

The data structure 'rep_value'

As it has been explained in section 5.4.1, the data structure 'rep_value' is used to represent the value of an arithmetic expression. A full description of the data structure 'rep_value' is given below.

```
type rep_value = record
      case def:boolean of
        true : (value : integer);
        false: ( )
    end;
```

The following operations are defined on the data structure 'rep_value' :

- procedure initun_value (var v : rep_value);
      V is initialized with the undefined value.

- procedure init_value (var v : rep_value; i : integer);
      V is initialized with the integer I.

- function undef_value (v : rep_value) : boolean;
      Return a boolean value indicating whether the value contained in V is the undefined value.

- <u>procedure</u> add_value (<u>var</u> v1 : rep_value; v2 : rep_value);
     Add the value of V2 to the value of V1 and store the result in
     V1. If either V1 or V2 contain the undefined value, or if an
     overflow occurs when performing the addition, the value contained
     in V1 will become the undefined value. Only in the latter case,
     an error message will be produced.

- <u>procedure</u> subtract_value (<u>var</u> v1 : rep_value; v2 : rep_value);
     Subtract the value of V2 from the value of V1 and store the
     result in V1. If either V1 or V2 contain the undefined value, or
     if an overflow occurs when performing the subtraction, the value
     contained in V1 will become the undefined value. Only in the
     latter case, an error message will be produced.

- <u>procedure</u> multiply_value (<u>var</u> v1 : rep_value; v2 : rep_value);
     Multiply the value of V1 with the value of V2 and store the
     result in V1. If either V1 or V2 contain the undefined value, or
     if an overflow occurs when performing the multiplication, the
     value contained in V1 will become the undefined value. Only in
     the latter case, an error message will be produced.

- <u>procedure</u> divide_value (<u>var</u> v1 : rep_value; v2 : rep_value);
     Integer divide the value of V1 by the value of V2 and store
     the result in V1. If either V1 or V2 contain the undefined
     value, or if the value contained in V2 equals 0, the value con-
     tained in V1 will become the undefined value. Only in the latter
     case, an error message will be produced.

- <u>procedure</u> print_value (v : rep_value);
     Print the value contained in V on the standard file 'output'.
     If the value contained in V is the undefined value, a question
     mark will be printed.

The data structure for the Symbol Table

     As it has been explained above, a table will be set up to contain
the values of all the variables defined during interpretation. Each
table entry contains the name of a variable and its current value.
The symbol table is defined as follows :

```
var
  symbtab : array [0 .. maxsymbt] of record
    name  : rep_name;
    value : rep_value;
  end;
```

The operations to manipulate the symbol table are described below.

- **procedure** add_symbtab (n : rep_name; v : rep_value);
    Add a new entry to the symbol table. The name field of the
  new entry will become N; the value field will be V. If an entry
  with name N already exists, it will be overridden. If there is
  no more room in the symbol table, the only effect is the production of an error message.

- **procedure** get_symbtab (n : rep_name; **var** v : rep_value);
    Assign the current value of the variable with name N to V. If
  the symbol table does not contain an entry with name N, an error
  message will be produced and the undefined value will be assigned
  to V.

- **procedure** print_symbtab;
    Print the contents of the symbol table on the file 'output'.

$$
$ LILA INPUT $
$ $
$ Interpreter for Arithmetic expressions : Syntax-semantic Analyser $
$$

###inputvocabulary rep(char);

  "identifier" = 2 : rep_name

  "constant" = 3 : rep_value

  "print" = 4   "value" = 5   "of" = 6

  "(" = 40   ")" = 41   "*" = 42   "+" = 43   "-" = 45
  "/" = 47   ";" = 59   "=" = 61
```
```

```
###syntax;

$ Definition of a program
  ##rule;
    <program> =
      <statement>+

$ Analysis of a print statement or an assignment statement
  ##rule;
    <statement> =
      ( "print"  "value"  "of"  <expression>    print
      | "identifier"  "="  <expression>    assign
      )  ";"

    ##action;
      #print;
        print_value(@<expression>1);
        writeln(output)

      #assign;
        add_symbtab( @"identifier", @<expression>2)

$ Calculation of the value of an expression
  ##rule;
    <expression> =
      <term>  pass_te
      ( "+" <term> add
      | "-" <term> subtract
      )*

    ##attribute;
      rep_value

    ##action;
      #pass_te;
        @<expression> := @<term>1

      #add;
        add_value( @<expression>, @<term>2)

      #subtract;
        subtract_value( @<expression>, @<term>3)

$ Calculation of the value of a term
  ##rule;
    <term> =
      <factor>  pass_ft
      ( "*" <factor> multiply
```

```
        | "/" <factor> divide
        )*

    ##attribute;
      rep_value

    ##action;
      #pass_ft;
        @<term> := @<factor>1

      #multiply;
        multiply_value( @<term>, @<factor>2)

      #divide;
        divide_value( @<term>, @<factor>3)

$ Calculation of the value of a factor
  ##rule;
    <factor> =
        "identifier"  identifier
      | "constant"  constant
      | "(" <expression> ")"  pass_ef

    ##attribute;
      rep_value

    ##action;
      #identifier;
        get_symbtab( @"identifier", @<factor>)

      #constant;
        @<factor> := @"constant"

      #pass_ef;
        @<factor> := @<expression>


###globalinfo;

  ##parameter;
    infile, output

  ##const;
    $ The Symbol Table
      idlength =    8;
      maxsymbt = 100

  ##type;
```

```
$ Message
  message = ( undef_var, arith_overfl, zero_divide, maxvar_exc);

$ Rep Value
  rep_value = record
    case  def:boolean  of
      true : ( value:integer);
      false: ( )
  end;

$ The Symbol Table
  rep_name = packed array [1..idlength] of char

##var;
  $ The Symbol Table
  symbtab : array [0..maxsymbt] of record
    name : rep_name;
    value: rep_value
  end;
  symbtabp: 0..maxsymbt

##routine;
  $ Message
  procedure error (m:message);
  begin
    writeln(output);
    writeln(output, linenumb:3, ' --> ERROR');
    write  (output,'         ');
    case  m  of
      undef_var:
        write(output, 'Undefined variable.');
      arith_overfl:
        write(output, 'Arithmetic overflow.');
      zero_divide:
        write(output, 'Zero division.');
      maxvar_exc:
        write(output, 'Allowed number of variables exceeded.')
    end;
    writeln(output)
  end; {error}

  $ Rep value
  procedure initun_value (var v:rep_value);
  begin
    v.def := false
  end; {initun_value}

  procedure init_value ( var v:rep_value; i:integer);
```

```
begin
  v.def := true;
  v.value := i
end; {init_value}

function undefined_value (v:rep_value): boolean;
begin
  undefined_value := not v.def
end; {undefined_value}

procedure add_value (var v1:rep_value; v2:rep_value);
begin
  v1.def := v1.def  and  v2.def;
  if  v1.def  then begin
        { Check for arithmetic overflow }
    if   (v1.value < 0) and (v2.value < 0)
      or (v1.value > 0) and (v2.value > 0)
        then v1.def := abs(v1.value) <= maxint - abs(v2.value);
    if  v1.def  then v1.value := v1.value + v2.value
    else error(arith_overfl)
  end
end; {add_value}

procedure subtract_value (var v1:rep_value; v2:rep_value);
begin
  if  v2.def  then v2.value := -v2.value;
  add_value( v1, v2)
end; {subtract_value}

procedure multiply_value (var v1:rep_value; v2:rep_value);
begin
  v1.def := v1.def  and  v2.def;
  if  v1.def  then begin
        { Check for arithmetic overflow }
    if (v2.value <> 0)
      then v1.def := abs(v1.value) <= maxint div abs(v2.value);
    if  v1.def  then v1.value := v1.value * v2.value
    else error(arith_overfl)
  end
end; {multiply_value}

procedure divide_value (var v1:rep_value; v2:rep_value);
begin
  v1.def := v1.def  and  v2.def;
  if  v1.def  then
    if (v2.value = 0) then begin
      error(zero_divide);
      v1.def := false
```

```
      end
      else vl.value := vl.value div v2.value
  end; {divide_value}


  procedure print_value (v:rep_value);
  begin
    if  v.def
      then write(output, v.value:5)
      else write(output, '?':5)
  end; {print_value}
```

$ The Symbol Table

```
  procedure add_symbtab (n:rep_name; v:rep_value);
  var i:0..maxsymbt;
  begin
    symbtab [symbtabp].name := n;
    i := 0;
    while (symbtab[i].name <> n)
      do i:=i+1;
    symbtab[i].value := v;
    if (i = symbtabp) then begin
      if (symbtabp = maxsymbt)
        then error(maxvar_exc)
        else symbtabp := symbtabp + 1
    end
  end; {add_symbtab}


  procedure get_symbtab (n:rep_name; var v:rep_value);
  var i:0..maxsymbt;
  begin
    with  symbtab[symbtabp]  do begin
      name := n;
      initun_value(value)
    end;
    i := 0;
    while (symbtab[i].name <> n)
      do i:=i+1;
    if (i = symbtabp) then error(undef_var);
    v := symbtab[i].value
  end; {get_symbtab}


  procedure print_symbtab;
  var i:0..maxsymbt;
  begin
    writeln(output);
    writeln(output,'SYMBOL TABLE');
    writeln(output,'************');
    for i:=0 to symbtabp-1 do
```

```
      with  symbtab [i]  do begin
         write(output, name:10, ' = ');
         print_value(value);
         writeln(output)
      end
   end {print_symbtab}

##prologue;
   $ The Symbol Table
      symbtabp := 0
         { first free entry in the symbol table }

##epilogue;
   $ The Symbol Table
      print_symbtab
```

5.4.4. One-Pass Interpreter

As it has been explained in section 5.4.2, the lexical analyser
will be integrated into the syntax-semantic analyser such that the
lexical analyser will override the read module of the syntax-
semantic analyser. For this reason, the lexical analyser program
module of section 5.4.3.1 must be turned into a procedure producing
the next attributed input symbol for the syntax-semantic analyser.
This is explained in section 5.4.4.1. The LILA input for the
syntax-semantic analyser, in which the lexical analyser overrides
the read module, is given in section 5.4.4.2.

5.4.4.1. The Lexical Analyser

In this section, the implementation of the lexical analyser in
the form of a procedure will be discussed. Each time the lexical
analyser is called, it will return the next input symbol for the
syntax-semantic analyser via the formal parameter 'outp'. The
interface between the lexical analyser and the syntax-semantic analyser is schematically illustrated below.

```
program synsem_analyser (input,output);
   ...
var inp : rep_syninp;
```

```
   ...
procedure lex_analyser (var outp:rep_syninp);
   ...
  var inp : record c:char end;
   ...
  procedure readin;
      ...
    get(input);
    if  eof(input)  then begin
      outp.c := chr(0);
      goto 9999
    end
    else inp.c := input^
      ...
  end; {readin}
   ...                              {prologue for the lexical analyser}
```

```
    if  eof(input)  then begin
      outp.c := chr(0);
      goto 9999
    end
    else inp.c := input^
      ...
```

```
    Produce an output symbol in outp from inp
```

```
end; {lex_analyser}
   ...
procedure readin;
   ...
  lex_analyser(inp)
   ...
end; {readin}
   ...                              {prologue for the syntax-semantic analyser}
```

```
    readin
```

```
    Produce the results of the print instructions
```

```
      ...
end.
```

The LILA input to produce the lexical analyser in the form of a procedure, differs from the LILA input to produce the lexical analyser program module, in the following ways :

1) The global options 'procedure' and 'name' are used in order to produce a procedure, which is called 'lex_analyser'. The formal parameters of the generated procedures are specified in the parameter part of globalinfo.

2) The syntax rule for program is changed such that it defines the lexical structure of exactly one input symbol for the syntax-semantic analyser.

3) The set of characters which can follow a lexically analysed input symbol for the syntax-semantic analyser is now explicitly defined in the follow part of the LILA input for the lexical analyser.

4) The read module is user-defined, because the input head of the lexical analyser must be initialized by <u>copying</u> the contents of the buffer variable ('input^') into the input head 'inp'. In the default read module, the input head is initialized with the <u>next</u> input symbol.

5) The write module is user-defined, It must be a dummy routine, since the generated output symbol should not be written on an output file.

6) The error module is user-defined; this module will generate a special symbol 'error' indicating that an error at the lexical level has been encountered.

```
$$$$$$$$$$$$$$$$$$$$$$$$$$$$$$$$$$$$$$$$$$$$$$$$$$$$$$$$$$$$$$$$$$$$$$$$$$$$$$$$$$$$$$$
$    LILA INPUT                                                                  $
$                                                                               $
$        Interpreter for Arithmetic expressions : Lexical Analyser              $
$$$$$$$$$$$$$$$$$$$$$$$$$$$$$$$$$$$$$$$$$$$$$$$$$$$$$$$$$$$$$$$$$$$$$$$$$$$$$$$$$$$$$$$


###options
```

```
  let,
  procedure,
  name(lex_analyser);
```

###inputvocabulary   rep(char);

| " " = 32 | "(" = 40 | ")" = 41 | "*" = 42 | "+" = 43 | "-" = 45 |
| "/" = 47 | ";" = 59 | "=" = 61 | | | |

| "0" = 48 | "1" = 49 | "2" = 50 | "3" = 51 | "4" = 52 | "5" = 53 |
| "6" = 54 | "7" = 55 | "8" = 56 | "9" = 57 | | |

"a" = 97	"b" = 98	"c" = 99	"d" =100	"e" =101	"f" =102
"g" =103	"h" =104	"i" =105	"j" =106	"k" =107	"l" =108
"m" =109	"n" =110	"o" =111	"p" =112	"q" =113	"r" =114
"s" =115	"t" =116	"u" =117	"v" =118	"w" =119	"x" =120
"y" =121	"z" =122				

###outputvocabulary rep(char);

  [identifier] = 2 : rep_name

  [constant] = 3 : rep_value

  [print] = 4   [value] = 5   [of] = 6

  [(] = 40   [)] = 41   [*] = 42   [+] = 43   [-] = 45
  [/] = 47   [;] = 59   [=] = 61

  [error] = 7

###syntax;

$ <u>Definition of the lexical structure of an input symbol</u>
  ##rule;
    <program> =
      " "*
        (<identifier keyword>
        | <constant>
        | <delimiter>
)

$ <u>Analysis of an identifier or a keyword</u>
  ##rule;
    <identifier keyword> =

```
      init_name  <letter>
        ( add_name  ( <letter> | <digit> )  )*
      out_idenkey

  ##var;
    nb_char : 0..maxint

  ##action;
    #init_name;
      @[identifier] := '         ';
      @[identifier] [1] := inp.c;
      nb_char:= 1

    #add_name;
      nb_char := nb_char + 1;
      if (nb_char <= idlength)
        then @[identifier] [nb_char] := inp.c

    #out_idenkey;
      if (nb_char > idlength) then error(iden_trunc);
             if ( @[identifier] = 'value  ') then out(%[value])
      else if ( @[identifier] = 'print  ') then out(%[print])
      else if ( @[identifier] = 'of     ') then out(%[of])
      else out(%[identifier])

$ Analysis of a constant
  ##rule;
    <constant> =
      init_value
        ( value  <digit> )+
      out_constant

  ##var;
    value : integer

  ##action;
    #init_value;
      value := 0

    #value;
      if (value <> -1) then
        if (value + 1) <= (maxint div 10)
          then value := value*10 + (ord(inp.c) - ord('0'))
          else begin
            error(maxconst_exc);
            value := -1
          end
```

```
        #out_constant;
          if (value = -1)
            then initun_value(@[constant])
            else init_value(@[constant], value);
          out(%[constant])
```

$ Analysis of a delimiter
  ##rule;
    <delimiter> =
      out_delimiter
        ("*" | "/" | "+" | "-" | "(" | ")" | "=" | ";")

    ##action;
      #out_delimiter;
        out(inp.c)

$ Definition of a letter
  ##rule;
    <letter> =
        "a" | "b" | "c" | "d" | "e" | "f" | "g" | "h" | "i"
      | "j" | "k" | "l" | "m" | "n" | "o" | "p" | "q" | "r"
      | "s" | "t" | "u" | "v" | "w" | "x" | "y" | "z"

$ Definition of a digit
  ##rule;
    <digit> =
      "0" | "1" | "2" | "3" | "4" | "5" | "6" | "7" | "8" | "9"

###globalinfo;

  ##parameter;
    var outp: rep_syninp

  ##var;
    inp : record
            c:char
          end

  ##prologue;
    if eof(input) then begin
      outp.c := chr(0); $$ virtual end-of-file symbol
      goto 9999
    end
    else inp.c := input^

###follow;
```
```

```
"(" ")" "*" "+" "-" "/" ";" "=" " "

"0" "1" "2" "3" "4" "5" "6" "7" "8" "9"

"a" "b" "c" "d" "e" "f" "g" "h" "i" "j"
"k" "l" "m" "n" "o" "p" "q" "r" "s" "t"
"u" "v" "w" "x" "y" "z"

"end-of-file"


###readroutine;

  if eoln(input) then linenumb := linenumb + 1;
  get(input);
  if  eof(input)  then begin
    outp.c := chr(0);   $$ virtual end-of-file symbol
    goto 9999
  end
  else inp.c := input^


###writeroutine;

  $ Dummy Routine


###errorroutine;

  error(inv_char);
  outp.c := %[error];
  readin;
  goto 9999
```

Notice that, since the lexical analyser is a subroutine of the syntax-semantic analyser, it can access the global information (constants, types, variables and routines) of the syntax-semantic analyser.

5.4.4.2. The Syntax-semantic Analyser

```
$$$$$$$$$$$$$$$$$$$$$$$$$$$$$$$$$$$$$$$$$$$$$$$$$$$$$$$$$$$$$$$$$$$$$$$$$$$$$$$$$$$$$$$
$   LILA INPUT                                                                    $
$                                                                                 $
$      Interpreter for Arithmetic expressions : Syntax-semantic Analyser          $
$$$$$$$$$$$$$$$$$$$$$$$$$$$$$$$$$$$$$$$$$$$$$$$$$$$$$$$$$$$$$$$$$$$$$$$$$$$$$$$$$$$$$$$
```

```
###inputvocabulary rep(char);

  "identifier" =  2 : rep_name

  "constant" = 3 : rep_value

  "print" = 4    "value" = 5    "of" = 6

  "(" = 40    ")" = 41    "*" = 42    "+" = 43    "-" = 45
  "/" = 47    ";" = 59    "=" = 61

  "error" = 7


###syntax;
```

$ Definition of a program
```
  ##rule;
    <program> =
      <statement>+
```

$ Analysis of a print statement or an assignment statement
```
  ##rule;
    <statement> =
      ( "print" "value" "of" <expression>      print
      | "identifier" "=" <expression>     assign
      )  ";"

    ##action;
      #print;
        print_value(@<expression>1);
        writeln(output)

      #assign;
        add_symbtab( @"identifier", @<expression>2)
```

$ Calculation of the value of an expression
```
  ##rule;
    <expression> =
      <term>  pass_te
        ( "+" <term> add
        | "-" <term> subtract
        )*

    ##attribute;
      rep_value

    ##action;
```

```
        #pass_te;
          @<expression> := @<term>1

        #add;
          add_value( @<expression>, @<term>2)

        #subtract;
          subtract_value( @<expression>, @<term>3)

$ Calculation of the value of a term
  ##rule;
    <term> =
      <factor>   pass_ft
        ( "*" <factor> multiply
        | "/" <factor> divide
        )*

  ##attribute;
    rep_value

  ##action;
    #pass_ft;
      @<term> := @<factor>1

    #multiply;
      multiply_value( @<term>, @<factor>2)

    #divide;
      divide_value( @<term>, @<factor>3)

$ Calculation of the value of a factor
  ##rule;
    <factor> =
        "identifier"   identifier
      | "constant"   constant
      | "(" <expression> ")"   pass_ef

  ##attribute;
    rep_value

  ##action;
    #identifier;
      get_symbtab( @"identifier", @<factor>)

    #constant;
      @<factor> := @"constant"

    #pass_ef;
```

```
        @<factor> := @<expression>


###globalinfo;

  ##parameter;
    input, output

  ##const;
    $ The Symbol Table
      idlength =   8;
      maxsymbt = 100

  ##type;
    $ Message
      message = ( undef_var, arith_overfl, zero_divide, iden_trunc,
        maxconst_exc, inv_char, maxvar_exc, end_of_prog);

    $ Rep Value
      rep_value = record
        case  def:boolean  of
          true : ( value:integer);
          false: ( )
      end;

    $ The Symbol Table
      rep_name = packed array [1..idlength] of char;

    $ Lexical Analyser
      nb_attr = 1..2;
      rep_syninp = record
        c : char;
        a : record
              case nb:nb_attr of
                1: (rep_name : rep_name);
                2: (rep_value:rep_value)
            end
      end

  ##var;
    $ The Symbol Table
      symbtab : array [0..maxsymbt] of record
        name : rep_name;
        value: rep_value
      end;
      symbtabp: 0..maxsymbt;

    $ Lexical Analyser
```

```
    inp : rep_syninp;
    linenumb : integer

##routine;
  $ Message
    procedure error (m:message);
    begin
      writeln(output);
      writeln(output, linenumb:3, ' --> ERROR');
      write  (output,'        ');
      case  m  of
        undef_var:
          write(output, 'Undefined variable.');
        arith_overfl:
          write(output, 'Arithmetic overflow.');
        zero_divide:
          write(output, 'Zero division.');
        iden_trunc:
          write(output, 'Identifier trunctated to ',idlength:1,'characters');
        maxconst_exc:
          write(output, 'Constant exceeds maximum value.');
        inv_char:
          write(output, 'Invalid character.');
        maxvar_exc:
          write(output, 'Allowed number of variables exceeded.');
        end_of_prog:
          write(output, 'End of program reached, before end of file.')
      end;
      writeln(output)
    end; {error}


  $ Rep value
    procedure initun_value (var v:rep_value);
    begin
      v.def := false
    end; {initun_value}

    procedure init_value ( var v:rep_value; i:integer);
    begin
      v.def := true;
      v.value := i
    end; {init_value}

    function undefined_value (v:rep_value): boolean;
    begin
      undefined_value := not v.def
    end; {undefined_value}
```

```
procedure add_value (var v1:rep_value; v2:rep_value);
begin
  v1.def := v1.def  and  v2.def;
  if  v1.def  then begin
         { Check for arithmetic overflow }
     if   (v1.value < 0) and (v2.value < 0)
       or (v1.value > 0) and (v2.value > 0)
         then v1.def := abs(v1.value) <= maxint - abs(v2.value);
     if  v1.def  then v1.value := v1.value + v2.value
     else error(arith_overfl)
   end
end; {add_value}

procedure subtract_value (var v1:rep_value; v2:rep_value);
begin
  if  v2.def  then v2.value := -v2.value;
  add_value( v1, v2)
end; {subtract_value}

procedure multiply_value (var v1:rep_value; v2:rep_value);
begin
  v1.def := v1.def  and  v2.def;
  if  v1.def  then begin
         { Check for arithmetic overflow }
     if (v2.value <> 0)
       then v1.def := abs(v1.value) <= maxint div abs(v2.value);
     if  v1.def  then v1.value := v1.value * v2.value
     else error(arith_overfl)
   end
end; {multiply_value}

procedure divide_value (var v1:rep_value; v2:rep_value);
begin
  v1.def := v1.def  and  v2.def;
  if  v1.def  then
    if (v2.value = 0) then begin
      error(zero_divide);
      v1.def := false
    end
    else v1.value := v1.value div v2.value
end; {divide_value}

procedure print_value (v:rep_value);
begin
  if  v.def  then write(output, v.value:5)
  else write(output, '?':5)
end; {print_value}
```

```
$ The Symbol Table
  procedure add_symbtab (n:rep_name; v:rep_value);
  var i:0..maxsymbt;
  begin
    symbtab [symbtabp].name := n;
    i := 0;
    while (symbtab[i].name <> n)
      do i:=i+1;
    symbtab[i].value := v;
    if (i = symbtabp) then begin
      if (symbtabp = maxsymbt)
        then error(maxvar_exc)
        else symbtabp := symbtabp + 1
    end
  end; {add_symbtab}

  procedure get_symbtab (n:rep_name; var v:rep_value);
  var i:0..maxsymbt;
  begin
    with symbtab[symbtabp] do begin
      name := n;
      initun_value(value)
    end;
    i := 0;
    while (symbtab[i].name <> n)
      do i:=i+1;
    if (i = symbtabp) then error(undef_var);
    v := symbtab[i].value
  end; {get_symbtab}

  procedure print_symbtab;
  var i:0..maxsymbt;
  begin
    writeln(output);
    writeln(output,'SYMBOL TABLE');
    writeln(output,'************');
    for i:=0 to symbtabp-1 do
      with symbtab [i] do begin
        write(output, name:10, ' = ');
        print_value(value);
        writeln(output)
      end
  end {print_symbtab}

$ Lexical Analysis
  $$$    Include the definition of the procedure 'lex_analyser',
  $$$ as it is produced by LILA, at this point.
```

```
##prologue;
   $ The Symbol Table
     symbtabp := 0;
        { first free entry in the symbol table }

   $ Lexical Analysis
     linenumb := 1;
     readin

##epilogue;
   $ The Symbol Table
     print_symbtab;
```

```
###readroutine;

   lex_analyser(inp)
```

5.4.5. Example

The execution of the interpreter for arithmetic expressions is illustrated below. The interpretation is performed on a 16-bit machine, which means that the maximum value for an integer is equal to 32767.

```
   s0 = 4000;
   a  =   10;
   t  =   75;
   print value of  (a/2*t + v0)*t + s0;

       4 --> ERROR
           Undefined variable.
         ?

   v0 =   15;
   print value of  (a/2*t + v0)*t + s0;

       6 --> ERROR
           Arithmetic overflow.
         ?

   s0 = 0;
   print value of  (a/2*t + v0)*t + s0;
```

29250

```
SYMBOL TABLE
************
   s0      =     0
   a       =    10
   t       =    75
   v0      =    15
```

5.5. <u>Pico Algol</u>.

In this example, the design and implementation of a compiler for Pico Algol will be discussed. Although Pico Algol is a small (pico) subset of an Algol-like language, this case study is representative as an illustration of storage allocation and address calculation in language processors. This example also illustrates how semantic error recovery is implemented in a systematic and reliable way. Syntactic error recovery and the interaction between syntactic and semantic error recovery is discussed in section 6.

The ECF syntax for Pico Algol is given below. Notice the difference between the <u>variable</u> declarations "integer" "iden" and "boolean" "iden" on the one hand, and the <u>constant</u> declarations "integer" "iden" "=" <expression> and "boolean" "iden" "=" <expression>, on the other hand.

```
<program> =
  "begin"
    ( <declaration> ";" )*
    <statement> ( ";" <statement> )*
  "end"

<declaration> =
    "integer" "iden"
      ( & | "=" <expression> )
  | "boolean" "iden"
      ( & | "=" <expression> )

<statement> =
    <compound statement>
  | <print statement>
  | <if statement>
  | <for statement>
  | <assign statement>

<compound statement> =
  "do"
    <statement> ( ";" <statement> )*
  "od"

<assign statement> =
  "iden" ":=" <expression>
```

```
<print statement> =
  "print" <expression>

<if statement> =
  "if" <expression>
    "then" <statement>
    "else" <statement>
  "fi"

<for statement> =
  "for" "iden"
    "from" <expression>
    "to" <expression>
    <compound statement>

<expression> =
  <term>
    ( "+" <term>
    | "-" <term>
    )*

<term> =
  <factor>
    ( "*" <factor>
    | "/" <factor>
    )*

<factor> =
    "iden"
  | "intct"
  | "true"
  | "false"
  | "(" <expression> ")"
```

An example of a Pico Algol program calculating some of the Fibonacci numbers is given below. Obviously, a more compact form of the program is possible. This program is written in such a way that the Pico Algol for statements and if statements are used in a nested way. It will also serve as an illustration of code generation, see later.

```
'begin'
  'integer' fib1;  'integer' fib2;
  'integer' k;
  'integer' number = 10;
  'boolean' switch;

  fib1 := 1;  fib2 := 2;
  'print' 1;  'print' 2;
  switch := 'true';

  'for' k 'from' 1 'to' number 'do'
    'if' switch
      'then' 'do'
        fib1 := fib1 + fib2;
        'print' fib1;
        switch := 'false'
      'od'
      'else' 'do'
        fib2 := fib2 + fib1;
        'print' fib2;
        switch := 'true'
      'od'
    'fi'
  'od'
'end'
```

5.5.1. The general structure of the Pico Algol compiler.

The compiler for Pico Algol is divided into two modules: a portable module, in which machine-dependent features are localized, and a machine-dependent module. The former will translate a Pico Algol program into an intermediate language; a program in this language can be executed on a hypothetical machine, called the 3-Address Machine. The latter part will translate a program for the 3-Address Machine into a (assembler) program for a real machine. In this example, the Intel 8085 microprocessor has been chosen. The general structure of the Pico Algol compiler is illustrated in Fig. 5.5.

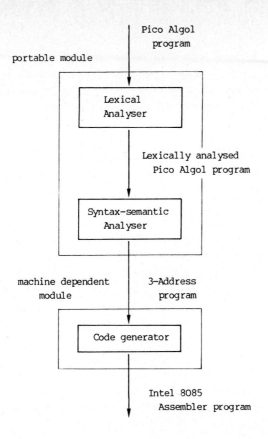

Fig 5.5.

Before discussing the implementation of the lexical analyser and the syntax-semantic analyser, we will study the structure of the 3-Address Machine in more detail.

5.5.2. The architecture of the 3-Address Machine.

The 3-Address Machine consists of a memory and a register PC
(Program Counter). The memory consists of two parts: a CODE part
containing the 3-Address instructions, and a DATA part containing
the data on which the 3-Address instructions operate.

The 3-Address instructions in the CODE part can only be reached
through the register PC, containing the address of the next instruction to be executed. Some 3-Address intructions may change the contents of the program counter.

The DATA part consists of 3 separate spaces: an idenspace, a
workspace and a table of constants. These spaces need not be con-
tiguous. The idenspace will contain the values associated with Pico
Algol identifiers (variable identifiers and constant identifiers).
The workspace will contain intermediate values, resulting from expression evaluation. The table of constants will contain the values
of all the constants used in the source program.

At compile-time, a value in the DATA part will be described by
means of two attributes: type and access.

-   The type attribute indicates how the addressed memory units
    must be interpreted. In our simple machine, this attribute
    will indicate whether an integer value (int), a boolean value
    (bool), a reference to an integer value (refint) or a refer-
    ence to a boolean value (refbool) is referred to.

-   The access attribute will indicate where the value can be
    reached during execution of the program. This specification
    consists of the name of the space in which the value resides,
    a level field indicating the number of indirections to be done
    in order to reach the value (in our simple machine there is
    only level 0 and level 1) and an offset within that space.

Examples of descriptions of values

- int (idenspace, 1, 10)

    The value is the contents of relative address 10 in the idenspace. This contents is interpreted as an integer.

- refint (idenspace, 0, 100)

    The value is the relative address 100 in the idenspace.

- refint (idenspace, 1, 100)

    The value is the contents of relative address 100 in the idenspace. This contents is interpreted as an address of a location.

- bool (worksp, 1, 1000)

    The value is the contents of the relative address 1000 in the workspace. This contents is interpreted as a boolean.

- undefined ( )

    An error has occured during the calculation of the description of the value.

The type and access description method in the Pico Algol compiler is a systematic and general method, that lends itself to a very reliable semantic error recovery. The description method has been used in an Algol 68 compiler (see Branquart et al. [1976]).

The 3-Address Instructions

The 3-Address instructions are divided into arithmetic operations, operations to change the flow of control and a print operation.

a) Arithmetic operations.

PLUS	type_left type_right	access_left	access_right	access_result
MINUS	type_left type_right	access_left	access_right	access_result
TIMES	type_left type_right	access_left	access_right	access_result
DIVIDE	type_left type_right	access_left	access_right	access_result
ASSIGN	type_right	access_left	access_right	
INCR	type	access		

b) Operations to change the flow of control.

JUMP	label		co	unconditional jump	co
JUMPP	label	access	co	jump if positive	co
JUMPF	label	access	co	jump if false	co
LABDEF	label		co	label definition	co

c) Print operation.

PRINT	type	access

5.5.3.   The lexical Analyser.

The lexical analyser will transform sequences of input characters into attributed input symbols for the syntax-semantic analyser. These input symbols are keywords, identifiers, integer constants and delimiters.

The LILA input to produce the attributed input symbols for the syntax-semantic analyser is given in section 5.5.3.2. In order to understand the implementation of the lexical analyser, the data structures used in it, are briefly discussed in section 5.5.3.1.

5.5.3.1.   Data structures in the lexical analyser of Pico Algol

In the lexical analysis of a Pico Algol program, the following data structures will be used:

-   rep keyname: description of the data structure for the names of Pico Algol keywords.

-   message: description of the data structure for error messages on the semantic level.

Now follows a brief description of the operations (procedures and functions) defined on the data structures of types 'rep_keyname' and 'message'.

rep_keyname

- <u>type</u> rep_keyname = <u>packed</u> <u>array</u> [1..keylength] <u>of</u> char;

- <u>function</u> key_code (n:rep_keyname): integer;
    The internal code, as it is specified in the outputvocabulary, of a keyword with name N is returned. If no such keyword exists, the constant 'max_keycode' is returned.

message

- <u>type</u> message = (inv_keyword, iden_trunc, maxint_exc);

- <u>procedure</u> error (m:message);
    Print the message M on the standard file 'output'.

5.5.3.2. <u>Implementation of the lexical analysis of Pico Algol</u>.

The LILA input for the lexical analyser of the Pico Algol compiler is given below. Notice that the ECF syntax rules defining the lexical structure of identifiers and constants, do not satisfy the ELL(1) conditions. The ELL(1) transducer generated by LILA will perform correctly however, since all the letters and digits (digits) not separated from one another, are considered to be part of the same identifier (constant). Therefore, the <u>let</u> option is specified in the LILA input, indicating that the lexical analyser has to be generated even if its translation syntax does not satisfy the ELL(1) conditions.

```
$$$$$$$$$$$$$$$$$$$$$$$$$$$$$$$$$$$$$$$$$$$$$$$$$$$$$$$$$$$$$$$$$$$$$$$$$$$$$$$$$$$$$$$$$$$
$    LILA INPUT                                                                      $
$                                                                                    $
$       Compiler for Pico Algol : Lexical Analyser                                   $
$$$$$$$$$$$$$$$$$$$$$$$$$$$$$$$$$$$$$$$$$$$$$$$$$$$$$$$$$$$$$$$$$$$$$$$$$$$$$$$$$$$$$$$$$$$
```

```
###options let;


###inputvocabulary  rep(char), file(input);

$ Delimiters
   " " = 32    "'" = 39    "(" = 40    ")" = 41    "*" = 42    "+" = 43
   "-" = 45    "/" = 47    ":" = 58    ";" = 59    "=" = 61

$ Digits
   "0" = 48    "1" = 49    "2" = 50    "3" = 51    "4" = 52    "5" = 53
   "6" = 54    "7" = 55    "8" = 56    "9" = 57

$ Letters
   "a" = 97    "b" = 98    "c" = 99    "d" =100    "e" =101    "f" =102
   "g" =103    "h" =104    "i" =105    "j" =106    "k" =107    "l" =108
   "m" =109    "n" =110    "o" =111    "p" =112    "q" =113    "r" =114
   "s" =115    "t" =116    "u" =117    "v" =118    "w" =119    "x" =120
   "y" =121    "z" =122


###outputvocabulary  rep(integer);

$ Keywords
   [begin]   = 2     [end]     = 3
   [boolean] = 4     [integer] = 5
   [true]    = 6     [false]   = 7
   [print]   = 8     [if]      = 9
   [then]    =10     [else]    =11
   [fi]      =12     [do]      =13
   [od]      =14     [for]     =15
   [from]    =16     [to]      =17

$ Delimiters
   [(] = 40    [)] = 41    [*] = 42    [+] = 43    [-] = 45    [/] = 47
   [:=]= 48    [;] = 59    [=] = 61

$ Integer Constant
   [intct] = 62 : integer
```

$ Identifier
  [iden] = 63 : rep_name

       $ Notice that the codes of the keywords must be identical to the
       $ corresponding indexes in the table of   keyword names 'keytab'
       $ (see prologue of the LILA input). Furthermore, the codes of the
       $ delimiters (except for the assignment operator) must be identical
       $ to the codes of the the corresponding delimiters in the input
       $ vocabulary.

###syntax;

$ Definition of the lexical structure of a Pico Algol program
  ##rule;
    <program> =
      (<keyword>
      | <identifier>
      | <constant>
      | <delimiter>
)*

$ Analysis of a keyword
  ##rule;
    <keyword> =
      "'" init_name
        (add_name <letter>)*
      "'" out_keyword

    ##var;
      key_name: rep_keyname;
      nb_char : integer;
      code   : integer;

    ##action;
      #init_name;
        key_name := '   ';
        nb_char := 0

      #add_name;
        nb_char := nb_char + 1;
        if (nb_char <= keylength)
          then key_name [nb_char] := inp.c

      #out_keyword;
                $ If the character string enclosed between quotes is not
                $ a Pico Algol keyword, an error message is issued and the
                $ lexical analysis will stop.

```
         if (nb_char <= keylength)
           then code := key_code(key_name)
           else code := max_keycode;
         if (code = max_keycode) then begin
           error(inv_keyword);
           goto 9999    $ STOP
         end
         else out(code)
```

$ Analysis of an identifier
  ##rule;
    <identifier> =
      init_name <letter>
        (add_name (<letter> | <digit>))*
      out_identifier

    ##var;
      nb_char : integer

    ##action;
      #init_name;
        @[iden] := '   ';
        @[iden] [1] := inp.c;
        nb_char := 1

      #add_name;
        nb_char := nb_char + 1;
        if (nb_char <= idlength)
          then @[iden] [nb_char] := inp.c

      #out_identifier;
        if (nb_char > idlength) then error(iden_trunc);
        out(%[iden])

$ Analysis of a constant
  ##rule;
    <constant> =
      init_val
        (val <digit>)+
      out_intct

    ##action;
      #init_val;
        @[intct] := 0

      #val;
        if (@[intct] <> -1) then
          if (@[intct] + 1) <= (maxint div 10)
```
```

```
        then @[intct] := @[intct]*10 + (ord(inp.c) - ord('0'))
        else begin
          error(maxint_exc);
                 $ Semantic error recovery: whenever the value of a
                 $ constant exceeds 'maxint', it will be set to -1.
          @[intct] := -1
        end

    #out_intct;
      out(%[intct])
```

$ Analysis of a delimiter
  ##rule;
    <delimiter> =
        out_delimiter
          ("+" | "-" | "*" | "/" | "=" | "(" | ")" | ";")
      | ":" "=" out_assign
      | " "+

  ##action;
    #out_delimiter;
      out(ord(inp.c))

    #out_assign;
      out(%[:=])

$ Definition of a letter
  ##rule;
    <letter> =
        "a" | "b" | "c" | "d" | "e" | "f" | "g" | "h" | "i"
      | "j" | "k" | "l" | "m" | "n" | "o" | "p" | "q" | "r"
      | "s" | "t" | "u" | "v" | "w" | "x" | "y" | "z"

$ Definition of a digit
  ##rule;
    <digit> =
      "0" | "1" | "2" | "3" | "4" | "5" | "6" | "7" | "8" | "9"

###globalinfo;

  ##parameter;
    input, output, outfile

  ##const;
    $ rep keyname
      keylength = 7;
      min_keycode = 2; $$ smallest code in the set of keywords.

```
      max_keycode =18;     $$ largest code in the set of keywords + 1.

  $ rep name
      idlength = 8

##type;
  $ rep keyname
      rep_keyname = packed array [1..keylength] of char;

  $ message
      message = (inv_keyword, iden_trunc, maxint_exc);

  $ rep name
      rep_name = packed array [1..idlength] of char

##var;
  $ rep keyname
      keytab : array [ min_keycode..max_keycode ] of rep_keyname

##routine;
  $ rep keyname
      function key_code (n:rep_keyname): integer;
      var i : min_keycode..max_keycode;
      begin
        keytab[ max_keycode ] := n;
        i := min_keycode;
        while (keytab[i] <> n)
          do i := succ(i);
        key_code := i
      end; {key_code}

  $ message
      procedure error (m:message);
      begin
        writeln(output);
        write(output, linenumb:4, ' *** ERROR *** : ');
        case  m  of
          inv_keyword:
            write('Invalid keyword used.');
          iden_trunc:
            write('Identifier truncated to',idlength:2,' characters.');
          maxint_exc:
            write('Constant exceeds maximum value.')
        end;
        writeln(output)
      end {error}

##prologue;
```

```
$ rep keyname
  keytab[ 2] := 'begin  ';   keytab[ 3] := 'end     ';
  keytab[ 4] := 'boolean';   keytab[ 5] := 'integer';
  keytab[ 6] := 'true   ';   keytab[ 7] := 'false  ';
  keytab[ 8] := 'print  ';   keytab[ 9] := 'if      ';
  keytab[10] := 'then   ';   keytab[11] := 'else   ';
  keytab[12] := 'fi     ';   keytab[13] := 'do      ';
  keytab[14] := 'od     ';   keytab[15] := 'for     ';
  keytab[16] := 'from   ';   keytab[17] := 'to      '
```

5.5.4. The Syntax-semantic Analyser.

The syntax-semantic analyser of the Pico Algol compiler will
translate a lexically analysed Pico Algol program into an equivalent
program for the 3-Address Machine. The LILA input producing the 3-
Address instructions, is given in section 5.5.4.2. In order to
understand the implementation of the syntax-semantic analyser, the
data structures used in it, are briefly discussed in section
5.5.4.1.

5.5.4.1. Data structures in the syntax-semantic analyser.

In the syntax-semantic analysis of a Pico Algol program, the following data structures will be used:

- rep type: a data structure for the type attribute of a 3-
  Address value.

- rep access: a data structure for the access attribute of a 3-
  Address value.

- rep description: a data structure for the compile-time
  description of a 3-Address value.

- rep label: a data structure for the label attribute of a 3-
  Address instruction.

- idenspace: a data structure to set up the idenspace.

- <u>workspace</u>: a data structure to set up the workspace.

- <u>constab</u>: a data structure to set up the table of constants.

- <u>symbtab</u>: a data structure to hold information about the identifiers (variable identifiers and constant identifiers) in the
  Pico Algol program.

- <u>message</u>: a data structure for handling error messages on the
  semantic level.

For each data structure, a brief description of the operations
(procedures and functions) defined on it, is given below. All these
data structures and their operations are defined in the globalinfo
part of the LILA input for the syntax-semantic analyser.

rep_type

The type attribute of a value dealt with in the Pico Algol program, describes at compile-time <u>how</u> the sequence of basic address-
able units (bau's) must be interpreted at run-time. In our simple
machine, a value is either of type int, bool, refint, refbool or undefined. The data structure 'rep_type' is described below.

- <u>type</u> rep_type = (int, bool, refint, refbool, undefined);

- <u>procedure</u> deref_type (<u>var</u> t:rep_type);
  Dereferencing of a type: the new type in T will become the
  type of the contents of a value, described by the old type in T.
  If the old type in T is not a locational type, i.e. refint or
  refbool, an error message will be produced and the new type in T
  will become the undefined type.

- <u>function</u> size_type (t:rep_type): integer;
  The number of bau's, needed to store a value of type T in the
  Intel 8085 microprocessor, is returned. This operation illustrates how machine-dependent features are localized in the portable part of the Pico Algol compiler.

- <u>procedure</u> print_type (t:rep_type);
    The type T is printed in a readable form on the standard file
    'output'.

rep_access

The access attribute of a value dealt with in the Pico Algol program, describes at compile-time <u>where</u> the value can be reached at
run-time. The access specification consists of the space in which
the value resides, the number of indirections to be applied in order
to reach the value and an offset within the space. The data structure 'rep_access' is described below.

- <u>type</u>
    rep_space = (idensp, worksp, constab);
    rep_level = 0..1;
    rep_offset= 0..maxint;
    rep_access= <u>record</u>
      <u>case</u> def:boolean <u>of</u>
        true :
        (space : rep_space;
         level : rep_level;
         offset: rep_offset);
        false : () $ undefined access
      <u>end</u>;

- <u>procedure</u> init_access
      (<u>var</u> a:rep_access; s:rep_space; l:rep_level; o:rep_offset);
    Initialize the access in A with [S, L, O].

- <u>procedure</u> deref_access (<u>var</u> a:rep_access);
    Dereferencing of an access: the new access in A will become
    the access of the contents of a value, described by the old ac-
    cess in A.

- <u>procedure</u> print_access (a:rep_access);
    The access A is printed in a readable form on the standard
    file 'output'.

rep_description

   As it has been described above, the Pico Algol compiler will as-
sociate with each value in the source program a type attribute and
an access attribute.   Type and access attributes constitute a
compile-time description of a 3-Address (run-time) value.   The data
structure 'rep_description' is discussed below.

- <u>type</u>
      rep_description = <u>record</u>
        typ : rep_type;
        acc : rep_access
      <u>end</u>;

- <u>procedure</u> deref_description (<u>var</u> d:rep_description);
      Dereferencing of a description : the new description in D will
   become the description of the contents of a value, described by
   the old description in D.   If the old description in D does not
   describe a locational value, an error message will be produced.
   In this case, the type and access attributes of the new description in D will become the undefined type and the undefined access, respectively.

- <u>procedure</u> coerce_description (<u>var</u> d:rep_description; t:rep_type);
      Coercion (type conversion) of a description : the new descrip-
   tion in D will become the description of the T coercion of a
   value described by the old description in D.   If the coercion is
   not allowed, an error message will be produced and the type and
   access attributes of the new description in D will become the undefined type and the undefined access, respectively.

Examples of coercions

<u>old D</u>   <u>T</u>   <u>new D</u>

(refint,(idensp,0,100))   int   (int,(idensp,1,100))
(refint,(idensp,0,100))   refint   (refint,(idensp,0,100))
(refint,(idensp,0,100))   bool   (undefined,( ))
(refint,(idensp,0,100))   undefined   (undefined,( ))

```
(int,(worksp,1,101))      int        (int,(worksp,1,101))
(int,(worksp,1,101))      bool       (undefined,( ))
(undefined,( ))           int        (undefined,( ))
(undefined,( ))           undefined  (undefined,( ))
```

rep_label

A label in a 3-Address Program is a symbolic name for the address of an instruction. The data structure 'rep_label' is described below.

- __type__ rep_label = 0..maxint;

- __function__ unique_label : rep_label;
    Create a new (unique) label value.

idenspace

Idenspace is a run-time space. However, the syntax-semantic analyser determines the address calculation in the idenspace; i.e., it will allocate a particular sequence of bau's in the idenspace for each value associated with a Pico Algol identifier. The data structure 'idenspace' is described below.

- __var__ idenp : rep_offset;

- __function__ idensp_loc (t:rep_type): rep_offset;
    Reserve an appropriate sequence of bau's in the idenspace, to contain a run-time value of type T. The address of the first bau of the storage for that value is returned.

workspace

Workspace is a run-time space. The syntax-semantic analyser determines the address calculation in the workspace; i.e., it will allocate a particular sequence of bau's in the workspace for each intermediate value, resulting from expression evaluation. The data structure 'workspace' is described below.

- <u>var</u> workp : rep_offset;

- <u>function</u> worksp_loc (t:rep_type): rep_offset;
     Reserve an appropriate sequence of bau's in the workspace, to
contain a run-time value of type T. The address of the first bau
of the storage for that value is returned.

constab

     Constab is a run-time space. The syntax-semantic analyser deter-
mines the address calculation in the table of constants; i.e., it
will allocate a particular sequence of bau's in the table of constants for each constant dealt with in the Pico Algol program. The
values of the constants will be passed from the syntax-semantic analyser to the code generator by means of the file 'value_file'. They
will provide for the appropriate initialization of the table of constants at run-time. The data structure 'constab' is described
below.

- <u>type</u>
     rep_value = <u>record</u>
        <u>case</u> typ:rep_type <u>of</u>
           int : (ival:integer);
           bool: (bval:boolean)
        <u>end</u>;

- <u>var</u> constp : rep_offset;
     value_file : <u>file</u> <u>of</u> rep_value;

- <u>function</u> constb_loc (t:rep_type; v:rep_value): rep_offset;
     Reserve an appropriate sequence of bau's in the table of con-
stants, to contain a run-time value of type T. The address of
the first bau of the storage for that value is returned. Furthermore, the value V of the constant is written on 'value_file'.

symbol table

    During the translation of a Pico Algol program, the compiler will set up a table, containing information about the Pico Algol identif- iers. After the syntax-semantic analysis of an identifier declara- tion, this information consists of the identifier and of the description of the value associated with it. The data structure 'symbol table' is described below.

- const maxsymbt = 100;

- var
    symbtab : array [0..maxsymbt] of record
     name : rep_name;
     desc : rep_description
    end;
    symbtabp: 0..maxsymbt;

- procedure add_symbt (n:rep_name; d:rep_description);
    Add the pair (N,D) to the symbol table. Error messages will be produced if a pair with name N is already in the symbol table or if a table overflow occurs.

- procedure search_symbt (n:rep_name; var d:rep_description);
    Return the description D of a pair with name N. If no such pair exists, an error message will be produced.

- procedure print_symbt;
    Print the contents of the symbol table on the standard file 'output'.

message

    Whenever a semantic error is detected, an error message will be produced. The data structure 'message' is described below.

- type message = (label_overfl, inv_deref, inv_coercion,
               redefinition, maxvar_exc, undef_obj);

- <u>procedure</u> error (m:message);
      Print the message M on the standard file 'output'.

5.5.4.2. <u>Implementation of the syntax-semantic analyser of Pico Al-</u>
<u>gol</u>


```
$$$$$$$$$$$$$$$$$$$$$$$$$$$$$$$$$$$$$$$$$$$$$$$$$$$$$$$$$$$$$$$$$$$$$$$$$$$$$$$$$$$$$
$   LILA INPUT                                                                  $
$                                                                              $
$     Compiler for Pico Algol : Syntax-semantic Analyser                        $
$$$$$$$$$$$$$$$$$$$$$$$$$$$$$$$$$$$$$$$$$$$$$$$$$$$$$$$$$$$$$$$$$$$$$$$$$$$$$$$$$$$$$
```

###inputvocabulary rep(integer);

$ <u>Keywords</u>
```
  "begin"   = 2     "end"      = 3
  "boolean" = 4     "integer"  = 5
  "true"    = 6     "false"    = 7
  "print"   = 8     "if"       = 9
  "then"    =10     "else"     =11
  "fi "     =12     "do"       =13
  "od"      =14     "for"      =15
  "from"    =16     "to"       =17
```

$ <u>Delimiters</u>
```
  "(" = 40   ")" = 41    "*" = 42    "+" = 43   "-" =45   "/" = 47
  ":="= 48   ";" = 59    "=" = 61
```

$ <u>Integer Constant</u>
```
  "intct" = 62 : integer
```

$ <u>Identifier</u>
```
  "iden"  = 63 : rep_name
```


###outputvocabulary rep(integer);

$ <u>Arithmetic instructions</u>
```
  [assign] = 2 : addr2
  [plus]   = 3 : addr3
  [minus]  = 4 : addr3
  [times]  = 5 : addr3
  [divide] = 6 : addr3
  [incr]   = 7 : addr1
```

$ <u>Instructions changing flow of control</u>
```
  [jump]   =10 : rep_label
  [jumpp]  =11 : lab_access
  [jumpf]  =12 : lab_access
  [labdef] =13 : rep_label
```

$ <u>Print instruction</u>
```
  [print]  = 8 : addr1
```


###syntax;

$ <u>Analysis of a Pico Algol program</u>
```
  ##rule;
    <program> =
      "begin"
        ( <declaration> ";" )*
        <statement>  ( ";" <statement> )*
      "end"
```

$ <u>Analysis of a declaration</u>
```
  ##rule;
    <declaration> =
      ( "integer" "iden" int_value
          ( &  |  "=" <expression> intct )
      | "boolean" "iden" bool_value
          ( &  |  "=" <expression> boolct )
      ) add_symbt

  ##var;
    id_name : rep_name;
    id_descr: rep_description

  ##action;
    #int_value;
      id_name := @"iden"1;
      id_descr.typ := refint;
      init_access(id_descr.acc, idensp, 0, idensp_loc(int))

    #intct;
      coerce_descr( @<expression>1, int);
      with @[assign]  do begin
        typ_right := int;
        acc_left  := id_descr.acc;
        acc_right := @<expression>1.acc
      end;
      out(%[assign]);
      deref_descr(id_descr)
```

```
      #bool_value;
        id_name := @"iden"2;
        id_descr.typ := refbool;
        init_access(id_descr.acc, idensp, 0, idensp_loc(bool))

      #boolct;
        coerce_descr( @<expression>2, bool);
        with @[assign]  do begin
          typ_right := bool;
          acc_left  := id_descr.acc;
          acc_right := @<expression>2.acc
        end;
        out(%[assign]);
        deref_descr(id_descr)

      #add_symbt;
        add_symbt( id_name, id_descr)

$ Analysis of a statement
  ##rule;
    <statement> =
        <compound statement>
      | <print statement>
      | <if statement>
      | <for statement>
      | <assign statement>

$ Analysis of a compound statement
  ##rule;
    <compound statement> =
      "do"
        <statement> ( ";" <statement> )*
      "od"

$ Analysis of an assignment statement
  ##rule;
    <assign statement> =
      "iden" ":=" <expression>  assign

    ##var;
      left_descr : rep_description

    ##action;
      #assign;
        search_symbt( @"iden", left_descr);
        coerce_descr( @<expression>, deref_type(left_descr.typ));
        with @[assign]  do begin
          typ_right := @<expression>.typ;
```

```
          acc_left  := left_descr.acc;
          acc_right := @<expression>.acc
        end;
      out(%[assign])
```

$ Analysis of a print statement
  ##rule;
    <print statement> =
      "print" <expression> print

    ##action;
      #print;
            $ Only integer values are allowed in a print statement.
          coerce_descr(@<expression>, int);
          @[print] := @<expression>;
          out(%[print])

$ Analysis of an if statement
  ##rule;
    <if statement> =
      "if" <expression> cond
        "then" <statement> then_part
        "else" <statement> else_part
      "fi"

    ##action;
      #cond;
        coerce_descr(@<expression>, bool);
        with @[jumpf] do begin
          lab := unique_lab;
          acc := @<expression>.acc
        end;
        out(%[jumpf])

      #then_part;
        @[jump]   := unique_label;
        out(%[jump]);
        @[labdef] := @[jumpf].lab;
        out(%[labdef])

      #else_part;
        @[labdef] := @[jump];
        out(%[labdef])

$ Analysis of a for statement
  ##rule;
    <for statement> =
      "for" "iden" for_iden
```
```

```
     "from"  <expression>  from_expr
     "to"    <expression>  to_expr
     <compound statement>    after_stat

##var;
  cvar_descr : rep_description

##action;
  #for_iden;
    search_symbt( @"iden", cvar_descr);
    coerce_descr( cvar_descr, refint)

  #from_expr;
    coerce_descr( @<expression>1, int);
    with  @[assign]  do begin
      typ_right := @<expression>1.typ;
      acc_left  := cvar_descr.acc;
      acc_right := @<expression>1.acc
    end;
    out(%[assign]);
    @[labdef] := unique_lab;
    out(%[labdef])

  #to_expr;
    coerce_descr( @<expression>2, int);
    with  @[minus]  do begin
      typ_left  := deref_type(cvar_descr.typ);
      typ_right := @<expression>2.typ;
      acc_left  := cvar_descr.acc;
      deref_access(acc_left);
      acc_right := @<expression>2.acc;
      init_access(acc_result, worksp, 1, worksp_loc(int))
    end;
    out(%[minus]);
    with  @[jumpp]  do begin
      lab := unique_lab;
      acc := @[minus].acc_result
    end;
    out(%[jumpp])

  #after_stat;
    with  @[incr]  do begin
      typ := deref_type(cvar_descr.typ);
      acc := cvar_descr.acc
    end;
    out(%[incr]);
    @[jump]    := @[labdef];
    out(%[jump]);
```

```
          @[labdef] := @[jumpp].lab;
          out(%[labdef])


$ Analysis of an expression
  ##rule;
    <expression> =
      <term>  pass_te
      ( "+" <term>  add
      | "-" <term>  subtract
      )*

    ##attribute;
      rep_description

    ##action;
      #pass_te;
        @<expression> := @<term>1

      #add;
        coerce_descr( @<expression>, int);
        coerce_descr( @<term>2, int);
        with  @[plus]  do begin
          typ_left  := @<expression>.typ;
          typ_right := @<term>2.typ;
          acc_left  := @<expression>.acc;
          acc_right := @<term>2.acc;
          init_access(acc_result, worksp, 1, worksp_loc(int))
        end;
        out(%[plus]);
        @<expression>.acc := @[plus].acc_result

      #subtract;
        coerce_descr( @<expression>, int);
        coerce_descr( @<term>3, int);
        with  @[minus]  do begin
          typ_left  := @<expression>.typ;
          typ_right := @<term>3.typ;
          acc_left  := @<expression>.acc;
          acc_right := @<term>3.acc;
          init_access(acc_result, worksp, 1, worksp_loc(int))
        end;
        out(%[minus]);
        @<expression>.acc := @[minus].acc_result

$ Analysis of a term
  ##rule;
    <term> =
```

```
        <factor>  pass_ft
          ( "*" <factor>  multiply
          | "/" <factor>  divide
          )*

    ##attribute;
      rep_description

    ##action;
      #pass_ft;
        @<term> := @<factor>1

      #multiply;
        coerce_descr( @<term>, int);
        coerce_descr( @<factor>2, int);
        with @[times]  do begin
          typ_left   := @<term>.typ;
          typ_right  := @<factor>2.typ;
          acc_left   := @<term>.acc;
          acc_right  := @<factor>2.acc;
          init_access(acc_result, worksp, 1, worksp_loc(int))
        end;
        out(%[times]);
        @<term>.acc := @[times].acc_result

      #divide;
        coerce_descr( @<term>, int);
        coerce_descr( @<factor>3, int);
        with @[divide]  do begin
          typ_left   := @<term>.typ;
          typ_right  := @<factor>3.typ;
          acc_left   := @<term>.acc;
          acc_right  := @<factor>3.acc;
          init_access(acc_result, worksp, 1, worksp_loc(int))
        end;
        out(%[divide]);
        @<term>.acc := @[divide].acc_result

$ Analysis of a factor
  ##rule;
    <factor> =
        "iden"  iden
      | "intct" intct
      | "true"  true
      | "false" false
      | "(" <expression> ")" pass_ef

    ##attribute;
```

```
    rep_description

  ##var;
    v : rep_value

  ##action;
    #iden;
      search_symbt( @"iden", @<factor>)

    #intct;
      @<factor>.typ := int;
      with v do begin
        typ  := int;
        ival := @"intct"
      end;
      init_access(@<factor>.acc, constab, 1, constb_loc( int, v))

    #true;
      @<factor>.typ := bool;
      with v do begin
        typ  := bool;
        bval := true
      end;
      init_access(@<factor>.acc, constab, 1, constb_loc( bool, v))

    #false;
      @<factor>.typ := bool;
      with v do begin
        typ  := bool;
        bval := false
      end;
      init_access(@<factor>.acc, constab, 1, constb_loc( bool, v))

    #pass_ef;
      @<factor> := @<expression>


###globalinfo;

  ##parameter;
    infile, outfile, output, value_file

  ##const;
    $ symbol table
      maxsymbt = 100;

    $ Miscelaneous
      idlength = 8
```

```
##type;
  $ message
    message = (label_overfl, inv_deref, inv_coercion,
      redefinition, maxvar_exc, undef_value);

  $ rep type
    rep_type = (int, bool, refint, refbool, undefined);

  $ rep access
    rep_space = (idensp, worksp, constab);
    rep_level = 0..maxint;
    rep_offset= 0..maxint;
    rep_access = record
      case  def:boolean of
        true :
          (space : rep_space;
           level : rep_level;
           offset: rep_offset);
        false: ( )
      end;

  $ rep label
    rep_label = 0..maxint;

  $ constab
    rep_value = record
      case  typ:rep_type  of
        int : (ival : integer);
        bool: (bval : boolean);
        refint,refbool,undefined : ()
      end;

  $ rep description
    rep_description = record
      typ : rep_type;
      acc : rep_access
    end;

  $ Miscelaneous
    rep_name = packed array [1..idlength] of char;

    addr1 = rep_description;
    addr2 = record
      typ_right : rep_type;
      acc_left  : rep_access;
      acc_right : rep_access
    end;
    addr3 = record
```

```
    typ_left  : rep_type;
    typ_right : rep_type;
    acc_left  : rep_access;
    acc_right : rep_access;
    acc_result: rep_access
  end;
  lab_access = record
    lab : rep_label;
    acc : rep_access
  end

##var;

  $ idenspace
    idenp : rep_offset;

  $ workspace
    workp : rep_offset;

  $ constab
    constp : rep_offset;
    value_file: file of rep_value;

  $ rep_label
    lab_counter : rep_label;

  $ symbol_table
    symbtab : array [O..maxsymbt] of record
      name : rep_name;
      desc : rep_description
    end;
    symbtabp: O..maxsymbt;

  $ Miscelaneous
    space_name : array [rep_space] of packed array [1..6] of char;
    type_name  : array [rep_type] of packed array [1..7] of char
        $   'space_name' and 'type_name' are used to print access and
        $ type information for debugging purposes.


##routine;
  $ message
    procedure error (m:message);
    begin
      writeln(output);
      write(output, linenumb:4, ' *** ERROR *** : ');
      case  m  of
        label_overfl:
```

```
        write('Label overflow. The compilation halts.');
      inv_deref:
        write('Locational value expected, but constant was found.');
      inv_coercion:
        write('Unallowed coercion specified.');
      redefinition:
        write('More than one declaration for the same identifier');
      maxvar_exc:
        write('Symbol table overflow. The compilation halts.');
      undef_value:
        write('Reference to an undefined value.')
    end;
    writeln(output)
  end; {error}
```

$ rep type
```
  function deref_type (t:rep_type): rep_type;
  begin
    case  t  of
      refint   :   deref_type:=int;
      refbool  :   deref_type:=bool;
      int,bool : begin
          error(inv_deref);
          deref_type := undefined
        end;
      undefined:  deref_type := undefined
    end
  end; {deref_type}

  function size_type (t:rep_type): integer;
  begin
    case  t  of
      int, bool :
        size_type := 1;
      refint, refbool :
        size_type := 2;
      undefined :
        size_type := 0 {arbitrary value}
    end
  end; {size_type}

  procedure print_type (t:rep_type);
  begin
    write(output, type_name[t])
  end; {print_type}
```

$ rep access
```
  procedure init_access
```

```
      (var a:rep_access; s:rep_space; l:rep_level; o:rep_offset);
begin
  with a do begin
    def     := true;
    space   := s;
    level   := l;
    offset  := o
  end
end; {init_access}

procedure deref_access (var a:rep_access);
begin
  if  a.def  then a.level := succ(a.level)
end; {deref_access}

procedure print_access (a:rep_access);
begin
  if a.def
    then write(output, '[', space_name [a.space], ',',
                  a.level:1, ',', a.offset:5, ']')
    else write(output,'[     ????     ]')
end; {print_access}
```

$ rep description
```
  procedure deref_descr (var d:rep_description);
  begin
    d.typ := deref_type(d.typ);
    if (d.typ <> undefined)
      then deref_access(d.acc)
      else d.acc.def := false
  end; {deref_descr}

  procedure coerce_descr (var d:rep_description; t:rep_type);
  begin
    if (t = undefined) then begin
      d.typ      := undefined;
      d.acc.def := false
    end
    else if (d.typ <> undefined) then begin
      if (d.typ <> t) then begin
          $ Dereferencing
        if (d.typ=refint) and (t=int) or (d.typ=refbool) and (t=bool)
          then  deref_descr(d)
          else begin
            error(inv_coercion);
            d.typ := undefined;
            d.acc.def := false
          end
```

```
      end
    end
  end; {coerce_descr}

  procedure print_descr (d:rep_description);
  begin
    print_type (d.typ);
    write(', ');
    print_access (d.acc)
  end; {print_descr}

$ rep label
  function unique_lab: rep_label;
  begin
    if (lab_counter = maxint) then begin
      error(label_overfl);
      goto 9999    $$ STOP
    end
    else begin
      unique_lab  := lab_counter;
      lab_counter := lab_counter + 1
    end
  end; {unique_lab}

$ storage allocation
  procedure align (var o:rep_offset; t:rep_type);
  begin
    { Since no alignments are required on the Intel 8085,
      this is a dummy routine. }
  end; {align}

$ idenspace
  function idensp_loc (t:rep_type): rep_offset;
  begin
    align( idenp, t);
    idensp_loc := idenp;
    idenp := idenp + size_type(t)
  end; {idensp_loc}

$ workspace
  function worksp_loc (t:rep_type): rep_offset;
  begin
    align( workp, t);
    worksp_loc := workp;
    workp := workp + size_type(t)
  end; {worksp_loc}

$ constab
```

```
function constb_loc (t:rep_type; v:rep_value): rep_offset;
begin
  align( constp, t);
  constb_loc := constp;
  constp := constp + size_type(t);
  write(value_file, v)
end; {constb_loc}
```

$ symbol table
```
  procedure add_symbt (n:rep_name; d:rep_description);
  var i:0..maxsymbt;
  begin
    symbtab [symbtabp].name := n;
    i := 0;
    while (symbtab[i].name <> n)
      do  i:=i+1;
    symbtab[i].desc := d;
    if (i < symbtabp) then error(redefinition)
    else begin
      if (symbtabp = maxsymbt) then begin
        error(maxvar_exc);
        goto 9999    $$ STOP
      end
      else symbtabp := symbtabp + 1
    end
  end; {add_symbt}

  procedure search_symbt (n:rep_name; var d:rep_description);
  var i:0..maxsymbt;
  begin
    symbtab [symbtabp].name := n;
    i := 0;
    while (symbtab[i].name <> n)
      do  i:=i+1;
    if (i <> symbtabp) then d := symbtab[i].desc
    else begin
      error(undef_value);
      d.typ := undefined;
      d.acc.def := false;
      add_symbt( n, d)
    end
  end; {search_symbt}

  procedure print_symbt;
  var i:0..maxsymbt;
  begin
    writeln(output,'SYMBOL TABLE');
    writeln(output,'************');
```

```
      writeln(output);
      for  i:=0 to symbtabp-1  do
        with  symbtab[i]  do begin
          writeln(output, '|---------|--------------------------|');
          write(output, '| ', name, '| ');
          print_descr(desc);
          writeln(output, ' |')
        end
      end {print_symbt}

##prologue;
  $ rep label
    lab_counter := 0;

  $ idenspace
    idenp := 0;

  $ workspace
    workp := 0;

  $ constab
    constp:= 0;
    rewrite(value_file);

  $ symbol table
    symbtabp := 0;

  $ Miscelaneous
    space_name [idensp] := 'idensp';
    space_name [worksp] := 'worksp';
    space_name [constab]:= 'constb';

    type_name [undefined] := '  ???  ';
    type_name [int]       := 'int    ';
    type_name [bool]      := 'bool   ';
    type_name [refint]    := 'refint ';
    type_name [refbool]   := 'refbool'

##epilogue;
  $ symbol table
    print_symbt
```

5.5.5. Example

The results of the different passes in the compilation of a Pico Algol program are illustrated below for the program to calculate some of the Fibonacci numbers.

Input program

```
'begin'
  'integer' fibl;  'integer' fib2;
  'integer' k;
  'integer' number = 10;
  'boolean' switch;

  fibl := 1;  fib2 := 2;
  'print' 1;  'print' 2;
  switch := 'true';

  'for'  k  'from' 1  'to' number  'do'
    'if' switch
      'then' 'do'
        fibl := fibl + fib2;
        'print' fibl;
        switch := 'false'
      'od'
      'else' 'do'
        fib2 := fib2 + fibl;
        'print' fib2;
        switch := 'true'
      'od'
    'fi'
  'od'
'end'
```

Results of the lexical analyser

```
                        'begin'
begin       2
                        'integer' fibl;  'integer' fib2;
integer     5
iden       63 fibl
;          59
integer     5
iden       63 fib2
;          59
```

```
                              'integer' k;
integer      5
iden        63 k
;           59
                              'integer' number = 10;
integer      5
iden        63 number
=           61
intct       62 10
;           59
                              'boolean' switch;
boolean      4
iden        63 switch
;           59
                              fib1 := 1;   fib2 := 2;
iden        63 fib1
:=          48
intct       62 1
;           59
iden        63 fib2
:=          48
intct       62 2
;           59
                              'print' 1;   'print' 2;
print        8
intct       62 1
;           59
print        8
intct       62 2
;           59
                              switch := 'true';
iden        63 switch
:=          48
true         6
;           59
                              'for'  k  'from' 1  'to' number   'do'
for         15
iden        63 k
from        16
intct       62 1
to          17
iden        63 number
do          13
                              'if' switch
if           9
iden        63 switch
                              'then' 'do'
then        10
```

```
do          13
                    fibl := fibl + fib2;
iden        63 fibl
:=          48
iden        63 fibl
+           43
iden        63 fib2
;           59
                    'print' fibl;
print        8
iden        63 fibl
;           59
                    switch := 'false'
iden        63 switch
:=          48
false        7
                    'od'
od          14
                    'else' 'do'
else        11
do          13
                    fib2 := fib2 + fibl;
iden        63 fib2
:=          48
iden        63 fib2
+           43
iden        63 fibl
;           59
                    'print' fib2;
print        8
iden        63 fib2
;           59
                    switch := 'true'
iden        63 switch
:=          48
true         6
                    'od'
od          14
                    'fi'
fi          12
                    'od'
od          14
                    'end'
end          3
```

Results of the syntax-semantic analyser

SYMBOL TABLE
****

fib1	refint , [idensp,0, 0]
fib2	refint , [idensp,0, 1]
k	refint , [idensp,0, 2]
number	int , [idensp,1, 3]
switch	refbool, [idensp,0, 4]

3-ADDRESS INSTRUCTIONS
****

```
                                          'begin'
                                          'integer' fib1;  'integer' fib2;
                                          'integer' k;
                                          'integer' number = 10;
        ASSIGN  int          [idensp,0,3]  [constb,1,0]
                                          'boolean' switch;
                                          fib1 := 1;  fib2 := 2;
        ASSIGN  int          [idensp,0,0]  [constb,1,1]
        ASSIGN  int          [idensp,0,1]  [constb,1,2]
                                          'print' 1;  'print' 2;
        PRINT   int          [constb,1,3]
        PRINT   int          [constb,1,4]
                                          switch := 'true';
        ASSIGN  bool         [idensp,0,4]  [constb,1,5]
                                          'for' k 'from' 1 'to' number  'do'
        ASSIGN  int          [idensp,0,2]  [constb,1,6]
LABDEF LO
        MINUS   int    int   [idensp,1,2] [idensp,1,3]  [worksp,1,0]
        JUMPP   L1           [worksp,1,0]
                                          'if' switch
        JUMPF   L2           [idensp,1,4]
                                          'then' 'do'
                                          fib1 := fib1 + fib2;
        PLUS    int    int   [idensp,1,0] [idensp,1,1]  [worksp,1,1]
        ASSIGN  int          [idensp,0,0] [worksp,1,1]
                                          'print' fib1;
        PRINT   int          [idensp,1,0]

                                          switch := 'false'
```

```
                                          'od'
   ASSIGN  bool            [idensp,0,4]  [constb,1,7]
   JUMP    L3
                                          'else' 'do'
LABDEF  L2
                                          fib2 := fib2 + fib1;
   PLUS    int    int      [idensp,1,1]  [idensp,1,0]  [worksp,1,2]
   ASSIGN  int             [idensp,0,1]  [worksp,1,2]
                                          'print' fib2;
   PRINT   int             [idensp,1,1]
                                          switch := 'true'
                                          'od'
   ASSIGN  bool            [idensp,0,4]  [constb,1,8]
                                          'fi'
LABDEF  L3
                                          'od'
   INCR    int             [idensp,0,2]
   JUMP    LO
LABDEF  L1
                                          'end'
```

CONSTANT TABLE
****

```
    |-------|
 0  |   10  |
    |-------|
 1  |    1  |
    |-------|
 2  |    2  |
    |-------|
 3  |    1  |
    |-------|
 4  |    2  |
    |-------|
 5  | TRUE  |
    |-------|
 6  |    1  |
    |-------|
 7  | FALSE |
    |-------|
 8  | TRUE  |
```

5.5.6.   The Syntax-semantic Analyser : Optimized version

In the previous version of the syntax-semantic analyser for Pico
Algol, the storage allocation for the intermediate values, resulting
from expression evaluation, has been kept very simple. For each intermediate value a different location in the workspace was allocat-
ed.   In this version of the syntax-semantic analyser, the storage
allocation for the intermediate values has been optimized.   This is
an example of an implementation of a run-time stack with compile-
time address calculation.

The optimization is based on the fact that in Pico Algol a value
on the workspace can only be used once as an operand in an intermediate instruction.   Therefore, the storage occupied by a value on
the workspace can be released after the 3-Address instruction, having that value as an operand, has been executed.   For this purpose,
a new operation ('free_worksp') is defined on the data structure
workspace; this operation is described below.

- procedure free_worksp (d:rep_descr);
      If the value described by D resides on top of the workspace,
      the storage occupied by that value will be recovered.

The translation syntax part of the LILA input for the optimized
version of the syntax-semantic analyser for Pico Algol is given
below.   The other parts of the LILA input are identical with those
of the non-optimized version, except for the implementation of the
operation 'free_worksp', which has to be added to the global routines.

```
$$$$$$$$$$$$$$$$$$$$$$$$$$$$$$$$$$$$$$$$$$$$$$$$$$$$$$$$$$$$$$$$$$$$$$$$$$$$$$$$$$
$   LILA INPUT                                                               $
$                                                                           $
$      Compiler for Pico Algol : Syntax-semantic Analyser, optimized version $
$$$$$$$$$$$$$$$$$$$$$$$$$$$$$$$$$$$$$$$$$$$$$$$$$$$$$$$$$$$$$$$$$$$$$$$$$$$$$$$$$$
```

###syntax;

$ Analysis of a Pico Algol program
   ##rule;
     <program> =

```
      "begin"
        ( <declaration> ";" )*
        <statement>  ( ";" <statement> )*
      "end"
```

$ Analysis of a declaration
  ##rule;
     <declaration> =
        ("integer" "iden" int_value
            (& | "=" <expression> intct)
        | "boolean" "iden" bool_value
            (& | "=" <expression> boolct)
) add_symbt

    ##var;
      id_name : rep_name;
      id_descr: rep_description

    ##action;
      #int_value;
        id_name := @"iden"1;
        id_descr.typ := refint;
        init_access(id_descr.acc, idensp, 0, idensp_loc(int))

      #intct;
        free_worksp(@<expression>1);
        coerce_descr(@<expression>1, int);
        with @[assign] do begin
          typ_right := int;
          acc_left := id_descr.acc;
          acc_right := @<expression>1.acc
        end;
        out(%[assign]);
        deref_descr(id_descr)

      #bool_value;
        id_name := @"iden"2;
        id_descr.typ := refbool;
        init_access(id_descr.acc, idensp, 0, idensp_loc(bool))

      #boolct;
        free_worksp(@<expression>2);
        coerce_descr(@<expression>2, bool);
        with @[assign] do begin
          typ_right := bool;
          acc_left := id_descr.acc;
          acc_right := @<expression>2.acc
        end;
```
```

```
        out(%[assign]);
        deref_descr(id_descr)

    #add_symbt;
        add_symbt( id_name, id_descr)
```

$ Analysis of a statement
```
  ##rule;
    <statement> =
        <compound statement>
      | <print statement>
      | <if statement>
      | <for statement>
      | <assign statement>
```

$ Analysis of a compound statement
```
  ##rule;
    <compound statement> =
        "do"
          <statement> ( ";" <statement> )*
        "od"
```

$ Analysis of an assignment statement
```
  ##rule;
    <assign statement> =
        "iden" ":=" <expression>   assign

    ##var;
      left_descr : rep_description

    ##action;
      #assign;
        free_worksp(@<expression>);
        search_symbt( @"iden", left_descr);
        coerce_descr( @<expression>, deref_type(left_descr.typ));
        with @[assign] do begin
          typ_right := @<expression>.typ;
          acc_left  := left_descr.acc;
          acc_right := @<expression>.acc
        end;
        out(%[assign])
```

$ Analysis of a print statement
```
  ##rule;
    <print statement> =
        "print" <expression>   print

    ##action;
```

```
    #print;
           $ Only integer values are allowed in a print statement.
       free_worksp(@<expression>);
       coerce_descr( @<expression>, int);
       @[print] := @<expression>;
       out(%[print])

$ Analysis of an if statement
  ##rule;
    <if statement> =
      "if" <expression>   cond
        "then" <statement>   then_part
        "else" <statement>   else_part
      "fi"

    ##action;
      #cond;
        free_worksp(@<expression>);
        coerce_descr( @<expression>, bool);
        with  @[jumpf]   do begin
          lab := unique_lab;
          acc := @<expression>.acc
        end;
        out(%[jumpf])

      #then_part;
        @[jump]    := unique_label;
        out(%[jump]);
        @[labdef] := @[jumpf].lab;
        out(%[labdef])

      #else_part;
        @[labdef] := @[jump];
        out(%[labdef])

$ Analysis of a for statement
  ##rule;
    <for statement> =
      "for" "iden"  for_iden
        "from" <expression>  from_expr
        "to"   <expression>  to_expr
        <compound statement>   after_stat

    ##var;
      cvar_descr : rep_description;
      help : rep_description

    ##action;
```

```
#for_iden;
  search_symbt( @"iden", cvar_descr);
  coerce_descr( cvar_descr, refint)

#from_expr;
  free_worksp(@<expression>1);
  coerce_descr( @<expression>1, int);
  with @[assign]  do begin
    typ_right := @<expression>1.typ;
    acc_left  := cvar_descr.acc;
    acc_right := @<expression>1.acc
  end;
  out(%[assign]);
  @[labdef] := unique_lab;
  out(%[labdef])

#to_expr;
  free_worksp(@<expression>2);
  coerce_descr( @<expression>2, int);
  with @[minus]  do begin
    typ_left  := deref_type(cvar_descr.typ);
    typ_right := @<expression>2.typ;
    acc_left  := cvar_descr.acc;
    deref_access(acc_left);
    acc_right := @<expression>2.acc;
    init_access(acc_result, worksp, 1, worksp_loc(int))
  end;
  out(%[minus]);
  with help  do begin
    typ := int;
    acc := @[minus].acc_result
  end;
  free_worksp(help);
  with @[jumpp]  do begin
    lab := unique_lab;
    acc := @[minus].acc_result
  end;
  out(%[jumpp])

#after_stat;
  with @[incr]  do begin
    typ := deref_type(cvar_descr.typ);
    acc := cvar_descr.acc
  end;
  out(%[incr]);
  @[jump]   := @[labdef];
  out(%[jump]);
  @[labdef] := @[jumpp].lab;
```

```
        out(%[labdef])

$ Analysis of an expression
  ##rule;
    <expression> =
      <term>  pass_te
        ( "+" <term>  add
        | "-" <term>  subtract
        )*

  ##attribute;
    rep_description

  ##action;
    #pass_te;
      @<expression> := @<term>1

    #add;
      free_worksp(@<term>2);
      free_worksp(@<expression>);
      coerce_descr( @<expression>, int);
      coerce_descr( @<term>2, int);
      with  @[plus]  do begin
        typ_left   := @<expression>.typ;
        typ_right  := @<term>2.typ;
        acc_left   := @<expression>.acc;
        acc_right  := @<term>2.acc;
        init_access(acc_result, worksp, 1, worksp_loc(int))
      end;
      out(%[plus]);
      @<expression>.acc := @[plus].acc_result

    #subtract;
      free_worksp(@<term>3);
      free_worksp(@<expression>);
      coerce_descr( @<expression>, int);
      coerce_descr( @<term>3, int);
      with  @[minus]  do begin
        typ_left   := @<expression>.typ;
        typ_right  := @<term>3.typ;
        acc_left   := @<expression>.acc;
        acc_right  := @<term>3.acc;
        init_access(acc_result, worksp, 1, worksp_loc(int))
      end;
      out(%[minus]);
      @<expression>.acc := @[minus].acc_result

$ Analysis of a term
```

```
##rule;
   <term> =
     <factor>  pass_ft
       ( "*" <factor>  multiply
       | "/" <factor>  divide
       )*

  ##attribute;
    rep_description

  ##action;
    #pass_ft;
      @<term> := @<factor>1

    #multiply;
      free_worksp(@<factor>2);
      free_worksp(@<term>);
      coerce_descr( @<term>, int);
      coerce_descr( @<factor>2, int);
      with @[times]  do begin
        typ_left   := @<term>.typ;
        typ_right  := @<factor>2.typ;
        acc_left   := @<term>.acc;
        acc_right  := @<factor>2.acc;
        init_access(acc_result, worksp, 1, worksp_loc(int))
      end;
      out(%[times]);
      @<term>.acc := @[times].acc_result

    #divide;
      free_worksp(@<factor>3);
      free_worksp(@<term>);
      coerce_descr( @<term>, int);
      coerce_descr( @<factor>3, int);
      with @[divide]  do begin
        typ_left   := @<term>.typ;
        typ_right  := @<factor>3.typ;
        acc_left   := @<term>.acc;
        acc_right  := @<factor>3.acc;
        init_access(acc_result, worksp, 1, worksp_loc(int))
      end;
      out(%[divide]);
      @<term>.acc := @[divide].acc_result

$ Analysis of a factor
  ##rule;
    <factor> =
        "iden"  iden
```

```
        | "intct"  intct
        | "true"   true
        | "false"  false
        | "(" <expression> ")"  pass_ef

  ##attribute;
    rep_description

  ##var;
    v : rep_value

  ##action;
    #iden;
      search_symbt( @"iden", @<factor>)

    #intct;
      @<factor>.typ  := int;
      with  v  do begin
        typ  := int;
        ival := @"intct"
      end;
      init_access(@<factor>.acc, constab, 1, constb_loc( int, v))

    #true;
      @<factor>.typ  := bool;
      with  v  do begin
        typ  := bool;
        bval := true
      end;
      init_access(@<factor>.acc, constab, 1, constb_loc( bool, v))

    #false;
      @<factor>.typ  := bool;
      with  v  do begin
        typ  := bool;
        bval := false
      end;
      init_access(@<factor>.acc, constab, 1, constb_loc( bool, v))

    #pass_ef;
      @<factor> := @<expression>


###globalinfo;

  $ see the non-optimized version, except for
  $
```

```
$ procedure free_worksp (d:rep_descr);
$ begin
$   if (d.acc.space = worksp) and (d.acc.offset = workp - size_type(d.typ))
$     then workp := d.acc.offset
$ end; {free_worksp}
```

6. ERROR RECOVERY

6.1. Introduction

The generation schemes discussed in sections 2,3 and 4 did not take error recovery into account. This means that parsers or transducers generated by these schemes halt at the first occurrence of a syntactic error. In the subsequent sections, we will extend these generation schemes so that parsers and transducers will be produced in which error recovery takes place.

The development of compiler writing systems that produce compilers with error recovery has always been a serious problem. Insertion of error recovery by hand in the generated compiler is impractical and in most cases impossible; it destroys the modular structure of the generated compiler. Each time a new version of the compiler is generated, the entire insertion process has to be redone. LILA offers an elegant solution for this error recovery problem. The very start of the error recovery strategy supported by LILA originates from the Algol 68 compiler project, see Branquart et al.[1976]. The error recovery in compilers generated by LILA is mechanically produced from the error recovery information in the LILA input. The use of this feature requires the knowledge of the error recovery strategy supported by LILA.

An adequate error recovery strategy must satisfy the following design objectives :

1) The error recovery strategy must be powerful. The input parts that are skipped during parsing must be as small as possible.

2) The error recovery strategy must be conceptually simple and the generation of ELL(1) parsers with error recovery must be transparent.

319

3) The LILA user must have a certain degree of control over the
error recovery performed in parsers generated by LILA. This
is conform with the main philosophy of LILA : in a translator
writing system, a number of important decisions must be the
user's responsibility.

4) The overhead in the parser due to the error recovery must be
within reasonable limits.

The general principles of the error recovery incorporated in compilers produced by LILA can be roughly explained as follows.
The parser of a compiler operates in two modes : the <u>parsing</u> mode
and the <u>error</u> mode.

1) The parser starts in the parsing mode. This corresponds to
the activation of the parsing routine for the start symbol A_0
of the ECF syntax. This parsing routine activates other parsing routines.

2) In the parsing mode, the error routine is activated as soon as
a syntactic error is detected and the error mode is entered
for that error.

3) In the error mode, input symbols are skipped until an <u>end-
marker</u> is found, terminating an activation of a given parsing
routine. From this moment, the parser is able to react as if
no syntactic error has occurred.
This process is called <u>synchronization</u> based on endmarkers.
As we will see later, the endmarkers are derived from the
error recovery information in the LILA input. There are two
kinds of endmarkers : lastmarkers and followmarkers. This is
explained later.

4) In the error mode, input symbols are skipped until a <u>begin-
marker</u> is found, characterizing the start of a given parsing
routine. Then the error mode is left and the parsing routine
is activated. When the parser returns from this parsing routine, the error mode is again entered.
This process is called <u>recognition</u> based on beginmarkers. As
we will see later, also the beginmarkers are derived from the

error recovery information in the LILA input.   There are two
kinds of beginmarkers : firstmarkers and precedemarkers.   This
is explained later.

The error recovery mechanism has a <u>recursive</u> <u>aspect</u>.   If during
recognition (see point 4) another syntactic error occurs, the whole
process applies recursively.   This is illustrated in Fig. 6.1.   In
this figure a_i, a_j, a_k represent beginmarkers, whereas b_i, b_j, b_k
represent endmarkers.

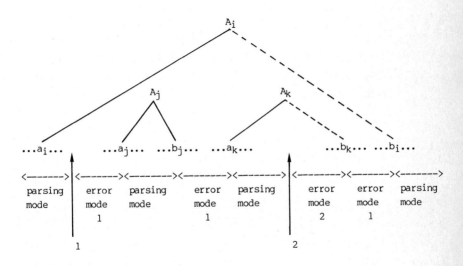

Fig. 6.1.

The choice of the beginmarkers and the endmarkers is very important.   How to choose these markers is explained and illustrated in
the subsequent sections.

6.2. The error recovery strategy supported by LILA

In this section, a family of error recovery strategies with growing complexity is discussed. We will start with a very simple one,
which will then be extended step by step to obtain the final error
recovery strategy as it is supported by LILA.

6.2.1. Synchronization based on LAST

The simplest error recovery strategy would be to skip input symbols until an input symbol is found belonging to $LAST(A_{x_n})$, where
A_{x_n} is the label (nonterminal symbol) of the nonterminal node x_n
immediately covering the syntactic error in the derivation tree.
$LAST(A_{x_n})$ is the set of all the input symbols that can terminate any
string derivable from A_{x_n}. These input symbols are called the lastmarkers of A_{x_n}.

First approach of the error recovery strategy

It is schematically described by the following algorithm :

<u>while</u> in $\notin LAST(A_{x_n})$ <u>do</u> read <u>od</u>;
read;
return from the nonterminal node x_n

After execution of this algorithm the parser assumes the nonterminal
node x_n to be parsed correctly and returns to its normal parsing
state.

Example

Let us consider the ECF syntax for Pico Algol. Suppose that
there is a syntactic error in a compound statement : two consecutive
statements within the compound statement are not separated from one
another by a semicolon. In this case, the parser will skip input
symbols until the lastmarker "od" of the compound statement is
found. This is illustrated in Fig. 6.2.

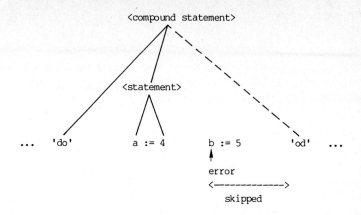

Fig. 6.2.

Definition of LAST

    Given an ECF expression e, LAST(e) specifies the set of input symbols that may terminate any string in L(e). LAST is defined by the following scheme of rules. The definition of LAST is analogous to the definition of FIRST, see section 2.5.

Axiomatic rules

1)   LAST(&) $= \emptyset$.

2)   LAST(a_i) = $\{a_i\}$, where $a_i \in$ VT.

2`) LAST(A_j) = LAST(e_j), where $A_j \in$ VN and $A_j = e_j \in$ P.

Composition rules

3)   LAST(($e_1 | e_2 | \ldots | e_n$)) = $\cup_{1 \leq i \leq n}$ LAST(e_i).

4) $LAST(e_1 e_2 \ldots e_n)$ = <u>if</u> <u>not</u> $EMPTY(e_n)$
        <u>then</u> $LAST(e_n)$
        <u>else</u> $LAST(e_n)$ U $LAST(e_1 \ldots e_{n-1})$
      <u>fi</u>.

5) $LAST((e)*)$ = $LAST(e)$.

6) $LAST((e)^+)$ = $LAST(e)$.

Second approach of the error recovery strategy

The error recovery strategy as it is explained above considers only the nonterminal node (labeled A_{x_n}) immediately covering a syntactic error. It would be better to consider all the nonterminal nodes covering a syntactic error. Let these nodes be x_0, x_1, ..., x_i, ..., x_n, where x_i covers x_{i+1}, for all i ($0 \leq i < n$). In a second approach of the error recovery strategy, the parser will skip input symbols until a lastmarker of one of the nonterminal symbols A_{x_0}, A_{x_1}, ..., A_{x_i}, ..., A_{x_n} is found. The parser returns from a nonterminal node as it is described by the following algorithm. In this way, the error recovery strategy takes care of missing lastmarkers.

```
while in ∉ U_{0≤i≤n} LAST(A_{x_i})  do read od;
case in
  when  LAST(A_{x_n})
    read;
    return from the nonterminal node x_n
  when · LAST(A_{x_{n-1}})
    read;
    return from the nonterminal node x_{n-1}
    .
    .
    .
  when  LAST(A_{x_1})
    read;
    return from the nonterminal node x_1
  otherwise
    read;
    return from the nonterminal node x_0
esac
```

After execution of this algorithm the parser assumes x_i for some i to be parsed correctly and returns to its normal parsing state. Notice that the sets $\text{LAST}(A_{x_i})$ $(0 \leq i \leq n)$ need not to be mutually disjoint. If a lastmarker is found which is a common element of several sets $\text{LAST}(A_{x_{k_1}})$, ... , $\text{LAST}(A_{x_{k_i}})$, ... , $\text{LAST}(A_{x_{k_m}})$ with $k_{i+1} > k_i$ for all i $(1 \leq i < m)$, then the parser returns from x_{k_m}.

Example

Let us consider the ECF syntax for Pico Algol. Suppose that the lastmarker "fi" of an if statement is missing. The if statement is nested within a compound statement. In this case, the parser will skip input symbols until either the lastmarker "fi" of the if statement, or the lastmarker "od" of the compound statement, or a lastmarker of a nonterminal symbol labeling a more covering nonterminal node is found. This is illustrated in Fig. 6.3.

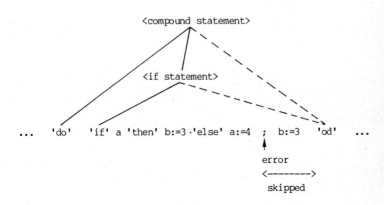

Fig. 6.3.

Third approach of the error recovery strategy

The error recovery strategies as they have been explained above assume that the end of an input part covered by any nonterminal node x_i can be detected simply by skipping input symbols until a symbol is found that belongs to LAST(A_{x_i}). This is however not always possible. As an example, suppose that there is an error in an if statement of a Pico Algol program, e.g., "then" is missing. The if statement is derived from program as shown in Fig. 6.4.

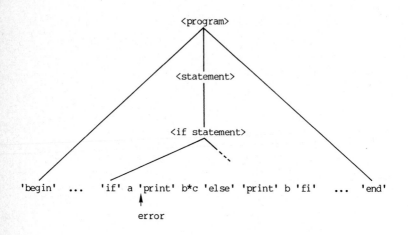

<program>

<statement>

<if statement>

'begin' ...   'if' a 'print' b*c 'else' 'print' b 'fi'   ... 'end'

↑
error

Fig. 6.4.

Skipping to the lastmarker "fi" of the if statement or to the last-marker "end" of the program is obviously a good choice, but skipping to the lastmarkers of statement, which contains "fi", "od", "iden", "intct", "true", "false" and ")" will not produce the expected result. Indeed, the identifier b will be interpreted as the last-marker of the statement with the result shown in Fig. 6.5.

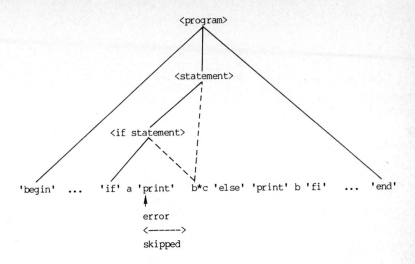

Fig. 6.5.

Such problems can be avoided by a synchronization based on LAST of only those nonterminal symbols, that are designated in the LILA input. Let us first illustrate this by an example. In Pico Algol, the nonterminal symbols designated to be synchronized on LAST are <program>, <compound statement>, <if statement> and <for statement>. For the input in Fig. 6.4, the parser will then only look for the lastmarkers "fi" or "end" with the good result shown in Fig. 6.6.

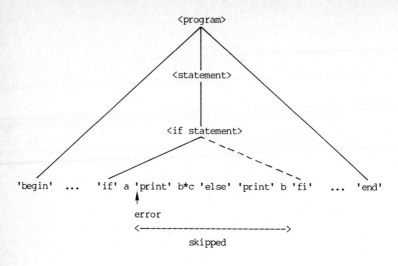

Fig. 6.6.

The <u>third approach</u> of the error recovery strategy is schematically described by the following algorithm :

<u>while</u> in ∉ $U_{0\leq i\leq m}$ LAST($A_{x_{s_i}}$) <u>do</u> read <u>od</u>;
<u>case</u> in
  <u>when</u> LAST($A_{x_{s_m}}$)
    read;
    return from the nonterminal node x_{s_m}
  <u>when</u> LAST($A_{x_{s_{m-1}}}$)
    read;
    return from the nonterminal node $x_{s_{m-1}}$
    .
    .
    .
  <u>when</u> LAST($A_{x_{s_1}}$)
    read;
    return from the nonterminal node x_{s_1}
  <u>otherwise</u>
    read;
    return from the nonterminal node x_{s_0}
  <u>esac</u>

x_{s_0}, x_{s_1}, ... and x_{s_m} are the nonterminal nodes covering the syntactic error, where x_{s_i} covers $x_{s_{i+1}}$ for all i ($1\leq i<m$), for which the

nonterminal symbols $A_{x_{s_0}}$, $A_{x_{s_1}}$, ..., $A_{x_{s_m}}$ are designated to be synchronized on LAST. After execution of this algorithm the parser assumes x_{s_i} for some i to be parsed correctly and returns to its normal parsing state.

It is the LILA user who must designate in the LILA input the nonterminal symbols that are to be synchronized on LAST.
For Pico Algol, this is specified as follows :

###syntax;

$ Analysis of a Pico Algol program
   ##rule;
     <program> =
       "begin"
         (<declaration> ";")*
         <statement>
         (";" <statement>)*
       "end"

   ##recovery last;

$ Analysis of a declaration
   ##rule;
     <declaration> =
         "integer" "iden"
           (& | "=" <expression>)
       | "boolean" "iden"
           (& | "=" <expression>)

$ Analysis of a statement
   ##rule;
     <statement> =
         <assign statement>
       | <print statement>
       | <compound statement>
       | <if statement>
       | <for statement>

$ Analysis of a compound statement
   ##rule;
     <compound statement> =
       "do"
         <statement>   (";" <statement>)*
       "od"

```
  ##recovery last;

$ Analysis of an assign statement
  ##rule;
    <assign statement> =
      "iden" ":=" <expression>

$ Analysis of a print statement
  ##rule;
    <print statement> =
      "print" <expression>

$ Analysis of an if statement
  ##rule;
    <if statement> =
      "if" <expression>
        "then" <statement>
        "else" <statement>
      "fi"

  ##recovery last;

$ Analysis of a for statement
  ##rule;
    <for statement> =
      "for" "iden"
        "from" <expression>
        "to"    <expression>
        <compound statement>

  ##recovery last;

$ Analysis of an expression
  ##rule;
    <expression> =
      <term>
        ( "+" <term>
        | "-" <term>
        )*

$ Analysis of a term
  ##rule;
    <term> =
      <factor>
        ( "*" <factor>
        | "/" <factor>
        )*
```

```
$ Analysis of a factor
  ##rule;
    <factor> =
        "iden"
      | "intct"
      | "true"
      | "false"
      | "(" <expression> ")"
```

Generation scheme

This generation scheme describes the generation of an ELL(1) parser with error recovery based on synchronization on LAST of designated nonterminal symbols. This generation scheme is an extension of the generation scheme in section 2.5. The generation schemes describing the generation of (attributed) ELL(1) transducers with error recovery can be obtained in a similar way.

```
proc ELL(1) parser = void :
begin
   mode VTset = set of char;
   char in := co leftmost symbol of the input string co;
   proc read = void :
      co
         The next symbol in the input string is put in the variable
         'in' (the input head is moved one symbol to the right).
      co;
   proc error = void :
      co This routine produces an appropriate error message. co;
   proc accept = void :
      co
         The input string has been parsed. Some appropriate actions
         are performed. Thereafter, the ELL(1) parser halts.
      co;
   A(A_0 = e_0);
   A(A_1 = e_1);
      .
      .
      .
   A(A_j = e_j);
      .
      .
      .
   A(A_m = e_m);
      co
```

The virtual end-of-file symbol "#" is always considered an
endmarker, as if there were a rule $Z = A_0$ "#", for which Z
is designated to be synchronized on LAST.

```
      co
if  in ∈ DIRSYMB(e₀)
   then if A₀ ({#})
          then skip
          else goto sync
        fi
   else goto prer
fi;
if  in = "#"
   then accept
   else goto prer
fi;
prer:error;
sync:while  in ∉ {#}  do read od
end
```

The program part surrounded by a dotted line is only generated if
the nonterminal symbol A_0 is designated to be synchronized on LAST.
The reason for this will be explained below.

For each ECF syntax rule $A_j = e_j$ in P of G, we produce an ELL(1)
<u>parsing</u> <u>routine</u>, denoted $A(A_j = e_j)$, as follows :

a) A_j is designated to be synchronized on LAST

```
    Aj = ej ∈ P  —>
      proc Aj = (VTset sp) boolean :
        begin
          VTset s := sp U LAST(ej);
          A(ej);
          return (true);
      prer:error;
      sync:while  in ∉ s  do read od;
           if  in ∈ LAST(ej)
             then read;
                  return (true)
           fi;
           return (false)
         end
```

b) A_j is <u>not</u> designated to be synchronized on LAST

```
Aj = ej ∈ P —>
   proc Aj = (VTset sp) boolean :
      begin
         VTset s := sp;
         A(ej);
         return (true);
      prer:error;
      sync:return (false)
         end
```

$A(e_j)$ is produced in a modular way by means of three axiomatic rules and four composition rules. These rules are the same as in the generation scheme in section 2.5, except for two axiomatic rules :

```
2) aᵢ ∈ Vin —>
     if  in = aᵢ
        then read
        else goto prer
     fi
```

```
2') Aj ∈ VN —>
      ┌if  in ∈ DIRSYMB(ej)┐
      │  then ┌if  Aj(s)   ┘
      │       │   then skip   co This is the empty statement co
      │       │   else goto sync
      │       │fi
      │  else  goto prer┐
      │fi ┌─────────────┘
      └──┘
```

The program part surrounded by a dotted line is only generated if the nonterminal symbol A_j is designated to be synchronized on LAST. In this way, a parsing routine corresponding to a nonterminal symbol designated to be synchronized on LAST is only activated if one of its direction symbols is under the input head. Indeed, the detection of a syntactic error at this point can no longer be postponed, if the nonterminal symbol A_j corresponding to the activated routine has been designated to be synchronized on LAST. If the detection of the syntactic error were delayed, the parsing situation could be incorrect and the parser would go on searching for one of the last-markers of A_j. This could give incorrect error recovery results as is illustrated below.

   Consider the rule defining a Pico Algol statement and suppose
that the if statement is the last alternative. From the generation
schemes in sections 2, 3 and 4, it follows that the analysis of an
if statement is activated for each input symbol different from the
direction symbols of a compound statement ("do"), a print statement
("print"), an assign statement ("iden") and a for statement ("for"),
whenever a statement is expected. This can lead to an incorrect
behavior of the error recovery in the syntax analyser for Pico Algol
as is illustrated in Fig. 6.7.

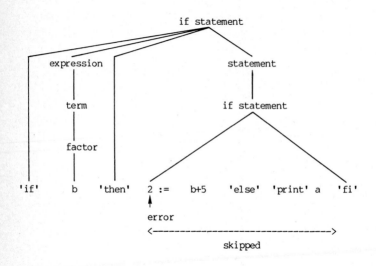

Fig. 6.7.

   A correct behavior of the error recovery in the syntax analyser
for Pico Algol is obtained by preceding each activation of the parsing routine for if statement by a test if the input symbol currently
under the input head belongs to the set of direction symbols {"if"}
of if statement. This is illustrated in Fig. 6.8.

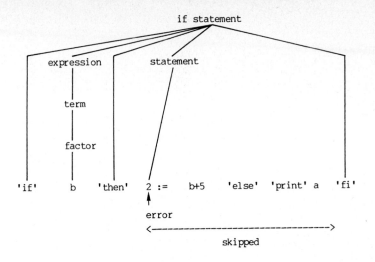

Fig. 6.8.

6.2.2. <u>Synchronization based on FOLLOW</u>

The error recovery strategy as it has been introduced in section 6.2.1, is based on the synchronization on LAST of designated nonter- minal symbols by looking for an input symbol that can <u>terminate</u> a sentence derivable from those nonterminal symbols. In the same way, an occurrence of a nonterminal symbol can also be synchronized by looking for an input symbol that can <u>follow</u> a sentence derivable from that nonterminal symbol occurrence. The input symbols that can follow an occurrence of a nonterminal symbol are called the <u>follow- markers</u> of that occurrence.

Example

Consider the expression (condition) of an if statement in Pico Algol. Obviously, an expression is not a good candidate to be syn- chronized on LAST. However, the expression occurring as the condi- tion of an if statement must be followed by the input symbol "then". This means that if an error is detected within the conditional

expression of an if statement, the parser can synchronize that
expression by looking for the input symbol "then". This is illustrated in Fig. 6.9.

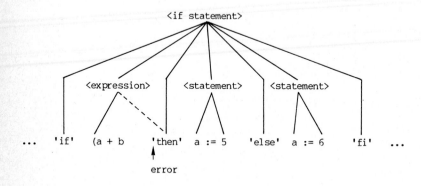

Fig. 6.9.

The LILA user must designate in the LILA input the nonterminal
symbol occurrences to be synchronized on FOLLOW. This is done by
writing '!' after the occurrence of the nonterminal symbol. The
syntax for Pico Algol becomes :

```
###syntax;

$ Analysis of a Pico Algol program
  ##rule;
    <program> =
      "begin"
        ( <declaration>! ";" )*
        <statement>!
        ( ";" <statement>! )*
      "end"

  ##recovery last;

$ Analysis of a declaration
  ##rule;
    <declaration> =
        "integer" "iden"
```

```
            ( &  | "=" <expression>  )
       | "boolean" "iden"
            ( &  | "=" <expression>  )
```

$ <u>Analysis of a statement</u>
```
  ##rule;
     <statement> =
         <assign statement>
       | <print statement>
       | <compound statement>
       | <if statement>
       | <for statement>
```

$ <u>Analysis of a compound statement</u>
```
  ##rule;
     <compound statement> =
       "do"
         <statement>!  ( ";" <statement>! )*
       "od"

  ##recovery last;
```

$ <u>Analysis of an assign statement</u>
```
  ##rule;
     <assign statement> =
       "iden" ":=" <expression>
```

$ <u>Analysis of a print statement</u>
```
  ##rule;
     <print statement> =
       "print" <expression>
```

$ <u>Analysis of an if statement</u>
```
  ##rule;
     <if statement> =
       "if" <expression>!
         "then" <statement>!
         "else" <statement>
       "fi"

  ##recovery last;
```

$ <u>Analysis of a for statement</u>
```
  ##rule;
     <for statement> =
       "for" "iden"
         "from" <expression>!
         "to"   <expression>!
```

```
         <compound statement>

   ##recovery last;

$ Analysis of an expression
  ##rule;
    <expression> =
      <term>
        ( "+" <term>
        | "-" <term>
        )*

$ Analysis of a term
  ##rule;
    <term> =
      <factor>
        ( "*" <factor>
        | "/" <factor>
        )*

$ Analysis of a factor
  ##rule;
    <factor> =
        "iden"
      | "intct"
      | "true"
      | "false"
      | "(" <expression>! ")"
```

Generation scheme

This generation scheme describes the generation of an ELL(1) parser with error recovery based on synchronization on LAST and on FOLLOW. This generation scheme is an extension of the preceding one.

```
    proc ELL(1) parser = void :
    begin
      mode VTset = set of char;
      char in := co leftmost symbol of the input string co;
      proc read = void :
        co
          The next symbol in the input string is put in the variable
          'in' (the input head is moved one symbol to the right).
        co;
      proc error = void :
```

```
        co This routine produces an appropriate error message. co;
    proc accept = void :
        co
            The input string has been parsed. Some appropriate actions
            are performed. Thereafter, the ELL(1) parser halts.
        co;
    A(A_0 = e_0);
    A(A_1 = e_1);
      .
      .
      .
    A(A_j = e_j);
      .
      .
      .
    A(A_m = e_m);
    if  in ∈ DIRSYMB(e_0)
        then if A_0 ({#} , Ø )
                then skip
                else goto sync
             fi
        else goto prer
    fi ;
    if  in = "#"
        then accept
        else goto prer
    fi;
    prer:error;
    sync:while  in ∉ {#}  do read od
    end
```

For each ECF syntax rule $A_j=e_j$ in P of G, we produce an ELL(1)
parsing routine, denoted $A(A_j = e_j)$, as follows :

a) A_j is designated to be synchronized on LAST

```
        A_j = e_j ∈ P  —>
           proc A_j = (VTset sp , f ) boolean :
              begin
                 VTset s := sp U LAST(e_j) U f ;
                 A(e_j);
                 return (true);
              prer:error;
              sync:while  in ∉ s  do read od;
                   if  in ∈ LAST(e_j)
```

```
          then read;
             return (true)
      fi;
     ┌─────────────────────┐
     │ if  in ∈ f          │
     │   then return (true)│
     │ fi;                 │
     └─────────────────────┘
       return (false)
    end
```

b) A_j is <u>not</u> designated to be synchronized on LAST

```
    A_j = e_j ∈ P  —>
       proc A_j = (VTset sp ⌐, f⌐) boolean :
          begin
             VTset s := sp ⌐U f⌐ ;
             A(e_j);
             return (true);
       prer:error;
       sync:┌───────────────────────────────────┐
            │ if  f ≠ ∅                          │
            │   then while  in ∉ s  do read od;  │
            │           if  in ∈ f               │
            │             then return (true)     │
            │           fi                       │
            │ fi;                                │
            └───────────────────────────────────┘
             return (false)
          end
```

As an optimization, the program parts within a rectangle are only
generated if there is at least one occurrence of A_j which is designated to be synchronized on FOLLOW.

For the axiomatic rules defining A(e_j) rule 2' must be changed
and rule 2" must be added, for A_j ∈ VN :

```
2') A_j ∈ VN  —>
    ┌─────────────────────────┐
    │ if  in ∈ DIRSYMB(e_j)    │
    │   then │ if  A_j(s ⌐, ∅⌐) │
    │        │   then skip      │
    │        │   else goto sync │
    │        │ fi               │
    │        └──────────────────┘
    │   else  goto prer │
    └─────────────────────────┘
     fi
```

```
2")  A_j!  —>
        if  in ∈ DIRSYMB(e_j)
          then if  A_j(s, FOLLOW(A_j!))
                   then skip
                   else goto sync
                fi
          else goto prer
        fi
```

Notice that the set $FOLLOW(A_j!)$ in rule 2" is the FOLLOW set of the given occurrence of the nonterminal symbol A_j.

6.2.3. Recognition based on FIRST

The error recovery strategies as they have been introduced in sections 6.2.1 and 6.2.2, simply skip input symbols until a symbol is found that indicates the end of an input part covered by a nonterminal node whose label is a nonterminal symbol designated to be synchronized on LAST, or whose label corresponds to a nonterminal symbol occurrence designated to be synchronized on FOLLOW. In the sequel, such a nonterminal node is said to be designated to be synchronized. We call the endmarkers of a nonterminal node x, the lastmarkers of A_x, if A_x is designated to be synchronized on LAST, together with the followmarkers of the nonterminal symbol occurrence corresponding to x, if that occurrence is designated to be synchronized on FOLLOW. The strategies introduced in sections 6.2.1 and 6.2.2 are not sufficient for two reasons :

1) a large part of the input may not be analysed.

2) if there is a nonterminal node designated to be synchronized, whose label (nonterminal symbol) is recursively defined, then an incorrect endmarker for that nonterminal node might be found.

Let us illustrate this last point by an example. Consider the following part of a Pico Algol program:

    ... 'do' a := 3 'do' ... 'od'; b := 4 'od' ...

The semicolon between the first and the second statement of the outermost compound statement is missing. Because the parser is

analysing a compound statement, it will search for the lastmarker
"od". With the error recovery strategies introduced in sections
6.2.1 and 6.2.2, the parser will find the lastmarker of the innermost compound statement, which is incorrect. The result is illustrated in Fig. 6.10.

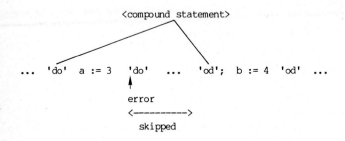

Fig. 6.10.

This can be avoided if the innermost compound statement is recognized as such by the parser during the skipping. In the error
recovery strategy as it is explained in this section, such a recognition of a nonterminal symbol is said to be based on FIRST. This
means that during the skipping of input symbols a nonterminal node
x_{n+1} is recognized, as soon as an input symbol is found that belongs
to the set FIRST of the nonterminal symbol $A_{x_{n+1}}$. Such an input
symbol is called a <u>firstmarker</u> for that nonterminal symbol. In the
example, the analysis of the innermost compound statement will then
be triggered by the "do" symbol with the good result shown in Fig.
6.11.

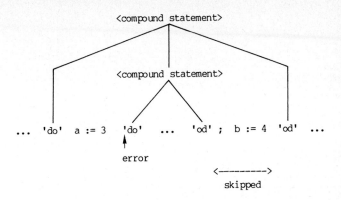

Fig. 6.11.

Notice the <u>recursive</u> <u>aspect</u> in the error recovery strategy explained above : if during recognition of a nonterminal node x_{n+1} another syntactic error is detected, the parser will try to recover from that error. This is illustrated in Fig. 6.12.

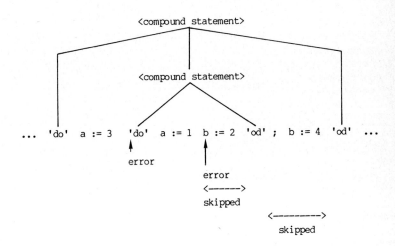

Fig. 6.12.

Again, the LILA user must designate in the LILA input the nonterminal symbols that are to be recognized on FIRST. The syntax for Pico Algol then becomes :

```
###syntax;

$ Analysis of a Pico Algol program
  ##rule;
     <program> =
       "begin"
         ( <declaration>! ";" )*
         <statement>!
         ( ";" <statement>! )*
       "end"

  ##recovery  last;

$ Analysis of a declaration
  ##rule;
     <declaration> =
         "integer" "iden"
           ( &  | "=" <expression>  )
       | "boolean" "iden"
           ( &  | "=" <expression>  )

  ##recovery  first;

$ Analysis of a statement
  ##rule;
     <statement> =
         <assign statement>
       | <print statement>
       | <compound statement>
       | <if statement>
       | <for statement>

$ Analysis of a compound statement
  ##rule;
     <compound statement> =
       "do"
         <statement>!  ( ";" <statement>! )*
       "od"

  ##recovery  first, last;

$ Analysis of an assign statement
  ##rule;
     <assign statement> =
       "iden" ":=" <expression>

$ Analysis of a print statement
  ##rule;
```

```
   <print statement> =
      "print" <expression>

  ##recovery  first;

$ Analysis of an if statement
  ##rule;
    <if statement> =
      "if" <expression>!
        "then" <statement>!
        "else" <statement>
      "fi"

  ##recovery  first, last;

$ Analysis of a for statement
  ##rule;
    <for statement> =
      "for"  "iden"
        "from" <expression>!
        "to"    <expression>!
        <compound statement>

  ##recovery  first, last;

$ Analysis of an expression
  ##rule;
    <expression> =
      <term>
        ( "+" <term>
        | "-" <term>
        )*

$ Analysis of a term
  ##rule;
    <term> =
      <factor>
        ( "*" <factor>
        | "/" <factor>
        )*

$ Analysis of a factor
  ##rule;
    <factor> =
        "iden"
      | "intct"
      | "true"
      | "false"
```

| "(" <expression>! ")"

The recognition of a nonterminal symbol A_j designated to be recognized on FIRST, is always performed local to a nonterminal node x_k designated to be synchronized. Let x_{s_0}, x_{s_1}, ... and x_{s_m} be the nonterminal nodes designated to be synchronized and covering a syntactic error, where x_{s_i} covers $x_{s_{i+1}}$, for all i ($0 \leq i < m$). If a firstmarker is found of a nonterminal symbol A_x, reachable from $A_{x_{s_m}}$, then the parsing of the node x is activated local to the nonterminal node x_{s_m}. If, however, a firstmarker is found of a nonterminal symbol $A_{x'}$ reachable from $A_{x_{s_i}}$ with i<m, but not reachable from $A_{x_{s_j}}$ for all j ($i<j \leq m$), then the parser concludes that the endmarkers of x_{s_j} for all j ($i<j \leq m$), are missing. In this case, the parsing of the node x' is activated local to x_{s_i}.

Let us illustrate this with an example. Consider the following Pico Algol program :

```
'begin'
    'boolean' switch;
    'integer' size = 256 *+ 2;
    'if' switch
        'then' 'print' size
        'else' switch := true
    'fi'
'end'
```

At the moment when the syntactic error is detected we have :

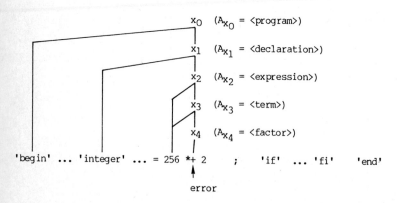

Notice that in this example x_{s_0} is x_0, x_{s_1} is x_1 and m is 1. The parser will skip the input symbols "+" and "intct", and synchronizes the node x_{s_1} with the ";".

Suppose, however, that this semicolon is also missing. We have the following input :

```
'begin'
    'boolean' switch;
    'integer' size = 256 *+ 2
    'if' switch
        'then' 'print' size
        'else' switch := true
    'fi'
'end'
```

In this case, the parser will skip input symbols until the input symbol "if" is found. This is a firstmarker of a nonterminal symbol, reachable from $A_{x_{s_0}}$ but not reachable from $A_{x_{s_1}}$. Therefore, the parser concludes that the semicolon following the declaration is missing. The if statement will then be parsed local to $A_{x_{s_0}}$ and the parsing situation becomes :

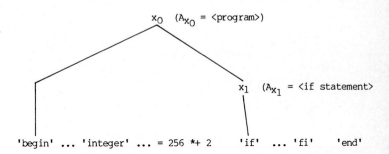

Hereafter, the input symbol "end" is found. This indicates the end of $A_{x_{s_0}}$ and terminates the parsing.

Generation scheme

This generation scheme is an extension of the preceding one with recognition of nonterminal symbols based on FIRST.

```
proc ELL(1) parser = void :
begin
  mode VTset = set of char;
  char in := co leftmost symbol of the input string co;
  proc read = void :
    co
      The next symbol in the input string is put in the variable
      'in' (the input head is moved one symbol to the right).
    co;
  proc error = void :
    co This routine produces an appropriate error message. co;
  proc accept = void :
    co
      The input string has been parsed. Some appropriate actions
      are performed. Thereafter, the ELL(1) parser halts.
    co;
  A(A₀ = e₀);
  A(A₁ = e₁);
      .
      .
      .
  A(Aⱼ = eⱼ);
      .
      .
      .
  A(Aₘ = eₘ);
  if  in ∈ DIRSYMB(e₀)
    then if A₀ ({#},  ∅,  BEGINMARKER(A₀))
          then skip
          else goto sync
        fi
    else goto prer
  fi;
  if  in = "#"
    then accept
    else goto prer
  fi;
  prer:error;
  sync:while  in ∉ {#}
        do if in ∈ BEGINMARKER(A₀)
            then RECOGNIZE(A₀)
            else read
          fi
        od
end
```

For each ECF syntax rule $A_j = e_j$ in P of G, we produce an ELL(1) parsing routine, denoted $A(A_j = e_j)$. The definitions of the set BEGINMARKER(A_j) and the program part RECOGNIZE(A_j) are given later.

a) A_j is designated to be synchronized on LAST

```
Aj = ej ∈ P  —>
  proc Aj = (VTset sp, f, bp) boolean :
    begin
      VTset s := sp U LAST(ej) U f ,
            b := bp U BEGINMARKER(Aj);
      A(ej);
      return (true);
  prer:error;
  sync:while  in ∉ s
          do  if  in ∈ b
                then if  in ∈ BEGINMARKER(Aj)
                        then RECOGNIZE(Aj)
                        else return (false)
                     fi
                else read
              fi
          od;
          if  in ∈ LAST(ej)
            then read;
                 return (true)
          fi;
          if  in ∈ f
            then return (true)
          fi;
          return (false)
    end
```

b) A_j is not designated to be synchronized on LAST

```
Aj = ej ∈ P  —>
  proc Aj = (VTset sp, f, bp) boolean :
    begin
      VTset s := sp U f ,
            b := bp;
      if  f ≠ ∅
        then b := b U BEGINMARKER(Aj)
      fi;
      A(ej);
```

```
          return (true);
prer:error;
sync: if  f ≠ ∅
        then  while  in ∉ s
                 do  if  in ∈ b
                       then if  in ∈ BEGINMARKER(Aⱼ)
                                 then RECOGNIZE(Aⱼ)
                                 else return (false)
                            fi
                       else read
                    fi
                 od;
              if  in ∈ f
                 then return (true)
              fi
      fi;
          return (false)
end
```

As an optimization, the program parts within a rectangle are only
generated if there is at least one occurrence of A_j which is designated to be synchronized on FOLLOW.

For the axiomatic rules defining $A(e_j)$ rules 2' and 2" must be
changed, for $A_j \in VN$:

2') $A_j \in VN \longrightarrow$
```
    if  in ∈ DIRSYMB(eⱼ)
      then  if  Aⱼ(s, ∅, b)
               then skip
               else goto sync
            fi
      else  goto prer
    fi
```

2") $A_j! \longrightarrow$
```
    if  in ∈ DIRSYMB(eⱼ)
      then if  Aⱼ(s, FOLLOW(Aⱼ!), b)
              then skip
              else goto sync
           fi
      else goto prer
    fi
```

The set BEGINMARKER(A_j) contains all the firstmarkers of the non-terminals that can be recognized local to the parsing routine A_j. The calculation of this set is described below. The program part RECOGNIZE(A_j) activates the parsing routine for the nonterminal symbol that can be recognized local to the parsing routine A_j and whose firstmarker has been found. RECOGNIZE(A_j) can be described by the following case statement :

```
case in
    when {"a₁"}
        A₁(s,[∅,]b)
    when {"a₂"}
        A₂(s,[∅,]b)
    .
    .
    .
    when {"aₙ"}
        Aₙ(s,[∅,]b)
esac
```

(a_1,A_1), (a_2,A_2), ... and (a_n,A_n) are all the members of the set $R_{first}(A_j)$ which is defined below.

Calculation of $R_{first}(A_j)$ and BEGINMARKER(A_j)

1. $Q_{first}(A_j) = \{(a_i,A_i) \mid A_i \in$ REACH(A_j) and
$$a_i \in \text{FIRST}(A_i) \text{ and}$$
$$A_i \text{ is designated}$$
$$\text{to be recognized on FIRST }\}$$
   REACH(A_j) is the set of all nonterminal symbols reachable from A_j. Formally,
$$\text{REACH}(A_j) = \{A_i \mid A_j =>^+ xA_iy \text{ and}$$
$$A_i,A_j \in \text{VN and}$$
$$x, y \in (\text{VT } \cup \text{ VN})^* \}$$

2. We obtain $R_{first}(A_j)$ by deleting from $Q_{first}(A_j)$ all tuples that have the same firstmarker. Formally,
$$R_{first}(A_j) = \{ (a_i,A_i) \mid (a_i,A_i) \in Q_{first}(A_j) \text{ and}$$
$$\nexists A_k ((a_i,A_k) \in Q_{first}(A_j) \text{ and}$$
$$A_i \neq A_k) \}$$

3. BEGINMARKER(A_j) = {a_i | $a_i \in$ VT and

$$\dagger A_i ((a_i, A_i) \in R_{first}(A_j))\}$$

6.2.4. Recognition based on PRECEDE

In the preceding section the parser was able to recognize nonterminal nodes the labels of which are designated to be recognized on
FIRST. The recognition is triggered by the appearance of a firstmarker in the input. In the same way, the recognition of a nonterminal node x can also be triggered by the appearance of an input
symbol that always precedes the corresponding occurrence of the nonterminal symbol A_x. Such an input symbol is called a <u>precedemarker</u>
for that nonterminal symbol occurrence.

In Pico Algol, for example, "then" and "else" are precedemarkers
for statement in the then part, respectively the else part of an if
statement, and ":=" is a precedemarker for expression occurring in
the right-hand side of an assign statement. In this way, the parser
is able to recognize the expression in the right-hand side of an
assign statement as is illustrated in Fig. 6.13.

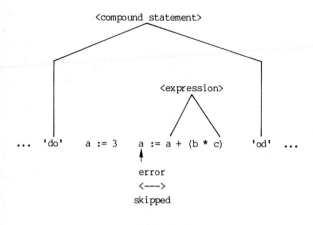

Fig. 6.13.

Definition of PRECEDE

The set PRECEDE(e) is the set of all the input symbols that can precede a given occurrence of e. The definition of PRECEDE is analogous to the definition of FOLLOW, see section 2.5.

1) $(e_1|e_2|\ldots|e_n)$
   For all i $(1 \leq i \leq n)$, PRECEDE(e_i) = PRECEDE$((e_1|e_2|\ldots|e_n))$

2) $e_1 e_2 \ldots e_n$
   For all i $(1 < i \leq n)$,
   $\quad$ PRECEDE(e_i) = $\underline{\text{if}}$ EMPTY(e_{i-1})
   $\qquad\qquad\qquad\qquad\underline{\text{then}}$ LAST(e_{i-1}) U PRECEDE(e_{i-1})
   $\qquad\qquad\qquad\qquad\underline{\text{else}}$ LAST(e_{i-1})
   $\qquad\qquad\qquad\underline{\text{fi}}$
   $\quad$ PRECEDE(e_1) = PRECEDE($e_1 e_2 \ldots e_n$)

3) e^x, where x is * or $^+$
   PRECEDE(e) = LAST(e) U PRECEDE$((e)^x)$

4) Assume that e_j is the right-hand side of an ECF syntax rule $A_j = e_j \in P$. PRECEDE(e_j) is the union of PRECEDE(A_j) for any occurrence of A_j in the right-hand side of the ECF syntax rules in P.

5) PRECEDE(A_0) = {"%"}
   The symbol "%" represents a virtual symbol preceding each input string.

Again, the LILA user must designate in the LILA input the nonterminal symbol occurrences to be recognized on PRECEDE. This is done by writing a '?' after the occurrence of the nonterminal symbol. The Pico Algol syntax with recognition based on precedemarkers is given below.

```
###syntax;

$ Analysis of a Pico Algol program
  ##rule;
    <program> =
      "begin"
        ( <declaration>! ";" )*
        <statement>!
        ( ";" <statement>! )*
      "end"

  ##recovery  last;

$ Analysis of a declaration
  ##rule;
    <declaration> =
        "integer" "iden"
          ( &  | "=" <expression>?  )
      | "boolean" "iden"
          ( &  | "=" <expression>?  )

  ##recovery  first;

$ Analysis of a statement
  ##rule;
    <statement> =
        <assign statement>
      | <print statement>
      | <compound statement>
      | <if statement>
      | <for statement>

$ Analysis of a compound statement
  ##rule;
    <compound statement> =
      "do"
        <statement>!  ( ";" <statement>! )*
      "od"

  ##recovery  first, last;

$ Analysis of an assign statement
  ##rule;
    <assign statement> =
      "iden" ":=" <expression>?

$ Analysis of a print statement
```

```
  ##rule;
    <print statement> =
      "print" <expression>

  ##recovery  first;

$ Analysis of an if statement
  ##rule;
    <if statement> =
      "if" <expression>!
        "then" <statement>!?
        "else" <statement>?
      "fi"

  ##recovery  first, last;

$ Analysis of a for statement
  ##rule;
    <for statement> =
      "for" "iden"
        "from" <expression>!?
        "to"   <expression>!?
        <compound statement>

  ##recovery  first, last;

$ Analysis of an expression
  ##rule;
    <expression> =
      <term>
        ( "+" <term>
        | "-" <term>
        )*

$ Analysis of a term
  ##rule;
    <term> =
      <factor>
        ( "*" <factor>
        | "/" <factor>
        )*

$ Analysis of a factor
  ##rule;
    <factor> =
        "iden"
      | "intct"
      | "true"
```

```
| "false"
| "(" <expression>!? ")"
```

Generation scheme

This generation scheme is the same as the preceding one, except
for the definition of the program part RECOGNIZE(A_j), which
becomes :

<u>case</u> in
  <u>when</u> {"a_{b1}"}
    A_{b1}(s,$\boxed{\emptyset,}$ b)
  <u>when</u> {"a_{b2}"}
    A_{b2}(s,$\boxed{\emptyset,}$ b)
    .
    .
    .
  <u>when</u> {"a_{bn}"}
    A_{bn}(s,$\boxed{\emptyset,}$ b)
  <u>when</u> {"a_{p1}"}
    read;
    A_{p1}(s,$\boxed{\emptyset,}$ b)
  <u>when</u> {"a_{p2}"}
    read;
    A_{p2}(s,$\boxed{\emptyset,}$ b)
    .
    .
    .
  <u>when</u> {"a_{pm}"}
    read;
    A_{pm}(s,$\boxed{\emptyset,}$ b)
<u>esac</u>

(a_{b1},A_{b1}), (a_{b2},A_{b2}), ... and (a_{bn},A_{bn}) are all the members of the
set $R_{first}(A_j)$ and (a_{p1},A_{p1}), (a_{p2},A_{p2}), ... and (a_{pm},A_{pm}) are all
the members of the set $R_{precede}(A_j)$. Both sets are defined below.

Calculation of $R_{first}(A_j)$, $R_{precede}(A_j)$ and BEGINMARKER(A_j)

1. $P_{first}(A_j) = \{(a_i,A_i) \mid A_i \in$ REACH(A_j) and
                                  $a_i \in$ FIRST(A_i) and
                                  A_i is designated

to be recognized on FIRST }

2. $P_{precede}(A_j) = \{ (a_i,A_i) \mid \nexists A_k \ (A_k \in REACH(A_j) \cup \{A_j\}$ and an occurrence of A_i in e_k, where $A_k = e_k \in P$, has been designated to be recognized on PRECEDE and a_i belongs to the set PRECEDE of that occurrence) $\}$

3. We obtain $Q_{first}(A_j)$ by deleting from $P_{first}(A_j)$ all tuples that have a firstmarker that is also a precedemarker in $P_{precede}(A_j)$. Formally,

$$Q_{first}(A_j) = \{ (a_i,A_i) \mid (a_i,A_i) \in P_{first}(A_j) \text{ and } \nexists A_k \ ((a_i,A_k) \in P_{precede}(A_j)) \}$$

4. We obtain $Q_{precede}(A_j)$ by deleting from $P_{precede}(A_j)$ all tuples that have a precedemarker that is also a firstmarker in $P_{first}(A_j)$. Formally,

$$Q_{precede}(A_j) = \{ (a_i,A_i) \mid (a_i,A_i) \in P_{precede}(A_j) \text{ and } \nexists A_k \ ((a_i,A_k) \in P_{first}(A_j)) \}$$

5. We obtain $R_{first}(A_j)$ by deleting from $Q_{first}(A_j)$ all tuples that have the same firstmarker. Formally,

$$R_{first}(A_j) = \{ (a_i,A_i) \mid (a_i,A_i) \in Q_{first}(A_j) \text{ and } \nexists A_k \ ((a_i,A_k) \in Q_{first}(A_j) \text{ and } A_i \neq A_k) \}$$

6. We obtain $R_{precede}(A_j)$ by deleting from $Q_{precede}(A_j)$ all tuples that have the same precedemarker. Formally,

$$R_{precede}(A_j) = \{ (a_i,A_i) \mid (a_i,A_i) \in Q_{precede}(A_j) \text{ and } \nexists A_k \ ((a_i,A_k) \in Q_{precede}(A_j) \text{ and } A_i \neq A_k) \}$$

7. $BEGINMARKER(A_j) = \{ a_i \mid a_i \in VT$ and $\nexists A_i \ ((a_i,A_i) \in R_{first}(A_j) \cup R_{precede}(A_j)) \}$

6.2.5. Rules of thumb

In the preceding subsections, the error recovery method has been
stepwise developed to arrive at the final scheme in section 6.2.4.
The effectiveness of the error recovery in a particular transducer
depends heavily on the error recovery information specified in the
LILA input. This section contains some rules of thumb that are
helpful in specifying this information.

1. Always start by selecting the nonterminal symbols that are to be
   synchronized. First specify the nonterminal symbols that are to
   be synchronized on their lastmarkers, then specify the nonterminal symbol occurrences that are to be synchronized on their followmarkers.

2. In general, all the nonterminal symbols with specific lastmarkers
   are candidates to be synchronized on their lastmarkers.
   One must be careful with recursively defined nonterminal symbols.
   If a recursively defined nonterminal symbol is designated to be
   synchronized on its lastmarkers, then it must also be recognizable. A nonterminal symbol is recognizable if it is recognizable
   from its firstmarkers, or if all its occurrences are recognizable
   from their precedemarkers.

3. A nonterminal symbol occurrence can be synchronized on its followmarkers if these followmarkers are specific for that
   occurrence. Take care that these followmarkers are not derivable
   from the selected nonterminal symbol.

4. After the synchronizable nonterminal symbols have been designated, select the nonterminal symbols that are to be recognized
   from their firstmarkers.
   Take care that there is only one nonterminal symbol that is
   recognized from a particular firstmarker in a particular context.
   For example, if both <statement> and <if statement> are designated to be recognized from their firstmarkers, then "if" will be
   removed from the firstmarkers because of the rules that calculate
   R_{first}. The result is that an <if statement> will never be
   recognized. In such a case it is always better to select the
   most enclosing nonterminal symbol, i.e. <statement>.

5. In a last step, select the nonterminal symbol occurrences that are to be recognized from their precedemarkers. These precede-markers must be specific for the nonterminal symbol occurrence and they may not be used as firstmarkers.

Other interesting points about the selection of the error recovery information can be found in sections 6.3 and 6.4.

6.3. The error recovery in Pico Algol

The Pico Algol compiler as it has been introduced in section 5.5, will halt as soon as a lexical or syntactic error is encountered. In order to detect as many errors as possible in a single compilation, both the lexical analyser and the syntax-semantic analyser must be synchronized in case of errors.

The error recovery in the syntax analyser of Pico Algol has already been discussed in section 6.2. In order to illustrate the error recovery strategy supported by LILA in all its power, we will illustrate what can be achieved with the recovery information in the LILA input for the syntax analyser. As it will be explained in section 6.3.2, this will result in a very powerful error recovery for Pico Algol. In section 6.3.3, the interaction between the syntactic error recovery and the semantic error recovery will be discussed.

The error recovery in the lexical analyser of Pico Algol is straightforward. However, since we want to detect as many errors as possible during a single compilation, it is necessary to activate the syntax-semantic analyser even if a lexical error is encountered. The error recovery in the lexical analyser of Pico Algol is discussed in section 6.3.1.

6.3.1. The error recovery in the lexical analyser

In this section, two different ways to synchronize the lexical analyser of Pico Algol will be discussed. In section 6.3.1.1, the lexical analyser will be synchronized by means of the error recovery strategy supported by LILA. In section 6.3.1.2, a more ad hoc error recovery strategy will be introduced, which is especially useful in synchronizing analysers as simple as the lexical analyser of Pico Algol.

An important aspect in the error recovery in the lexical analyser is the interaction between the lexical analyser and the syntax-semantic analyser of Pico Algol. As it has been mentioned above, the syntax-semantic analyser must be activated even if a lexical error is encountered. Therefore, the lexical analyser will produce a special symbol, called the <u>error</u> symbol, for each lexical error.

Each appearance of the error symbol in the input for the syntax-semantic analyser will force the latter in the error state.

6.3.1.1. The error recovery in the lexical analyser : Version 1

The lexical analyser of Pico Algol can be synchronized using the error recovery strategy supported by LILA. The option 'syncflow' is discussed later.

```
$$$$$$$$$$$$$$$$$$$$$$$$$$$$$$$$$$$$$$$$$$$$$$$$$$$$$$$$$$$$$$$$$$$$$$$$$$$$$$$$$$
$   LILA INPUT                                                                $
$                                                                            $
$       Compiler for Pico Algol : Lexical Analyser, synchronized version.    $
$$$$$$$$$$$$$$$$$$$$$$$$$$$$$$$$$$$$$$$$$$$$$$$$$$$$$$$$$$$$$$$$$$$$$$$$$$$$$$$$$$


###options
  let,
  syncflow;


###inputvocabulary  rep(char), file(input);

$ Delimiters
  " " = 32    "'" = 39    "(" = 40    ")" = 41    "*" = 42    "+" = 43
  "-" = 45    "/" = 47    ":" = 58    ";" = 59    "=" = 61

$ Digits
  "0" = 48    "1" = 49    "2" = 50    "3" = 51    "4" = 52    "5" = 53
  "6" = 54    "7" = 55    "8" = 56    "9" = 57

$ Letters
  "a" = 97    "b" = 98    "c" = 99    "d" =100    "e" =101    "f" =102
  "g" =103    "h" =104    "i" =105    "j" =106    "k" =107    "l" =108
  "m" =109    "n" =110    "o" =111    "p" =112    "q" =113    "r" =114
  "s" =115    "t" =116    "u" =117    "v" =118    "w" =119    "x" =120
  "y" =121    "z" =122

$ Erroneous input characters
                "stx"= 2    "etx"= 3    "eot"= 4    "enq"= 5    "ack"= 6    "bel"= 7
  "bs" = 8     "ht" = 9     "lf" =10    "vt" =11    "ff" =12    "cr" =13    "so" =14
  "si" =15     "dle"=16     "dc1"=17    "dc2"=18    "dc3"=19    "dc4"=20    "nak"=21
  "syn"=22     "etb"=23     "can"=24    "em" =25    "sub"=26    "esc"=27    "fs" =28
  "gs" =29     "rs" =30     "us" =31    "!" =33     "\"" =34    "\#" =35    "\$" =36
  "%" =37      "&" =38      "," =44     "." =46     "<" =60     ">" =62     "?" =63
  "@" =64      "A" =65      "B" =66     "C" =67     "D" =68     "E" =69     "F" =70
  "G" =71      "H" =72      "I" =73     "J" =74     "K" =75     "L" =76     "M" =77
```

```
"N"  =78  "O"  =79  "P"  =80  "Q"  =81  "R"  =82  "S"  =83  "T"  =84
"U"  =85  "V"  =86  "W"  =87  "X"  =88  "Y"  =89  "Z"  =90  "["  =91
"\\"  =92  "]"  =93  "^"  =94  "_"  =95  "`"  =96  "{"  =123  "|"  =124
"}"  =125  " "  =126  "del"= 127
```

###syntax;

$ <u>Definition of the lexical structure of a Pico Algol program</u>
  ##rule;
    <program> =
      (<keyword>!
      | <identifier>
      | <constant>
      | <delimiter>!
)*

$ <u>Analysis of a keyword</u>
  ##rule;
    <keyword> =
      "'"
        <letter>*
      "'"

  ##recovery first;

$ <u>Analysis of an identifier</u>
  ##rule;
    <identifier> =
      <letter>
        (<letter> | <digit>)*

  ##recovery first;

$ <u>Analysis of a constant</u>
  ##rule;
    <constant> =
      <digit>+

  ##recovery first;

$ <u>Analysis of a delimiter</u>
  ##rule;
    <delimiter> =
        ("+" | "-" | "*" | "/" | "=" | "(" | ")" | ";")
      | ":" "="
      | " "+
```
```

```
##recovery first;
```

$ Definition of a letter
```
  ##rule;
    <letter> =
      "a" | "b" | "c" | "d" | "e" | "f" | "g" | "h" | "i"
    | "j" | "k" | "l" | "m" | "n" | "o" | "p" | "q" | "r"
    | "s" | "t" | "u" | "v" | "w" | "x" | "y" | "z"
```

$ Definition of a digit
```
  ##rule;
    <digit> =
      "0" | "1" | "2" | "3" | "4" | "5" | "6" | "7" | "8" | "9"
```

```
###globalinfo;

  ##parameter;
    input, output
```

For each error inside a keyword or a delimiter the lexical analyser will skip input characters until a character is found which can start a keyword, an identifier, a constant or a delimiter. Whenever a character not part of the inputvocabulary is under the input head, the lexical analyser will recognize keywords, identifiers, constants and delimiters from their respective firstmarkers until the virtual end-of-file symbol is found.

In this section, only the syntactic phase of the lexical analyser is discussed. In a second step, semantic actions producing the input symbols for the syntax-semantic analyser will be added to the LILA input. In order to accomplish the interaction between the lexical analyser and the syntax-semantic analyser, the LILA input will also contain a user-defined error routine. This routine will print an error message and will produce the special input symbol 'error' for the syntax-semantic analyser.

6.3.1.2.   The error recovery in the lexical analyser : Version 2

The error recovery strategy supported by LILA for a syntax which is as simple as the lexical structure of Pico Algol, is too heavy. Examining the lexical analyser in more detail reveals that there are only three lexical errors:

1) a keyword not terminated by a quote.

2) a colon not followed by an equal sign.

3) a character not part of the input vocabulary under the input
   head.

In such cases, a more direct approach to synchronize the analyser
generated by LILA, is to make the syntax error-<u>free</u>. This is illustrated below for the lexical analyser of Pico Algol.

```
$$$$$$$$$$$$$$$$$$$$$$$$$$$$$$$$$$$$$$$$$$$$$$$$$$$$$$$$$$$$$$$$$$$$$$$$$$$$$$$$$$$$$
$    LILA INPUT                                                                 $
$                                                                              $
$      Compiler for Pico Algol : Lexical Analyser, error-free version.         $
$$$$$$$$$$$$$$$$$$$$$$$$$$$$$$$$$$$$$$$$$$$$$$$$$$$$$$$$$$$$$$$$$$$$$$$$$$$$$$$$$$$$$
```

```
###options
  let,
  nolast;
```

```
###inputvocabulary  rep(char), file(input);
```

$ <u>Delimiters</u>
```
" " = 32    "'" = 39    "(" = 40    ")" = 41    "*" = 42    "+" = 43
"-" = 45    "/" = 47    ":" = 58    ";" = 59    "=" = 61
```

$ <u>Digits</u>
```
"0" = 48    "1" = 49    "2" = 50    "3" = 51    "4" = 52    "5" = 53
"6" = 54    "7" = 55    "8" = 56    "9" = 57
```

$ <u>Letters</u>
```
"a" = 97    "b" = 98    "c" = 99    "d" =100    "e" =101    "f" =102
"g" =103    "h" =104    "i" =105    "j" =106    "k" =107    "l" =108
"m" =109    "n" =110    "o" =111    "p" =112    "q" =113    "r" =114
"s" =115    "t" =116    "u" =117    "v" =118    "w" =119    "x" =120
"y" =121    "z" =122
```

$ <u>Erroneous input characters</u>
```
            "stx"= 2   "etx"= 3   "eot"= 4   "enq"= 5   "ack"= 6   "bel"= 7
"bs" = 8    "ht" = 9   "lf" =10   "vt" =11   "ff" =12   "cr" =13   "so" =14
"si" =15    "dle"=16   "dc1"=17   "dc2"=18   "dc3"=19   "dc4"=20   "nak"=21
"syn"=22    "etb"=23   "can"=24   "em" =25   "sub"=26   "esc"=27   "fs" =28
"gs" =29    "rs" =30   "us" =31   "!"  =33   "\"" =34   "\#" =35   "\$" =36
```

```
"%"  =37  "&"  =38  ","  =44  "."  =46  "<"  =60  ">"  =62  "?"  =63
"@"  =64  "A"  =65  "B"  =66  "C"  =67  "D"  =68  "E"  =69  "F"  =70
"G"  =71  "H"  =72  "I"  =73  "J"  =74  "K"  =75  "L"  =76  "M"  =77
"N"  =78  "O"  =79  "P"  =80  "Q"  =81  "R"  =82  "S"  =83  "T"  =84
"U"  =85  "V"  =86  "W"  =87  "X"  =88  "Y"  =89  "Z"  =90  "["  =91
"\\" =92  "]"  =93  "^"  =94  "_"  =95  "`"  =96  "{"  =123 "|"  =124
"}"  =125 " "  =126 "del"= 127
```

###syntax;

$ Definition of the lexical structure of a Pico Algol program
  ##rule;
    <program> =
      (<keyword>
      | <identifier>
      | <constant>
      | <delimiter>
      | <erroneous symbol>
)*

$ Analysis of a keyword
  ##rule;
    <keyword> =
      "'"
        <letter>*
      ("'" | &)

$ Analysis of an identifier
  ##rule;
    <identifier> =
      <letter>
        (<letter> | <digit>)*

$ Analysis of a constant
  ##rule;
    <constant> =
      <digit>+

$ Analysis of a delimiter
  ##rule;
    <delimiter> =
        ("+" | "-" | "*" | "/" | "=" | "(" | ")" | ";")
      | ":" ("=" | &)
      | " "+

$ Definition of a letter
  ##rule;
```
```

```
<letter> =
    "a" | "b" | "c" | "d" | "e" | "f" | "g" | "h" | "i"
  | "j" | "k" | "l" | "m" | "n" | "o" | "p" | "q" | "r"
  | "s" | "t" | "u" | "v" | "w" | "x" | "y" | "z"
```

$ Definition of a digit
```
##rule;
    <digit> =
    "0" | "1" | "2" | "3" | "4" | "5" | "6" | "7" | "8" | "9"
```

$ Definition of an erroneous symbol
```
##rule;
    <erroneous symbol> =
                "stx" | "etx" | "eot" | "enq" | "ack" | "bel" | "bs"  | "ht"
      | "lf"  | "vt"  | "ff"  | "cr"  | "so"  | "si"  | "dle" | "dc1" | "dc2"
      | "dc3" | "dc4" | "nak" | "syn" | "etb" | "can" | "em"  | "sub" | "esc"
      | "fs"  | "gs"  | "rs"  | "us"  | "!"   | "\""  | "\#"  | "\$"  | "%"
      | "&"   | ","   | "."   | "<"   | ">"   | "?"   | "@"   | "A"   | "B"
      | "C"   | "D"   | "E"   | "F"   | "G"   | "H"   | "I"   | "J"   | "K"
      | "L"   | "M"   | "N"   | "O"   | "P"   | "Q"   | "R"   | "S"   | "T"
      | "U"   | "V"   | "W"   | "X"   | "Y"   | "Z"   | "["   | "\\"  | "]"
      | "^"   | "_"   | "`"   | "{"   | "|"   | "}"   | " "   | "del"
```

###globalinfo;

```
    ##parameter;
     input, output
```

###errorroutine;
```
    $   Since there are no syntactic errors, the error routine
    $ becomes a dummy routine.
```

Obviously, the lexical analyser as it is described above, will accept any string of characters. We are now able to add semantic actions in order to translate a stream of characters into a sequence of input symbols for the syntax-semantic analyser. In contrast with the non-synchronized version of the lexical analyser, some of the semantic actions generate error diagnostic messages and produce the special input symbol 'error' for the syntax-semantic analyser.

```
$$$$$$$$$$$$$$$$$$$$$$$$$$$$$$$$$$$$$$$$$$$$$$$$$$$$$$$$$$$$$$$$$$$$$$$$$$$$$$$$$$$$$
$    LILA INPUT                                                                 $
$                                                                              $
$       Compiler for Pico Algol : Lexical Analyser, error-free version         $
$$$$$$$$$$$$$$$$$$$$$$$$$$$$$$$$$$$$$$$$$$$$$$$$$$$$$$$$$$$$$$$$$$$$$$$$$$$$$$$$$$$$$
```

###options
  let,
  nolast;

###inputvocabulary rep(char), file(input);

$ Delimiters
  " " = 32   "'" = 39   "(" = 40   ")" = 41   "*" = 42   "+" = 43
  "-" = 45   "/" = 47   ":" = 58   ";" = 59   "=" = 61

$ Digits
  "0" = 48   "1" = 49   "2" = 50   "3" = 51   "4" = 52   "5" = 53
  "6" = 54   "7" = 55   "8" = 56   "9" = 57

$ Letters
  "a" = 97   "b" = 98   "c" = 99   "d" =100   "e" =101   "f" =102
  "g" =103   "h" =104   "i" =105   "j" =106   "k" =107   "l" =108
  "m" =109   "n" =110   "o" =111   "p" =112   "q" =113   "r" =114
  "s" =115   "t" =116   "u" =117   "v" =118   "w" =119   "x" =120
  "y" =121   "z" =122

$ Erroneous input characters
          "stx"= 2   "etx"= 3   "eot"= 4   "enq"= 5   "ack"= 6   "bel"= 7
  "bs" = 8   "ht" = 9   "lf" =10   "vt" =11   "ff" =12   "cr" =13   "so" =14
  "si" =15   "dle"=16   "dc1"=17   "dc2"=18   "dc3"=19   "dc4"=20   "nak"=21
  "syn"=22   "etb"=23   "can"=24   "em" =25   "sub"=26   "esc"=27   "fs" =28
  "gs" =29   "rs" =30   "us" =31   "!" =33   "\"" =34   "\#" =35   "\$" =36
  "%" =37   "&" =38   "," =44   "." =46   "<" =60   ">" =62   "?" =63
  "@" =64   "A" =65   "B" =66   "C" =67   "D" =68   "E" =69   "F" =70
  "G" =71   "H" =72   "I" =73   "J" =74   "K" =75   "L" =76   "M" =77
  "N" =78   "O" =79   "P" =80   "Q" =81   "R" =82   "S" =83   "T" =84
  "U" =85   "V" =86   "W" =87   "X" =88   "Y" =89   "Z" =90   "[" =91
  "\\" =92   "]" =93   "^" =94   "_" =95   "`" = 96   "{" =123   "|" =124
  "}" =125 " " =126 "del"= 127

###outputvocabulary rep(integer);

$ Keywords

```
[begin]    = 2      [end]      = 3
[boolean]  = 4      [integer]  = 5
[true]     = 6      [false]    = 7
[print]    = 8      [if]       = 9
[then]     =10      [else]     =11
[fi]       =12      [do]       =13
[od]       =14      [for]      =15
[from]     =16      [to]       =17
```

$ <u>Delimiters</u>
```
[(] = 40    [)] = 41    [*] = 42    [+] = 43    [-] = 45    [/] = 47
[:=]= 48    [;] = 59    [=] = 61
```

$ <u>Integer Constant</u>
```
[intct] = 62 : integer
```

$ <u>Identifier</u>
```
[iden]  = 63 : rep_name
```

$ <u>Miscellaneous</u>
```
[error] = 18
```

```
     $   Notice that the codes of the keywords must be identical to  the
     $ corresponding indices in the table of   keyword  names  'keytab'
     $ (see prologue of the LILA input). Furthermore, the codes  of  the
     $ delimiters (except for the assignment operator) must be identical
     $ to the codes of the corresponding  delimiters  in  the  input
     $ vocabulary.
```

###syntax;

$ <u>Definition of the lexical structure of a Pico Algol program</u>
```
  ##rule;
    <program> =
      ( <keyword>
      | <identifier>
      | <constant>
      | <delimiter>
      | <erroneous symbol>   inv_symbol
      )*

    ##action;
    #inv_symbol;
      error(inv_symbol);
      out(%[error])
```

$ <u>Analysis of a keyword</u>

```
##rule;
  <keyword> =
    "'"  init_name
      ( add_name  <letter> )*
    ( "'" out_keyword | quote_exp )

  ##var;
    key_name: rep_keyname;
    nb_char : integer;
    code    : integer

  ##action;
    #init_name;
      key_name := '        ';
      nb_char   := 0

    #add_name;
      nb_char := nb_char + 1;
      if (nb_char <= keylength)
        then key_name [nb_char] := inp.c

    #out_keyword;
              $    If the character string enclosed between quotes is not
              $ a Pico Algol keyword, an error message is issued and  the
              $ error symbol is produced.
      if (nb_char <= keylength)
        then code := key_code(key_name)
        else code := max_keycode;
      if (code = max_keycode) then begin
        error(inv_keyword);
        out(%[error])
      end
      else out(code)

    #quote_exp;
      error(quote_exp);
      out(%[error])

$ Analysis of an identifier
  ##rule;
    <identifier> =
      init_name  <letter>
        ( add_name  ( <letter> | <digit> )  )*
      out_identifier

    ##var;
      nb_char : integer
```

```
##action;
  #init_name;
    @[iden] := '        ';
    @[iden] [1] := inp.c;
    nb_char := 1

  #add_name;
    nb_char := nb_char + 1;
    if (nb_char <= idlength)
      then @[iden] [nb_char] := inp.c

  #out_identifier;
    if (nb_char > idlength) then error(iden_trunc);
    out(%[iden])
```

$ Analysis of a constant
```
  ##rule;
    <constant> =
      init_val
        (  val  <digit>  )+
      out_intct

  ##action;
    #init_val;
      @[intct] := 0

    #val;
      if (@[intct] <> -1) then
        if (@[intct] + 1) <= (maxint div 10)
          then @[intct] := @[intct]*10 + (ord(inp.c) - ord('0'))
          else begin
            error(maxint_exc);
                      $ Semantic error recovery: whenever the value of a
                      $ constant exceeds 'maxint', it will be set to -1.
            @[intct] := -1
          end

    #out_intct;
      out(%[intct])
```

$ Analysis of a delimiter
```
  ##rule;
    <delimiter> =
        out_delimiter
          ( "+" | "-" | "*" | "/" | "=" | "(" | ")" | ";" )
      | ":" ( "=" out_assign | equal_exp )
      | " "+
```

```
##action;
  #out_delimiter;
    out(ord(inp.c))

  #out_assign;
    out(%[:=])

  #equal_exp;
    error(equal_exp);
    out(%[error])
```

$ Definition of a letter
```
  ##rule;
    <letter> =
       "a" | "b" | "c" | "d" | "e" | "f" | "g" | "h" | "i"
     | "j" | "k" | "l" | "m" | "n" | "o" | "p" | "q" | "r"
     | "s" | "t" | "u" | "v" | "w" | "x" | "y" | "z"
```

$ Definition of a digit
```
  ##rule;
    <digit> =
       "0" | "1" | "2" | "3" | "4" | "5" | "6" | "7" | "8" | "9"
```

$ Definition of an erroneous symbol
```
  ##rule;
    <erroneous symbol> =
                  "stx" | "etx" | "eot" | "enq" | "ack" | "bel" | "bs"  | "ht"
       | "lf"  | "vt"  | "ff"  | "cr"  | "so"  | "si"  | "dle" | "dc1" | "dc2"
       | "dc3" | "dc4" | "nak" | "syn" | "etb" | "can" | "em"  | "sub" | "esc"
       | "fs"  | "gs"  | "rs"  | "us"  | "!"   | "\""  | "\#"  | "\$"  | "%"
       | "&"   | ","   | "."   | "<"   | ">"   | "?"   | "@"   | "A"   | "B"
       | "C"   | "D"   | "E"   | "F"   | "G"   | "H"   | "I"   | "J"   | "K"
       | "L"   | "M"   | "N"   | "O"   | "P"   | "Q"   | "R"   | "S"   | "T"
       | "U"   | "V"   | "W"   | "X"   | "Y"   | "Z"   | "["   | "\\"  | "]"
       | "^"   | "_"   | "`"   | "{"   | "|"   | "}"   | " "   | "del"
```

```
###global info;

  ##parameter;
    input, output, outfile

  ##const;
    $ rep keyname
      keylength   = 7;
      min_keycode = 2;    $$ smallest code in the set of keywords.
      max_keycode =18;    $$ largest code in the set of keywords + 1.
```

```
   $ rep name
     idlength = 8

##type;
  $ rep keyname
    rep_keyname = packed array [1..keylength] of char;

  $ message
    message = (inv_keyword, iden_trunc, maxint_exc,
                inv_symbol,  quote_exp, equal_exp);

  $ rep name
    rep_name = packed array [1..idlength] of char

##var;
  $ rep keyname
    keytab : array [ min_keycode..max_keycode ] of rep_keyname

##routine;
  $ rep keyname
    function key_code (n:rep_keyname): integer;
    var i : min_keycode..max_keycode;
    begin
      keytab[ max_keycode ] := n;
      i := min_keycode;
      while (keytab[i] <> n)
        do i := succ(i);
      key_code := i
    end; {key_code}

  $ message
    procedure error (m:message);
    begin
      writeln(output);
      write(output, linenumb:4, ' *** ERROR *** : ');
      case  m  of
        inv_keyword:
          write('Invalid keyword used.');
        iden_trunc:
          write('Identifier truncated to',idlength:2,' characters.');
        maxint_exc:
          write('Constant exceeds maximum value.');
        inv_symbol:
          write('Invalid character in input stream.');
        quote_exp:
          write('Quote expected to terminate keyword.');
        equal_exp:
          write('Equal sign expected after colon.')
```

```
        end;
        writeln(output)
      end {error}

  ##prologue;
    $ rep keyname
      keytab[ 2] := 'begin ';   keytab[ 3] := 'end    ';
      keytab[ 4] := 'boolean';  keytab[ 5] := 'integer';
      keytab[ 6] := 'true  ';   keytab[ 7] := 'false ';
      keytab[ 8] := 'print ';   keytab[ 9] := 'if     ';
      keytab[10] := 'then  ';   keytab[11] := 'else  ';
      keytab[12] := 'fi    ';   keytab[13] := 'do    ';
      keytab[14] := 'od    ';   keytab[15] := 'for   ';
      keytab[16] := 'from  ';   keytab[17] := 'to     '
```

###errorroutine;

```
  $   Since there are no syntactic errors, the error routine
  $ becomes a dummy routine.
```

6.3.2. The error recovery in the syntax analyser

The syntax analyser of the Pico Algol compiler, as it has been introduced in section 5.5.3, will halt as soon as a syntactic error is encountered. In order to detect as many syntactic errors as possible in a single compilation, recovery information must be added to the LILA input for the syntax analyser.

The design of appropriate error recovery information is always a compromise between the resolution of the error recovery (only small parts of the input program are skipped) and efficiency of the compiler (time and space). Such a compromise for the syntax analyser of Pico Algol has already been introduced in section 6.2. This section discusses the design of recovery information for the syntax analyser, such that only small parts of Pico Algol programs are skipped. Thereafter, the behavior of the error recovery for Pico Algol will be illustrated by a number of examples.

program

A Pico Algol program will be recognized from its firstmarker "begin" and synchronized on its lastmarker "end". Furthermore, each declaration within a program will be synchronized on its follow-marker ";". The LILA input for the rule for program, extended with the appropriate recovery information is given below.

```
##rule;
  <program> =
    "begin"
      ( <declaration>! ";" )*
      <statement>  ( ";" <statement> )*
    "end"

##recovery  last, first;
```

Notice that we cannot synchronize a Pico Algol statement on all its followmarkers (";" and "end"), because the semicolon can appear within a (compound) statement.

declaration

In the rule for declaration, each expression will be recognized from its precedemarker ("="). Furthermore, a declaration itself will be recognized from its firstmarkers ("integer" and "boolean".) The LILA input for the rule for declaration, extended with the appropriate recovery information is given below.

```
##rule;
  <declaration> =
      "integer" "iden"
        ( & | "=" <expression>? )
    | "boolean" "iden"
        ( & | "=" <expression>? )

##recovery  first;
```

statement

As it has been explained above, a statement in a Pico Algol program cannot be synchronized on its followmarkers (";" and "end"), because a semicolon can appear within a compound statement. Some of the Pico Algol statements (assign statement and print statement), however, will never contain a semicolon; in fact, they will never contain any of the followmarkers of a Pico Algol statement (";", "end", "else", "fi" and "od"). Therefore, an assign statement and a print statement will be synchronized on their followmarkers.

The LILA input for the rule for statement, extended with the appropriate recovery information is given below.

```
##rule;
  <statement> =
      <compound statement>
  | <if statement>
  | <for statement>
  | <print statement>!
  | <assign statement>!
```

compound statement

The treatment of the rule for compound statement is analogous to the treatment of the rule for program: a compound statement is recognized from its firstmarker ("do") and synchronized on its lastmarker ("od"). The LILA input for the rule for compound statement, extended with the appropriate recovery information is given below.

```
##rule;
  <compound statement> =
    "do"
      <statement>  ( ";" <statement> )*
    "od"

##recovery  last, first;
```

if statement

In the rule for if statement, the boolean expression will be synchronized on its followmarker ("then"). Furthermore, the statements in the then-part and the else-part will be recognized from their respective precedemarkers ("then" and "else"). At last, the if statement itself will be recognized from its firstmarker ("if") and synchronized on its lastmarker ("fi").

The LILA input for the rule for if statement, extended with the appropriate recovery information is given below.

```
##rule;
 <if statement> =
   "if" <expression>!
     "then" <statement>?
     "else" <statement>?
   "fi"

##recovery last, first;
```

for statement

In the rule for for statement, the expressions determining the initial value and the final value of the control variable will be synchronized on their respective followmarkers ("to" and "do") and recognized from their respective precedemarkers ("from" and "to"). Notice that the for statement itself should not be synchronized on its lastmarker ("od"). This symbol is part of the compound statement at the end of the for statement. Whenever a compound statement is recognized within a for statement, The input symbol "od" is analysed within the scope of that compound statement; it is, however, not interpreted as the end of the for statement.

The LILA input for the rule for for statement, extended with the appropriate recovery information is given below.

```
##rule;
 <for statement> =
   "for" "iden"
     "from" <expression>!?
     "to"   <expression>!?
     <compound statement>
```

```
##recovery first;
```

print statement

A Pico Algol print statement will be recognized from its first-marker ("print"). The LILA input for the rule for print statement, extended with the appropriate recovery information is given below.

```
##rule;
  <print statement> =
    "print" <expression>
```

```
##recovery first;
```

assign statement

In the rule for assign statement, each expression will be recognized from its precedemarker (":="). The LILA input for the rule for assign statement, extended with the appropriate recovery information is given below.

```
##rule;
  <assign statement> =
    "iden" ":=" <expression>?
```

Obviously, an assign statement cannot be recognized from its firstmarker, because an identifier can be used at more than one place in a Pico Algol program.

expression

In the rule for expression, each term will be recognized from its precedemarkers ("+" and "-"). The LILA input for the rule for expression, extended with the appropriate recovery information is given below.

```
##rule;
  <expression> =
    <term>
```

```
( "+" <term>?
| "-" <term>?
)*
```

term

In the rule for term, each factor will be recognized from its precedemarkers ("*" and "/") The LILA input for the rule for term, extended with the appropriate recovery information is given below.

```
##rule;
  <term> =
    <factor>
      ( "*" <factor>?
      | "/" <factor>?
      )*
```

factor

In the error recovery for Pico Algol, an expression between parentheses is synchronized on its followmarker ")" and recognized from its precedemarker "(". The LILA input for the rule for factor extended with the appropriate recovery information is given below.

```
##rule;
  <factor> =
      "intct"
    | "true"
    | "false"
    | "iden"
    | "(" <expression>!? ")"
```

Remark

The resolution of the error recovery performed in the syntax analyser for Pico Algol can still be increased if the syntax rules defining a Pico Algol program and a Pico Algol declaration are changed. Then, the semicolon <u>following</u> a Pico Algol declaration is no longer specified after the analysis of a declaration; instead, it is specified as a <u>terminator</u> in the rule for declaration itself.

The LILA input for the rule for program and the rule for declaration then becomes :

```
##rule;
  <program> =
    "begin"
      <declaration>*
      <statement> ( ";" <statement> )*
    "end"

##recovery last, first;


##rule;
  <declaration> =
    ( "integer" "iden"
        ( & | "=" <expression>? )
    | "boolean" "iden"
        ( & | "=" <expression>? )
    ) ";"

##recovery last, first;
```

In this way, an error message can be produced whenever a declaration <u>recognized</u> from one of its beginmarkers "integer" or "boolean", is not terminated by a semicolon.

The behavior of the error recovery in the syntax analyser for Pico Algol will now be illustrated by a number of examples. For each example, the error messages produced by the lexical analyser and the syntax analyser for Pico Algol will be given. These messages are produced by the LILA default error module; they have the following form :

k: *** error *** : The input symbol a_i is invalid after
$$a_{i-4} \; a_{i-3} \; a_{i-2} \; a_{i-1}$$

where k is the number of the line in which the error has occurred, a_i is the erroneous input symbol and a_{i-4}, a_{i-3}, a_{i-2} and a_{i-1} are the symbols immediately preceding the input symbol a_i in the input string. Notice the importance of the symbolic names chosen for the input symbols in the LILA input. They determine the readability of

the error messages as they are produced by the LILA default error
module.

Furthermore, if the 'syncflow' option is specified in the LILA
input, the error diagnostics will contain three other kind of messages. These messages are intended for the LILA user to understand
the error recovery performed in the syntax analyser generated by
LILA.

  - *** synchronized : A
       The syntax analyser has synchronized the rule for the non-
       terminal symbol A.

  - *** recognized : A
       The syntax analyser has recognized in the error state the
       start of a sentence derivable from the nonterminal symbol A.
       It will parse that sentence.

  - *** skipped : a
       The syntax analyser skips the input symbol a in the error
       state.

  Example 1 : Lexical errors

  This example illustrates the behavior of the error recovery in
the lexical analyser and in the syntax analyser, if the input does
not meet the lexical structure of Pico Algol . The input program is
given below.

```
1   'begin
2     'integer' a = 100000;
3     'bool'    b $ 'true';
4     'integer' toolongidentifier;
5     toolongidentifier : 10
6   'end'
```

The error diagnostic messages produced by the lexical analyser are
listed below :

```
2 *** error *** : quote expected to terminate keyword.

2 *** error *** : constant exceeds maximum value.

3 *** error *** : invalid keyword used.

3 *** error *** : invalid character in input stream.

4 *** error *** : identifier truncated to 8 characters.

5 *** error *** : identifier truncated to 8 characters.

5 *** error *** : equal sign expected after colon.
```

The diagnostics produced by the syntax analyser are given below.

```
**skipped : "error"
**recognized : <declaration>
**skipped : ";"
**skipped : "error"
**skipped : "iden"
**skipped : "error"
**skipped : "true"
**skipped : ";"
**recognized : <declaration>
**skipped : ";"
**skipped : "iden"
**skipped : "error"
**skipped : "intct"
**skipped : "end"
```

Example 2 : Errors in declarations

This example illustrates the behavior of the error recovery in the syntax analyser for some errors in declaring variables and constants. The input program is given below.

```
1  'begin'
2    'integer' 100;
3    'boolean' b c = 'true';
4    'integer' d = 10 +;
5    'integer' e = 10 d;
6    'print' 10
7  'end'
```

The diagnostics generated by the syntax analyser are given below.

```
    2: *** error ***: the input symbol "intct" is invalid after
                        "begin" "integer"
**skipped : "intct"
**synchronized : <declaration>

    3: *** error ***: the input symbol "iden" is invalid after
                        "intct" ";" "boolean" "iden"
**skipped : "iden"
**recognized : <expression>
**synchronized : <declaration>

    4: *** error ***: the input symbol ";" is invalid after
                        "iden" "=" "intct" "+"
**synchronized : <declaration>

    5: *** error ***: the input symbol "iden" is invalid after
                        "integer" "iden" "=" "intct"
**skipped : "iden"
**skipped : ";"
**recognized : <print statement>
**synchronized : <program>
```

Example 3 : Errors in a nested construct

This example illustrates the behavior of the error recovery in the syntax analyser for errors in a nested if statement. The input program is given below.

```
 1   'begin'
 2     'integer' a;
 3     'boolean' b;
 4     'if' b
 5       then a := 4
 6       'else' 'if' b
 7               'then' a := 5
 8               'else' b 6
 9             'fi'
10     'fi'
11   'end'
```

The diagnostics generated by the syntax analyser are given below.

```
    5: *** error ***: the input symbol "iden" is invalid after
                        "iden" ";" "if" "iden"
**skipped : "iden"
**skipped : "iden"
**recognized : <expression>
**recognized : <statement>

    9: *** error ***: the input symbol "intct" is invalid after
                        ":=" "intct" "else" "iden"
**skipped : "intct"
**synchronized : <assign statement>
**synchronized : <if statement>
```

Example 4 : Errors against synchronization markers

In the previous examples the behavior of the error recovery in the syntax analyser has been illustrated for programs in which there are no errors against firstmarkers, precedemarkers, lastmarkers and followmarkers. The following two examples illustrate the behavior of the error recovery in the syntax analyser if some markers are missing. These examples show that, even in complex situations the parser still behaves well. The input program for the first example is given below.

```
 1  'begin'
 2    'integer' a = (4+5;
 3    'boolean' b c
 4    'do'
 5      'if' b
 6        'then' c:='true'
 7        'else' c:='false'
 8      'print' a
 9    'od'
10  'end'
```

The diagnostics generated by the syntax analyser are given below.

```
    2: *** error ***: the input symbol ";" is invalid after
                        "(" "intct" "+" "intct"
**synchronized : <declaration>

    4: *** error ***: the input symbol "iden" is invalid after
                        "intct" ";" "boolean" "iden"
**skipped : "iden"
```

```
**recognized : <compound statement>

    8: *** error ***: the input symbol "print" is invalid after
                       "else" "iden" ":=" "false"
**recognized : <print statement>
**synchronized : <compound statement>
**synchronized : <program>
```

The input program for the second example is given below.

```
 1   'begin'
 2     'integer' a;
 3     'boolean' b;
 4     'do'
 5       'if' b
 6         'then' a:=3
 7         'else' a:=4
 8       'print' a;
 9       'if' b
10         'then' if b
11                   'then' a:=4
12                   'else' a:=5
13                'fi'
14         'else' 'print' a
15       'fi'
16     'od'
17   'end'
```

The diagnostics generated by the syntax analyser are given below.

```
    8: *** error ***: the input symbol "print" is invalid after
                       "else" "iden" ":=" "intct"
**recognized : <print statement>
**skipped : ";"
**recognized : <if statement>

   11: *** error ***: the input symbol "iden" is invalid after
                      "if" "iden" "then" "iden"
**skipped : "iden"
**recognized : <statement>
**recognized : <statement>
**synchronized : <if statement>
**recognized : <statement>
**synchronized : <if statement>
```

The behavior of the syntax analyser is further explained in Fig.
6.14.

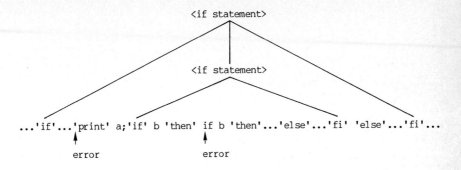

Fig. 6.14.

6.3.3. The error recovery in the syntax-semantic analyser

The syntax-semantic analyser of Pico Algol as it has been introduced in section 5.5.3 halts as soon as a syntactic error is encountered. In section 6.3.2 we illustrated how the syntax analyser can be extended with recovery information in order to recover from syntactic errors. If semantic actions are added to the syntax analyser, the environment consisting of attribute variables and the global information must be forced into a well-defined state, whenever the syntax-semantic analyser recovers from a syntactic error.

For this reason, special actions forcing the environment into an appropriate state have to be taken whenever a rule is synchronized. These actions are specified in the exit-part of the recovery information local to a rule.

In Pico Algol, the rule for expression needs a special action to give an appropriate value to the synthesized attribute associated with an expression. This attribute will be the undefined value, giving rise to semantic error recovery. The undefined value is identified in the output produced by the syntax-semantic analyser for Pico Algol by means of three consecutive question marks. In this way, an interaction between syntactic and semantic error recovery is accomplished in the syntax-semantic analyser for Pico

Algol. This is illustrated in the example below.

Input Progam

```
 1  'begin'
 2    'integer' a;
 3    'integer' b;
 4    'integer' c;
 5
 6    'if'  2 * (b + 4  +/  (c - 3)
 7      'then' a := 3
 8      'else' a := 4
 9    'fi'
10  'end'
```

Results of the syntax-semantic analyser

```
    6: *** error ***: the input symbol "/" is invalid after
                       "iden" "+" "intct" "+"
```

SYMBOL TABLE
****

```
|---------|-------------------------|
| a       | refint , [idensp,0,    0] |
|---------|-------------------------|
| b       | refint , [idensp,0,    1] |
|---------|-------------------------|
| c       | refint , [idensp,0,    2] |
```

3-ADDRESS INSTRUCTIONS
****

```
    PLUS    int    int    [idensp,1,1]  [constb,1,1]  [worksp,1,0]
    MINUS   int    int    [idensp,1,2]  [constb,1,2]  [worksp,1,1]
    JUMPF   L0            [   ????   ]
    ASSIGN  int           [idensp,0,0]  [constb,1,3]
    JUMP    L1
LABDEF  L0
    ASSIGN  int           [idensp,0,0]  [constb,1,4]
LABDEF  L1
```

The syntax part of the LILA input for the synchronized version of the syntax-semantic analyser is given below. The other parts of the LILA input are identical to those given in section 5.5.3.

```
$$$$$$$$$$$$$$$$$$$$$$$$$$$$$$$$$$$$$$$$$$$$$$$$$$$$$$$$$$$$$$$$$$$$$$$$$$$$$$$$
$   LILA INPUT                                                              $
$                                                                          $
$   Compiler for Pico Algol : Syntax-semantic Analyser, synchronized version $
$$$$$$$$$$$$$$$$$$$$$$$$$$$$$$$$$$$$$$$$$$$$$$$$$$$$$$$$$$$$$$$$$$$$$$$$$$$$$$$$
```

```
###syntax;

$ Analysis of a Pico Algol program
  ##rule;
    <program> =
      "begin"
        ( <declaration>! ";" )*
        <statement>  ( ";" <statement> )*
      "end"

    ##recovery  last, first;

$ Analysis of a declaration
  ##rule;
    <declaration> =
      ( "integer" "iden" int_value
          ( &  |  "=" <expression>? intct )
      | "boolean" "iden" bool_value
          ( &  |  "=" <expression>? boolct )
      ) add_symbt

    ##var;
      id_name : rep_name;
      id_descr: rep_description

    ##action;
      #int_value;
        id_name := @"iden"1;
        id_descr.typ := refint;
        init_access(id_descr.acc, idensp, 0, idensp_loc(int))

      #intct;
        coerce_descr( @<expression>1, int);
        with  @[assign]  do begin
          typ_right := int;
          acc_left  := id_descr.acc;
          acc_right := @<expression>1.acc
        end;
```

```
    out(%[assign]);
    deref_descr(id_descr)

  #bool_value;
    id_name := @"iden"2;
    id_descr.typ := refbool;
    init_access(id_descr.acc, idensp, 0, idensp_loc(bool))

  #boolct;
    coerce_descr( @<expression>2, bool);
    with @[assign]  do begin
      typ_right := bool;
      acc_left  := id_descr.acc;
      acc_right := @<expression>2.acc
    end;
    out(%[assign]);
    deref_descr(id_descr)

  #add_symbt;
    add_symbt( id_name, id_descr)

##recovery  first;
```

$ Analysis of a statement
```
  ##rule;
    <statement> =
        <compound statement>
    | <if statement>
    | <for statement>
    | <print statement>!
    | <assign statement>!
```

$ Analysis of a compound statement
```
  ##rule;
    <compound statement> =
      "do"
        <statement> ( ";" <statement> )*
      "od"

  ##recovery  last, first;
```

$ Analysis of an assignment statement
```
  ##rule;
    <assign statement> =
      "iden" ":=" <expression>?  assign

  ##var;
    left_descr : rep_description
```

```
  ##action;
    #assign;
      search_symbt( @"iden", left_descr);
      coerce_descr( @<expression>, deref_type(left_descr.typ));
      with @[assign]  do begin
        typ_right := @<expression>.typ;
        acc_left  := left_descr.acc;
        acc_right := @<expression>.acc
      end;
      out(%[assign])
```

$ Analysis of a print statement
```
  ##rule;
    <print statement> =
      "print" <expression>  print


    ##action;
      #print;
            $ Only integer values are allowed in a print statement.
        coerce_descr( @<expression>, int);
        @[print] := @<expression>;
        out(%[print])


    ##recovery  first;
```

$ Analysis of an if statement
```
  ##rule;
    <if statement> =
      "if" <expression>!  cond
        "then" <statement>?  then_part
        "else" <statement>?  else_part
      "fi"


    ##action;
      #cond;
        coerce_descr( @<expression>, bool);
        with @[jumpf]  do begin
          lab := unique_lab;
          acc := @<expression>.acc
        end;
        out(%[jumpf])

      #then_part;
        @[jump]    := unique_label;
        out(%[jump]);
        @[labdef] := @[jumpf].lab;
        out(%[labdef])
```

```
    #else_part;
      @[labdef] := @[jump];
      out(%[labdef])


  ##recovery  last, first;

$ Analysis of a for statement
  ##rule;
    <for statement> =
      "for"  "iden"   for_iden
        "from" <expression>!?  from_expr
        "to"    <expression>!?  to_expr
        <compound statement>    after_stat


  ##var;
    cvar_descr : rep_description


  ##action;
    #for_iden;
      search_symbt( @"iden", cvar_descr);
      coerce_descr( cvar_descr, refint)


    #from_expr;
      coerce_descr( @<expression>1, int);
      with @[assign]  do begin
        typ_right := @<expression>1.typ;
        acc_left  := cvar_descr.acc;
        acc_right := @<expression>1.acc
      end;
      out(%[assign]);
      @[labdef] := unique_lab;
      out(%[labdef])


    #to_expr;
      coerce_descr( @<expression>2, int);
      with @[minus]  do begin
        typ_left  := deref_type(cvar_descr.typ);
        typ_right := @<expression>2.typ;
        acc_left  := cvar_descr.acc;
        deref_access(acc_left);
        acc_right := @<expression>2.acc;
        init_access(acc_result, worksp, 1, worksp_loc(int))
      end;
      out(%[minus]);
      with @[jumpp]  do begin
        lab := unique_lab;
        acc := @[minus].acc_result
      end;
```

```
        out(%[jumpp])

    #after_stat;
      with @[incr]  do begin
        typ := deref_type(cvar_descr.typ);
        acc := cvar_descr.acc
      end;
      out(%[incr]);
      @[jump]   := @[labdef];
      out(%[jump]);
      @[labdef] := @[jumpp].lab;
      out(%[labdef])

  ##recovery  first;

$ Analysis of an expression
  ##rule;
    <expression> =
      <term>  pass_te
      ( "+" <term>?  add
      | "-" <term>?  subtract
      )*

  ##attribute;
    rep_description

  ##action;
    #pass_te;
      @<expression> := @<term>1

    #add;
      coerce_descr( @<expression>, int);
      coerce_descr( @<term>2, int);
      with @[plus]  do begin
        typ_left  := @<expression>.typ;
        typ_right := @<term>2.typ;
        acc_left  := @<expression>.acc;
        acc_right := @<term>2.acc;
        init_access(acc_result, worksp, 1, worksp_loc(int))
      end;
      out(%[plus]);
      @<expression>.acc := @[plus].acc_result

    #subtract;
      coerce_descr( @<expression>, int);
      coerce_descr( @<term>3, int);
      with @[minus]  do begin
        typ_left  := @<expression>.typ;
```

```
       typ_right := @<term>3.typ;
       acc_left  := @<expression>.acc;
       acc_right := @<term>3.acc;
       init_access(acc_result, worksp, 1, worksp_loc(int))
     end;
     out(%[minus]);
     @<expression>.acc := @[minus].acc_result

  ##recovery;
    #exit;
      @<expression>.typ := undefined;
      @<expression>.acc.def := false
```

$ Analysis of a term
  ##rule;
    <term> =
      <factor> pass_ft
      ("*" <factor>? multiply
      | "/" <factor>? divide
)*

```
  ##attribute;
    rep_description
```

```
  ##action;
    #pass_ft;
      @<term> := @<factor>1

    #multiply;
      coerce_descr( @<term>, int);
      coerce_descr( @<factor>2, int);
      with @[times]  do begin
        typ_left  := @<term>.typ;
        typ_right := @<factor>2.typ;
        acc_left  := @<term>.acc;
        acc_right := @<factor>2.acc;
        init_access(acc_result, worksp, 1, worksp_loc(int))
      end;
      out(%[times]);
      @<term>.acc := @[times].acc_result

    #divide;
      coerce_descr( @<term>, int);
      coerce_descr( @<factor>3, int);
      with @[divide]  do begin
        typ_left  := @<term>.typ;
        typ_right := @<factor>3.typ;
        acc_left  := @<term>.acc;
```

```
        acc_right := @<factor>3.acc;
        init_access(acc_result, worksp, 1, worksp_loc(int))
    end;
    out(%[divide]);
    @<term>.acc := @[divide].acc_result
```

$ <u>Analysis of a factor</u>
```
  ##rule;
    <factor> =
        "intct" intct
      | "true"  true
      | "false" false
      | "iden"  iden
      | "(" <expression>!? ")" pass_ef

    ##attribute;
      rep_description

    ##var;
      v : rep_value

    ##action;
      #iden;
        search_symbt( @"iden", @<factor>)

      #intct;
        @<factor>.typ  := int;
        with  v  do begin
          typ  := int;
          ival := @"intct"
        end;
        init_access(@<factor>.acc, constab, 1, constb_loc( int, v))

      #true;
        @<factor>.typ  := bool;
        with  v  do begin
          typ  := bool;
          bval := true
        end;
        init_access(@<factor>.acc, constab, 1, constb_loc( bool, v))

      #false;
        @<factor>.typ  := bool;
        with  v  do begin
          typ  := bool;
          bval := false
        end;
        init_access(@<factor>.acc, constab, 1, constb_loc( bool, v))
```

```
#pass_ef;
    @<factor> := @<expression>
```

6.4.   The error recovery in Pascal

The principles of error recovery as they have been illustrated in
the syntax analyser of Pico Algol have been applied on a more
representative example: a syntax analyser for Pascal. The LILA
input for the syntax analyser for Pascal is briefly discussed in
section 6.4.1. Thereafter, some examples illustrating the behavior
of the error recovery in the syntax analyser will be given in section 6.4.2.

6.4.1.   The syntax analyser for Pascal

In this section, the implementation of a syntax analyser for Pascal by means of LILA will be discussed. The implementation is based
on the definition of Pascal as it is introduced in the Draft Proposal of Pascal by the International Standards Organization (ISO) (see
Addyman [1980]). In the ECF syntax for Pascal, a difference is made
between six kinds of identifiers:
- constant identifier
- type identifier
- variable identifier
- procedure identifier
- function identifier
- identifier (the identifier has not been declared yet)

Whenever the lexical analyser recognizes an identifier in the
input program, it will produce the appropriate input symbol by examining the attributes currently associated with that identifier in
the symbol table. Differentiation between certain kinds of identifiers makes it easier to write an ECF syntax satisfying the ELL(1)
conditions. Otherwise, some rules would have to be factorized,
resulting in a rather obscure ECF syntax.

```
$$$$$$$$$$$$$$$$$$$$$$$$$$$$$$$$$$$$$$$$$$$$$$$$$$$$$$$$$$$$$$$$$$$$$$$$$$$$$$$$$$$
$    LILA INPUT                                                                $
$                                                                             $
$      Compiler for PASCAL : Syntax Analysis, synchronized version            $
```

$$

```
###options
  let,
  syncflow;



###inputvocabulary rep(integer);
```

$ Keywords

"and"	= 23	"array"	= 24	"begin"	= 25	"case"	= 26
"const"	= 28	"div"	= 30	"do"	= 31	"downto"	= 32
"else"	= 33	"end"	= 34	"file"	= 36	"for"	= 37
"function"	= 38	"goto"	= 40	"if"	= 41	"in"	= 42
"label"	= 43	"mod"	= 44	"nil"	= 45	"not"	= 46
"of"	= 47	"or"	= 48	"packed"	= 50	"procedure"	= 52
"program"	= 54	"record"	= 56	"repeat"	= 57	"set"	= 58
"then"	= 61	"to"	= 62	"type"	= 63	"until"	= 68
"var"	= 69	"while"	= 71	"with"	= 72		

$ Delimiters

"("	= 2	")"	= 3	"*"	= 4	"+"	= 5	","	= 6	"-"	= 7	"."	= 8
".."	= 9	"/"	= 10	":"	= 11	":="	= 12	";"	= 13	"<"	= 14	"<="	= 15
"<>"	= 16	"="	= 17	">"	= 18	">="	= 19	"["	= 20	"]"	= 21	"^"	= 22

$ Identifiers

"constant identifier"	= 29	"type identifier"	= 49
"variable identifier"	= 35	"procedure identifier"	= 53
"function identifier"	= 39	"identifier"	= 67

$ Constants

"string"	= 27	"unsigned integer"	= 65	"unsigned real"	= 66
"character"	= 59				

```
###syntax;
```

$ Analysis of a Pascal PROGRAM

```
  ##rule;
    <program> =
      <program heading>!
      <block> "."

  ##recovery  first;
```

```
$ Analysis of a PROGRAM HEADING
  ##rule;
    <program heading> =
      "program" <identifier>
        ( &
        | <program parameters>
        )
      ";"


  ##recovery  first, last;


$ Analysis of the PROGRAM PARAMETERS
  ##rule;
    <program parameters> =
      "("
          <identifier>  ( "," <identifier> )*
      ")"



  ##recovery  first, last;


$ Analysis of a BLOCK
  ##rule;
    <block> =
      ( <label declaration part>! | & )
      ( <constant def part>! | & )
      ( <type definition part>! | & )
      ( <variable decl part>! | & )
      ( <procedure declaration>! | <function declaration>! )*
      <compound statement>


$ Analysis of a LABEL DECLARATION PART
  ##rule;
    <label declaration part> =
      "label"
        "unsigned integer"  ( "," "unsigned integer" )*
      ";"

  ##recovery  first, last;


$ Analysis of a CONSTANT DEFINITION PART
  ##rule;
    <constant def part> =
      "const"  <constant definition>+
```

```
  ##recovery  first;


$ Analysis of a CONSTANT DEFINITION
  ##rule;
    <constant definition> =
      <identifier>  "="  <constant>?  ";"

  ##recovery  last;


$ Analysis of a CONSTANT
  ##rule;
    <constant> =
        ( "+"  |  "-"  |  & )
          <unsigned constant>
      | "string"
      | "character"


$ Analysis of a TYPE DEFINITION PART
  ##rule;
    <type definition part> =
      "type"  <type definition>+

  ##recovery  first;


$ Analysis of a TYPE DEFINITION
  ##rule;
    <type definition> =
      <identifier>  "="  <type>?  ";"

  ##recovery  last;


$ Analysis of a TYPE
  ##rule;
    <type> =
        "type identifier"
      | <enumerated type>
      | <subrange type>
      | ( "packed"  |  & )
          ( <array type>
          | <record type>
          | <set type>
          | <file type>
          )
```

```
    | "^"  <identifier>


$ Analysis of an ENUMERATED TYPE
  ##rule;
    <enumerated type> =
      "("
        <identifier>  ( "," <identifier> )*
      ")"

  ##recovery  first, last;


$ Analysis of a SUBRANGE TYPE
  ##rule;
    <subrange type> =
      <constant> ".." <constant>?


$ Analysis of an ARRAY TYPE
  ##rule;
    <array type> =
      "array"
        <index type specification>!
        "of" <type>?

  ##recovery  first;


$ Analysis of an INDEX TYPE SPECIFICATION
  ##rule;
    <index type specification> =
      "["
        <type>  ( "," <type>? )*
      "]"

  ##recovery  first, last;


$ Analysis of a RECORD TYPE
  ##rule;
    <record type> =
      "record"
        <field list>
      "end"

  ##recovery  first, last;
```

```
$ Analysis of a FIELD LIST
  ##rule;
    <field list> =
        <record section>!
          ( ";"  ( <field list> | & )
          | &
          )
      | <variant part>


$ Analysis of a RECORD SECTION
  ##rule;
    <record section> =
      <identifier>  ( "," <identifier> )*
        ":" <type>?


$ Analysis of a VARIANT PART
  ##rule;
    <variant part> =
      "case"  <identifier> ( ":" "type identifier" | & )  "of"
        <variant list>?

  ##recovery  first;


$ Analysis of a VARIANT LIST
  ##rule;
    <variant list> =
      <variant>!
        ( ";"  ( <variant list> | & )
        | &
        )


$ Analysis of a VARIANT
  ##rule;
    <variant> =
      <constant>  ( "," <constant>? )*  ":"
        "("  ( <field list>!? | & )  ")"


$ Analysis of a SET TYPE
  ##rule;
    <set type> =
      "set"  "of"  <type>?

  ##recovery  first;
```

```
$ Analysis of a FILE TYPE
  ##rule;
    <file type> =
      "file"  "of"  <type>?

  ##recovery  first;


$ Analysis of a VARIABLE DECLARATION PART
  ##rule;
    <variable decl part> =
      "var" <variable declaration>+

  ##recovery  first;


$ Analysis of a VARIABLE DECLARATION
  ##rule;
    <variable declaration> =
      <identifier>  ( "," <identifier> )*
        ":"  <type>?  ";"

  ##recovery  last;


$ Analysis of a PROCEDURE DECLARATION
  ##rule;
    <procedure declaration> =
      <procedure heading> ";"
        ( <identifier>
        | <block>
        )
      ";"

  ##recovery  first;


$ Analysis of a PROCEDURE HEADING
  ##rule;
    <procedure heading> =
      "procedure"  <identifier>
        ( <formal parameter list> | & )


$ Analysis of a FUNCTION DECLARATION
  ##rule;
    <function declaration> =
      <function heading>  ";"
```

```
        ( <identifier>
        | <block>
        )
      ";"

  ##recovery  first;


$ Analysis of a FUNCTION HEADING
  ##rule;
    <function heading> =
      "function"  <identifier>
        ( ( <formal parameter list> | & )
          ":"  "type identifier"
        | &
        )


$ Analysis of a FORMAL PARAMETER LIST
  ##rule;
    <formal parameter list> =
      "("
        <formal parameter section>  ( ";" <formal parameter section>? )*
      ")"

  ##recovery  first, last;


$ Analysis of a FORMAL PARAMETER SECTION
  ##rule;
    <formal parameter section> =
        <value parameter specification>
      | <variable parameter specification>
      | <procedure heading>
      | <function heading>


$ Analysis of a VALUE PARAMETER SPECIFICATION
  ##rule;
    <value parameter specification> =
      <identifier>  ( "," <identifier> )*
        ":" "type identifier"


$ Analysis of a VARIABLE PARAMETER SPECIFICATION
  ##rule;
    <variable parameter specification> =
      "var"
```

```
             <identifier>  ( "," <identifier> )*
          ":" ( "type identifier"
              | <conformant array schema>
              )
```

$ Analysis of a CONFORMANT ARRAY SCHEMA
```
  ##rule;
    <conformant array schema> =
      "array"
        <conformant index type specification>!
        "of" ( "type identifier" | <conformant array schema> )
```

$ Analysis of a CONFORMANT INDEX TYPE SPECIFICATION
```
  ##rule;
    <conformant index type specification> =
      "["
        <conf. index type>  ( ";" <conf. index type>? )*
      "]"

  ##recovery  first, last;
```

$ Analysis of a CONFORMANT INDEX TYPE
```
  ##rule;
    <conf. index type> =
      <identifier> ".." <identifier>
        ":" "type identifier"
```

$ Analysis of a COMPOUND STATEMENT
```
  ##rule;
    <compound statement> =
      "begin"
        <statement>  ( ";" <statement> )*
      "end"

  ##recovery  first, last;
```

$ Analysis of a STATEMENT
```
  ##rule;
    <statement> =
      ( "unsigned integer" ":"  |  & )
        ( <simple statement>!
        | <structured statement>
        )
```

```
$ Analysis of a SIMPLE STATEMENT
  ##rule;
    <simple statement> =
        <assignment statement>
      | <procedure statement>
      | <goto statement>
      | &                        $ empty statement


$ Analysis of an ASSIGNMENT STATEMENT
  ##rule;
    <assignment statement> =
        ( <variable access> | "function identifier" )
          ":="  <expression>?


$ Analysis of a VARIABLE ACCESS
  ##rule;
    <variable access> =
      "variable identifier"
        ( <index specification>
        | "." <identifier>
        | "^"
        )*


$ Analysis of an INDEX SPECIFICATION
  ##rule;
    <index specification> =
      "["
        <expression>  ( "," <expression>? )*
      "]"

  ##recovery  first, last;


$ Analysis of a PROCEDURE STATEMENT
  ##rule;
    <procedure statement> =
      "procedure identifier"
        ( <actual parameter list> | & )


$ Analysis of an ACTUAL PARAMETER LIST
  ##rule;
    <actual parameter list> =
      "("
        <actual parameter>  ( "," <actual parameter>? )*
```

```
     ")"

  ##recovery  first, last;


$ Analysis of an ACTUAL PARAMETER
  ##rule;
    <actual parameter> =
        <expression>  ( <format list> | & )
      | "procedure identifier"


$ Analysis of a FORMAT LIST
  ##rule;
    <format list> =
      ":" <expression>?
        ( ":" <expression>?
        | &
        )


$ Analysis of a GOTO STATEMENT
  ##rule;
    <goto statement> =
      "goto" "unsigned integer"

  ##recovery  first;


$ Analysis of a STRUCTURED STATEMENT
  ##rule;
    <structured statement> =
        <compound statement>
      | <if statement>
      | <case statement>
      | <repeat statement>
      | <while statement>
      | <for statement>
      | <with statement>


$ Analysis of an IF STATEMENT
  ##rule;
    <if statement> =
      "if" <expression>!
        "then" <statement>?
        ( "else" <statement>? | & )
```

```
##recovery  first;


$ Analysis of a CASE STATEMENT
  ##rule;
    <case statement> =
      "case"  <expression>!  "of"
        <case list>?
      "end"

  ##recovery  first, last;


$ Analysis of a CASE LIST
  ##rule;
    <case list> =
      <case list element>!
        ( ";"  ( <case list> | & )
        | &
        )


$ Analysis of a CASE LIST ELEMENT
  ##rule;
    <case list element> =
      <constant>  ( ","  <constant>? )*
        ":"  <statement>?


$ Analysis of a REPEAT STATEMENT
  ##rule;
    <repeat statement> =
      "repeat"  <statement>
        ( ";"  <statement> )*
      "until"  <expression>?

  ##recovery  first;


$ Analysis of a WHILE STATEMENT
  ##rule;
    <while statement> =
      "while"  <expression>!  "do"
        <statement>?

  ##recovery  first;
```

```
$ Analysis of a FOR STATEMENT
  ##rule;
    <for statement> =
      "for"  "variable identifier"  ":="  <expression>!?
         ( "to" | "downto" )  <expression>!?  "do"
         <statement>?

  ##recovery  first;


$ Analysis of a WITH STATEMENT
  ##rule;
    <with statement> =
      "with"  <variable access>! ( ","  <variable access>!? )*  "do"
         <statement>?

  ##recovery  first;


$ Analysis of an EXPRESSION
  ##rule;
    <expression> =
      <simple expression>
         ( ( "=" | "<>" | "<" | "<=" | ">" | ">=" | "in" )
             <simple expression>?
         | &
         )


$ Analysis of a SIMPLE EXPRESSION
  ##rule;
    <simple expression> =
      ( "+" | "-" | & )  <term>
         ( ( "+" | "-" | "or" )   <term>? )*


$ Analysis of a TERM
  ##rule;
    <term> =
      <factor>
         ( ( "*" | "/" | "div" | "mod" | "and" )   <factor>? )*


$ Analysis of a FACTOR
  ##rule;
    <factor> =
         <variable access>
      | <unsigned constant>
```

```
        | "string"
        | "character"
        | "nil"
        | <function designator>
        | <set constructor>
        | "(" <expression>!? ")"
        | "not" <factor>?
```

$ Analysis of an UNSIGNED CONSTANT
```
  ##rule;
     <unsigned constant> =
         "unsigned real"
       | "unsigned integer"
       | "constant identifier"
```

$ Analysis of a FUNCTION DESIGNATOR
```
  ##rule;
     <function designator> =
       "function identifier"
          ( <actual parameter list> | & )
```

$ Analysis of a SET CONSTRUCTOR
```
  ##rule;
     <set constructor> =
       "["
         ( <member designator>  ( "," <member designator>? )*
         | &
         )
       "]"

  ##recovery  first, last;
```

$ Analysis of a MEMBER DESIGNATOR
```
  ##rule;
     <member designator> =
       <expression>
          ( ".." <expression>?
          | &
          )
```

$ Analysis of an IDENTIFIER
```
  ##rule;
     <identifier> =
```

```
            "constant identifier"
         |  "function identifier"
         |  "type identifier"
         |  "procedure identifier"
         |  "variable identifier"
         |  "identifier"


###global info;


  ##parameter;
     infile, output
```

6.4.2. Examples

In this section, the behavior of the error recovery in the syntax analyser for Pascal, as it is described in section 6.4.1, will be illustrated by two examples. The first example illustrates the behavior of the error recovery in the syntax analyser for some minor errors in the input program, such as a missing semicolon. In the second example, the input program contains some bigger mistakes.

Example 1


```
 1   program treesearch (input output);
 2   type ref = ^word;
 3     word = record
 4       key : integer;
 5       count:integer
 6       left,right : ref
 7     end;
 8   var root : ref;
 9     k : integer
10   procedure printtree (w:ref;l:integer);
11   var i : integer;
12   begin
13     if  w <> nil then
14       with  w^  do begin
15         printtree(left,l+1)
16         for i:=1 to l do write('    ');
```

```
17        writeln(key);
18        printtree(right,l+1)
19     end
20  end {printtree}
21  procedure search (x:integer; var p:ref);
22  begin
23    if  p = nil then begin
24      new(p;
25      with  p^  do begin
26        key := x;
27        count := 1;
28        left := nil;
29        right := nil
30      end
31    end
32    else if (x < p^.key  then search(x,p^.left)
33    else if (x > p^.key) then search(x p^.right)
34    else p^.count := p^.count + 1
35  end {search};
36  begin
37    root := nil;
38    while  not eof(input)  do begin
39      read(k);
40      search(k,root
41    end;
42    printtree(root,0)
43  end
```

The diagnostics generated by the syntax analyser for Pascal are
given below.

```
      1: *** error ***: the input symbol "variable identifier" is invalid after
                       "program" "identifier" "(" "variable identifier"
  **skipped : "variable identifier"
  **synchronized : <program parameters>

      6: *** error ***: the input symbol "variable identifier" is invalid after
                       ";" "variable identifier" ":" "type identifier"
  **skipped : "variable identifier"
  **skipped : ","
  **skipped : "variable identifier"
  **recognized : <type>
  **synchronized : <record type>

     10: *** error ***: the input symbol "procedure" is invalid after
                       ";" "variable identifier" ":" "type identifier"
  **synchronized : <variable decl part>
```

```
   16: *** error ***: the input symbol "for" is invalid after
                      "variable identifier" "+" "unsigned integer" ")"
**recognized : <for statement>
**skipped : ";"
**skipped : "procedure identifier"
**skipped : "("
**skipped : "variable identifier"
**skipped : ")"
**skipped : ";"
**skipped : "procedure identifier"
**skipped : "("
**skipped : "variable identifier"
**skipped : ","
**skipped : "variable identifier"
**recognized : <term>
**skipped : ")"
**synchronized : <compound statement>

   21: *** error ***: the input symbol "procedure" is invalid after
                      "unsigned integer" ")" "end" "end"
**synchronized : <procedure declaratio>

   24: *** error ***: the input symbol ";" is invalid after
                      "begin" "procedure identifier" "(" "variable identifier"
**synchronized : <simple statement>

   32: *** error ***: the input symbol "then" is invalid after
                      "variable identifier" "^" "." "variable identifier"
**synchronized : <expression>

   33: *** error ***: the input symbol "variable identifier" is invalid after
                      "then" "procedure identifier" "(" "variable identifier"
**skipped : "variable identifier"
**skipped : "^"
**skipped : "."
**skipped : "variable identifier"
**synchronized : <actual parameter lis>

   41: *** error ***: the input symbol "end" is invalid after
                      "(" "variable identifier" "," "variable identifier"
**synchronized : <simple statement>

   44: *** error ***: the input symbol is invalid after
                      "," "unsigned integer" ")" "end"
```

Example 2

```
1   program treesearch (input,output);
2   type ref = ^word;
3     word = record
4       key : integer;
5       count:integer;
6       left,right : ref;
7     end;
8   var root : ref;
9     k : integer;
10  procedure printtree (w:ref;l:integer);
11  vra i : integer;
12  begin
13    if  w <> nil then
14      with  w^  begin
15        printtree(left,l+1);
16        for i:=1 to l do write('   ');
17        writeln(key);
18        printtree(right,l+1)
19  end {printtree};
20  procedure search (x:integer; var p:ref);
21  begin
22    if  p = nil then begin
23      new(p);
24      with  p^  do
25        key := x;
26        count := 1;
27        left := nil;
28        right := nil
29      end
30    end
31    else if (x < p^.key)  then search(x,p^.left)
32          if (x > p^.key) then search(x p^.right)
33    else p^.count := p^.count + 1
34  end {search};
35    root := nil
36    while  not eof(input)  do begin
37      read(k);
38      search(k,root)
39    end;
40    printtree(root,0)
41  end.
```

The diagnostics generated by the syntax analyser for Pascal are given below.

```
    11: *** error ***: the input symbol "variable identifier" is invalid after
                      "type identifier" ")" ";" "identifier"
**skipped : "variable identifier"
**skipped : ":"
**skipped : "type identifier"
**skipped : ";"
**synchronized : <procedure declaratio>

    14: *** error ***: the input symbol "begin" is invalid after
                      "then" "with" "variable identifier" "^"
**recognized : <compound statement>
**skipped : ";"
**recognized : <procedure declaratio>

    31: *** error ***: the input symbol "else" is invalid after
                      ":=" "nil" "end" "end"
**recognized : <statement>
**recognized : <if statement>

    32: *** error ***: the input symbol "variable identifier" is invalid after
                      "then" "procedure identifier" "(" "variable identifier"
**skipped : "variable identifier"
**skipped : "^"
**skipped : "."
**skipped : "variable identifier"
**synchronized : <actual parameter lis>
**skipped : "end"
**skipped : ";"
**skipped : "variable identifier"
**recognized : <expression>
**recognized : <while statement>
**skipped : ";"
**skipped : "procedure identifier"
**skipped : "("
**skipped : "variable identifier"
**skipped : ","
**skipped : "unsigned integer"
**skipped : ")"
**skipped : "end"
**skipped : "."
```

For the sake of completeness, the error messages generated by the syntax analyser for Pascal if the syncflow option had not been specified in the LILA input, are given below.

11: *** error ***: the input symbol "variable identifier" is invalid after
                   "type identifier" ")" ";" "identifier"

14: *** error ***: the input symbol "begin" is invalid after
                   "then" "with" "variable identifier" "^"

31: *** error ***: the input symbol "else" is invalid after
                   ":=" "nil" "end" "end"

32: *** error ***: the input symbol "variable identifier" is invalid after
                   "then" "procedure identifier" "(" "variable identifier"

7. SYNTAX-DIRECTED DESCRIPTION OF LILA

7.1. Introduction

LILA has been designed as a tool to develop transducers (compilers, interpreters) in the form of programs of high quality. By quality of programs, we mean that programs must be simple, reliable and adaptable, at the first place. In addition, it is desirable that programs are also efficient and portable. Simplicity, reliability and adaptability make it possible to understand what programs do and guarantee that they can be changed and extended at a reasonable cost. Simplicity, reliability and adaptability are the essential requirements that make programs manageable.

There are two main aspects in LILA :

1) at the first place, LILA represents a methodology in the area of compiler construction. With the basic principles of LILA in mind, one is able to develop programs of high quality. These basic principles have been treated in sections 2, 3 and 4.

2) at the same time, LILA is a software tool, supporting the above methodology. This has been illustrated in sections 5 and 6.

The main point here is that LILA itself is a transducer. The input of this transducer is a generalized AECF translation syntax, written in a form which is described in the LILA Reference Guide (see appendix). The output of the transducer is an ELL(1) transducer in the form of a Pascal program.

Since LILA itself is a transducer, it is obvious to develop the program LILA with the underlying methodology of LILA. The result of this experience has two important aspects. First, we obtained a program LILA of high quality. Secondly, we proved that the methodology of LILA is powerful enough to describe LILA itself.

415

LILA as a black box, is pictured in Fig. 7.1.

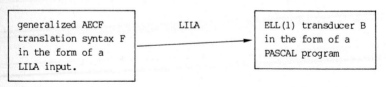

Fig. 7.1.

The system LILA has been designed and documented as a multi-pass transducer. Each transducer pass is described in one of the subsequent sections. In the actual implementation, some of the passes are combined for efficiency reasons.

In a first pass, the LILA input is lexically analysed, followed by a syntax analysis pass. A next pass will test if the input syntax is reduced. Then, in subsequent passes the boolean attribute EMPTY and the sets of terminal symbols FIRST, FOLLOW and DIRSYMB are calculated from the LILA input. In the next pass, the ELL(1) conditions are tested, followed by the generation pass.

This is a first approximation of the partitioning of LILA into nine passes. Most of these passes are in turn partitioned into several passes, as we will explain later.

This macroscopic view of LILA as a nine-pass transducer is schematically illustrated in Fig. 7.2.

LILA input   LILA

generalized AECF
translation
syntax F

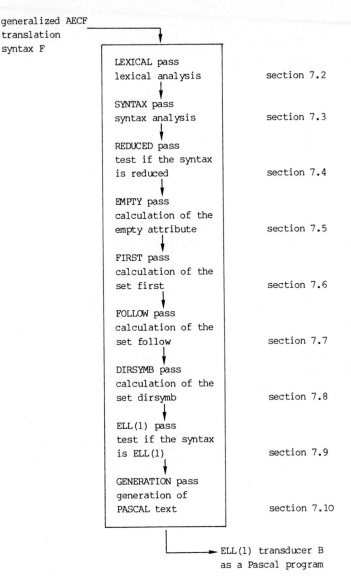

LEXICAL pass lexical analysis	section 7.2
SYNTAX pass syntax analysis	section 7.3
REDUCED pass test if the syntax is reduced	section 7.4
EMPTY pass calculation of the empty attribute	section 7.5
FIRST pass calculation of the set first	section 7.6
FOLLOW pass calculation of the set follow	section 7.7
DIRSYMB pass calculation of the set dirsymb	section 7.8
ELL(1) pass test if the syntax is ELL(1)	section 7.9
GENERATION pass generation of PASCAL text	section 7.10

ELL(1) transducer B
as a Pascal program

Fig. 7.2.

The description of each pass of LILA is syntax-directed. This description is in the form of a LILA input, as it is described in the Reference Guide in the appendix, except for one extension. This extension concerns attribute handling. It simplifies the description upto a great extent, thereby making the description a powerfull tool for LILA documentation and LILA maintenance. We assume that the syntax analyser produces a derivation tree and that this derivation tree is transmitted through all the next passes. Each of the following passes may calculate attributes in the derivation tree in the normal way. In addition we assume that each pass has access to the attributes calculated in the preceeding passes as if they were calculated in the current pass.

A further simplification of the algorithms presented in this section is the omission of the implementation description of the attribute mechanism, the error recovery, the output vocabulary and other features whose implementation description is less interesting.

7.2. LEXICAL pass

The LILA input is first lexically analysed. The input of the lexical analyser is a string of characters from the input vocabulary, whereas the output is a string of output symbols; some of them are attributed. The set of all possible output symbols is described in the output vocabulary.

The input vocabulary of the lexical analyser contains all the characters of the Pascal vocabulary (letters, digits and special symbols) and all the characters used in the specific LILA input parts as described in the LILA Reference Guide.

The output vocabulary of the lexical analyser consists of all the symbols that were called LILA input symbols in the LILA Reference Guide. The output vocabulary is then :

```
[###]   [##]   [#]   [;]   [,]   [:]   [=]   [+]   [*]   [&]   [(]   [)]   [|]
[OPTIONS]   [PRINVOC]   [PROUTVOC]   [PRTREE]   [LET]   [PROCEDURE]   [NAME]
[NOGENERATE]   [NOOPTIMIZE]   [SOURCE]   [GSLN]
[INPUTVOCABULARY]   [OUTPUTVOCABULARY]
[REP]   [INTEGER]   [CHAR]   [FILE]   [EOF]
[SYNTAX]   [RULE]   [ATTRIBUTE]
[LABEL]   [CONST]   [TYPE]   [VAR]   [ROUTINE]   [ACTION]
[GLOBALINFO]   [PARAMETER]   [PROLOGUE]   [EPILOGUE]
[FOLLOW]   [READROUTINE]   [WRITEROUTINE]   [ERRORROUTINE]
[input symbol name]   : VT
[output symbol name]
[nonterminal symbol name]   : VN
[semantic action name]   : VA
[unsigned integer]   [character constant]
[pascal text]   : string
```

Notice that the representations are omitted in this list since they
are not relevant. Notice also that all Pascal portions are
described by the output symbol [pascal text].
A number of these output symbols are attributed. We have however
only indicated the attribute type of those output symbols that will
be used in the subsequent sections.
The type VT identifies an input symbol, VN identifies a nonterminal
symbol and VA a semantic action. For simplicity, we suppose that
they are defined as :

> type VT = 0..n;
>   VN = 0..m;
>   VA = 1..k

where n is the number of input symbols, m+1 is the number of nonterminal symbols and k is the number of semantic actions. The symbol #
is represented by 0. The start nonterminal symbol is represented by
0.

7.3. SYNTAX pass

The output of the lexical analyser is the input of the syntax
analyser. Therefore, the input vocabulary of the syntax analyser is
identical with the output vocabulary of the lexical analyser.

The output of the syntax analyser for a syntactically correct input string is the derivation tree of that input string. The syntax-directed description of the syntax analyser is given below. The semantic actions building the derivation tree are omitted here. They represent a level of detail which is irrelevant for the documentation, we are interested in.

```
###syntax;
##rule;
  <LILA input> =
      ( <global options> | & )
      <input vocabulary>
      ( <output vocabulary> | & )
      <syntax>
      ( <globalinfo> | & )
      ( <follow> | & )
      ( <readroutine> | & )
      ( <writeroutine> | & )
      ( <errorroutine> | & )


##rule;
  <global options> =
      "###" "OPTIONS" <global option> ( "," <global option> )* ";"


##rule;
  <global option> =
        "PRINVOC" | "PROUTVOC" | "PRTREE"
      | "PROCEDURE"
      | "NAME" "(" <identifier> ")"
      | "LET" | "NOOPTIMIZE" | "NOGENERATE"
      | "SOURCE" | "GSLN"


##rule;
  <input vocabulary> =
      "###" "INPUTVOCABULARY" <input vocabulary options> ";"
      <input symbol definition>+


##rule;
  <input vocabulary options> =
      <input vocabulary option> ( "," <input vocabulary option> )*
```

```
##rule;
  <input vocabulary option> =
       <rep option>
     | <file option>
     | <eof option>


##rule;
  <input symbol definition> =
     "input symbol name" "=" <representation> ( ":" <type identifier> | & )


##rule;
  <output vocabulary> =
     "###" "OUTPUTVOCABULARY" <output vocabulary options> ";"
     <output symbol definition>+


##rule;
  <output vocabulary options> =
     <output vocabulary option> ( "," <output vocabulary option> )*


##rule;
  <output vocabulary option> =
       <rep option>
     | <file option>


##rule;
  <output symbol definition> =
     "output symbol name" "=" <representation> ( ":" <type identifier> | & )


##rule;
  <representation> =
     "unsigned integer" | "character constant"


##rule;
  <rep option> =
     "REP" "(" ( "INTEGER" | "CHAR" ) ")"


##rule;
  <file option> =
     "FILE" "(" <file identifier> ")"
```

```
##rule;
  <eof option> =
     "EOF" "(" "unsigned integer" ")"


##rule;
  <syntax> =
     "###" "SYNTAX" ";"
     <translation syntax module>+


##rule;
  <translation syntax module> =
     <rule definition>
     ( <attribute definition> | & )
     ( <local label definitions> | & )
     ( <local const definitions> | & )
     ( <local type definitions> | & )
     ( <local var definitions> | & )
     ( <local routine definitions> | & )
     ( <semantic action definitions> | & )


##rule;
  <rule definition> =
     "##" "RULE" ";"
     "nonterminal symbol name" "=" <expression>


##rule;
  <expression> =
     <alternative> ( "|" <alternative> )*


##rule;
  <alternative> =
     <factor>+


##rule;
  <factor> =
     <primary> ( & | "+" | "*" )
```

```
##rule;
  <primary> =
        "&"
     |  "semantic action name"
     |  "nonterminal symbol name"
     |  "input symbol name"
     |  "(" <expression> ")"


##rule;
  <attribute definition> =
     "##" "ATTRIBUTE" ";"
     <type>


##rule;
  <local label definitions> =
     "##" "LABEL" ";"
     <labels>


##rule;
  <local const definitions> =
     "##" "CONST" ";"
     <constant definitions>


##rule;
  <local type definitions> =
     "##" "TYPE" ";"
     <type definitions>


##rule;
  <local var definitions> =
     "##" "VAR" ";"
     <variable declarations>


##rule;
  <local routine definitions> =
     "##" "ROUTINE" ";"
     <procedure or function declarations>
```

```
##rule;
  <semantic action definitions> =
     "##" "ACTION" ";"
     <semantic action definition>+


##rule;
  <semantic action definition> =
     "#" "semantic action name" ";"
     <statements>


##rule;
  <globalinfo> =
     "###" "GLOBALINFO" ";"
     ( <parameter definitions> | & )
     ( <global label definitions> | & )
     ( <global const definitions> | & )
     ( <global type definitions> | & )
     ( <global var definitions> | & )
     ( <global routine definitions> | & )
     ( <prologue definition> | & )
     ( <epilogue definition> | & )


##rule;
  <parameter definitions> =
     "##" "PARAMETER" ";"
     <parameters>


##rule;
  <global label definitions> =
     "##" "LABEL" ";"
     <labels>


##rule;
  <global const definitions> =
     "##" "CONST" ";"
     <constant definitions>


##rule;
  <global type definitions> =
     "##" "TYPE" ";"
     <type definitions>
```

```
##rule;
  <global var definitions> =
      "##" "VAR" ";"
      <variable declarations>


##rule;
  <global routine definitions> =
      "##" "ROUTINE" ";"
      <procedure or function declarations>


##rule;
  <prologue definition> =
      "##" "PROLOGUE" ";"
      <statements>


##rule;
  <epilogue definition> =
      "##" "EPILOGUE" ";"
      <statements>


##rule;
  <follow> =
      "###" "FOLLOW" ";"
      "input symbol name"+


##rule;
  <readroutine> =
      "###" "READROUTINE" ";"
      <statements>


##rule;
  <writeroutine> =
      "###" "WRITEROUTINE" ";"
      <statements>


##rule;
  <errorroutine> =
      "###" "ERRORROUTINE" ";"
      <statements>
```

```
##rule;
  <type> =
     "pascal text"


##rule;
  <type identifier> =
     "pascal text"


##rule;
  <file identifier> =
     "pascal text"


##rule;
  <identifier> =
     "pascal text"


##rule;
  <labels> =
     "pascal text"


##rule;
  <constant definitions> =
     "pascal text"


##rule;
  <type definitions> =
     "pascal text"


##rule;
  <variable declarations> =
     "pascal text"


##rule;
  <procedure or function declarations> =
     "pascal text"


##rule;
  <statements> =
     "pascal text"
```

```
##rule;
  <parameters> =
    "pascal text"
```

The <u>output</u> of the syntax analyser is the attributed derivation
tree. The values of the attributes, associated with the nodes of
the derivation tree, will be calculated during the next passes.

Each of the following passes represents an algorithm that calculates new attributes in terms of old ones, i.e., attribute values
calculated in preceeding passes. The input of each algorithm is the
attributed input string and its attributed derivation tree, whereas
the output is the same derivation tree, in which new attribute
values are calculated.

Each algorithm is described in a syntax-directed way. Obviously,
the syntax rules in each syntax-directed description are identical,
only the semantic actions and global information will be different.
The syntax rules used in the syntax-directed description of each
algorithm is precisely <syntax>.

The algorithms described in the subsequent sections, only deal
with a part of <syntax>. In the syntax-directed description of
these algorithms, we will use only that part of <syntax>, that is
necessary. This part is given below.

```
##rule;
  <syntax> =
    "###" "SYNTAX" ";"
    <rule definition>+
```

```
##rule;
  <rule definition> =
    "##" "RULE" ";"
    "nonterminal symbol name" "=" <expression>
```

```
##rule;
  <expression> =
    <alternative> ( "|" <alternative> )*
```

```
##rule;
  <alternative> =
    <factor>+
```

```
##rule;
  <factor> =
    <primary> ( & | "+" | "*" )
```

```
##rule;
  <primary> =
       "&"
    | "input symbol name"
    | "nonterminal symbol name"
    | "semantic action name"
    | "(" <expression> ")"
```

7.4. REDUCED pass

As it has been defined in section 4, a generalized AECF translation syntax F is <u>reduced</u> if there are no useless symbols.
Therefore, the following two sets of conditions must be fulfilled :

1) each nonterminal symbol in F must derive at least one string over
   VT.

2) each nonterminal symbol in F must appear at least once in a sentential form in F.

The algorithm testing whether a generalized AECF translation syntax
F is reduced, is called REDUCED. It is designed in two passes
called REDUCED1 and REDUCED2. The algorithm REDUCED1 tests if each
nonterminal symbol in F derives at least one string over VT. The
algorithm REDUCED2 tests if each nonterminal symbol in F appears at
least once in a sentential form in F.

7.4.1. <u>REDUCED1 pass</u>

We calculate the set N_e of all nonterminal symbols from which no string over VT can be derived. The following algorithm constructs the sets N_0, N_1, ... iteratively as follows :

step 1 Let $N_0 = \emptyset$ and set i = 1

step 2 Let N_i^1 be the set of all nonterminal symbols A for which there exists a string x ∈ (VT U N_{i-1})*, such that A = s is a rule in P and x is an element of L(G'), where G' = (VT U VN,e) and e is derived from s by replacing each semantic action symbol by &.
Let $N_i = N_i^1$ U N_{i-1}.
Formally, we have

$$N_i = \{A \mid \not{\exists} x \in (N_{i-1} \cup VT)^*, \text{ such that}$$
$$A = s \text{ is in P, } x \in L(G') \text{ and } G' = (VT \cup VN,e)\} \cup N_{i-1}$$

step 3 If $N_i \not= N_{i-1}$ then set i = i+1 and go to step 2.
Otherwise, let $N_e = VN-N_i$.

Now, we have the following subproblem : given a rule A = s in P and a set N_{i-1} U VT, determine whether there exists a string x ∈ (N_{i-1} U VT)* such that x ∈ L(G') with G' = (VT U VN,e). Our problem is that L(G') is an infinite set. Therefore, we transform each rule A = s into a finite set V of strings over (VT U VN). This transformation T is defined below :

axiomatic rules
    T(&)   -> {&}
    T(a_i)   -> {a_i}   where a_i ∈ VT
    T(A_j)   -> {A_j}   where A_j ∈ VN
    T(r)   -> {&}

```
composition rules
    T((s₁|s₂| ... |sₙ))  ->  T(s₁) U T(s₂) U ... U T(sₙ)
    T(s₁s₂ ... sₙ)        ->  T(s₁).T(s₂). ... .T(sₙ)
    T((s)*)              ->  {&}
    T((s)⁺)              ->  T(s)
```

This transformation results in a finite set V of strings over (VT U VN) such that the process of looking after a string x over (N_{i-1} U VT) in L(G') is reduced to the process of looking after a string x over (N_{i-1} U VT) in V.

The syntax-directed description of the algorithm REDUCED1 is straightforward and is left to the reader.

7.4.2.   REDUCED2 pass

We calculate the set V_a of all nonterminal symbols which are accessible from the start symbol of F. The following algorithm constructs the sets V_0, V_1, ... iteratively as follows :

step 1 Let V_0 = {A_0}, where A_0 is the start symbol of F, and set i = 1.

step 2 Let V_i' be the set of all nonterminal symbols X for which there exists a string x $\in$ (VT U VN)* and a nonterminal symbol A $\in$ V_{i-1}, such that X appears in x, A = s is in P and x $\in$ L(G'), where G' = (VT U VN,e) and where e is derived from s by replacing each semantic action symbol by &.
       Let V_i = V_i' U V_{i-1}.
       Formally,

       V_i = {X | ∃x $\in$ (VT U VN)*{X}(VT U VN)* and ∃ A $\in$ V_{i-1}
              such that A = s is in P, x $\in$ L(G') and G' = (VT U VN,e)}
              U V_{i-1}.

step 3 If V_i ≠ V_{i-1} then set i = i+1 and go to step 2.
       Otherwise, let V_a = V_i.

VN-V_a is the set of all nonterminal symbols for which there is no sentential form in which they occur.

Now follows a syntax-directed description of the algorithm REDUCED2. The semantic actions build for each nonterminal symbol A_j a set of nonterminals that occur in the right hand side s_j of the syntax rule $A_j = s_j$.

These sets are represented by the type 'reachset'. The operations defined on the data structure 'reachset' are :

1) <u>function</u> reachset_element (x : VN) : reachset;
   This function returns a reachset containing the nonterminal symbol x.

2) <u>function</u> reachset_union (x,y : reachset) : reachset;
   This function returns a reachset composed of the reachsets x and y.

3) <u>nil</u> is the empty reachset.

The sets of reachable nonterminal symbols are available in the following table :

```
reachtable : array [VN] of record
                          reach : reachset;
                          reachable : boolean
                    end
```

The algorithm first calculates the immediately reachable nonterminal symbols from each nonterminal symbol. Then it calculates the closure of the set of reachable symbols from the start symbol. All nonterminal symbols must be in this set.

The semantic actions that operate on 'reachtable' are 'init_reachtable', 'add_reachtable', 'closure_reachtable' and 'check_reachtable'.

```
###syntax;

$ Treatment of the syntax
  ##rule;
    <syntax> =
        init_reachtable
        "###" "SYNTAX" ";"
        <rule definition>+
        closure_reachtable
        check_reachtable


  ##var;
    i : VN
  ##action;
    #init_reachtable;
      reachtable[0].reachable := true;
      {Remember that A_0 is the start symbol}
      for i:=1 to m do reachtable[i].reachable := false

    #closure_reachtable;
      {This action calculates from 'reachtable' the fields
       'reachable' for each reachable nonterminal symbol A_j
       from the start symbol A_0 }
       ...

    #check_reachtable;
      for i:=1 to m do if not reachtable[i].reachable
        then {error message :
               the nonterminal symbol A_i is not reachable
               from the start symbol A_0}


$ Treatment of a rule definition
  ##rule;
    <rule definition> =
        "##" "RULE" ";"
        "nonterminal symbol name" "=" <expression> add_reachtable


  ##action;
    #add_reachtable;
      reachtable[@"nonterminal symbol name"].reach := @<expression>
```

```
$ Treatment of an expression
  ##rule;
    <expression> =
       <alternative> pass_a_e ( "|" <alternative> concat_a )*


  ##attribute;
     reachset


  ##action;
    #pass_a_e;
      @<expression> := @<alternative>1

    #concat_a;
      @<expression> := reachset_union (@<expression>,@<alternative>2)


$ Treatment of an alternative
  ##rule;
    <alternative> =
       <factor> pass_f_a
       (<factor> concat_f)*


  ##attribute;
     reachset


  ##action;
    #pass_f_a;
      @<alternative> := @<factor>1

    #concat_f;
      @<alternative> := reachset_union (@<alternative>,@<factor>2)


$ Treatment of a factor
  ##rule;
    <factor> =
       <primary> pass_p_f ( &
                          | "+"
                          | "*"
                          )


  ##attribute;
     reachset
```

```
       ##action;
         #pass_p_f;
           @<factor> := @<primary>


$ Treatment of a primary
       ##rule;
         <primary> =
               "&" reachset_empty
             | "input symbol name" reachset_empty
             | "nonterminal symbol name" reachset_element
             | "semantic action name" reachset_empty
             | "(" <expression> ")" pass_e_p


       ##attribute;
         reachset


       ##action;
         #reachset_empty;
           @<primary> := nil

         #reachset_element;
           @<primary> := reachset_element (@"nonterminal symbol name")

         #pass_e_p;
           @<primary> := @<expression>


###global info;
       ##type;
         reachset = ...


       ##var;
         reachtable : array [VN] of record
                                     reach : reachset;
                                     reachable : boolean
                                 end


       ##routine;
         function reachset_union (x,y : reachset) : reachset;
           ...
         function reachset_element (x : VN) : reachset;
           ...
```

7.5.   EMPTY pass

The algorithm EMPTY calculates EMPTY(s) for each ECF translation subexpression s of the right hand side of each syntax rule $A_j = s_j$ in F. The algorithm EMPTY is designed in two passes, called EMPTY1 and EMPTY2.

EMPTY1 constructs a boolean expression for each ECF translation subexpression s of the right hand side of each syntax rule $A_j = s_j$ in F. Such a boolean expression describes the calculation of EMPTY(s) in function of the boolean expressions describing the calculation of EMPTY for the nonterminals.

EMPTY2 evaluates the boolean expression for each ECF translation subexpression.

7.5.1.   EMPTY1 pass

EMPTY1 constructs a boolean expression for each ECF translation subexpression s of the right hand side of each syntax rule $A_j = s_j$ in F. Such a boolean expression describes the calculation of EMPTY(s) in function of the boolean expressions describing the calculation of EMPTY for the nonterminals. The expressions for the nonterminals will be available in the table :

  emptytable : <u>array</u> [VN] <u>of</u> boolexpr

The data type 'boolexpr' describes a boolean expression. The operations defined on this type are :

1) <u>function</u> boolexpr_true : boolexpr;
   This function returns the expression <u>true</u>.

2) <u>function</u> boolexpr_false : boolexpr;
   This function returns the expression <u>false</u>.

3) <u>function</u> boolexpr_or (el, e2 : boolexpr) : boolexpr;
   This function returns the expression el <u>or</u> e2.

4) <u>function</u> boolexpr_and (el, e2 : boolexpr) : boolexpr;
   This function returns the expression el <u>and</u> e2.

5) <u>function</u> boolexpr_evaluate (e : boolexpr) : boolean;
   This function evaluates the boolean expression e.

6). <u>nil</u> is an uninitialized boolean expression.

7) If z is a boolean expression which is the composition (<u>and</u> or <u>or</u>)
   of two other boolean expressions, then z^.left and z^.right
   reference the composing boolean expressions. The following relations hold :

$$
\begin{aligned}
\text{boolexpr\_or}(x,y)^.\text{left} &= x \\
\text{boolexpr\_or}(x,y)^.\text{right} &= y \\
\text{boolexpr\_and}(x,y)^.\text{left} &= x \\
\text{and boolexpr\_and}(x,y)^.\text{right} &= y
\end{aligned}
$$

The   semantic   actions   that   operate   on   'emptytable'   are
'init_emptytable' and 'add_emptytable'.

###syntax;

$ <u>Treatment of the syntax</u>
  ##rule;
    <syntax> = init_emptytable
      "###" "SYNTAX" ";"
      <rule definition>+

  ##var;
   i : VN

  ##action;
   #init_emptytable;
    <u>for</u> i:=0 <u>to</u> m <u>do</u> emptytable[i] := boolexpr_or (boolexpr_false, <u>nil</u>)

$ <u>Treatment of a rule definition</u>
  ##rule;
    <rule definition> =
      "##" "RULE" ";"
      "nonterminal symbol name" "=" <expression> add_emptytable

```
##action;
  #add_emptytable;
    emptytable [@"nonterminal symbol name"]^.right := @<expression>.expr
```

$ Treatment of an expression
```
  ##rule;
    <expression> =
      <alternative> pass_a_e ( "|" <alternative> or )*
```

```
  ##attribute;
    record
      expr : boolexpr
    end
```

```
  ##action;
    #pass_a_e;
      @<expression>.expr := @<alternative>1.expr

    #or;
      @<expression>.expr := boolexpr_or (@<expression>.expr,
                                         @<alternative>2.expr)
```

$ Treatment of an alternative
```
  ##rule;
    <alternative> =
      <factor> pass_f_a ( <factor> and )*
```

```
  ##attribute;
    record
      expr : boolexpr
    end
```

```
  ##action;
    #pass_f_a;
      @<alternative>.expr := @<factor>1.expr

    #and;
      @<alternative>.expr := boolexpr_and (@<alternative>.expr,
                                          @<factor>2.expr)
```

```
$ Treatment of a factor
  ##rule;
    <factor> =
       <primary> ( & pass_p_f
                  | "+" pass_p_f
                  | "*" closure
                  )


  ##attribute;
    record
      expr : boolexpr
    end


  ##action;
    #pass_p_f;
      @<factor>.expr := @<primary>.expr

    #closure;
      @<factor>.expr := boolexpr_true


$ Treatment of a primary
  ##rule;
    <primary> =
         "&" empty
       | "input symbol name" terminal
       | "nonterminal symbol name" nonterminal
       | "semantic action name" empty
       | "(" <expression> ")" pass_e_p


  ##attribute;
    record
      expr : boolexpr
    end
```

```
##action;
  #empty;
    @<primary>.expr := boolexpr_true

  #terminal;
    @<primary>.expr := boolexpr_false

  #nonterminal;
    @<primary>.expr := emptytable [@"nonterminal symbol name"]

  #pass_e_p;
    @<primary>.expr := @<expression>.expr


###globalinfo;
  ##type;
    boolexpr = ...

  ##var;
    emptytable : array [VN] of boolexpr

  ##routine;
    function boolexpr_true : boolexpr;
       ...
    function boolexpr_false : boolexpr;
       ...
    function boolexpr_or (el, e2 : boolexpr) : boolexpr;
       ...
    function boolexpr_and (el, e2 : boolexpr) : boolexpr;
       ...
    function boolexpr_evaluate (e : boolexpr) : boolean;
       ...
```

7.5.2. EMPTY2 pass

This pass evaluates the boolean expression for each ECF translation subexpression.

###syntax;

$ Treatment of the syntax
```
  ##rule;
    <syntax> =
        "###" "SYNTAX" ";"
        <rule definition>+
```

$ Treatment of a rule definition
  ##rule;
     <rule definition> =
         "##" "RULE" ";"
         "nonterminal symbol name" "=" <expression> evaluate_e

  ##action;
     #evaluate_e;
        @<expression>.empty := boolexpr_evaluate (@<expression>.expr)

$ Treatment of an expression
  ##rule;
     <expression> =
         <alternative> evaluate_al ("|" <alternative> evaluate_a2)*

  ##attribute;
     record
       expr : boolexpr;
       empty : boolean
     end

  ##action;
     #evaluate_al;
        @<alternative>1.empty := boolexpr_evaluate (@<alternative>1.expr)

     #evaluate_a2;
        @<alternative>2.empty := boolexpr_evaluate (@<alternative>2.expr)

$ Treatment of an alternative
  ##rule;
     <alternative> =
         (<factor> evaluate_f)+

  ##attribute;
     record
       expr : boolexpr;
       empty : boolean
     end

```
##action;
  #evaluate_f;
    @<factor>.empty := boolexpr_evaluate (@<factor>.expr)
```

$ Treatment of a factor
```
  ##rule;
    <factor> =
      <primary> evaluate_p ( &
                             | "+"
                             | "*"
                             )
```

```
  ##attribute;
    record
      expr : boolexpr;
      empty : boolean
    end
```

```
  ##action;
    #evaluate_p;
      @<primary>.empty := boolexpr_evaluate (@<primary>.expr)
```

$ Treatment of a primary
```
  ##rule;
    <primary> =
          "&"
        | "input symbol name"
        | "nonterminal symbol name"
        | "semantic action name"
        | "(" <expression> ")" evaluate_e
```

```
  ##attribute;
    record
      expr : boolexpr;
      empty : boolean
    end
```

```
  ##action;
    evaluate_e;
      @<expression>.empty := boolexpr_evaluate (@<expression>.expr)
```

```
###globalinfo;
  ##type;
    boolexpr = ...



  ##routine;
    function boolexpr_evaluate (e : boolexpr) : boolean;
    ...
```

7.6. FIRST pass

The algorithm FIRST calculates the set FIRST(s) for each ECF translation subexpression s of the right hand side of each syntax rule $A_j = s_j$ in F.

These sets are calculated in the form of set expressions of type 'setexpr'. Such a set expression describes the calculation of FIRST(s) in terms of the set expressions describing the calculation of FIRST for the nonterminals. The set expressions for the nonterminals will be available in the table :

firsttable : array [VN] of setexpr

The semantic actions that operate on this table are 'init_firsttable' and 'add_firsttable'.

The operations defined on the data structure 'setexpr' are :

1) function setexpr_element (x : VT) : setexpr;
   This function returns a set expression containing the input (terminal) symbol x.

2) function setexpr_union (x,y : setexpr) : setexpr;
   This function returns a set expression composed of the set expressions x and y.

3) nil is the empty set expression.

4) If z is a set expression which is the composition of two other set expressions, then z^.left and z^.right reference the composing set expressions. The following relations hold :

$$setexpr\_union(x,y)\hat{}.left = x$$
$$and\ setexpr\_union(x,y)\hat{}.right = y$$

5) <u>procedure</u> setexpr_to_set (x : setexpr; <u>var</u> y : VTset);
   This procedure initializes the set y with all the elements in the set expression x.

   The algorithm FIRST uses EMPTY(s) calculated as an attribute during the previous pass EMPTY2.

###syntax;

$ <u>Treatment of the syntax</u>
  ##rule;
    <syntax> = init_firsttable
      "###" "SYNTAX" ";"
      <rule definition>+

  ##var;
    i : VN

  ##action;
    #init_firsttable;
      <u>for</u> i:=0 <u>to</u> m <u>do</u> firsttable[i] := setexpr_union(<u>nil</u>,<u>nil</u>)

$ <u>Treatment of a rule definition</u>
  ##rule;
    <rule definition> =
      "##" "RULE" ";"
      "nonterminal symbol name" "=" <expression> add_firsttable

  ##action;
    #add_firsttable;
      firsttable[@"nonterminal symbol name"]^.right := @<expression>.first

```
$ Treatment of an expression
  ##rule;
    <expression> =
      <alternative> pass_a_e ( "|" <alternative> union )*


  ##attribute;
    record
      empty : boolean;
      first : setexpr
    end


  ##action;
    #pass_a_e;
      @<expression>.first := @<alternative>1.first

    #union;
      @<expression>.first := setexpr_union (@<expression>.first,
                                            @<alternative>2.first)

$ Treatment of an alternative
  ##rule;
    <alternative> =
      <factor> pass_f_a ( <factor> concatenate )*


  ##attribute;
    record
      empty : boolean;
      first : setexpr
    end


  ##var;
    empty_f : boolean


  ##action;
    #pass_f_a;
      @<alternative>.first := @<factor>1.first;
      empty_f := @<factor>1.empty
```

```
##concatenate;
  if empty_f then begin
    @<alternative>.first := setexpr_union (@<alternative>.first,
                                    @<factor>2.first);
    empty_f := @<factor>2.empty
    end
```

$ Treatment of a factor
```
  ##rule;
    <factor> =
      <primary> pass_p_f ( &
                         | "+"
                         | "*"
                         )
```

```
  ##attribute;
    record
      empty : boolean;
      first : setexpr
    end
```

```
  ##action;
    #pass_p_f;
      @<factor>.first := @<primary>.first
```

$ Treatment of a primary
```
  ##rule;
    <primary> =
        "&" empty
      | "input symbol name" terminal
      | "nonterminal symbol name" nonterminal
      | "semantic action name" empty
      | "(" <expression> ")" pass_e_p
```

```
  ##attribute;
    record
      empty : boolean;
      first : setexpr
    end
```

```
##action;
  #empty;
    @<primary>.first := nil

  #terminal;
    @<primary>.first := setexpr_element(@"input symbol name")

  #nonterminal;
    @<primary>.first := firsttable[@"nonterminal symbol name"]

  #pass_e_p;
    @<primary>.first := @<expression>.first


###globalinfo;
  ##type;
    setexpr = ...

  ##var;
    firsttable : array [VN] of setexpr

  ##routine;
    function setexpr_element (x : VT) : setexpr;
      ...
    function setexpr_union (x,y : setexpr) : setexpr;
      ...
```

7.7.   FOLLOW pass

The algorithm FOLLOW calculates the set FOLLOW(s) for each ECF
translation subexpression s of the right hand side of each syntax
rule $A_j = s_j$ in F.
As for FIRST(s), the sets FOLLOW(s) are calculated in the form of
set expressions of type 'setexpr'. This type is explained in section 7.6.

The algorithm to calculate FOLLOW(s) is different in nature from
the algorithm to calculate EMPTY(s) and FIRST(s). The set expression to calculate FOLLOW(s) is constructed from the right context of
s. One of these right contexts is the set expression to calculate
FOLLOW(A_j). These expressions will be available in the table :

followtable : <u>array</u> [VN] <u>of</u> setexpr

The semantic actions that operate on this table are
'init_followtable' and 'add_followtable'.

The algorithm FOLLOW uses EMPTY(s) and the set FIRST(s), calculated as attributes during the previous passes EMPTY2 and FIRST,
respectively.

###syntax;

$ <u>Treatment of the syntax</u>
  ##rule;
    <syntax> = init_followtable
      "###" "SYNTAX" ";"
      <rule definition>+

  ##var;
   i : VN

  ##action;
    #init_followtable;
     <u>for</u> i:= 0 <u>to</u> m <u>do</u> followtable[i] := setexpr_union(<u>nil</u>,<u>nil</u>);
     followtable[0]^.right := setexpr_element(0)

$ <u>Treatment of a rule definition</u>
  ##rule;
    <rule definition> =
      "##" "RULE" ";"
      "nonterminal symbol name" "=" pass_e <expression>

  ##action;
    #pass_e;
     @<expression>.follow := followtable[@"nonterminal symbol name"]

$ <u>Treatment of an expression</u>
  ##rule;
    <expression> = pass_e_al
      <alternative> ("|" pass_e_a2 <alternative>)*

```
##attribute;
  record
    empty : boolean;
    first,follow : setexpr
  end


##action;
  #pass_e_al;
    @<alternative>1.follow := @<expression>.follow

  #pass_e_a2;
    @<alternative>2.follow := @<expression>.follow
```

$ Treatment of an alternative
```
##rule;
  <alternative> = follow_f1
    <factor> ( follow_f2 <factor> )* follow_fn


##attribute;
  record
    empty : boolean;
    first,follow : setexpr
  end


##var;
  follow_f : setexpr;
    {the local variable 'follow_f' of an alternative is used
     to calculate the union of the follow sets of the
     subsequent factors, for which empty is true.}


##action;
  #follow_f1;
    @<factor>1.follow := setexpr_union(nil,nil);
    follow_f := @<factor>1.follow

  #follow_f2;
    @<factor>2.follow := setexpr_union(nil,nil);
    follow_f^.left := @<factor>2.first;
    if @<factor>2.empty
      then follow_f^.right := @<factor>2.follow;
    follow_f := @<factor>2.follow
```

```
  #follow_fn;
     follow_f^.left := @<alternative>.follow
```

$ Treatment of a factor
```
  ##rule;
     <factor> = follow_p
        <primary> ( &
                   | "+" iteration
                   | "*" iteration
                   )
```

```
  ##attribute;
    record
      empty : boolean;
      first,follow : setexpr
    end
```

```
  ##action;
    #follow_p;
      @<primary>.follow := setexpr_union(@<factor>.follow,nil)

    #iteration;
      @<primary>.follow^.right := @<primary>.first
```

$ Treatment of a primary
```
  ##rule;
     <primary> =
          "&"
        | "input symbol name"
        | add_followtable "nonterminal symbol name"
        | "semantic action name"
        | "(" pass_a_e <expression> ")"
```

```
  ##attribute;
    record
      empty : boolean;
      first,follow : setexpr
    end
```

```
##action;
  #add_followtable;
    followtable[@"nonterminal symbol name"]^.left :=
      setexpr_union(followtable[@"nonterminal symbol name"]^.left,
                @<primary>.follow)

  #pass_p_e;
    @<expression>.follow := @<primary>.follow


###globalinfo;
  ##type;
    setexpr = ...

  ##var;
    followtable : array [VN] of setexpr

  ##routine;
    function setexpr_element (x : VT) : setexpr;
      ...
    function setexpr_union (x,y : setexpr) : setexpr;
      ...
```

7.8. DIRSYMB pass

The algorithm DIRSYMB calculates the set DIRSYMB(s) for some ECF translation subexpressions s of the right hand side of each syntax rule $A_j = s_j$ in F. The sets DIRSYMB(s) are calculated in the form of an attribute 'dirsymb' of type 'VTset'. The algorithm DIRSYMB uses EMPTY(s) and the set expressions FIRST(s) and FOLLOW(s) calculated as attributes during the previous passes EMPTY2, FIRST and FOLLOW, respectively.

```
###syntax;

$ Treatment of the syntax
  ##rule;
    <syntax> =
      "###" "SYNTAX" ";"
      <rule definition>+
```

$ <u>Treatment of a rule definition</u>
  ##rule;
    <rule definition> =
       "##" "RULE" ";"
       "nonterminal symbol name" "=" <expression>

$ <u>Treatment of an expression</u>
  ##rule;
    <expression> =
       <alternative> ("|" <alternative>)*

  ##attribute;
    <u>record</u>
      empty : boolean;
      first, follow : setexpr
    <u>end</u>

$ <u>Treatment of an alternative</u>
  ##rule;
    <alternative> =
       dirsymb
       <factor>+

  ##attribute;
    <u>record</u>
      empty : boolean;
      first, follow : setexpr;
      dirsymb : VTset
    <u>end</u>

  ##action;
    #dirsymb;
      <u>if</u> @<alternative>.empty
        <u>then</u> setexpr_to_set (setexpr_union (@<alternative>.first,
                                        @<alternative>.follow),
                           @<alternative>.dirsymb)
      <u>else</u> setexpr_to_set (@<alternative>.first,
                          @<alternative>.dirsymb)

$ Treatment of a factor
  ##rule;
    <factor> =
      <primary> (&
                | "+"
                | "*"
)

  ##attribute;
    record
      empty : boolean;
      first, follow : setexpr
    end

$ Treatment of a primary
  ##rule;
    <primary> =
      dirsymb
      ("&"
      | "input symbol name"
      | "nonterminal symbol name"
      | "semantic action name"
      | "(" <expression> ")")

  ##attribute;
    record
      empty : boolean;
      first, follow : setexpr;
      dirsymb : VTset
    end

  ##action;
    #dirsymb;
      if @<primary>.empty
        then setexpr_to_set (setexpr_union (@<primary>.first,
                                            @<primary>.follow),
                             @<primary>.dirsymb)
        else setexpr_to_set (@<primary>.first,
                             @<primary>.dirsymb)

```
###globalinfo;
  ##type;
    setexpr = ...

  ##routine;
    function setexpr_union (x,y : setexpr) : setexpr;
      ...
    procedure setexpr_to_set (x : setexpr; var y : VTset);
      ...
```

7.9. ELL(1) pass

The algorithm ELL(1) tests the ELL(1) conditions in F exhaustively.

- For each ECF translation subexpression s of the form $(s_1| \ldots |s_i| \ldots |s_n)$, all sets $DIRSYMB(s_i)$ must be disjoint.

- For each ECF translation subexpression s of the form $(s_1)*$, $DIRSYMB(s_1)$ and $FOLLOW((s_1)*)$ must be disjoint. The same condition must hold for $(s_1)^+$.

The algorithm ELL(1) uses the attributes EMPTY(s), FOLLOW(s) and DIRSYMB(s), calculated during the previous passes.

```
###syntax;
```

$ Treatment of the syntax
```
  ##rule;
    <syntax> =
        "###" "SYNTAX" ";"
        <rule definition>+
```

$ Treatment of a rule definition
```
  ##rule;
    <rule definition> =
        "##" "RULE" ";"
        "nonterminal symbol name" "=" <expression>
```

$ <u>Treatment of an expression</u>
  ##rule;
    <expression> =
      <alternative> check_al ("|" <alternative> check_a2)* check_a

  ##attribute;
    <u>record</u>
      empty : boolean;
      first, follow : setexpr
    <u>end</u>

  ##var;
    union, common : VTset

  ##action;
    #check_al;
      union := @<alternative>1.dirsymb;
      common := [ ]

    #check_a2;
      common := union * @<alternative>2.dirsymb + common;
      union := union + @<alternative>2.dirsymb

    #check_a;
      <u>if</u> common <> [ ]
        <u>then</u> error1

$ <u>Treatment of an alternative</u>
  ##rule;
    <alternative> =
      <factor>+

  ##attribute;
    <u>record</u>
      empty : boolean;
      first, follow : setexpr;
      dirsymb : VTset
    <u>end</u>

```
$ Treatment of a factor
  ##rule;
    <factor> =
       <primary> ( &
                   | "+" check_p
                   | "*" check_p
                   )


  ##attribute;
    record
      empty : boolean;
      first, follow : setexpr
    end


  ##var;
    fol : VTset


  ##action;
    #check_p;
      if @<primary>.empty
        then error2
      else begin
        setexpr_to_set (@<factor>.follow,fol);
        if fol * @primary>.dirsymb <> [ ]
          then error3
        end


$ Treatment of a primary
  ##rule;
    <primary> =
         "&"
       | "input symbol name"
       | "nonterminal symbol name"
       | "semantic action name"
       | "(" <expression> ")"


  ##attribute;
    record
      empty : boolean;
      first, follow : setexpr;
      dirsymb : VTset
    end
```

```
###globalinfo;
  ##routine;
    procedure error1;
      { The DIRSYMB sets of alternatives are not disjoint }
      ...
    procedure error2;
      { EMPTY(s) is true for (s)* or (s)+ }
      ...
    procedure error3;
      { DIRSYMB(s) and FOLLOW((s)*) (or FOLLOW((s)+)) are not disjoint }
      ...
```

7.10. GENERATION pass, simple version

This algorithm is a syntax-directed description of the generation of a nonoptimized ELL(1) transducer in the form of a Pascal program from a generalized AECF translation syntax without attributes, error recovery, output vocabulary and other features whose implementation description is less interesting. Only the generation of the transducer routines is described.

The simple version is straightforward and serves as a skeleton for the optimized version (described in section 7.11), which is much more sophisticated.

At the start of the generation we assume that two attributes have been calculated in the SYNTAX pass. The attribute 'last_a', of type boolean, of an <alternative> indicates whether the alternative is the last one or not. The attribute 'operator', of type (plus,star,empty), of a <factor> indicates which operator, if any, is associated with the <factor>.

```
###syntax;

$ Treatment of the syntax
  ##rule;
    <syntax> =
        program_heading
        "###" "SYNTAX" ";"
        <rule definition>+
        program_body
```

```
##action;
  #program_heading;
    { This semantic action generates the program heading
      of the transducer.
      This heading contains the global information and the
      declarations of the read and error routines. }
    ...


  #program_body;
    { This semantic action generates the statement part
      of the transducer.
      It contains the necessary initializations and
      the call of the transducer routine of the start
      nonterminal symbol. }
    ...
```

$ Treatment of a rule definition
```
  ##rule;
    <rule definition> =
       "##" "RULE" ";"
       "nonterminal symbol name" "=" head_e <expression> tail_e


  ##action;
    #head_e;
      write (gener, 'procedure', routname[@"nonterminal symbol name"], '; begin')


    #tail_e;
      write (gener, 'end;')
```

$ Treatment of an expression
```
  ##rule;
    <expression> = head_a1
       <alternative> tail_a1 ( "|" head_a2 <alternative> tail_a2 )*


  ##action;
    #head_a1;
      if not @<alternative>1.last_a then begin
        write (gener, 'if');
        generate_test (@<alternative>1.dirsymb);
        write (gener, 'then begin')
        end
```

```
#tail_a1;
  if not @<alternative>1.last_a then write (gener, 'end')


#head_a2;
  write (gener, 'else')
  if not @<alternative>2.last_a then begin
    write (gener, 'if');
    generate_test (@<alternative>2.dirsymb);
    write (gener, 'then')
    end;
  write (gener, 'begin')


#tail_a2;
  write (gener, 'end')
```

$ Treatment of an alternative
```
##rule;
  <alternative> =
    <factor>
    ( separate <factor> )*


##attribute;
  record
    dirsymb : VTset;
    last_a : boolean
  end


##action;
  #separate;
    write (gener, ';')
```

$ Treatment of a factor
```
##rule;
  <factor> =
    head_p
    <primary> ( &
              | "+"
              | "*"
              ) tail_p
```

```
##attribute;
   record
     operator : (plus,star,empty)
   end


##action;
   #head_p;
     case @<factor>.operator of
           plus : write (gener, 'repeat');
           star : begin
                    write (gener, 'while');
                    generate_test (@<primary>.dirsymb);
                    write (gener, 'do begin')
                    end;
           empty :
     end


   #tail_p;
     case @<factor>.operator of
           plus : begin
                    write (gener, 'until not (' )
                    generate_test (@<primary>.dirsymb);
                    write (gener, ')')
                    end;
           star : write (gener, 'end');
           empty :
     end


$ Treatment of a primary
  ##rule;
     <primary> =
          "&"
        | "input symbol name" terminal
        | "nonterminal symbol name" nonterminal
        | "semantic action name" action
        | "(" <expression> ")"


   ##attribute;
     record
       dirsymb : VTset
     end
```

```
  ##action;
    #terminal;
      write (gener, 'if inp.c =', repr[@"input symbol name"],
                      'then readin  else error')


    #nonterminal;
      write (gener, routname[@"nonterminal symbol name"])


    #action;
      generate_action (@"action symbol name")


###globalinfo;
  ##var;
    routname : array [VN] of string;
      { This table contains the names of the transducer
        procedure for the nonterminals }
    repr : array [VT] of string;
      { This table contains the representations of the input symbols }
    gener : text
      { This file will contain the generated transducer }

  ##routine;
    procedure generate_test (x : VTset);
      { This procedure generates :
          (inp.c = a_1) or (inp.c = a_2) or ... or (inp.c = a_k)
        where a_1,a_2, ... ,a_k are all the elements of x
        For an optimization of this test, see section 7.11}
      ...


    procedure generate_action (x : VA);
      { This procedure copies the semantic action definition for x }
      ...
```

7.11.   GENERATION pass, optimized version

The generation algorithm, simple version (see section 7.10), produces a Pascal program that can still be optimized in space and
time. The present generation algorithm produces a Pascal program
that is optimized up to a large extent. Our experience is that the
ELL(1) transducers generated by the optimized version are competitive with handwritten ELL(1) transducers.

The optimizations are divided into four categories :

1) <u>type</u> 1 <u>optimizations</u> : terminal alternatives

The ECF translation expression is of the form '$(s_1 \mid s_2 \mid \ldots \mid s_n)$', where each s_i is a simple terminal symbol or a nonterminal symbol defining an ECF translation expression of the form as described above.
Suppose that the terminal symbols directly or indirectly involved are a_1, a_2, $\ldots$, a_k. Then, the optimized generated Pascal program part will be

<u>if</u> (inp.c = a_1) <u>or</u> (inp.c = a_2) <u>or</u> $\ldots$ <u>or</u> (inp.c = a_k)
  <u>then</u> readin
  <u>else</u> error

The information necessary to perform this kind of optimization, is calculated by means of the two-pass algorithm TERMINAL-ALTERNATIVES, described in section 7.11.1. This information is then used in the algorithm GENERATION, described in section 7.11.3.

2) <u>type</u> 2 <u>optimizations</u> : redundant tests

In the nonoptimized version, the Pascal text generated for a terminal symbol will always be :

<u>if</u> inp.c = a_i
  <u>then</u> readin
  <u>else</u> error

In many cases, the test on 'inp.c = a_i' is redundant, in which case it can be deleted. The optimized generated Pascal text for a terminal symbol will then become :

readin

The information necessary to perform this kind of optimization, is calculated by means of the two-pass algorithm REDUNDANT-TESTS, described in section 7.11.2. This information is then used in the algorithm GENERATION, described in section 7.11.3.

3) type 3 optimizations : optimized tests

In the nonoptimized version, the Pascal expression generated to test whether inp.c belongs to the set of symbols $\{a_1, a_2, ..., a_k\}$ is always of the form :

(inp.c = a_1) or (inp.c = a_2) or ... or (inp.c = a_k)

If there are consecutive symbols $a_{i1}, a_{i2}, ..., a_{in}$ in this set, then the test for these symbols can be replaced by

(inp.c >= a_{i1}) and (inp.c <= a_{in})

This optimization will be carried out in the procedure 'generate_test' which is defined in the algorithm GENERATION, described in section 7.11.3.

4) type 4 optimizations : combination of type 1 and 2

Then the optimized generated Pascal text from '(s_1 | s_2 | ... | s_n)' is simply

    readin

This optimization is local in the algorithm GENERATION, described in section 7.11.3.

7.11.1. TERMINAL-ALTERNATIVES pass

This algorithm calculates in each <expression>-node of the attributed derivation tree a boolean attribute called 'term_alternatives', indicating whether type 1 optimizations are applicable. The attribute 'term_alternatives' is defined by the following scheme of rules.

Axiomatic rules

0) TERM_ALTERNATIVES(r) = <u>false</u>, where r $\in$ V$_{action}$

1) TERM_ALTERNATIVES(&) = <u>false</u>

2) TERM_ALTERNATIVES(a$_i$) = <u>true</u>, where a$_i$ $\in$ VT

2') TERM_ALTERNATIVES(A$_j$) = TERM_ALTERNATIVES(s$_j$), where A$_j$ $\in$ VN and A$_j$=s$_j$ $\in$ P. Notice that this is a recursive definition.

Composition rules

3) TERM_ALTERNATIVES((s$_1$|s$_2$| ... |s$_n$)) =
        AND$_{1 \leq i \leq n}$ TERM_ALTERNATIVES(s$_i$)

4) TERM_ALTERNATIVES(s$_1$s$_2$ ... s$_n$) = <u>false</u>

5) TERM_ALTERNATIVES((s)*) = <u>false</u>

6) TERM_ALTERNATIVES((s)$^+$) = <u>false</u>

The algorithm TERMINAL-ALTERNATIVES is designed in two passes, called TERMINAL-ALTERNATIVES1 and TERMINAL-ALTERNATIVES2.

TERMINAL-ALTERNATIVES1 constructs a boolean expression for each ECF translation subexpression of the right hand side of each syntax rule A$_j$ = s$_j$ in F. Such a boolean expression describes the calculation of TERMINAL_ALTERNATIVES(s) in terms of the boolean expressions to calculate TERMINAL-ALTERNATIVES for the nonterminals.

TERMINAL-ALTERNATIVES2 evaluates these boolean expressions in each <expression>-node of the attributed derivation tree. The boolean result will be stored in the attribute 'term_alternatives'.

This algorithm is very similar to the calculation of EMPTY in section 7.5.

7.11.1.1. <u>TERMINAL-ALTERNATIVES1 pass</u>

TERMINAL-ALTERNATIVES1 constructs a boolean expression for each
ECF translation subexpression of the right hand side of each syntax
rule $A_j = s_j$ in F. Such a boolean expression describes the calculation of TERMINAL_ALTERNATIVES(s) in terms of the boolean expressions
to calculate TERMINAL-ALTERNATIVES for the nonterminals. The
expressions for the nonterminals will be available in the table :

   alternativetable : <u>array</u> [VN] <u>of</u> boolexpr

The data type 'boolexpr' describes a boolean expression. This type
is defined in section 7.5.1.

###syntax;

$ <u>Treatment of the syntax</u>
  ##rule;
    <syntax> =
      init_alternativetable
      "###" "SYNTAX" ";"
      <rule definition>+

  ##var;
   i : VN

  ##action;
   #init_alternativetable;
    <u>for</u> i:=0 <u>to</u> m <u>do</u> alternativetable[i] := boolexpr_or (boolexpr_false, <u>nil</u>)

$ <u>Treatment of a rule definition</u>
  ##rule;
    <rule definition> =
      "##" "RULE" ";"
      "nonterminal symbol name" "=" <expression> add_alternativetable

  ##action;
   #add_alternativetable;
    alternativetable [@"nonterminal symbol name"]^.right := @<expression>.expr

$ <u>Treatment of an expression</u>
  ##rule;
    <expression> =
      <alternative> pass_a_e ("|" <alternative> and)*

  ##attribute;
   <u>record</u>
     expr : boolexpr
   <u>end</u>

  ##action;
   #pass_a_e;
    @<expression>.expr := @<alternative>1.expr

   #and;
    @<expression>.expr := boolexpr_and (@<expression>.expr,
                             @<alternative>2.expr)

$ <u>Treatment of an alternative</u>
  ##rule;
    <alternative> =
      <factor> first_f
      (<factor> more_f)*
      expr_a

  ##attribute;
   <u>record</u>
     expr : boolexpr
   <u>end</u>

  ##var;
   one_factor : boolean

  ##action;
   #first_f;
    one_factor := true

   #more_f;
    one_factor := false

```
#expr_a;
  if one_factor then @<alternative>.expr := @<factor>1.expr
    else @<alternative>.expr := boolexpr_false
```

$ Treatment of a factor
```
  ##rule;
    <factor> =
      <primary> ( & pass_p_f
                 | "+" false
                 | "*" false
                 )


  ##attribute;
    record
      expr : boolexpr
    end


  ##action;
    #pass_p_f;
      @<factor>.expr := @<primary>.expr


    #false;
      @<factor> := boolexpr_false
```

$ Treatment of a primary
```
  ##rule;
    <primary> =
        ( "&" false
        | "input symbol name" terminal
        | "nonterminal symbol name" nonterminal
        | "semantic action name" false
        | "(" <expression> ")" pass_e_p


  ##attribute;
    record
      expr : boolexpr
    end


  ##action;
    #false;
      @<primary>.expr := boolexpr_false
```

```
  #terminal;
     @<primary>.expr := boolexpr_true


  #nonterminal;
     @<primary>.expr := alternativetable [@"nonterminal symbol name"]


  #pass_e_p;
     @<primary>.expr := @<expression>.expr
```

```
###globalinfo;
  ##type;
     boolexpr = ...

  ##var;
     alternativetable : array [VN] of boolexpr

  ##routine;
     function boolexpr_true : boolexpr;
        ...
     function boolexpr_false : boolexpr;
        ...
     function boolexpr_and (e1, e2 : boolexpr) : boolexpr;
        ...
```

7.11.1.2.   TERMINAL-ALTERNATIVES2 pass

This pass evaluates the boolean expressions in each
<expression>-node of the attributed derivation tree. The boolean
result will be stored in the attribute 'term_alternatives'.

###syntax;

$ Treatment of the syntax
```
  ##rule;
     <syntax> =
        "###" "SYNTAX" ";"
        <rule definition>+
```

```
$ Treatment of a rule definition
  ##rule;
    <rule definition> =
        "##" "RULE" ";"
        "nonterminal symbol name" "=" <expression>


$ Treatment of an expression
  ##rule;
    <expression> =
        eval_e
        <alternative> ( "|" <alternative> )*


  ##attribute;
    record
      expr : boolexpr;
      term_alternatives : boolean
    end


  ##action;
    #eval_e;
      @<expression>.term_alternatives := boolexpr_evaluate (@<expression>.expr)

$ Treatment of an alternative
  ##rule;
    <alternative> =
        <factor>+


$ Treatment of a factor
  ##rule;
    <factor> =
        <primary> ( &
                  | "+"
                  | "*"
                  )
```

```
$ Treatment of a primary
  ##rule;
    <primary> =
        "&"
      | "input symbol name"
      | "nonterminal symbol name"
      | "semantic action name"
      | "(" <expression> ")"


###globalinfo;
  ##type;
    boolexpr = ...

  ##routine;
    function boolexpr_evaluate (e : boolexpr) : boolean;
      ...
```

7.11.2. REDUNDANT-TESTS pass

This algorithm calculates in each <expression>-node and <primary>-node of the attributed derivation tree a boolean attribute called 'redundant_test'. This attribute indicates whether at the moment the transducing module for the expression or primary concerned is activated, one of its direction symbols is guaranteed to be under the input head. The algorithm REDUNDANT-TESTS is designed in two passes, called REDUNDANT-TESTS1 and REDUNDANT-TESTS2.

REDUNDANT-TESTS1 constructs a boolean expression for each ECF translation subexpression of the right hand side of each syntax rule $A_j = s_j$ in F. Such a boolean expression describes the calculation of REDUNDANT-TESTS(s) in terms of the boolean expressions to calculate REDUNDANT-TESTS for the nonterminals. These boolean expressions are defined by the following scheme :

<rule> -> A_j = <expression>

   boolexpr (<expression>) = the boolexpr defining A_j

<expression> -> <alternative>1 | <alternative>2 | ... | <alternative>n

```
boolexpr (<alternative>i) = true   for 1≤i<n
boolexpr (<alternative>n) = boolexpr (<expression>)
```

```
<alternative> -> <factor>1 <factor>2 ... <factor>n
```

```
boolexpr (<factor>1) = boolexpr (<alternative>)
boolexpr (<factor>i) = false   for 1<i≤n
```

```
<factor> -> <primary>*
```

```
boolexpr (<primary>) = true
```

```
<factor> -> <primary>+
```

```
boolexpr (<primary>) = boolexpr (<factor>)
```

```
<factor> -> <primary>
```

```
boolexpr (<primary>) = boolexpr (<factor>)
```

```
<primary> -> Aj
```

```
boolexpr defining Aj = boolexpr defining Aj
                       ___ boolexpr (<primary>)
```

```
<primary> -> "(" <expression> ")"
```

```
boolexpr (<expression>) = boolexpr (<primary>)
```

REDUNDANT-TESTS2 evaluates these boolean expressions in each <expression>-node and <primary>-node of the attributed derivation tree. The boolean result will be stored in the attribute 'redundant_test'.

7.11.2.1. REDUNDANT-TESTS1 pass

REDUNDANT-TESTS1 constructs a boolean expression for each ECF translation subexpression of the right hand side of each syntax rule $A_j = s_j$ in F. Such a boolean expression describes the calculation of REDUNDANT-TESTS(s) in terms of the boolean expressions to calculate REDUNDANT-TESTS for the nonterminals. The expressions for the nonterminals are available in the table :

  redundant_testtable : <u>array</u> [VN] <u>of</u> boolexpr

The data type 'boolexpr' describes a boolean expression. This type is defined in section 7.5.1.

###syntax;

$ <u>Treatment of the syntax</u>
  ##rule;
    <syntax> =
      init
      "###" "SYNTAX" ";"
      <rule definition>+

  ##var;
   i : VN

  ##action;
   #init;
    redundant_testtable [0] := boolexpr_and (boolexpr_false, boolexpr_true);
    <u>for</u> i:=1 <u>to</u> m <u>do</u> redundant_testtable [i] :=
      boolexpr_and (boolexpr_true, boolexpr_true)

$ <u>Treatment of a rule definition</u>
  ##rule;
    <rule definition> =
      "##" "RULE" ";"
      "nonterminal symbol name" "=" init_e <expression>

  ##action;
   #init_e;
    @<expression>.expr := redundant_testtable [@"nonterminal symbol name"]

$ <u>Treatment of an expression</u>
  ##rule;
    <expression> = optimize_a1
      <alternative> ("|" optimize_a2 <alternative>)*

```
##attribute;
  record
    expr : boolexpr
  end


##action;
  #optimize_a1;
    if @<alternative>1.last_a
      then @<alternative>1.expr := @<expression>.expr
      else @<alternative>1.expr := boolexpr_true


  #optimize_a2;
    if @<alternative>2.last_a
      then @<alternative>2.expr := @<expression>.expr
      else @<alternative>2.expr := boolexpr_true
```

$ Treatment of an alternative
```
  ##rule;
    <alternative> =
        optimize_f1 <factor>
        (optimize_f2 <factor> )*


  ##attribute;
    record
      last_a : boolean;
      expr : boolexpr
    end


  ##action;
    #optimize_f1;
      @<factor>1.expr := @<alternative>.expr


    #optimize_f2;
      @<factor>2.expr := boolexpr_false
```

```
$ Treatment of a factor
   ##rule;
     <factor> = optimize_p
        <primary> ( &
                  | "+"
                  | "*"
                  )


   ##attribute;
      record
        operator : (plus,star,empty);
        expr : boolexpr
      end


   ##action;
     #optimize_p;
        case @<factor>.operator of
           star : @<primary>.expr := boolexpr_true;
           plus, empty : @<primary>.expr := @<factor>.expr
        end


$ Treatment of a primary
   ##rule;
     <primary> =
           "&"
        | "input symbol name"
        | "nonterminal symbol name" nonterminal
        | "semantic action name"
        | "(" optimize_e <expression> ")"


   ##attribute;
      record
        expr : boolexpr
      end


   ##action;
     #nonterminal;
        redundant_testtable [@"nonterminal symbol name"]^.right :=
           boolexpr_and (@<primary>.expr,
                         redundant_testtable [@"nonterminal symbol name"]^.right)
```

```
    #optimize_e;
       @<expression>.expr := @<primary>.expr


###globalinfo;
  ##type;
     boolexpr = ...

  ##var;
     redundant_testtable : array [VN] of boolexpr

  ##routine;
     function boolexpr_true : boolexpr;
       ...
     function boolexpr_false : boolexpr;
       ...
     function boolexpr_and (e1, e2 : boolexpr) : boolexpr;
       ...
```

7.11.2.2.   REDUNDANT-TESTS2 pass

The boolean expressions in each <expression>-node and <primary>-
node of the attributed derivation tree are evaluated.

```
###syntax;

$ Treatment of the syntax
  ##rule;
     <syntax> =
        "###" "SYNTAX" ";"
        <rule definition>+


$ Treatment of a rule definition
  ##rule;
     <rule definition> =
        "##" "RULE" ";"
        "nonterminal symbol name" "=" <expression>


$ Treatment of an expression
  ##rule;
     <expression> =
        eval_e
        <alternative> ( "|" <alternative> )*
```

```
##attribute;
   record
     expr : boolexpr;
     redundant_test : boolean
   end


##action;
   #eval_e;
     @<expression>.redundant_test := boolexpr_evaluate (@<expression>.expr)
```

$ Treatment of an alternative
```
##rule;
   <alternative> =
     <factor>+
```

$ Treatment of a factor
```
##rule;
   <factor> =
     <primary> ( &
               | "+"
               | "*"
               )
```

$ Treatment of a primary
```
##rule;
   <primary> =
     eval_p
     ( "&"
     | "input symbol name"
     | "nonterminal symbol name"
     | "semantic action name"
     | "(" <expression> ")" )


##attribute;
   record
     expr : boolexpr;
     redundant_test : boolean
   end
```

```
##action;
  #eval_p;
    @<primary>.redundant_test := boolexpr_evaluate (@<primary>.expr)


###globalinfo;
  ##type;
    boolexpr = ...

  ##routine;
    function boolexpr_evaluate (e : boolexpr) : boolean;
      ...
```


7.11.3. GENERATION pass


```
###syntax;

$ Treatment of the syntax
  ##rule;
    <syntax> =
        program_heading
        "###" "SYNTAX" ";"
        <rule definition>+
        program_body


  ##action;
    #program_heading;
      { This semantic action generates the program heading
        of the transducer.
        This heading contains the global information and the
        declarations of the read and error routines. }
      ...


    #program_body;
      { This semantic action generates the statement part
        of the transducer.
        It contains the necessary initializations and
        the call of the transducer routine of the start
        nonterminal symbol. }
      ...
```

```
$ Treatment of a rule definition
  ##rule;
    <rule definition> =
       "##" "RULE" ";"
       "nonterminal symbol name" "=" head_e <expression> tail_e


  ##action;
    #head_e;
      write (gener, 'procedure', routname[@"nonterminal symbol name"], '; begin');
      @<expression>.gener := true


    #tail_e;
      write (gener, 'end;')


$ Treatment of an expression
  ##rule;
    <expression> = begin head_al
       <alternative> tail_al ( "|" head_a2 <alternative> tail_a2 )*
       end


  ##attribute;
    record
       term_alternatives : boolean;
       redundant_test : boolean;
       gener : boolean
    end


  ##var;
    s : VTset

  ##action;
    #begin;
      @<alternative>1.gener := @<expression>.gener;
      @<alternative>2.gener := @<expression>.gener
```

```
#head_a1;
  if @<expression>.gener then
  if @<expression>.term_alternatives then @<alternative>1.gener := false
  else if not @<alternative>1.last_a then begin
    write (gener, 'if');
    generate_test (@<alternative>1.dirsymb);
    write (gener, 'then begin')
    end


#tail_a1;
  if @<expression>.gener then
  if @<expression>.term_alternatives then s := @<alternative>1.dirsymb
  else if not @<alternative>1.last_a then write (gener, 'end')


#head_a2;
  if @<expression>.gener then
  if @<expression>.term_alternatives then @<alternative>2.gener := false
  else begin
    write (gener, 'else')
    if not @<alternative>2.last_a then begin
      write (gener, 'if');
      generate_test (@<alternative>2.dirsymb);
      write (gener, 'then')
      end;
    write (gener, 'begin')
    end


#tail_a2;
  if @<expression>.gener then
  if @<expression>.term_alternatives then s := s + @<alternative>2.dirsymb
  else write (gener, 'end')


#end;
  if @<expression>.gener then
  if @<expression>.term_alternatives then
  if @<expression>.redundant_test then write (gener, 'readin')
  else begin
    write (gener, 'if');
    generate_test (s);
    write (gener, 'then readin else error ')
    end
```

```
$ Treatment of an alternative
   ##rule;
     <alternative> =
         begin
         <factor>
         ( separate <factor> )*


   ##attribute;
       record
         dirsymb : VTset;
         last_a : boolean;
         gener : boolean
       end


   ##action;
     #begin;
       @<factor>1.gener := @<alternative>.gener;
       @<factor>2.gener := @<alternative>.gener


     #separate;
       if @<alternative>.gener then write (gener, ';')


$ Treatment of a factor
   ##rule;
     <factor> =
         begin
         head_p
         <primary> ( &
                    | "+"
                    | "*"
                    ) tail_p


   ##attribute;
       record
         operator : (plus,star,empty);
         gener : boolean
       end


   ##action;
     #begin;
       @<primary>.gener := @<factor>.gener
```

```
#head_p;
  if @<factor>.gener then
  case @<factor>.operator of
        plus : write (gener, 'repeat');
        star : begin
                  write (gener, 'while');
                  generate_test (@<primary>.dirsymb);
                  write (gener, 'do begin')
                  end;
        empty :
  end


#tail_p;
  if @<factor>.gener then
  case @<factor>.operator of
        plus : begin
                  write (gener, 'until not (' )
                  generate_test (@<primary>.dirsymb);
                  write (gener, ')')
                  end;
        star : write (gener, 'end');
        empty :
  end


$ Treatment of a primary
  ##rule;
    <primary> =
          "&"
        | "input symbol name" terminal
        | "nonterminal symbol name" nonterminal
        | "semantic action name" action
        | begin_e "(" <expression> ")"


  ##attribute;
      record
        dirsymb : VTset;
        redundant_test : boolean;
        gener : boolean
      end
```

```
##action;
  #terminal;
    if @<primary>.gener then
    if @<primary>.redundant_test then write (gener, 'readin')
    else write (gener, 'if inp.c =', repr[@"input symbol name"],
                  'then readin else error')


  #nonterminal;
    if @<primary>.gener then
    write (gener, routname[@"nonterminal symbol name"])


  #action;
    if @<primary>.gener then
    generate_action (@"action symbol name")


  #begin_e;
    @<expression>.gener := @<primary>.gener


###global info;
  ##var;
    routname : array [VN] of string;
      { This table contains the names of the transducer
        procedure for the nonterminals }
    repr : array [VT] of string;
      { This table contains the representations of the input symbols }
    gener : text
      { This file will contain the generated transducer }

  ##routine;
    procedure generate_test (x : VTset);
      { This procedure generates
          (inp.c = a₁) or (inp.c = a₂) or ... or (inp.c = aₖ)
        where a₁,a₂, ... ,aₖ are all the elements of x.
        The type 3 optimization can be carried out in this procedure}
      ...

    procedure generate_action (x : VA);
      { This procedure copies the semantic action definition for x }
      ...
```

CONCLUSION

A first objective of the LILA project was to look for a methodology in compiler construction. This methodology has a conceptual aspect, as it is described in Part 1, and an engineering aspect, which is described in Part 2. A second objective was to develop a compiler writing tool LILA to support this methodology. One of the main design philosophies is the trade-off between the degree of automation and the degree of user interaction offered by the compiler writing tool. From our experience, we may conclude that LILA offers the user an appropriate infrastructure on which compilers can be developed in an elegant way. This means that the system LILA promotes the writing of compilers which are modular, reliable, efficient, easy to modify and to maintain. What compile time as well as run time efficiency is concerned, measurements have indicated that compilers produced by LILA are competitive with hand coded compilers.

Part 2 contains information on three different levels:
1) A reference guide that describes how correct LILA inputs must be written.
2) A set of case studies that show how compilers can be produced by LILA.
3) A description of LILA by means of LILA itself.
These three levels describe LILA as it is available now. The LILA program is written in standard Pascal. This implies that it can be installed on a wide variety of machines. LILA implementations already exist on DEC, IBM, Siemens and CDC machines.

A number of extensions of the current LILA system are envisaged. Among these are an alternate error recovery mechanism, improved error diagnostic facilities in the generated compilers and a LILA version with ADA as metalanguage.

APPENDIX

L I L A
REFERENCE GUIDE

INTRODUCTION

In sections 2, 3 and 4 of the book we have studied the generalized attributed extended context-free (AECF) translation syntax and the ELL(1) transducer. Also, the generation scheme to produce an ELL(1) transducer from such a translation syntax has been thoroughly discussed. The viewpoint of this study is a conceptual one.

The generation scheme producing ELL(1) transducers from generalized AECF translation syntaxes has been tuned towards a practical engineering tool called LILA, a Language Implementation LAboratory. The skeleton of the LILA input is the generalized AECF translation syntax, on which a number of software engineering features are added.

This Reference Guide contains three sections: the first section describes the LILA input, the second section describes the overall structure of the generated ELL(1) transducer and the third section describes the diagnostics that are generated by LILA. These three sections correspond to the LILA-input-file, the LILA-output-file and the LILA-diagnostics-file, respectively.

In the description of the LILA input, normal and advanced applications are distinguished. For advanced applications, a number of design decisions that are taken by LILA for the normal applications can be overridden by the user.

To avoid the possible ambiguity between references to sections of this appendix and the sections of the book, we adopt the convention that a section number always refers to a section of this appendix unless it is indicated otherwise.

The execution of LILA can be roughly divided in four phases:

Phase 1:
   The LILA input is lexically and syntactically analysed.

Phase 2:

A test is performed whether the translation syntax is reduced.

Phase 3:

The ELL(1) conditions on the translation syntax are checked.

Phase 4:

The ELL(1) transducer is generated.

1. LILA INPUT DESCRIPTION

1.1. Lexical considerations

At the lowest level, the LILA input is basically a stream of characters divided into lines, i.e. a textfile in Pascal terminology. Each portion of this character stream beginning with a '$' upto the end of the line is treated as comment. This is the only place where the end-of-line in the LILA input is significant. In all other places the end-of-line is equivalent to a space.

Some characters have a special meaning throughout the whole LILA input stream. These characters are: '$', '#' and '\'. Other characters have a special meaning only in particular portions of the input stream. These characters are: '@', '%', '"', '[', ']', '<' and '>'. To deprive a character of its special meaning it must be preceded by the escape character ('\').

At a higher level, the LILA input is a sequence of LILA input symbols where each input symbol is composed of one or more characters. Spaces may be used to separate input symbols from each other. The LILA input symbols can be divided into four categories:

* Special LILA input symbols:

     "###", "##", "#",
     ";", ",", ":", "=",
     "+", "*", "&", "(", ")", "|", "!", "?"

* LILA keywords:

     "OPTIONS", "PRINVOC", "PROUTVOC", "PRTREE", "LET",
     "PROCEDURE", "NAME", "NOOPTIMIZE", "NOGENERATE",
     "SOURCE", "GSLN", "SYNCFLOW", "SYNCSETS", "NOLAST",

```
"INPUTVOCABULARY", "OUTPUTVOCABULARY",
"REP", "INTEGER", "CHAR", "FILE", "EOF",
"SYNTAX", "RULE", "ATTRIBUTE", "LABEL", "CONST", "TYPE", "VAR",
"ROUTINE", "ACTION",
"RECOVERY", "LAST", "FIRST", "ENTRY", "EXIT",
"GLOBALINFO", "PARAMETER", "PROLOGUE", "EPILOGUE",
"FOLLOW",
"READROUTINE",
"WRITEROUTINE",
"ERRORROUTINE"
```

The keywords must be represented in the <u>system-case</u>. This is an installation defined characteristic and is either lower case or upper case. Lower case will be used in the examples of this Reference Guide.

* Other LILA input symbols:

```
"input symbol name", "output symbol name",
"nonterminal symbol name", "semantic action name",
"unsigned integer", "character constant"
```

An "input symbol name" is any string of characters enclosed between double quotes ("). Consecutive spaces in such a name are equivalent to one single space. The maximum length of this string is the installation defined characteristic <u>max-name-length</u>. If the character '"' is part of the name, it must be preceded by the escape-character.

An "output symbol name" is any string of characters enclosed between '[' and ']'. Consecutive spaces in such a name are equivalent to one single space. The maximum length of this string is the installation defined characteristic max-name-length. If the character ']' is part of the name, it must be preceded by the escape-character.

A "nonterminal symbol name" is any string of characters enclosed between '<' and '>'. Consecutive spaces in such a name are equivalent to one single space. The maximum length of this string is the installation defined characteristic max-name-length. If the character '>' is part of the name, it must be preceded by the escape-character.

A "semantic action name" is a string of letters, digits or under-
scores ('_'), starting with a letter. The letters must be in the
system-case. The maximum length of this string is the installation defined characteristic max-name-length.

An "unsigned integer" is a string of digits, such that the
corresponding integer value is less than or equal to the installation defined characteristic <u>max-integer</u>.

A "character constant" is any character enclosed between single
quotes (').

<u>Examples</u>

"a", "A", "identifier", "+", "integer number", "\"", "'", "aBc"
and "ABC" are different input symbol names.
"real number" and "real   number" are identical input symbol
names.

[identifier], [boolean], ["], [[] and [\]] are output symbol
names.

<type>, <if statement>, <BEGIN> are nonterminal symbol names.

OUT_NUMBER, ASSIGN, TYPE and TRANSFORM3 are semantic action names
if the system-case is upper case.

342, 2, 0 and 56 are unsigned integers.

'b', 'B', '%', ''' and '7' are character constants.

* Pascal input symbols:

The LILA input also contains portions of <u>Pascal-text</u>, composed of
elements of the Pascal vocabulary. These portions of Pascal-text
are defined by the following Pascal nonterminals (see Jensen and
Wirth [1978]):

```
<type>, <type identifier>, <file identifier>, <identifier>,
<label>, <constant definition>, <type definition>,
<variable declaration>, <procedure or function declaration>,
<statement>, <program parameters>, <formal parameter section>
```

Only the first 8 characters of <type identifier>, <file identif-
ier> and <identifier> are significant. The letters in these
identifiers must be in the system-case and the use of '_' is
allowed.

These Pascal-text input portions are not checked for Pascal
correctness by LILA.

1.2. The LILA input

The LILA input consists of up to nine different input parts, two of which are obligatory. The first five LILA input parts are for normal applications (see 1.3), whereas the other four are for advanced applications (see 1.4).

```
<LILA input> =
    ( <global options> | & )
    <input vocabulary>
    ( <output vocabulary> | & )
    <syntax>
    ( <globalinfo> | & )
    ( <follow> | & )
    ( <readroutine> | & )
    ( <writeroutine> | & )
    ( <errorroutine> | & )
```

Each LILA input part has a specific function.

<global options> specifies options that apply to the generation.

<input vocabulary> defines the input symbols of the generated ELL(1) transducer.

<output vocabulary> defines the output symbols of the generated ELL(1) transducer.

<syntax> defines the translation syntax modules.

<globalinfo> defines the global information for the semantic actions of the translation syntax.

<follow> defines the set of input symbols that can follow any sentence of the input language.

<readroutine> defines a user-defined read routine in the generated ELL(1) transducer.

<writeroutine> defines a user-defined write routine in the generated ELL(1) transducer.

<errorroutine> defines a user-defined error routine in the generated ELL(1) transducer.

Each LILA input part is identified with a <u>LILA</u> <u>control</u> <u>statement</u>. At the first level, a control statement starts with the symbol "###", followed by the name of the LILA input part and possibly some options concerning it. Such an input part may in turn contain other input parts starting with a LILA control statement at the second

level. This control statement must start with the symbol "##".
An input part that starts with a second level control statement may
in turn contain other input parts that start with a third level control statement. A third level control statement must start with the
symbol "#".

This hierarchy of control statements is an important aspect of the
LILA input. It will be defined more precisely in the following sections.

Examples of complete LILA inputs are given in section 5 of the book.

1.3.   Normal applications

1.3.1.   The input vocabulary

The input vocabulary defines all the input symbols of the generated ELL(1) transducer.

```
<input vocabulary> =
    "###" "INPUTVOCABULARY" <input vocabulary options> ";"
    <input symbol definition>+


<input symbol definition> =
    "input symbol name" "=" <representation> ( ":" <type identifier> | & )


<representation> =
    "unsigned integer" | "character constant"


<input vocabulary options> =
    <input vocabulary option> ( "," <input vocabulary option> )*


<input vocabulary option> =
        <rep option>
    | <file option>
    | <eof option>


<rep option> =
    "REP" "(" ( "INTEGER" | "CHAR" ) ")"


<file option> =
    "FILE" "(" <file identifier> ")"


<eof option> =
    "EOF" "(" "unsigned integer" ")"
```

Each input symbol consists of a representation and possibly an
attribute. The input symbol has also a symbolic name, the input
symbol name.

* The "input symbol name" is used to refer to the input symbol in
  the LILA input. All input symbol names must be different.

* The <representation> describes how the input symbol is
  represented.
  All the input symbol representations must be of the same type:
  integer or character.   This type is called the input-
  representation-type and must be defined in the REP option.
  If the input-representation-type is INTEGER, the "unsigned
  integer" is the integer representation of the defined input symbol.
  If the input-representation-type is CHAR, the "unsigned integer"
  is the ordinal value of the character representation of the
  defined input symbol. In this case, the representation may also
  be a "character constant". The ordinal value of the representation of the defined input symbol will then be the ordinal value
  of the "character constant" on the machine on which LILA is executed.
  All input symbols must have a different representation.
  The representation of an input symbol can be referred to in the
  pascal-text by a constant of the input-representation-type. This
  constant is denoted by:

     "%" "input symbol name"

* The <type identifier> defines the type of the attribute of the
  input symbol. This type identifier may be defined in GLOBALINFO.
  If the ":" <type identifier> part is absent, the defined input
  symbol has no attribute.
  The semantic actions and the local routines may access the attributes of the input symbols (see 1.3.3.4).

The ELL(1) transducer reads the input symbols one by one and stores
them in the input-head INP, which has a component INP.C of the
input-representation-type and possibly a component INP.A to hold the
attribute, if any (see 1.3.4). This read routine can be defined by
the user by means of the LILA input part READROUTINE (see 1.4.2).
If no READROUTINE is specified in the LILA input, a default read
routine will be generated. This default read routine reads the
input symbols from the input-symbol-file INFILE. The declaration of

this file and all actions concerning it are generated by LILA. The
file name must however appear among the program parameters (see
1.3.4).
The input-symbol-file can be given another name in the FILE option.

There is also a virtual input symbol, end-of-file, that is used to
represent the end of the input-symbol-file. This end-of-file input
symbol must have a representation different from all defined input
symbol representations. This representation can be defined by the
EOF option. Its default value is O.
Each sentence of the input language as defined by the translation
syntax, must always be followed by this end-of-file input symbol or
by one of the input symbols defined in the follow set (see 1.4.1).

Remarks

1. If the default read routine is generated, i.e. when no READROU-
   TINE is defined, 1 may not be used as representation of an input
   symbol. It has a special meaning to the default read routine: 1
   is used to represent line markers. These line markers are virtual input symbols that are skipped when reading input symbols.
   However, each time such a line marker occurs in the input, the
   LILA-defined global variable LINENUMB is incremented by 1 (see
   1.3.4).

2. The representations of the input symbols and the representation
   of the end-of-file input symbol should be chosen as small as possible. This decreases both memory usage and execution time during generation.

3. If the installation, where the generated ELL(1) transducer will
   be executed, requires information about the internal structure of
   the input-symbol-file, this information can be extracted from the
   file declaration in the generated ELL(1) transducer.

4. The input-symbol-file will be of type TEXT if the option
   REP(CHAR) is used and if none of the input symbols is attributed.
   A line marker is represented by an end-of-line in such a file.
   Such a line marker is not skipped but considered as a space

character.

Example 1

This example illustrates an input vocabulary of characters. Since none of the input symbols is attributed, the input-symbol-file will be a textfile.

    ###inputvocabulary rep(char), file(input);

    "bl"= ' '   "(" = '('   ")" = ')'   "*" = '*'   "+" = '+'   "," = ','
    "-" = '-'   "." = '.'   "/" = '/'   "0" = '0'   "1" = '1'   "2" = '2'
    "3" = '3'   "4" = '4'   "5" = '5'   "6" = '6'   "7" = '7'   "8" = '8'
    "9" = '9'   "=" = '='   "?" = '?'   "^" = '^'   "a" = 'a'   "b" = 'b'
    "c" = 'c'   "d" = 'd'   "e" = 'e'   "f" = 'f'   "g" = 'g'   "h" = 'h'
    "i" = 'i'   "j" = 'j'   "k" = 'k'   "l" = 'l'   "m" = 'l'   "n" = 'n'
    "o" = 'o'   "p" = 'p'   "q" = 'q'   "r" = 'r'   "s" = 's'   "t" = 't'
    "u" = 'u'   "v" = 'v'   "w" = 'w'   "x" = 'x'   "y" = 'y'   "z" = 'z'

Example 2

The following input vocabulary is equivalent with the one above if the ASCII character representation is used on the machine on which LILA is executed:

    ###inputvocabulary rep(char), file(input);

    "bl"= 32   "(" = 40   ")" = 41   "*" = 42   "+" = 43   "," = 44
    "-" = 45   "." = 46   "/" = 47   "0" = 48   "1" = 49   "2" = 50
    "3" = 51   "4" = 52   "5" = 53   "6" = 54   "7" = 55   "8" = 56
    "9" = 57   "=" = 61   "?" = 63   "^" = 94   "a" = 97   "b" = 98
    "c" = 99   "d" =100   "e" =101   "f" =102   "g" =103   "h" =104
    "i" =105   "j" =106   "k" =107   "l" =108   "m" =109   "n" =110
    "o" =111   "p" =112   "q" =113   "r" =114   "s" =115   "t" =116
    "u" =117   "v" =118   "w" =119   "x" =120   "y" =121   "z" =122

Example 3

This example illustrates an input vocabulary where the input symbols
are represented by integers and where some of them are attributed:

```
###inputvocabulary rep(integer);

  "identifier" = 2 : rep_name

  "number" = 3 : real

  "how"  = 4     "many" = 5     "in" = 6
  "kg"   = 7     "m"    = 8     "s"  = 9

  "(" = 10     ")" = 11     "*" = 12     "+" = 13     "," = 14
  "-" = 15     "/" = 16     "=" = 17     "?" = 18     "^" = 19
```

1.3.2. The output vocabulary

The output vocabulary defines all the output symbols of the generated ELL(1) transducer.

```
<output vocabulary> =
  "###" "OUTPUTVOCABULARY" <output vocabulary options> ";"
  <output symbol definition>+


<output symbol definition> =
  "output symbol name" "=" <representation> ( ":" <type identifier> | & )


<representation> =
  "unsigned integer" | "character constant"


<output vocabulary options> =
  <output vocabulary option> ( "," <output vocabulary option> )*


<output vocabulary option> =
    <rep option>
  | <file option>
```

```
<rep option> =
   "REP" "(" ( "INTEGER" | "CHAR" ) ")"


<file option> =
   "FILE" "(" <file identifier> ")"
```

Each output symbol consists of a representation and possibly an attribute. The output symbol has also a symbolic name, the output symbol name.

* The "output symbol name" is used to refer to the output symbol in the LILA input. All output symbol names must be different.

* The <representation> describes how the output symbol is represented.
  All the output symbol representations must be of the same type: integer or character. This type is called the output-representation-type and must be defined in the REP option.
  If the output-representation-type is INTEGER, the "unsigned integer" is the integer representation of the defined output symbol.
  If the output-representation-type is CHAR, the "unsigned integer" is the ordinal value of the character representation of the defined output symbol. In this case, the representation may also be a "character constant". The ordinal value of the representation of the defined output symbol will then be the ordinal value of the "character constant" on the machine on which LILA is executed.
  All output symbols must have a different representation.
  The representation of an output symbol can be referred to in the pascal-text by a constant of the output-representation-type. This constant is denoted by:

      "%" "output symbol name"

* The <type identifier> defines the type of the attribute of the output symbol. This type identifier may be defined in GLO-BALINFO. If the ":" <type identifier> part is absent, the defined output symbol has no attribute.
  The semantic actions and the local routines may access the

attributes of the output symbols (see 1.3.3.4).

The ELL(1) transducer can output an output symbol by the LILA-defined procedure OUT in the semantic actions (see 1.3.3.4). This procedure stores the output symbol in the <u>output-head</u> OUTP, which has a component OUTP.C of the output-representation-type and possibly a component OUTP.A to hold the attribute, if any (see 1.3.4). Then it activates the write routine to output the output-head. This write routine can be defined by the user by means of the LILA input part WRITEROUTINE (see 1.4.3).

If no WRITEROUTINE is specified in the LILA input, a default write routine will be generated. This default write routine writes the output symbols on the <u>output-symbol-file</u> OUTFILE. The declaration of this file and all actions concerning it are generated by LILA. The file name must however appear among the program parameters (see 1.3.4).

The output-symbol-file can be given another file name by the FILE option.

<u>Remarks</u>

1. If the default read and write routines are generated, i.e. when no READROUTINE or WRITEROUTINE are defined, then 1 may not be used as representation of an output symbol. It has a special meaning to the default write routine: 1 is used to represent line markers.

2. If the installation, where the generated ELL(1) transducer will be executed, requires information about the internal structure of the output-symbol-file, this information can be extracted from the file declaration in the generated ELL(1) transducer.

3. The output-symbol-file will be of type TEXT if the option REP(CHAR) is used and if none of the output symbols is attributed. A line marker is represented by an end-of-line in such a file.

Example

The following output vocabulary corresponds to the input vocabulary in example 3 in 1.3.1:

 ###outputvocabulary rep(integer);

 [identifier] = 2 : rep_name

 [number] = 3 : real

| [how] | = 4 | [many] | = 5 | [in] | = 6 |
| [kg] | = 7 | [m] | = 8 | [s] | = 9 |

| [(] = 10 | [)] = 11 | [*] = 12 | [+] = 13 | [,] = 14 |
| [-] = 15 | [/] = 16 | [=] = 17 | [?] = 18 | [^] = 19 |

1.3.3. The syntax

The syntax defines the translation syntax module for each nonterminal symbol :

<syntax> =
 "###" "SYNTAX" ";"
 <translation syntax module>+

<translation syntax module> =
 <rule definition>
 (<attribute definition> | &)
 (<local label definitions> | &)
 (<local const definitions> | &)
 (<local type definitions> | &)
 (<local var definitions> | &)
 (<local routine definitions> | &)
 (<semantic action definitions> | &)
 (<error recovery> | &)

The first <translation syntax module> defines the start symbol of the translation syntax.

The <rule definition> is the translation syntax rule for the defined nonterminal symbol.

The <attribute definition> defines the type of the attribute of the defined nonterminal symbol, if any.

The <semantic action definitions> are the definitions of all the semantic actions that are used in the <rule definition>.

Labels, constants, types, variables and routines may also be defined local to the translation syntax module,

1.3.3.1. Rule definition

The rule definition describes the translation syntax rule for the defined nonterminal symbol.

```
<rule definition> =
    "##" "RULE" ";"
    "nonterminal symbol name" "=" <expression>


<expression> =
    <alternative> ( "|" <alternative> )*


<alternative> =
    <factor>+


<factor> =
    <primary> ( & | "+" | "*" )


<primary> =
      "&"
    | "semantic action name"
    | "nonterminal symbol name" ( <follow or precede indication> | & )
    | "input symbol name"
    | "(" <expression> ")"


<follow or precede indication> =
    "!" | "?" | "!" "?" | "?" "!"
```

The <follow or precede indication> has to do with error recovery. The "!" indicates that this nonterminal symbol occurrence must be synchronized on its followmarkers. The "?" indicates that this non-terminal symbol occurrence must be recognized from its

precedemarkers.   For more information on error recovery, see section
6 of the book.

1.3.3.2.   Attribute definition

The attribute definition describes the type of the attribute of
the defined nonterminal symbol.

```
<attribute definition> =
   "##" "ATTRIBUTE" ";"
   <type>
```

Types and constants defined in GLOBALINFO may be used in this type
definition.
The start symbol of the translation syntax may not have an attribute.

1.3.3.3.   Local information

The local information may consist of labels, constants, types,
variables and routines that are only accessible in the translation
syntax module.

```
<local label definitions> =
   "##" "LABEL" ";"
   <label> ( "," <label> )*
```

```
<local const definitions> =
   "##" "CONST" ";"
   <constant definition> ( ";" <constant definition> )*
```

```
<local type definitions> =
   "##" "TYPE" ";"
   <type definition> ( ";" <type definition> )*
```

```
<local var definitions> =
   "##" "VAR" ";"
   <variable declaration> ( ";" <variable declaration> )*
```

```
<local routine definitions> =
   "##" "ROUTINE" ";"
   <procedure or function declaration>
   ( ";" <procedure or function declaration> )*
```

The names for the user-defined constants, types, variables and routines may not start with 'PP'.
The attributes of the symbols of the translation syntax rule are
accessible in the local routines. The OUT procedure may also be
used in the local routines if there is an output vocabulary. All
this must be done in the same way as in the semantic actions (see
1.3.3.4).

1.3.3.4. Semantic action definitions

All the semantic actions that are used in the translation syntax
rule must be defined here.

```
<semantic action definitions> =
   "##" "ACTION" ";"
   <semantic action definition>+
```

```
<semantic action definition> =
   "#" "semantic action name" ";"
   <statement> ( ";" <statement> )*
```

There may be several occurrences of the same semantic action symbol
name in a translation syntax rule. The semantic actions are defined
in the scope of the local information which in turn is defined in
the scope of the global information (see 1.3.4).
A semantic action may access the attributes of the input and nonterminal symbols of the translation syntax rule and may produce output
symbols.

The attribute of an input symbol is accessible by means of a variable that is local to the translation syntax module. This attribute
variable is referenced by:

```
   "@" "input symbol name" ( "unsigned integer" | & )
```

The type of this variable is defined in INPUTVOCABULARY. If the input symbol occurs more than once in the translation syntax rule, an "unsigned integer" must be used to indicate which occurrence is meant. Different occurrences of the same input symbol within a translation syntax rule are numbered from left to right, starting with 1.

Remark that it follows from the generation scheme in section 4.4 of the book that the input symbol attribute is stored in its attribute variable after the input symbol has been analysed. This means that references to this variable can only be meaningful in semantic actions that are used after the input symbol occurrence in the translation syntax rule.

The attribute of a nonterminal symbol is accessible by means of a variable that is local to the translation syntax module. This attribute variable is referenced by:

   "@" "nonterminal symbol name" ("unsigned integer" | &)

The type of this variable is defined in the <attribute definition> of the translation syntax module for that nonterminal symbol. If the nonterminal symbol occurs more than once in the translation syntax rule, an "unsigned integer" must be used to indicate which occurrence is meant. Different occurrences of the same nonterminal symbol within a translation syntax rule are numbered from left to right, starting with 1.

The attribute mechanism has been thoroughly discussed in section 4 of the book. Let us summarize the main points of the attribute handling. An inherited component of the attribute of the defined nonterminal symbol must have been calculated before the rule is entered. A synthesized component of the attribute of the defined nonterminal symbol must be calculated by the semantic actions of the rule. An inherited component of the attribute of a nonterminal symbol on the right hand side of the rule must be calculated by the semantic actions prior to the nonterminal symbol occurrence in the rule. A synthesized component of the attribute of a nonterminal symbol on the right hand side of the rule can only be used after the nonterminal symbol occurrence in the rule.

If an output vocabulary is defined, then an output symbol can be output in a semantic action by the LILA-defined procedure OUT:

    PROCEDURE OUT(C:output-representation-type);

This procedure is local to the translation syntax module. The parameter C is the representation of the output symbol to be produced. If this output symbol is attributed, then the attribute value must be assigned to the attribute variable:

    "@" "output symbol name"

prior to the activation of OUT. The type of this variable is defined in OUTPUTVOCABULARY. This attribute variable is local to the translation syntax module. The procedure OUT initializes the global variable OUTP and activates WRITEOUT (see 1.3.4).

1.3.3.5. Error recovery

The error recovery of the defined nonterminal symbol is specified in <error recovery> and in <rule definition> (see 1.3.3.1).

```
<error recovery> =
    "##" "RECOVERY" <error recovery options> ";"
    ( <entry action> | & )
    ( <exit action> | & )


<error recovery options> =
    <error recovery option> ("," <error recovery option>)*
    | &


<error recovery option> =
    "LAST"
    | "FIRST"


<entry action> =
    "#" "ENTRY" ";"
    <statement> ( ";" <statement> )*
```

```
<exit action> =
  "#" "EXIT" ";"
  <statement> ( ";" <statement> )*
```

The LAST option specifies that the defined nonterminal symbol must be synchronized on its lastmarkers.

The FIRST option specifies that the defined nonterminal symbol must be recognized from its firstmarkers.

The <entry action> is a semantic action that is executed prior to the recognition of the defined nonterminal symbol during error recovery.

The <exit action> is a semantic action that is executed after the recovery of the defined nonterminal symbol.

For more information on error recovery, see section 6 of the book. Section 6 also contains a number of examples worked out with LILA, illustrating the error recovery mechanism.

Examples of translation syntax modules

Example 1

This example describes a lexical analysis of identifiers or keywords. The input vocabulary is that of example 1 or 2 in 1.3.1. The output vocabulary is that of the example in 1.3.2. The nonterminals <letter> and <digit> have an attribute of type char. This example is extracted from section 1.4 in the book.

```
##rule;
  <identifier keyword> =
    <letter> init_name
      ( <letter> add_letter | <digit> add_digit )*
    out_idkey

##var;
  nb_chars : 1..maxint

##action;
  #init_name;
    @[identifier] := '        ';
    @[identifier] [1] := @<letter>1;
```

```
   nb_chars := 1

#add_letter;
  nb_chars := nb_chars + 1;
  if (nb_chars <= idlength)
    then @[identifier] [nb_chars] := @<letter>2

#add_digit;
  nb_chars := nb_chars + 1;
  if (nb_chars <= idlength)
    then @[identifier] [nb_chars] := @<digit>

#out_idkey;
  if (nb_chars > idlength) then error(iden_truncated);
  if      ( @[identifier]='how    ' ) then out(%[how])
  else if ( @[identifier]='many   ' ) then out(%[many])
  else if ( @[identifier]='in     ' ) then out(%[in])
  else if ( @[identifier]='kg     ' ) then out(%[kg])
  else if ( @[identifier]='m      ' ) then out(%[m])
  else if ( @[identifier]='s      ' ) then out(%[s])
  else out(%[identifier])
```

Example 2

This example illustrates two translation syntax modules where the
input vocabulary is that of example 3 in 1.3.1. This example is
extracted from section 1.2 in the book.

```
$ Assignment
  ##rule;
    <assignment> =
      "identifier" "=" <expression> assign

    ##action;
      #assign;
        if in_symbtab( @"identifier")
          then error(re_assignment)
          else add_symbtab( @"identifier", @<expression>)


$ Expression
  ##rule;
    <expression> =
      <term>  trans_et
        ( "+" <term> add  |  "-" <term> subtract )*
```

```
##attribute;
  rep_unit

##action;
  #trans_et;
    @<expression>  := @<term>1;

  #add;
    add_unit( @<expression>, @<term>2)

  #subtract;
    subtr_unit( @<expression>, @<term>3)
```

1.3.4. The global information

The global information defines the parameters and the global labels, constants, types, variables and routines. Also a prologue and epilogue may be defined.

```
<globalinfo> =
  "###" "GLOBALINFO" ";"
  ( <parameter definitions> | & )
  ( <global label definitions> | & )
  ( <global const definitions> | & )
  ( <global type definitions> | & )
  ( <global var definitions> | & )
  ( <global routine definitions> | & )
  ( <prologue definition> | & )
  ( <epilogue definition> | & )


<parameter definitions> =
  "##" "PARAMETER" ";"
  ( <program parameters>
  | <formal parameter section> ( ";" <formal parameter section> )* )


<global label definitions> =
  "##" "LABEL" ";"
  <label> ( "," <label> )*


<global const definitions> =
  "##" "CONST" ";"
  <constant definition> ( ";" <constant definition> )*
```

```
<global type definitions> =
    "##" "TYPE" ";"
    <type definition> ( ";" <type definition> )*


<global var definitions> =
    "##" "VAR" ";"
    <variable declaration> ( ";" <variable declaration> )*


<global routine definitions> =
    "##" "ROUTINE" ";"
    <procedure or function declaration>
    ( ";" <procedure or function declaration> )*


<prologue definition> =
    "##" "PROLOGUE" ";"
    <statement> ( ";" <statement> )*


<epilogue definition> =
    "##" "EPILOGUE" ";"
    <statement> ( ";" <statement> )*
```

If the global option PROCEDURE (see 1.3.6) is not specified, then <parameter definitions> defines the parameters of the generated ELL(1) transducer as a Pascal program. These parameters must include the input-symbol-file and possibly the output-symbol-file. If the default read routine or error routine are generated, i.e. when not both the LILA input parts READROUTINE and ERRORROUTINE are defined, then also the Pascal file 'output' must be included in the <program parameters>.
If the global option PROCEDURE is specified, then <parameter definitions> defines the parameters of the generated ELL(1) transducer as a Pascal procedure.

The <prologue definition> defines a number of statements to be executed prior to the activation of the ELL(1) transducer routine for the start symbol of the translation syntax.

The <epilogue definition> defines a number of statements to be executed after the activation of the ELL(1) transducer routine for the start symbol of the translation syntax.

The names for the user-defined constants, types, variables and routines may not start with 'PP'.

LILA-defined global information

Some global information is defined by LILA. This information consists of:

* VAR INP:PPINPTP;

   This is the input-head of the ELL(1) transducer. INP and the
   type PPINPTP are only defined if there is no LILA input part
   READROUTINE. PPINPTP is a record type such that INP.C is of the
   input-representation-type. See 1.4.2 for more information.

* PROCEDURE READIN;

   This procedure reads the next input symbol (representation and
   attribute, if any) from the input-symbol-file and stores it in
   INP. The body of this procedure can be overwritten by the user
   by means of the LILA input part READROUTINE. See 1.4.2 for more
   information.

* VAR INFILE:FILE OF PPINPTP; or VAR INFILE:TEXT;

   This is the input-symbol-file. It may be given another name in
   the FILE option of INPUTVOCABULARY (see 1.3.1). It is only
   defined if there is no LILA input part READROUTINE. See 1.3.1
   remark 4 and 1.4.2 for more information.

* VAR OUTP:PPOUTPTP;

   This is the output-head of the ELL(1) transducer. It exists only
   if there is an output vocabulary. OUTP and the type PPOUTPTP are
   only defined if there is no LILA input part WRITEROUTINE.
   PPOUTPTP is a record type such that OUTP.C is of the output-

representation-type. See 1.4.3 for more information.

* PROCEDURE WRITEOUT;

This procedure writes the output symbol that is stored in OUTP on
the output-symbol-file. It exists only if there is an output
vocabulary. The body of this procedure can be overwritten by the
user by means of the LILA input part WRITEROUTINE. See 1.4.3 for
more information.

* VAR OUTFILE:FILE OF PPOUTPTP; or VAR OUTFILE:TEXT;

This is the output-symbol-file. It exists only if there is an
output vocabulary. It may be given another name in the FILE
option of OUTPUTVOCABULARY (see 1.3.2). It is only defined if
there is no LILA input part WRITEROUTINE. See 1.3.2 remark 3 and
1.4.3 for more information.

* VAR LINENUMB:INTEGER;

This variable contains the sequence number of the current input
line. It is initialized with 0 and incremented by 1 each time an
end-of-line input symbol has been analysed. It is only defined
if there is no LILA input part READROUTINE.

* VAR NBERRORS:INTEGER;

This variable is used to count the number of errors. It is initialized with 0 and incremented by 1 each time a syntactic error
occurs. It is only defined if there is no LILA input part ERROR-
ROUTINE.

* LABEL 9999;

A jump to this label terminates the execution of the ELL(1)
transducer immediately.

1.3.5.   <u>The global options</u>

   The global options are used to specify certain options that apply
to the generation.

<global options> =
    "###" "OPTIONS" <global option> ("," <global option>)* ";"

<global option> =
      "PRINVOC" | "PROUTVOC" | "PRTREE"
    | "PROCEDURE"
    | "NAME" "(" <identifier> ")"
    | "LET" | "NOOPTIMIZE" | "NOGENERATE"
    | "SOURCE"
    | "GSLN"
    | "SYNCFLOW" | "SYNCSETS" | "NOLAST"

The meaning of these options is as follows:

PRINVOC   produces a list of the input symbols on the LILA-
             diagnostics-file, sorted by name.

PROUTVOC   produces a list of the output symbols on the LILA-
             diagnostics-file, sorted by name.

PRTREE   produces the attributed tree of the translation syntax
             rules on the LILA-diagnostics-file.

PROCEDURE   indicates that the ELL(1) transducer is to be generated
             as a Pascal procedure instead of a Pascal program.

NAME   specifies the name that is to be given to the generated
             ELL(1) transducer program or procedure.   Default is
             NAME(PARSER).

LET   indicates that violated ELL(1) conditions (i.e. level D
             errors) may not prohibit generation.

NOOPTIMIZE   indicates that optimizations in the syntax analysis may
             not be performed during generation (see section 7.10 of

the book).

NOGENERATE   indicates that no generation is to take place.

SOURCE   indicates that the LILA input must be listed on the LILA-diagnostics-file.

GSLN   indicates that the LILA input line numbers must be included as commentary in the generated transducer.

SYNCFLOW   indicates that the generated transducer must produce diagnostic messages that describe the error recovery.

SYNCSETS   indicates that Pascal sets will be used in the generated transducer to store the recovery information. If the input-representation-type is integer, then these sets will be of type <u>set</u> <u>of</u> (0..greatest input symbol representation). If the input-representation-type is char, then these sets will be of type <u>set</u> <u>of</u> char.

NOLAST   indicates that the virtual start symbol may not be synchronized on its lastmarkers.

1.4.   Advanced applications

1.4.1.   The follow set

   The follow set defines the input symbols that can follow any sentence of the input language.   In other words, it defines all the
input symbols that may be the contents of the input-head INP.C when
the transducing routine of the start nonterminal symbol is terminated.

```
<follow> =
   "###" "FOLLOW" ";"
   "input symbol name"+
```

If the virtual input symbol end-of-file is to be included in this
follow set, then one of the listed input symbol names must be "end-
of-file".   This is the only place where this virtual input symbol
may be referenced by an input symbol name.   Note however that, if
there is a user-defined input symbol with the same name, then "end-
of-file" will refer to that user-defined symbol.

If this follow set is not defined, then any sentence of the input
language can only be followed by the virtual end-of-file input symbol.

1.4.2.   The read routine

   This LILA input part contains the user-defined read routine.

```
<readroutine> =
   "###" "READROUTINE" ";"
   <statement> ( ";" <statement> )*
```

The specified statements will be the body of the READIN procedure.
This procedure must obtain the next input symbol and store it in the
input-head INP.

This input-head INP must be defined by the user.   It must be of a
record type such that:

1. INP.C is of the input-representation-type. This field must contain the representation of the input symbol.

2. INP.A must be defined if there are attributed input symbols. It must be of a record type such that there exists a field for each input symbol attribute type. The field selector for such a field must be the <type identifier> of the input symbol attribute type. The type of such a field is the type of the input symbol attribute.

For example, a possible declaration of the input-head for the input vocabulary of example 3 in 1.3.1 is:

```
var inp:record
           c:integer;
           a:record
               rep_name:rep_name;
               real:real
           end
        end
```

The use of the read routine can best be explained by examples. Each example contains two LILA inputs, one without a user-defined read routine and one with a user-defined read routine. The two inputs are equivalent in the sense that the user-defined read routine is the same as the default read routine. As the examples show, the declarations of INP, INFILE and LINENUMB disappear. Also the initialization of INP in the prologue is not generated.

Example 1

The input vocabulary consists of nonattributed characters.

The LILA input without user-defined read routine is:

```
###inputvocabulary  rep(char);

  "a" = 'a'   "b" = 'b'   "c" = 'c'

###syntax;
##rule;
```

```
    <start> = "a" | "b" | "c"

 ###globalinfo;
 ##parameter; infile,output
```

The equivalent LILA input with user-defined read routine is:

```
 ###inputvocabulary  rep(char);

   "a" = 'a'  "b" = 'b'  "c" = 'c'

 ###syntax;
 ##rule;

   <start> = "a" | "b" | "c"

 ###globalinfo;

   ##parameter; infile,output

   ##type;
     inptp=record
       c:char end

   ##var;
     linenumb:integer;
     inp:inptp;
     infile:text

   ##prologue;
     linenumb:=1;
     reset(infile);
     readin

 ###readroutine;
   if eof(infile) then if inp.c=chr(0) then begin
     writeln(output);
     write(output,linenumb,':');
     writeln(output,' *** error ***:',
     'End of input file reached before end of program');
     goto 9999
     end
   else inp.c:=chr(0)
   else begin
     if eoln(infile) then linenumb:=linenumb+1;
```

```
    inp.c:=infile^;
    get(infile)
    end
```

Example 2

This example differs from the first one in that the input-symbol-file is the standard input.

The LILA input without user-defined read routine is:

```
  ###inputvocabulary  rep(char), file(input);

   "a" = 'a'   "b" = 'b'   "c" = 'c'

  ###syntax;
  ##rule;

    <start> = "a" | "b" | "c"

  ###globalinfo;
  ##parameter; input,output
```

The equivalent LILA input with user-defined read routine is:

```
  ###inputvocabulary  rep(char), file(input);

   "a" = 'a'   "b" = 'b'   "c" = 'c'

  ###syntax;
  ##rule;

    <start> = "a" | "b" | "c"

  ###globalinfo;

    ##parameter; input,output

    ##type;
      inptp=record
        c:char end
```

```
##var;
  linenumb:integer;
  inp:inptp

##prologue;
  linenumb:=1;
  readin
```

```
###readroutine;
  if eof(input) then if inp.c=chr(0) then begin
    writeln(output);
    write(output,linenumb,':');
    writeln(output,' *** error ***:',
    'End of input file reached before end of program');
    goto 9999
    end
  else inp.c:=chr(0)
  else begin
    if eoln(input) then linenumb:=linenumb+1;
    inp.c:=input^;
    get(input)
    end
```

Example 3

The input vocabulary consists of attributed integers.

The LILA input without user-defined read routine is:

```
###inputvocabulary  rep(integer);

  "identifier" = 2 : rep_name
  "number" = 3 : real

  "how" = 4     "many" = 5    "in" = 6
  "kg"  = 7     "m"   = 8     "s"  = 9

  "(" = 10   ")" = 11    "*" = 12   "+" = 13   "," = 14
  "-" = 15   "/" = 16    "=" = 17   "?" = 18   "^" = 19
```

```
###syntax;

  ##rule;
    <program> = "identifier" | "number"
```

```
   ###globalinfo;

      ##parameter;   infile,output

      ##const;
        idlength=8

      ##type;
        rep_name=packed array [1..idlength] of char
```

The equivalent LILA input with user-defined read routine is:

```
   ###inputvocabulary  rep(integer);

      "identifier" = 2 : rep_name
      "number" = 3 : real

      "how" = 4     "many" = 5     "in" = 6
      "kg"  = 7     "m"    = 8     "s"  = 9

      "(" = 10    ")" = 11    "*" = 12    "+" = 13    "," = 14
      "-" = 15    "/" = 16    "=" = 17    "?" = 18    "^" = 19

   ###syntax;

      ##rule;
        <program> = "identifier" | "number"

   ###globalinfo;

      ##parameter;   infile,output

      ##const;
        idlength=8

      ##type;
        rep_name=packed array [1..idlength] of char;
        type1=1..2;
        type2=real;
        type3=rep_name;
        inptp=record
          c:integer;
          a:record case tagid:type1 of
            1:(real:type2);
            2:(rep_name:type3) end
```

```
    end

  ##var;
    linenumb:integer;
    inp:inptp;
    infile:file of inptp

  ##prologue;
    linenumb:=1;
    reset(infile);
    readin

###readroutine;
  repeat
  if eof(infile) then if inp.c=0 then begin
    writeln(output);
    write(output,linenumb,':');
    writeln(output,' *** error ***:',
    'End of input file reached before end of program');
    goto 9999
    end
  else inp.c:=0
  else begin
    inp:=infile^;
    get(infile);
    if inp.c=1 then linenumb:=linenumb+1
    end
  until inp.c<>1
```

Note that the types type2 and type3 have been introduced to get round a common Pascal compiler error where field identifiers may not be used as type identifiers inside a record definition.

Example 4

The input vocabulary consists of characters and there is an output vocabulary of attributed integers.

The LILA input without user-defined read routine is:

```
  ###inputvocabulary  rep(char), file(input);

  "a" = 'a'  "b" = 'b'  "c" = 'c'
```

```
###outputvocabulary  rep(integer);

   [identifier] = 2 : rep_name
   [number]  = 3 : real

   [how]  = 4     [many] = 5     [in] = 6
   [kg]   = 7     [m]    = 8     [s]  = 9

   [(] = 10    [)] = 11    [*] = 12    [+] = 13    [,] = 14
   [-] = 15    [/] = 16    [=] = 17    [?] = 18    [^] = 19

###syntax;
##rule;

   <start> = "a" | "b" | "c"

###globalinfo;

   ##parameter; input,output

   ##const;
     idlength=8

   ##type;
     rep_name=array[1..idlength] of char
```

The equivalent LILA input with user-defined read routine is:

```
   ###inputvocabulary  rep(char), file(input);

   "a" = 'a'   "b" = 'b'   "c" = 'c'

   ###outputvocabulary  rep(integer);

      [identifier] = 2 : rep_name
      [number]  = 3 : real

      [how] = 4     [many] = 5     [in] = 6
      [kg]  = 7     [m]    = 8     [s]  = 9

      [(] = 10    [)] = 11    [*] = 12    [+] = 13    [,] = 14
      [-] = 15    [/] = 16    [=] = 17    [?] = 18    [^] = 19

   ###syntax;
   ##rule;
```

```
  <start> = "a" | "b" | "c"

###global info;

  ##parameter; input,output

  ##const;
    idlength=8

  ##type;
    rep_name=array[1..idlength] of char;
    inptp=record
      c:char end

  ##var;
    linenumb:integer;
    inp:inptp

  ##prologue;
    linenumb:=1;
    readin

###readroutine;
  if eof(input) then if inp.c=chr(0) then begin
    writeln(output);
    write(output,linenumb,':');
    writeln(output,' *** error ***:',
    'End of input file reached before end of program');
    goto 9999
    end
  else inp.c:=chr(0)
  else begin
    if eoln(input) then begin
      linenumb:=linenumb+1;
      outp.c:=1;
      writeout
      end;
    inp.c:=input^;
    get(input)
    end
```

Example 5

The input vocabulary consists of attributed integers and the global
EOF option is used.

The LILA input without user-defined read routine is:

```
###inputvocabulary  rep(integer), eof(32);

  "identifier" = 2
  "number" = 3

  "how" = 4     "many" = 5      "in" = 6
  "kg"  = 7     "m"    = 8      "s"  = 9

  "(" = 10    ")" = 11    "*" = 12    "+" = 13    "," = 14
  "-" = 15    "/" = 16    "=" = 17    "?" = 18    "^" = 19

###syntax;

  ##rule;
    <program> = "identifier" | "number"

###globalinfo;

  ##parameter;  infile,output
```

The equivalent LILA input with user-defined read routine is:

```
###inputvocabulary  rep(integer), eof(32);

  "identifier" = 2
  "number" = 3

  "how" = 4     "many" = 5      "in" = 6
  "kg"  = 7     "m"    = 8      "s"  = 9

  "(" = 10    ")" = 11    "*" = 12    "+" = 13    "," = 14
  "-" = 15    "/" = 16    "=" = 17    "?" = 18    "^" = 19

###syntax;
```

```
  ##rule;
    <program> = "identifier" | "number"

 ###globalinfo;

  ##parameter;  infile,output

  ##type;
    inptp=record
      c:integer end

  ##var;
    linenumb:integer;
    inp:inptp;
    infile:file of inptp

  ##prologue;
    linenumb:=1;
    reset(infile);
    readin

 ###readroutine;
    repeat
    if eof(infile) then if inp.c=32 then begin
      writeln(output);
      write(output,linenumb,':');
      writeln(output,' *** error ***:',
      'End of input file reached before end of program');
      goto 9999
      end
    else inp.c:=32
    else begin
      inp:=infile^;
      get(infile);
      if inp.c=1 then linenumb:=linenumb+1
      end
    until inp.c<>1
```

1.4.3.   The write routine

   This LILA input part contains the user-defined write routine.

```
<writeroutine> =
  "###" "WRITEROUTINE" ";"
  <statement> ( ";" <statement> )*
```

The specified statements will be the body of the WRITEOUT procedure. This procedure must produce the next output symbol from the output-head OUTP.

This output-head OUTP must be defined by the user. It must be of a record type such that:

1. OUTP.C is of the output-representation-type. This field must contain the representation of the output symbol.

2. OUTP.A must be defined if there are attributed output symbols. It must be of a record type such that there exists a field for each output symbol attribute type. The field selector for such a field must be the <type identifier> of the output symbol attribute type. The type of such a field is the type of the output symbol attribute.

For example, a possible declaration of the output-head for the output vocabulary of example 3 in 1.3.1 is:

```
var outp:record
          c:integer;
          a:record
              rep_name:rep_name;
              real:real
          end
     end
```


Example

This example is the same as example 4 in 1.4.2. The write routine is now also user-defined.

The LILA input without user-defined read and write routine is:

```
###inputvocabulary  rep(char), file(input);

  "a" = 'a'  "b" = 'b'  "c" = 'c'
```

```
###outputvocabulary  rep(integer);

   [identifier] = 2 : rep_name
   [number]    = 3 : real

   [how] = 4      [many] = 5      [in] = 6
   [kg]  = 7      [m]    = 8      [s]  = 9

   [(] = 10    [)] = 11    [*] = 12    [+] = 13    [,] = 14
   [-] = 15    [/] = 16    [=] = 17    [?] = 18    [^] = 19

###syntax;
##rule;

   <start> = "a" | "b" | "c"

###globalinfo;

   ##parameter; input,output

   ##const;
     idlength=8

   ##type;
     rep_name=array[1..idlength] of char
```

The equivalent LILA input with user-defined read and write routine
is:

```
###inputvocabulary  rep(char), file(input);

   "a" = 'a'   "b" = 'b'   "c" = 'c'

###outputvocabulary  rep(integer);

   [identifier] = 2 : rep_name
   [number]    = 3 : real

   [how] = 4      [many] = 5      [in] = 6
   [kg]  = 7      [m]    = 8      [s]  = 9

   [(] = 10    [)] = 11    [*] = 12    [+] = 13    [,] = 14
   [-] = 15    [/] = 16    [=] = 17    [?] = 18    [^] = 19

###syntax;
```

```
##rule;

   <start> = "a" | "b" | "c"

###globalinfo;

  ##parameter; input,output

  ##const;
    idlength=8

  ##type;
    rep_name=array[1..idlength] of char;
    inptp=record
      c:char end;
    type1=1..2;
    type2=real;
    type3=rep_name;
    outptp=record
      c:integer;
      a:record case tagid:type1 of
        1:(real:type2);
        2:(rep_name:type3) end
    end

  ##var;
    linenumb:integer;
    inp:inptp;
    outp:outptp;
    outfile:file of outptp

  ##prologue;
    rewrite(outfile);
    linenumb:=1;
    readin

###readroutine;
  if eof(input) then if inp.c=chr(0) then begin
    writeln(output);
    write(output,linenumb,':');
    writeln(output,' *** error ***:',
    'End of input file reached before end of program');
    goto 9999
    end
  else inp.c:=chr(0)
  else begin
    if eoln(input) then begin
      linenumb:=linenumb+1;
```

```
        outp.c:=1;
        writeout
        end;
    inp.c:=input^;
    get(input)
    end

###writeroutine;
    write(outfile,outp)
```

1.4.4. The error routine

This LILA input part contains the user-defined error routine.

```
<errorroutine> =
    "###" "ERRORROUTINE" ";"
    <statement> ( ";" <statement> )*
```

These statements define the body of the error routine of the generated ELL(1) transducer. This routine is called when a syntactic
error is detected.
The default error routine writes a message on the file output. This
is illustrated by the example.

Example

This example is the same as example 1 in 1.4.2. The error routine
is now also user-defined.

The LILA input without user-defined read and error routine is:

```
    ###inputvocabulary  rep(char);

    "a" = 'a'   "b" = 'b'   "c" = 'c'

    ###syntax;
    ##rule;

    <start> = "a" | "b" | "c"

    ###globalinfo;
    ##parameter; infile,output
```

The equivalent LILA input with user-defined read and error routine is:

```
###inputvocabulary rep(char);

  "a" = 'a'   "b" = 'b'   "c" = 'c'

###syntax;
##rule;

  <start> = "a" | "b" | "c"

###globalinfo;

  ##parameter; infile,output

  ##const;
    condim=5

  ##type;
    inptp=record
      c:char end

  ##var;
    linenumb:integer;
    inp:inptp;
    infile:text;
    nberrors,i,cursmb:integer;
    contxt:array[1..condim] of char;
    term:array[1..3] of record
     cd:char;
     nm:packed array[1..20] of char end

  ##routine;
    procedure pnm(s:char);
    label 1,2;
    var i,j:integer;
    begin
      if s=chr(0) then goto 1;
      if s=chr(1) then goto 1;
      for i:=1 to 3 do with term[i] do if cd=s then begin
        write(output,' "');
        for j:=1 to 19 do
        if (nm[j]<>' ')or(nm[j+1]<>' ')or(j=1) then write(output,nm[j])
```

```
     else if (nm[j]=' ')and(nm[j+1]=' ') then goto 2;
     if nm[20]<>' ' then write(output,nm[20]);
     2:write(output,'"');
     goto 1
     end;
   write(output,' [unknown input symbol with representation = ',ord(s),']');
   1:
   end; {pnm}

procedure error;
var i,j:integer;
begin
  nberrors:=nberrors+1;
  writeln(output);
  write(output,linenumb,':');
  write(output,' *** error ***: the input symbol');
  pnm(contxt[cursmb]);
  writeln(output,' is invalid after');
  write(output,' ':23);
  i:=cursmb;
  for j:=2 to condim do begin
    i:=i+1;
    if i>condim then i:=1;
    pnm(contxt[i])
    end;
  writeln(output)
  end {error}

##prologue;
  nberrors:=0; cursmb:=0;
  for i:=2 to condim do contxt[i]:=chr(0);
  with term[1] do begin nm:='a                 ';cd:=chr(97) end;
  with term[2] do begin nm:='b                 ';cd:=chr(98) end;
  with term[3] do begin nm:='c                 ';cd:=chr(99) end;
  linenumb:=1;
  reset(infile);
  readin

###readroutine;
  if eof(infile) then if inp.c=chr(0) then begin
    writeln(output);
    write(output,linenumb,':');
    writeln(output,' *** error ***:',
    'End of input file reached before end of program');
    goto 9999
    end
  else inp.c:=chr(0)
  else begin
```

```
    if eoln(infile) then linenumb:=linenumb+1;
    inp.c:=infile^;
    get(infile)
    end;
 cursmb:=(cursmb mod condim)+1;
 contxt[cursmb]:=inp.c

###errorroutine;
 error
```

2. THE GENERATED ELL(1) TRANSDUCER

The generated ELL(1) transducer is a Pascal program or procedure on the LILA-output-file. It is conform to both the Pascal User Manual and Report by Jensen and Wirth [1978] and the Draft ISO Pascal Standard (Addyman [1980]).

The LILA input portions which are Pascal-text are not checked by LILA on Pascal correctness. Therefore the user must ensure that these are conform with its own Pascal implementation.
Errors in these portions will therefore only be detected by the Pascal compiler when the generated ELL(1) transducer is translated.

Overall program structure

There is an ELL(1) transducer routine for each translation syntax module. This routine is represented as a Pascal boolean function. The semantic actions of the module are local to this function. The nonterminal symbol name is added as comment to the heading of its ELL(1) transducer function. The semantic action name is also added as comment where the semantic action appears in the ELL(1) transducer function. References to attributes in the semantic actions are transformed by LILA, but the symbol name is added as comment. This will be illustrated in the example.

The global information is global to these ELL(1) transducer functions.

Example

This example illustrates part of the generated ELL(1) transducer program of the example in section 1.2 in the book. The illustrated program sections correspond to the two syntax modules of example 2 in 1.3.3.

```
program parser(output,infile );
  .
  .
  .
function pp000030;{assignment}
var ...
x : rep_unit
  .
  .
  .
{assign}if  in_symbtab( pp000037{identifier}, x)
        then error(re_assignment)
        else add_symbtab( pp000037{identifier}, pp000041{expression})
  .
  .
  .
function pp000039;{expression}
  .
  .
  .
{trans_et}pp000049{expression}   := pp000052{term-1};
  .
  .
  .
{add}add_unit( pp000049{expression}, pp000054{term-2})
  .
  .
  .
{subtract}subtract_unit( pp000049{expression}, pp000056{term-3})
  .
  .
  .
end.
```

The ELL(1) transducer function for <assignment> is pp000030 and the
ELL(1) transducer function for <expression> is pp000039.

3. DIAGNOSTICS

All the LILA error messages are written on the LILA-diagnostics-file. Only the error number is written in the message. The complete list of the error messages is given at the end of this section. There are six levels of errors:

* Level A errors cause immediate termination.

* Level B errors cause termination after phase 1 (see introduction).

* Level C errors cause termination after phase 2.

* Level D errors cause termination after phase 3, unless the LET option is specified.

* Level E errors cause termination after phase 3.

* Level W errors are only warnings.

An ELL(1) transducer is only generated when there are no errors or level W errors only. A message at the end of the LILA-diagnostics-file confirms the generation.

Example 1

This example shows some error messages for the following LILA input. This LILA input is the example from section 1.2 of the book where some errors were introduced. Only the changed parts are shown below:

###inputvocabulary rep(integer);

  "identifier" = 2 : rep_name

```
  "number" = 3 : real

  "how" = 4      "many" = 5      "in" = 6
  "kg"  = 7      "m"    = 8      "s"  = 9


  "(" = 10     ")" = 11     "*" = 12     "+" = 13     "," = 14
  "-" = 15     "/" = 15     "=" = 17     "?" = 18     "^" = 19



###syntax;


     .
     .
     .


$ Assignment
  ##rule;
    <assignment> =
      "identifier" "=" <expression> assign

    ##action;
      #assig;
        if  in_symbtab(@"identifier")
           then error(re_assignment)
           else add_symbtab( @"identifier", @<expression>)


$ Question
  ##rule;
    <question> =
      "how" "many"  <expression>  "in"  <expression> "?"  print_result

    ##action;
      #print_result;
        writeln(output, convert_unit(@<expression>1,@<expression>2):9)


$ Expression
  ##rule;
    <expression> =
      <term>  trans_et
        ( "+" <term> add  |  "-" <term> subtract )*

    ##attribute;
      rep_unit

    ##action;
      #trans_et;
```

```
      @<expression>  := @<term>1;

   #add;
     add_unit( @ expression>, @<term>2)

   #subtract;
     subtr_unit( @<expression>, @<term>4)
```

  .
  .
  .

The resulting LILA-diagnostics-file is:

   ***error 42 (B)
   representation=   15 for symbols: '-' and '/'

      52:          #assig;
                      ^
   ***error 35 (E)
   Action name is 'assig'

      81:              add_unit(@ expression>, @<term>2)
                          ^
   ***error 64 (E)

      85:              subtr_unit(@<expression>, @<term>4)
                                                    ^
   ***error 45 (E)
   Symbol name is 'term'

   ***error 37 (E)
   Action name is 'assign'

   Errors detected:
      1 of level B
      4 of level E
   No generation done

The first error is error number 42. It is a level B error that says
that two input or output symbols are defined with the same representation. The additional information tells that the multiple used
representation is 15 for the input symbols "-" and "/". Indeed, in
the input vocabulary "/" = 16 was changed to "/" = 15.
The following three errors also contain the LILA input line with the
error location. The input line is preceded by the line number.

Example 2

This example illustrates the error messages for a translation syntax
that is not reduced.   The LILA input is:

```
###inputvocabulary  rep(integer);

  "identifier" = 2
  "number" = 3

  "how" = 4      "many" = 5      "in" = 6
  "kg" = 7       "m"  = 8        "s" = 9

  "(" = 10    ")" = 11    "*" = 12    "+" = 13    "," = 14
  "-" = 15    "/" = 16    "=" = 17    "?" = 18    "^" = 19

###syntax;

  ##rule;
    <program> =
      <statement>  ( "," <statement> )*

  ##rule;
    <statement> =
      <assignment>

  ##rule;
    <assignment> =
      "identifier" "=" <expression>

  ##rule;
    <question> =
      "how" "many" <expression>  "in"  <expression> "?"

  ##rule;
    <expression> =
      <term>
        ( "+" <term>   |  "-" <term>  )*

  ##rule;
    <term> =
      <factor>
        ( "*" <factor>  |  "/" <factor>  )*

  ##rule;
```

```
<factor> =
  <secondary>
    ( "^" <factor> | & )

##rule;
  <secondary> =
      "-" <primary>
    | <primary>

##rule;
  <primary> =
    "(" <expression> ")"

###globalinfo;

  ##parameter;
    output,infile
```

The LILA-diagnostics-file is:


```
***error  17 (W)
Symbol name is 'kg'
Symbol name is 'm'
Symbol name is 'number'
Symbol name is 's'

***error  28 (C)
Symbol name is 'program'

***error  28 (C)
Symbol name is 'statement'

***error  28 (C)
Symbol name is 'assignment'

***error  28 (C)
Symbol name is 'expression'

***error  28 (C)
Symbol name is 'question'

***error  28 (C)
Symbol name is 'term'

***error  28 (C)
Symbol name is 'factor'
```

```
***error  28  (C)
Symbol name is 'secondary'

***error  28  (C)
Symbol name is 'primary'

***error  29  (C)
Symbol name is 'question'

Errors detected:
         10 of level C
          1 of level W
No generation done
```

Example 3

This example illustrates the error messages for violations of the ELL(1) conditions, i.e., level D errors. The LILA input is:

```
###inputvocabulary  rep(integer);

   "identifier" = 2
   "number" = 3

   "how" = 4    "many" = 5    "in" = 6
   "kg"  = 7    "m"    = 8    "s"  = 9

   "(" = 10    ")" = 11    "*" = 12    "+" = 13    "," = 14
   "-" = 15    "/" = 16    "=" = 17    "?" = 18    "^" = 19

###syntax;

   ##rule;
     <program> =
       <statement>  ( "," <statement> )*

   ##rule;
     <statement> =
       <assignment> | <question>

   ##rule;
     <assignment> =
       "identifier" "=" <expression>
```

```
##rule;
  <question> =
    <expression>  "in"  <expression> "?"

##rule;
  <expression> =
    <term>
      ( "*" <term>   |   "-" <term>  )*

##rule;
  <term> =
    <factor>
      ( "*" <factor>   |  "/" <factor>  )*

##rule;
  <factor> =
    <secondary>
      ( "^" <factor>  |  & )

##rule;
  <secondary> =
      "-" <primary>
    | <primary>

##rule;
  <primary> =
      "identifier"
    | "number"
    | "kg"
    | "m"
    | "s"
    | "(" <expression> ")"

  ###globalinfo;

  ##parameter;
    output,infile
```

The LILA-diagnostics-file is:


```
***error  17 (W)
Symbol name is '+'
Symbol name is 'how'
Symbol name is 'many'

***error  26 (D)
In rule defining <statement> for following alternatives:
```

```
    <assignment>   dirsymb= "identifier"
  |<question>   dirsymb= "identifier" "number" "kg" "m" "s" "(" "-"
Common input symbols are: "identifier"
```

***error   27 (D)
In rule defining <term> for the factor :("*"<factor>|"/"<factor>)*
dirsymb(primary)= "*" "/"
follow(factor)= "end-of-file" "in" ")" "*" "," "-" "?"
Common input symbols are: "*"

```
Errors detected:
     2 of level D
     1 of level W
No generation done
```

Example 4

This example illustrates the output produced by the PRTREE option.
The LILA input is:

```
###options prtree;
###inputvocabulary  rep(integer);

  "identifier" = 2
  "number" = 3

  "how" = 4     "many" = 5    "in" = 6
  "kg"  = 7     "m"    = 8     "s" = 9

  "(" = 10    ")" = 11    "*" = 12    "+" = 13    "," = 14
  "-" = 15    "/" = 16    "=" = 17    "?" = 18    "^" = 19

###syntax;

  ##rule;
    <program> =
      <statement>  ( "," <statement> )*

  ##rule;
    <statement> =
      <assignment> | <question>

  ##rule;
    <assignment> =
      "identifier" "=" <expression>
```

```
##rule;
  <question> =
    "how" "many" <expression>  "in"  <expression> "?"

##rule;
  <expression> =
    <term>
      ( "+" <term>  |  "-" <term>  )*

##rule;
  <term> =
    <factor>
      ( "*" <factor>  |  "/" <factor>  )*

##rule;
  <factor> =
    <secondary>
      ( "^" <factor>  |  & )

##rule;
  <secondary> =
      "-" <primary>
    | <primary>

##rule;
  <primary> =
      "identifier"
    | "number"
    | "kg"
    | "m"
    | "s"
    | "(" <expression> ")"

  ###globalinfo;

  ##parameter;
    output,infile
```

The LILA-diagnostics-file is:

```
  program              last= "identifier" "number" "kg" "m" "s" ")" "?"
  =
  <expression>:
    empty= false
    first= "identifier" "how"
    follow= "end-of-file"
    term_alternatives= false
```

```
redundant_test= false
<alternative>:
  empty= false
  first= "identifier" "how"
  follow= "end-of-file"
  dirsymb= "identifier" "how"
  <factor>:
    empty= false
    first= "identifier" "how"
    follow= "end-of-file" ","
    <primary>:
      empty= false
      first= "identifier" "how"
      follow= "end-of-file" ","
      dirsymb= "identifier" "how"
      precede=
      statement
  <factor>:
    empty= true
    first= ","
    follow= "end-of-file"
    <primary>:
      empty= false
      first= ","
      follow= "end-of-file" ","
      dirsymb= ","

      (
      <expression>:
        empty= false
        first= ","
        follow= "end-of-file" ","
        term_alternatives= false
        redundant_test= true
        <alternative>:
          empty= false
          first= ","
          follow= "end-of-file" ","
          dirsymb= ","
          <factor>:
            empty= false
            first= ","
            follow= "identifier" "how"
            <primary>:
              empty= false
              first= ","
              follow= "identifier" "how"
              dirsymb= ","
              redundant_test= true
```

```
                       ,
              <factor>:
                empty= false
                first= "identifier" "how"
                follow= "end-of-file" ","
                <primary>:
                  empty= false
                  first= "identifier" "how"
                  follow= "end-of-file" ","
                  dirsymb= "identifier" "how"
                  precede= ","
                  statement              )*


statement                 last= "identifier" "number" "kg" "m" "s" ")" "?"
=
 <expression>:
   empty= false
   first= "identifier" "how"
   follow= "end-of-file" ","
   term_alternatives= false
   redundant_test= false
   <alternative>:
     empty= false
     first= "identifier"
     follow= "end-of-file" ","
     dirsymb= "identifier"
     <factor>:
       empty= false
       first= "identifier"
       follow= "end-of-file" ","
       <primary>:
         empty= false
         first= "identifier"
         follow= "end-of-file" ","
         dirsymb= "identifier"
         precede= ","
         assignment
    |
    <alternative>:
      empty= false
      first= "how"
      follow= "end-of-file" ","
      dirsymb= "how"
      <factor>:
        empty= false
        first= "how"
        follow= "end-of-file" ","
```

```
        <primary>:
          empty= false
          first= "how"
          follow= "end-of-file" ","
          dirsymb= "how"
          precede= ","
          question


assignment                 last= "identifier" "number" "kg" "m" "s" ")"
=
 <expression>:
   empty= false
   first= "identifier"
   follow= "end-of-file" ","
   term_alternatives= false
   redundant_test= true
   <alternative>:
     empty= false
     first= "identifier"
     follow= "end-of-file" ","
     dirsymb= "identifier"
     <factor>:
       empty= false
       first= "identifier"
       follow= "="
       <primary>:
         empty= false
         first= "identifier"
         follow= "="
         dirsymb= "identifier"
         redundant_test= true
         identifier
     <factor>:
       empty= false
       first= "="
       follow= "identifier" "number" "kg" "m" "s" "(" "-"
       <primary>:
         empty= false
         first= "="
         follow= "identifier" "number" "kg" "m" "s" "(" "-"
         dirsymb= "="
         redundant_test= false
         =
     <factor>:
       empty= false
       first= "identifier" "number" "kg" "m" "s" "(" "-"
       follow= "end-of-file" ","
```

```
      <primary>:
        empty= false
        first= "identifier" "number" "kg" "m" "s" "(" "-"
        follow= "end-of-file" ","
        dirsymb= "identifier" "number" "kg" "m" "s" "(" "-"
        precede= "="
        expression


question                last= "?"
=
 <expression>:
   empty= false
   first= "how"
   follow= "end-of-file" ","
   term_alternatives= false
   redundant_test= false
   <alternative>:
     empty= false
     first= "how"
     follow= "end-of-file" ","
     dirsymb= "how"
     <factor>:
       empty= false
       first= "how"
       follow= "many"
       <primary>:
         empty= false
         first= "how"
         follow= "many"
         dirsymb= "how"
         redundant_test= false
         how
     <factor>:
       empty= false
       first= "many"
       follow= "identifier" "number" "kg" "m" "s" "(" "-"
       <primary>:
         empty= false
         first= "many"
         follow= "identifier" "number" "kg" "m" "s" "(" "-"
         dirsymb= "many"
         redundant_test= false
         many
     <factor>:
       empty= false
       first= "identifier" "number" "kg" "m" "s" "(" "-"
       follow= "in"
```

```
        <primary>:
          empty= false
          first= "identifier" "number" "kg" "m" "s" "(" "-"
          follow= "in"
          dirsymb= "identifier" "number" "kg" "m" "s" "(" "-"
          precede= "many"
          expression
      <factor>:
        empty= false
        first= "in"
        follow= "identifier" "number" "kg" "m" "s" "(" "-"
        <primary>:
          empty= false
          first= "in"
          follow= "identifier" "number" "kg" "m" "s" "(" "-"
          dirsymb= "in"
          redundant_test= false
          in
      <factor>:
        empty= false
        first= "identifier" "number" "kg" "m" "s" "(" "-"
        follow= "?"
        <primary>:
          empty= false
          first= "identifier" "number" "kg" "m" "s" "(" "-"
          follow= "?"
          dirsymb= "identifier" "number" "kg" "m" "s" "(" "-"
          precede= "in"
          expression
      <factor>:
        empty= false
        first= "?"
        follow= "end-of-file" ","
        <primary>:
          empty= false
          first= "?"
          follow= "end-of-file" ","
          dirsymb= "?"
          redundant_test= false
          ?



  expression                 last= "identifier" "number" "kg" "m" "s" ")"
  =
   <expression>:
     empty= false
     first= "identifier" "number" "kg" "m" "s" "(" "-"
     follow= "end-of-file" "in" ")" "," "?"
```

```
term_alternatives= false
redundant_test= false
<alternative>:
  empty= false
  first= "identifier" "number" "kg" "m" "s" "(" "-"
  follow= "end-of-file" "in" ")" "," "?"
  dirsymb= "identifier" "number" "kg" "m" "s" "(" "-"
  <factor>:
    empty= false
    first= "identifier" "number" "kg" "m" "s" "(" "-"
    follow= "end-of-file" "in" ")" "+" "," "-" "?"
    <primary>:
      empty= false
      first= "identifier" "number" "kg" "m" "s" "(" "-"
      follow= "end-of-file" "in" ")" "+" "," "-" "?"
      dirsymb= "identifier" "number" "kg" "m" "s" "(" "-"
      precede= "many" "in" "(" "="
      term
  <factor>:
    empty= true
    first= "+" "-"
    follow= "end-of-file" "in" ")" "," "?"
    <primary>:
      empty= false
      first= "+" "-"
      follow= "end-of-file" "in" ")" "+" "," "-" "?"
      dirsymb= "+" "-"

      (
      <expression>:
        empty= false
        first= "+" "-"
        follow= "end-of-file" "in" ")" "+" "," "-" "?"
        term_alternatives= false
        redundant_test= true
        <alternative>:
          empty= false
          first= "+"
          follow= "end-of-file" "in" ")" "+" "," "-" "?"
          dirsymb= "+"
          <factor>:
            empty= false
            first= "+"
            follow= "identifier" "number" "kg" "m" "s" "(" "-"
            <primary>:
              empty= false
              first= "+"
              follow= "identifier" "number" "kg" "m" "s" "(" "-"
              dirsymb= "+"
```

```
                       redundant_test= true
                       +
            <factor>:
               empty= false
               first= "identifier" "number" "kg" "m" "s" "(" "-"
               follow= "end-of-file" "in" ")" "+" "," "-" "?"
               <primary>:
                  empty= false
                  first= "identifier" "number" "kg" "m" "s" "(" "-"
                  follow= "end-of-file" "in" ")" "+" "," "-" "?"
                  dirsymb= "identifier" "number" "kg" "m" "s" "(" "-"
                  precede= "+"
                  term
               |
            <alternative>:
               empty= false
               first= "-"
               follow= "end-of-file" "in" ")" "+" "," "-" "?"
               dirsymb= "-"
               <factor>:
                  empty= false
                  first= "-"
                  follow= "identifier" "number" "kg" "m" "s" "(" "-"
                  <primary>:
                     empty= false
                     first= "-"
                     follow= "identifier" "number" "kg" "m" "s" "(" "-"
                     dirsymb= "-"
                     redundant_test= true
                     -
               <factor>:
                  empty= false
                  first= "identifier" "number" "kg" "m" "s" "(" "-"
                  follow= "end-of-file" "in" ")" "+" "," "-" "?"
                  <primary>:
                     empty= false
                     first= "identifier" "number" "kg" "m" "s" "(" "-"
                     follow= "end-of-file" "in" ")" "+" "," "-" "?"
                     dirsymb= "identifier" "number" "kg" "m" "s" "(" "-"
                     precede= "-"
                     term                 )*


    term                      last= "identifier" "number" "kg" "m" "s" ")"
    =
    <expression>:
       empty= false
       first= "identifier" "number" "kg" "m" "s" "(" "-"
```

```
follow= "end-of-file" "in" ")" "+" "," "-" "?"
term_alternatives= false
redundant_test= false
<alternative>:
  empty= false
  first= "identifier" "number" "kg" "m" "s" "(" "-"
  follow= "end-of-file" "in" ")" "+" "," "-" "?"
  dirsymb= "identifier" "number" "kg" "m" "s" "(" "-"
  <factor>:
    empty= false
    first= "identifier" "number" "kg" "m" "s" "(" "-"
    follow= "end-of-file" "in" ")" "*" "+" "," "-" "/" "?"
    <primary>:
      empty= false
      first= "identifier" "number" "kg" "m" "s" "(" "-"
      follow= "end-of-file" "in" ")" "*" "+" "," "-" "/" "?"
      dirsymb= "identifier" "number" "kg" "m" "s" "(" "-"
      precede= "many" "in" "(" "+" "-" "="
      factor
<factor>:
  empty= true
  first= "*" "/"
  follow= "end-of-file" "in" ")" "+" "," "-" "?"
  <primary>:
    empty= false
    first= "*" "/"
    follow= "end-of-file" "in" ")" "*" "+" "," "-" "/" "?"
    dirsymb= "*" "/"

    (
    <expression>:
      empty= false
      first= "*" "/"
      follow= "end-of-file" "in" ")" "*" "+" "," "-" "/" "?"
      term_alternatives= false
      redundant_test= true
      <alternative>:
        empty= false
        first= "*"
        follow= "end-of-file" "in" ")" "*" "+" "," "-" "/" "?"
        dirsymb= "*"
        <factor>:
          empty= false
          first= "*"
          follow= "identifier" "number" "kg" "m" "s" "(" "-"
          <primary>:
            empty= false
            first= "*"
            follow= "identifier" "number" "kg" "m" "s" "(" "-"
```

```
                    dirsymb= "*"
                    redundant_test= true
                    *
            <factor>:
              empty= false
              first= "identifier" "number" "kg" "m" "s" "(" "-"
              follow= "end-of-file" "in" ")" "*" "+" "," "-" "/" "?"
              <primary>:
                empty= false
                first= "identifier" "number" "kg" "m" "s" "(" "-"
                follow= "end-of-file" "in" ")" "*" "+" "," "-" "/" "?"
                dirsymb= "identifier" "number" "kg" "m" "s" "(" "-"
                precede= "*"
                factor
        |
          <alternative>:
            empty= false
            first= "/"
            follow= "end-of-file" "in" ")" "*" "+" "," "-" "/" "?"
            dirsymb= "/"
            <factor>:
              empty= false
              first= "/"
              follow= "identifier" "number" "kg" "m" "s" "(" "-"
              <primary>:
                empty= false
                first= "/"
                follow= "identifier" "number" "kg" "m" "s" "(" "-"
                dirsymb= "/"
                redundant_test= true
                /
            <factor>:
              empty= false
              first= "identifier" "number" "kg" "m" "s" "(" "-"
              follow= "end-of-file" "in" ")" "*" "+" "," "-" "/" "?"
              <primary>:
                empty= false
                first= "identifier" "number" "kg" "m" "s" "(" "-"
                follow= "end-of-file" "in" ")" "*" "+" "," "-" "/" "?"
                dirsymb= "identifier" "number" "kg" "m" "s" "(" "-"
                precede= "/"
                factor                 )*


factor                  last= "identifier" "number" "kg" "m" "s" ")"
=
  <expression>:
    empty= false
```

```
first= "identifier" "number" "kg" "m" "s" "(" "-"
follow= "end-of-file" "in" ")" "*" "+" "," "-" "/" "?"
term_alternatives= false
redundant_test= false
<alternative>:
  empty= false
  first= "identifier" "number" "kg" "m" "s" "(" "-"
  follow= "end-of-file" "in" ")" "*" "+" "," "-" "/" "?"
  dirsymb= "identifier" "number" "kg" "m" "s" "(" "-"
  <factor>:
    empty= false
    first= "identifier" "number" "kg" "m" "s" "(" "-"
    follow= "end-of-file" "in" ")" "*" "+" "," "-" "/" "?" "^"
    <primary>:
      empty= false
      first= "identifier" "number" "kg" "m" "s" "(" "-"
      follow= "end-of-file" "in" ")" "*" "+" "," "-" "/" "?" "^"
      dirsymb= "identifier" "number" "kg" "m" "s" "(" "-"
      precede= "many" "in" "(" "*" "+" "-" "/" "=" "^"
      secondary
  <factor>:
    empty= true
    first= "^"
    follow= "end-of-file" "in" ")" "*" "+" "," "-" "/" "?"
    <primary>:
      empty= true
      first= "^"
      follow= "end-of-file" "in" ")" "*" "+" "," "-" "/" "?"
      dirsymb= "end-of-file" "in" ")" "*" "+" "," "-" "/" "?" "^"

      (
      <expression>:
        empty= true
        first= "^"
        follow= "end-of-file" "in" ")" "*" "+" "," "-" "/" "?"
        term_alternatives= false
        redundant_test= false
        <alternative>:
          empty= false
          first= "^"
          follow= "end-of-file" "in" ")" "*" "+" "," "-" "/" "?"
          dirsymb= "^"
          <factor>:
            empty= false
            first= "^"
            follow= "identifier" "number" "kg" "m" "s" "(" "-"
            <primary>:
              empty= false
              first= "^"
```

```
                      follow= "identifier" "number" "kg" "m" "s" "(" "_"
                      dirsymb= "^"
                      redundant_test= true
                      ^

            <factor>:
              empty= false
              first= "identifier" "number" "kg" "m" "s" "(" "_"
              follow= "end-of-file" "in" ")" "*" "+" "," "_" "/" "?"
              <primary>:
                empty= false
                first= "identifier" "number" "kg" "m" "s" "(" "_"
                follow= "end-of-file" "in" ")" "*" "+" "," "_" "/" "?"
                dirsymb= "identifier" "number" "kg" "m" "s" "(" "_"
                precede= "^"
                factor
         |
        <alternative>:
          empty= true
          first=
          follow= "end-of-file" "in" ")" "*" "+" "," "_" "/" "?"
          dirsymb= "end-of-file" "in" ")" "*" "+" "," "_" "/" "?"
          <factor>:
            empty= true
            first=
            follow= "end-of-file" "in" ")" "*" "+" "," "_" "/" "?"
            <primary>:
              empty= true
              first=
              follow= "end-of-file" "in" ")" "*" "+" "," "_" "/" "?"
              dirsymb= "end-of-file" "in" ")" "*" "+" "," "_" "/" "?"
              &)


secondary              last= "identifier" "number" "kg" "m" "s" ")"
=
 <expression>:
   empty= false
   first= "identifier" "number" "kg" "m" "s" "(" "_"
   follow= "end-of-file" "in" ")" "*" "+" "," "_" "/" "?" "^"
   term_alternatives= false
   redundant_test= false
   <alternative>:
     empty= false
     first= "_"
     follow= "end-of-file" "in" ")" "*" "+" "," "_" "/" "?" "^"
     dirsymb= "_"
     <factor>:
       empty= false
```

```
      first= "-"
      follow= "identifier" "number" "kg" "m" "s" "("
      <primary>:
        empty= false
        first= "-"
        follow= "identifier" "number" "kg" "m" "s" "("
        dirsymb= "-"
        redundant_test= true
        -
    <factor>:
      empty= false
      first= "identifier" "number" "kg" "m" "s" "("
      follow= "end-of-file" "in" ")" "*" "+" "," "-" "/" "?" "^"
      <primary>:
        empty= false
        first= "identifier" "number" "kg" "m" "s" "("
        follow= "end-of-file" "in" ")" "*" "+" "," "-" "/" "?" "^"
        dirsymb= "identifier" "number" "kg" "m" "s" "("
        precede= "-"
        primary
  |
  <alternative>:
    empty= false
    first= "identifier" "number" "kg" "m" "s" "("
    follow= "end-of-file" "in" ")" "*" "+" "," "-" "/" "?" "^"
    dirsymb= "identifier" "number" "kg" "m" "s" "("
    <factor>:
      empty= false
      first= "identifier" "number" "kg" "m" "s" "("
      follow= "end-of-file" "in" ")" "*" "+" "," "-" "/" "?" "^"
      <primary>:
        empty= false
        first= "identifier" "number" "kg" "m" "s" "("
        follow= "end-of-file" "in" ")" "*" "+" "," "-" "/" "?" "^"
        dirsymb= "identifier" "number" "kg" "m" "s" "("
        precede= "many" "in" "(" "*" "+" "-" "/" "=" "^"
        primary


primary                    last= "identifier" "number" "kg" "m" "s" ")"
=
 <expression>:
   empty= false
   first= "identifier" "number" "kg" "m" "s" "("
   follow= "end-of-file" "in" ")" "*" "+" "," "-" "/" "?" "^"
   term_alternatives= false
   redundant_test= false
   <alternative>:
```

```
        empty= false
        first= "identifier"
        follow= "end-of-file" "in" ")" "*" "+" "," "-" "/" "?" "^"
        dirsymb= "identifier"
        <factor>:
          empty= false
          first= "identifier"
          follow= "end-of-file" "in" ")" "*" "+" "," "-" "/" "?" "^"
          <primary>:
            empty= false
            first= "identifier"
            follow= "end-of-file" "in" ")" "*" "+" "," "-" "/" "?" "^"
            dirsymb= "identifier"
            redundant_test= true
            identifier
    |
<alternative>:
  empty= false
  first= "number"
  follow= "end-of-file" "in" ")" "*" "+" "," "-" "/" "?" "^"
  dirsymb= "number"
  <factor>:
    empty= false
    first= "number"
    follow= "end-of-file" "in" ")" "*" "+" "," "-" "/" "?" "^"
    <primary>:
      empty= false
      first= "number"
      follow= "end-of-file" "in" ")" "*" "+" "," "-" "/" "?" "^"
      dirsymb= "number"
      redundant_test= true
      number
    |
<alternative>:
  empty= false
  first= "kg"
  follow= "end-of-file" "in" ")" "*" "+" "," "-" "/" "?" "^"
  dirsymb= "kg"
  <factor>:
    empty= false
    first= "kg"
    follow= "end-of-file" "in" ")" "*" "+" "," "-" "/" "?" "^"
    <primary>:
      empty= false
      first= "kg"
      follow= "end-of-file" "in" ")" "*" "+" "," "-" "/" "?" "^"
      dirsymb= "kg"
      redundant_test= true
```

```
        kg
|
<alternative>:
  empty= false
  first= "m"
  follow= "end-of-file" "in" ")" "*" "+" "," "-" "/" "?" "^"
  dirsymb= "m"
  <factor>:
    empty= false
    first= "m"
    follow= "end-of-file" "in" ")" "*" "+" "," "-" "/" "?" "^"
    <primary>:
      empty= false
      first= "m"
      follow= "end-of-file" "in" ")" "*" "+" "," "-" "/" "?" "^"
      dirsymb= "m"
      redundant_test= true
      m
|
<alternative>:
  empty= false
  first= "s"
  follow= "end-of-file" "in" ")" "*" "+" "," "-" "/" "?" "^"
  dirsymb= "s"
  <factor>:
    empty= false
    first= "s"
    follow= "end-of-file" "in" ")" "*" "+" "," "-" "/" "?" "^"
    <primary>:
      empty= false
      first= "s"
      follow= "end-of-file" "in" ")" "*" "+" "," "-" "/" "?" "^"
      dirsymb= "s"
      redundant_test= true
      s
|
<alternative>:
  empty= false
  first= "("
  follow= "end-of-file" "in" ")" "*" "+" "," "-" "/" "?" "^"
  dirsymb= "("
  <factor>:
    empty= false
    first= "("
    follow= "identifier" "number" "kg" "m" "s" "(" "-"
    <primary>:
      empty= false
      first= "("
```

```
            follow= "identifier" "number" "kg" "m" "s" "(" "-"
            dirsymb= "("
            redundant_test= false
            (
    <factor>:
      empty= false
      first= "identifier" "number" "kg" "m" "s" "(" "-"
      follow= ")"
      <primary>:
        empty= false
        first= "identifier" "number" "kg" "m" "s" "(" "-"
        follow= ")"
        dirsymb= "identifier" "number" "kg" "m" "s" "(" "-"
        precede= "("
        expression
    <factor>:
      empty= false
      first= ")"
      follow= "end-of-file" "in" ")" "*" "+" "," "-" "/" "?" "^"
      <primary>:
        empty= false
        first= ")"
        follow= "end-of-file" "in" ")" "*" "+" "," "-" "/" "?" "^"
        dirsymb= ")"
        redundant_test= false
        )
No errors detected
Generation completed
```

Explanation of the error message numbers

1: End of LILA-input-file encountered.
   Level is A

2: The first LILA input line must be a LILA control statement.
   Level is A

3: The name of this LILA control statement is longer than 20 characters. Name shortened to 20 characters.
   Level is W

4: Integer greater than max-integer.
   Level is A

5: LILA control statement not terminated with a semicolon. Prob-
   ably a missing comma between options.
   Level is A

6: Invalid option.
   Level is B

7: Invalid option specification.
   Level is B

8: This must be a first level LILA control statement.
   Level is A

9: The LILA input must start with the definition of the global
   options or the inputvocabulary.
   Level is A

10: Options of a first level LILA input part have not been taken
    into account. The name of the LILA input part is printed fol-
    lowed by a list of the options.
    Level is W

11: This first level LILA control statement must define the transla-
    tion syntax.
    Level is A

12: Missing ')' after option specification. A ')' is assumed.
    Level is B

13: This first level LILA control statement has an invalid name or
    is misplaced.
    Level is A

14: Multiple definition of a semantic action.
    Level is E

15: The translation syntax must start with a second level LILA con-
    trol statement defining rule.
    Level is A

16: This second level LILA control statement must define rule.
    Level is A

17: Input symbols have not been used as terminal symbols in the
    translation syntax.
    Level is W

18: The LILA input is incomplete.
    Level is A

19: The definition of the global options must be followed by a first
    level LILA control statement defining inputvocabulary.
    Level is A

20: This symbol name is longer than 20 characters. Name shortened
    to 20 characters.
    Level is W

21: This semantic action name is longer than 20 characters. Name
    shortened to 20 characters.
    Level is W

22: Invalid symbol. Symbol is ignored.
Level is B

23: ELL(1) condition violated: a primary within an iteration can derive the empty string. The primary is printed.
Level is D

24: Invalid syntactic structure of a translation syntax rule. The complete module is ignored.
Level is B

25: The referenced input symbol is not defined in inputvocabulary.
Level is B

26: ELL(1) condition violated: the dirsymb sets of alternatives are not disjoint. The alternatives are printed with their dirsymb sets. The set with common symbols is also printed.
Level is D

27: ELL(1) condition violated: the dirsymb set of a primary in an iteration is not disjoint with the follow set of the enclosing factor. The factor is printed with the dirsymb and follow set. The set of common symbols is also printed.
Level is D

28: The translation syntax is not reduced: a nonterminal symbol cannot derive a finite string of input symbols.
Level is C

29: The translation syntax is not reduced: a nonterminal symbol is not reachable from the start nonterminal symbol.
Level is C

30: A nonterminal symbol is not defined.
Level is B

31: Two input or output symbols are defined with the same name.
Level is B

32: The REP option must specify 'char' or 'integer'.
   Level is A

33: The REP option must be specified.
   Level is A

34: Multiple definition of a nonterminal symbol.
   Level is B

35: Definition of a semantic action which is not used in the translation syntax rule.
   Level is E

36: This must be the start of a semantic action definition.
   Level is A

37: Undefined semantic action.
   Level is E

38: This must be a second level LILA control statement defining one
   of the globalinfo parts.
   Level is A

39: Invalid LILA control statement name in globalinfo.
   Level is A

40: An input symbol is defined with the end-of-file representation.
   Level is B

41: The start nonterminal symbol may not have attributes.
   Level is A

42: Two input or output symbols are defined with the same representation.
   Level is B

43: This symbol does not occur in the translation syntax rule.
   Level is E

44: Invalid symbol in follow set definition.
   Level is A

45: This reference to an input or nonterminal symbol is not followed
   by its correct sequence number in the translation syntax rule.
   Level is E

46: The referred input symbol has no attributes.
   Level is E

47: The referred nonterminal symbol has no attributes.
   Level is E

48: This input symbol is not defined.
   Level is E

49: The NAME option must specify the name of the generated transducer.
   Level is A

50: Invalid use of the escape character.
   Level is A

51: Identifier contains more than 8 characters.   Other characters
   ignored.
   Level is W

52: This character constant is not terminated with a single quote.
   A quote is assumed.
   Level is B

53: A character constant may not be used as representation with
   REP(INTEGER).
   Level is A

54: Invalid symbol in the representation.
   Level is A

55: The symbol name is not followed by '='.
   Level is A

56: Invalid symbol in a vocabulary definition.
    Level is A

57: An input symbol with representation 1 may not be defined when
    there is no user defined read routine.
    Level is B

58: The type identifier for the attribute of an input or output sym-
    bol must start with a letter.   .
    Level is A

59: The referred nonterminal has no attributes.
    Level is E

60: The referred output symbol is not defined.
    Level is E

61: A '%' must be followed by '"' or '['.
    Level is E

62: The referred output symbol has no attributes.
    Level is E

63: At least one input symbol must be given in the follow set.
    Level is B

64: An '@' must be followed by '"', '<' or '['.
    Level is E

65: Start of a LILA control statement inside a symbol name.
    Level is A

66: The FILE option is given without a file name.
    Level is A

67: The EOF option is given without a value.
    Level is A

68: The EOF option must specify an unsigned integer number.
    Level is A

69: Writeroutine may not be defined when there is no output vocabulary.
Level is A

70: An output symbol with representation 1 may not be defined when
there is no user defined read and write routine.
Level is B

71: This input symbol is not defined and different from "end-of-
file".
Level is B

72: This must be a LILA control statement.
Level is A

73: Invalid symbol in the list of begin markers.
Level is A

74: A begin-marker does not belong to FIRST of its goal.
Level is E

REFERENCES

ADDYMAN, A.M. [1980]. A Draft Proposal for Pascal. SIGPLAN
Notices, Volume 15, number 4, april, pp. 1-66.

BRANQUART, P., CARDINAEL, J.P., LEWI, J., DELESCAILLE, J.P., VANBE-
GIN, M. [1976]. An optimized translation process and its appli-
cation to Algol 68. Lecture Notes in Computer Science, 38,
Springer-Verlag, Berlin.

COHEN, J. [1973]. Syntax-directed unit conversion. Information
Processing Letters 2, North-Holland Publishing Co., Amsterdam,
pp. 100-102.

JENSEN, K., WIRTH, N. [1974]. Pascal user manual and report. Lecture Notes in Computer Science 18, Springer-Verlag, New York.

KNUTH, D.E. [1968]. Semantics of context-free languages. Mathematical Systems Theory Journal 2:2, pp. 127-146.

LEWI, J., DE VLAMINCK, K., HUENS, J., HUYBRECHTS, M. [1978]. The
ELL(1) parser generator and the error recovery mechanism. Acta
Informatica 10, pp. 209-228.

LEWI, J., DE VLAMINCK, K., HUENS, J., HUYBRECHTS, M. [1979]. A Programming Methodology in Compiler Construction. Part 1 : Concepts. North-Holland Publishing Company, Amsterdam.

WARSHALL, S. [1962]. A theorem of boolean matrices. JACM 9:1, pp.
11-12.

- [1980]. Reference Manual for the Ada Programming Language. Proposed standard document. U.S. Department of Defense, july 1980.

Note: More references about the subject treated in this the book can
be found in Part 1.